How to Do *Everything* with FrontPage 2002

David Plotkin

Osborne/**McGraw-Hill**

New York Chicago San Francisco Lisbon
London Madrid Mexico City Milan New Delhi
San Juan Seoul Singapore Sydney Toronto

Osborne/**McGraw-Hill**
2600 Tenth Street
Berkeley, California 94710
U.S.A.

To arrange bulk purchase discounts for sales promotions, premiums, or fund-raisers, please contact Osborne/**McGraw-Hill** at the above address. For information on translations or book distributors outside the U.S.A., please see the International Contact Information page immediately following the index of this book.

How to Do Everything with FrontPage® 2002

567890 FGR FGR 0198765432

ISBN 0-07-213364-3

Publisher:	Brandon A. Nordin
Associate Publisher	
and Editor-in-Chief:	Scott Rogers
Acquisitions Editor:	Jane Brownlow
Project Editor:	Mark Karmendy
Acquisitions Coordinator:	Emma Acker
Technical Editor:	Bill Bruns
Copy Editor:	Dennis Weaver
Proofreaders:	John Gildersleeve, John Schindel, Stefany Otis
Indexer:	Rebecca Plunkett
Computer Designers:	Jean Butterfield, Lucie Ericksen, John Patrus, Dick Schwartz
Illustrators:	Michael Mueller, Alex Putney, Lyssa Sieben-Wald, Beth Young
Series Design:	Mickey Galicia
Cover Design:	Cristina Deh-Lee

This book was composed with Corel VENTURA™ Publisher.

This book is for Marisa, my wife. Making a book is a team effort, because someone has to pick up the load for the extra work while I do my writing. Marisa did that, and provided constant encouragement when the beta version of FrontPage kept crashing! Thanks, hon!

About the Author

David Plotkin is the Manager of Data Administration for Longs Drug Stores. He designs computer systems and databases for a living, and is a self-taught Web-tool user. He maintains Web sites for various non-profit and charitable organizations, and has written several other computer books on database topics and graphics.

About the Technical Reviewer

Bill Bruns is the Assistant Director for Business Systems at the University of Illinois' College of Medicine. In addition, he runs Jacob Marlie Financial, Inc. (http://www.jacobmarlie.com), an invoicing and collections agency for fraternal organizations. He has been involved in the Web since 1993, when he would routinely sit up all night surfing with wonder and amazement. He has tech-edited over 45 books relating to the Internet and HTML, as well as to creating and searching for Web pages. Bill lives with his wife Debbie, daughter Marlie, and bearded dragon Cookie in Champaign, Illinois.

Contents

Acknowledgments

Seven people deserve special mention. My agent, Carole McClendon, found the contract and negotiated some great terms. Jane Brownlow helped me through the process of revising the book and following the rules for OMH. I think the results speak for themselves, and I am grateful for their help!

Acquisitions Coordinator Emma Acker, though new, did a good job of pulling everything together for the book.

Copy Editor Dennis Weaver not only had the "eagle eyes" required of a copy editor (spotting stuff even missed by the tech editor), but punched up my prose to make it read better. Thanks, Dennis!

Executive Project Editor Mark Karmendy really made a difference, keeping everything straight, resolving any issues, and in general, just keeping everything on track. An experienced editor like Mark can make all the difference between having a good experience as you go through final proofreading or suffering the horror of realizing that everything is mixed up. Believe me, I know.

Now, if you're counting, you'll notice that we're two short on the number of people to acknowledge. First of all, a very special acknowledgement goes to Marty Williams, author of *FrontPage Developer's Guide*. He provided constant help and guidance as I wrestled with the new version of FrontPage, and endless patience as he educated me on getting Windows 2000 Professional up and working with IIS 5. This, despite writing his own book and running his own business. Thanks every so much, Marty!

And lastly, I need to acknowledge the efforts of my sister-in-law, Brenda Plotkin, who got me most of the material that appears in the screenshots for the Web site in this book. She is a remarkably capable woman, who is secretary of her local swim team, and has done a great job in raising my three nieces.

Introduction

- What a Web site is

- How the World Wide Web works

- What you need to build your own Web site

- Who should read this book

- How this book is organized

The fact that you bought this book—or are considering buying it—means you are ready to join the ranks of the huge number of people who are building and maintaining Web sites using Microsoft FrontPage 2002. Whether you bought FrontPage 2002 as a standalone package or as part of Office XP, you have one of the premier packages available for putting yourself, your family, or your business on the World Wide Web.

What Is a Web Site?

But just what is a Web site? This may seem like a strange question to ask—after all, you see Web sites every day, so you probably think you know what a Web site is, and maybe you do. But it is helpful to understand what a Web site *really* is, because it will be much easier for you to build a Web site if you understand (at least a little bit) what is happening behind the scenes.

What Is a Web Page?

First, let's answer the question, what is a Web page? Believe it or not, a Web page is a text file. It doesn't have pictures, buttons, or any of the other "fancies" you see on your screen. Instead, the text file contains a description of the Web page in a special programming language called Hypertext Markup Language (HTML). HTML uses programming commands, called *tags*, to describe the page layout, and includes other information, such as onscreen text and paths to the locations of graphics. A page's HTML also includes the destinations for links to other locations (called hyperlinks). Of course, the programming can become very complex when special features such as frames, tables, scripts written in other languages, and dynamic effects are included on the page. Nevertheless, if you are competent in HTML, you can code your own Web pages—and that is exactly how all Web pages were created in the early days of the Internet.

As with any other programming language, writing code in HTML is a trial-and-error process. First, you design the page, gather up the elements you will need (such as graphics), and write the code. Then you have to try and load that code in a browser (a tool for viewing Web pages), find the coding errors, fix them, and try again. Once you find all your coding errors, you still aren't done. Perhaps your page doesn't look the way you intended—the table cells are too narrow, or the text doesn't have the right effects. Back to the code/debug cycle.

Fortunately for you (and me too), there is an easier way. FrontPage 2002 implements a *WYSIWYG* (what you see is what you get) environment for building Web pages. With FrontPage 2002, you can type in your text, add graphics, format the text, align the paragraphs, build hyperlinks, and construct the rest of your Web page in an interactive environment where you can see what your Web page will look like as you build it and even test most features. When you are done, FrontPage 2002 writes the HTML code that describes the Web page for you. It never makes a syntax error, and you never even have to see the code (although you can if you want to). Further, if you make changes to the Web page, FrontPage 2002 automatically regenerates the HTML; you never have to worry about it.

Constructing a Web Site

A Web site is a set of related Web pages. Starting with a *home* page—the page that opens when you navigate to a Web site—you can build a set of pages related to each other through hyperlinks. Hyperlinks are points on the page you can click to navigate to another page. The home page is just a regular Web page with a special name, so the hosting Web server knows to display that page first. (The special name, by the way, is either Default.htm or Index.htm.)

FrontPage 2002 contains a set of tools for relating Web pages together into a Web site. It also includes templates for building special-purpose Web sites, such as a Web site for customer service or for hosting a discussion group. These templates actually build sets of related Web pages for you, making your job much easier.

Special Features of FrontPage 2002

If all FrontPage 2002 did was provide a great environment for building Web pages and Web sites, it would still be a pretty good tool. But wait, there's more. One of the main problems with building Web sites is that the most sophisticated features, such as forms, site searches, guest books, and hit counters (a feature that counts how many times someone has viewed your page), require a sophisticated interaction with the server hosting the site (more on this topic shortly). Prior to FrontPage 2002, you had to know how to write programs in a scripting language that could communicate with the Common Gateway Interface (CGI). This wasn't too much of a problem for professional Web developers, but for the average builder of a Web site, this requirement basically put these advanced features out of reach.

FrontPage solved this problem by introducing the *FrontPage server extensions*. This is a package of programs the service hosting your Web site installs on their server. Once these extensions have been installed, implementing forms and other sophisticated features is simply a matter of stepping through a Wizard: following specific instructions and answering a few questions. Of course, the hosting company has to install these extensions on their server or your forms won't work. But, perhaps because FrontPage became popular very quickly and carries the weight of the Microsoft marketing machine behind it, many hosting companies have installed the extensions. They also advertise this fact. If you see "FrontPage enabled" or "Supports FrontPage" or something to that effect, you can be sure all your special features will work.

Getting Your Site onto the Web

Normally, you build your Web site and its pages on your local machine. However, this does not make your site available to people using the Internet. To make your site available on the Internet, it must be present on a host computer that is connected to the Internet on a more-or-less continuous basis. Your Web site must have a fixed *address* (formally known as an *IP address*) so that people can consistently find it. While it is just barely possible to host your Web site on your own local machine, there are some really good reasons not to, especially if you are limited to a dial-up modem and would like to turn your computer off once in a while. The better option is to contract with a *Web Presence Provider* (WPP). These companies own computers (servers) on which they can host your site. These servers are online all of the time, have very fast Internet connections, and can usually provide you with statistics, such as how many times your site was viewed and which pages are the most popular. Of course, hosting your site on someone else's computer is usually going to cost you some money, typically in the neighborhood of $10 to $30 a month for a personal site. There are a number of free WPPs, but most do not support the FrontPage server extensions. In Chapter 17, we'll look at how to find a WPP to host your Web site.

FrontPage makes it easy to move your Web site to a host computer, a process known as *publishing*. In fact, another advance that FrontPage has made popular is to make publishing easy. Using FrontPage's publishing function, you can upload your Web site to the host over an Internet connection, refresh individual pages as necessary, and remove pages that are no longer included in your Web site.

Once your Web site is present on the host computer, the hosting company will give you a way to find the Web site on the World Wide Web. While technically this amounts to the IP address of your site (a rather odd-looking number you can't possibly remember), the hosting company will provide you with an easier address, usually beginning with *www*. For example, www.osborne.com takes you to the home page for Osborne/McGraw-Hill. Hosting companies will often provide you with an address that appends your username to the hosting company's own address, such as www.hostingcompany.com/dplotkin. At any rate, this address, provided by the hosting company, is what you can give to your friends, family, and co-workers so they can find your site in their browsers. The actual IP address of your site is resolved to this more-friendly text string by computers known as *domain name servers*. If you don't care for this method of identification, you can register for your own *domain name*. Your WPP will usually help you with this, as a special form has to be forwarded to the organization that monitors and assigns domain names. And you have to pay a fee to register and keep your own domain name. But provided that the domain you want is not in use (and you can afford it), this is the easiest way for people to find your site. For example, my domain name is www.dplotkin.com. This is exactly how the big boys do it.

Who Should Read this Book

Every author would like to believe that everyone who wants to use the software about which the book is written is the target audience, but most of the time that is not true. This book is targeted at people who want to build moderately sophisticated sites using FrontPage 2002, and it assumes you know nothing about the program, other than how to install it on your computer. It will explain all the features you need to create and maintain complex sites, including publishing the site to a WPP. This book will teach you how to build pages, maintain your site, check for all kinds of errors, and even find resources on the Internet to dress up your site.

If you just want a "quick and dirty" Web site that you can create in a day or two, you can skim Parts I and II and read enough of Chapter 17 to learn how to publish your site. When you need more details, you can refer to the other parts of the book as appropriate. This book does not really cover advanced development topics, as it does not cover the intricacies of using Java and JavaScript (although it does cover the basics). Nor does it cover the collaborative features of FrontPage 2002, which are more appropriate to businesses running an Intranet.

How this Book Is Organized

This book is broken into four parts. Part I introduces you to the general features of FrontPage 2002. This part also tells you how to build Web pages, using all the tools provided. These tools include adding and formatting text, adding graphics, working with lists, using themes to achieve a unified look, and adding and formatting tables.

Part II tells you how to connect pages together into a Web site, using such features as hyperlinks, shared borders, and image maps. This part also tells you how to use link bars to set up a structure for your site and create reusable sets of hyperlinks, and how to include forms to gather user feedback. You also learn how to implement frames to display multiple pages at once.

Part III covers advanced topics, such as FrontPage's components, page options, and using databases with FrontPage. You will learn how to incorporate Java applets and ActiveX controls (many of which can be found on the Internet). You will also learn the fine points of managing your Web site using reports and tasks you can assign to members of your team or use to keep track of items that need to be completed. Finally, you'll learn the ins and outs of publishing your Web site to a host server.

Part IV covers how to route information from your Web site to a database, and search the contents of a database on the Web. An additional chapter is available on the Osborne/McGraw-Hill Web site (www.osborne.com) that details implementing Cascading Style Sheets.

The appendixes (also available on the Web site) provide some additional important information. It's pretty easy to design an ugly Web site that serves no apparent purpose and loads slowly in the bargain. Appendix A provides a whole host of tips to help you design and implement a high-quality Web site. Finally, Appendix B tells you how to install the Microsoft Personal Web Server, so you can try out various features of your site on your local machine—features that require a Web server in order to function properly.

Part 1

Build Web Pages

Chapter 1

Navigate in FrontPage 2002

How to...

- Understand menus and toolbars
- Use the FrontPage views
- Configure the editors
- Create and customize toolbars

FrontPage 2002 is a powerful tool for creating and maintaining intranet Web sites as well as sites on the World Wide Web. Using FrontPage 2002, you can create Web pages, complete with formatted text and graphics, tables, buttons, and animations. You can add frames, borders, and hyperlinks to connect the pages into a Web site—or connect the pages to other Web sites. But probably the most seductive feature of FrontPage (if your Web site is running on a specially enabled server) is its ability to provide sophisticated Web functionality—such as forms, a guestbook, and even special-purpose Web sites (such as a Corporate Presence Web site)—without writing any code. If you are familiar with HTML, JavaScript, Java, or other supported scripting languages and you enjoy creating such special touches manually, you can add your own programs to a FrontPage Web project. Once you have built your site, FrontPage provides management tools such as reports and tasks to help you maintain the site. Finally, FrontPage automates the process of publishing your Web site to a Web presence provider (WPP) so it will be accessible to Internet browsers.

As you can probably imagine, FrontPage needs a capable and flexible interface to enable you to perform all these functions without being overwhelmed. This chapter introduces you to all the aspects of this interface and demonstrates how to customize it to your own way of working.

Understand the Interface

The main FrontPage window (shown in Figure 1-1) displays all the standard features of a Windows program as well as all the main FrontPage elements. Not all the elements are visible in every view, and you can configure the window to turn certain elements on and off. For example, if you don't want to see the Folder List, you can turn it off.

1

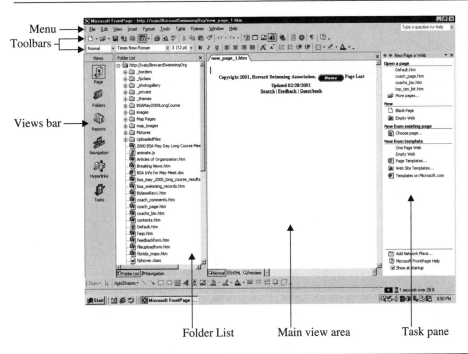

Menu →
Toolbars →

Views bar →

Folder List   Main view area   Task pane

FIGURE 1-1   The FrontPage main window is your "home base" for navigating in FrontPage.

The Menu Bar

As with virtually every other Windows program, the top of the active window is occupied by the *menu bar*. To choose a command, click the menu heading (such as File), and then select the menu command you want (such as Save). In this book, we will refer to this action like this: "Choose File | Save." To make a menu selection without using the mouse, press and hold the ALT key while pressing the letter key displayed as underlined in the menu bar. For example, to cause the File menu to drop down, press ALT-F. Then press S to choose Save from the File menu. Many menu commands also have single-key equivalents. The single-key equivalent is visible in the menu alongside the menu item it triggers. For example, you can press CTRL-S to save a file.

FrontPage 2002 does implement one nonstandard menu feature: the *tear-off menu*. The submenu Insert | Form displays a title bar (see Figure 1-2). To convert a submenu into a toolbar, click on its title bar and "tear off" (drag) the submenu from the menu. Using the submenu as a toolbar has the advantage of making the commands instantly available with a single mouse click. On the other hand, the toolbar takes up valuable screen space.

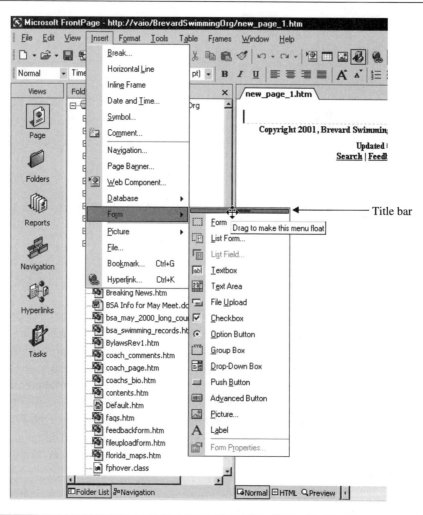

FIGURE 1-2   Click the title bar of a submenu and drag to create a toolbar.

When you are through working with the elements in a tear-off toolbar, you can click the Close button in the upper-right corner to close the toolbar and remove it from the screen. The submenu remains available from the main menu at all times, even when the toolbar equivalent is visible.

One of the more controversial menu features of all Office XP programs is the Recent Commands option. When this option is enabled, the menu commands you frequently use migrate to the top of the menu, and menu commands you don't frequently use disappear from the menu. Many people find these changes disconcerting (I am one of those people!). Fortunately, you can disable this feature. To do so, choose Tools | Customize to open the Customize dialog box. Click the Options tab and select the Always Show Full Menus checkbox.

The Toolbars

Just below the menu bar are the toolbars. Toolbars contain buttons for the most-often-used functions in FrontPage 2002. It is easier to click a toolbar button than to hunt down a command in the menu bar. A small down arrow appears next to some of the buttons in the toolbar. Clicking the button performs the default task associated with it, while clicking the down arrow displays a submenu of additional buttons. If you can't remember the function of a button in a toolbar, simply hover your mouse pointer over the button to see a *ScreenTip* that tells you the purpose of the button.

If you find the ScreenTips annoying, you can turn them off. From the Options tab of the Customize dialog box, clear the Show ScreenTips On Toolbars checkbox.

As you'll see later in this chapter, you can configure the toolbars to your liking, turning them off and on, adding and removing buttons, changing their position on the screen, and even creating your own custom toolbars.

The Standard and Formatting Toolbars

By default, FrontPage 2002 displays only two of its many toolbars: the Standard toolbar and the Formatting toolbar. The Standard toolbar contains common functions you use throughout FrontPage 2002: creating a new page; opening Web sites and files; saving files; running the spell checker; cutting, copying, and pasting; printing; inserting special FrontPage components and tables; previewing your work in a browser; working with hyperlinks; and "publishing" Web pages to the World Wide Web or to your intranet.

The Formatting toolbar is similar to the Formatting toolbars in other Microsoft Office programs. Its primary purpose is to help you format text and paragraphs. Using the Formatting toolbar, you can change a text font; choose effects such as bold, italics, and underline; modify the text size; change the paragraph alignment; format bullets and numbered lists; indent paragraphs; and change the text color. The main difference between the Formatting toolbar in FrontPage and the same toolbar in other applications is that the available text styles conform to HTML standards. The Formatting toolbar is discussed more in Chapter 2.

Other Toolbars

FrontPage provides other toolbars that perform specialized tasks. You can see a list of these toolbars by right-clicking a blank space at the end of any FrontPage toolbar. Each of these toolbars is covered later in the book, but here is a brief introduction to the other toolbars you can use:

- **DHTML Effect toolbar** Dynamic HTML (DHTML) allows you to add dynamic effects to your documents. For example, you can set up a button to glow whenever you move the mouse pointer over it, or you can cause text to fly off the page. The DHTML Effect toolbar lets you choose and configure the effect you want. This toolbar is covered in more detail in Chapter 13.

- **Drawing toolbar** You can draw right in a Web page using the tools in the Drawing toolbar. From this toolbar, you can add shapes such as arrows, flowchart symbols, stars, banners, lines, and callouts. You can change the weight, fill color, style, and other properties of the shapes, and add a drop shadow to any shape. Finally, you can add and customize the properties of text as well. The Drawing toolbar is covered in more detail in Chapter 3.

NOTE *When you click the AutoShapes selection in the Drawing toolbar, a pop-up list of available AutoShapes appears. You can tear off this list of AutoShapes to turn the list into a toolbar. As with other tear-off menus, clicking the "x" in the upper-right corner closes the toolbar.*

- **Drawing Canvas toolbar** When you create a drawing in a Web page, it resides on a "canvas"—an area of the page that you can modify independently of the rest of the page. The Drawing Canvas toolbar enables you to change the size of the canvas, as well as crop the drawing to any size you wish. The Drawing Canvas toolbar is covered in Chapter 3.

- **Navigation toolbar**   The Navigation toolbar provides tools for working the navigation view (discussed briefly later in this chapter). Using the Navigation toolbar, you can set up the structure of your Web site and determine how pages connect to one another. This toolbar, and the associated Navigation view, are discussed in more detail in Chapter 9.

- **Pictures toolbar**   Whenever you select a graphical element on a Web page, the Pictures toolbar appears. It contains tools for modifying graphics and attaching *hyperlinks* to areas of a graphic. The Pictures toolbar and the use of graphics with FrontPage 2002 are discussed in more detail in Chapters 3, 4, and 8.

NOTE   *A hyperlink is a way to jump to another section of the Web site or to another Web site.*

- **Positioning toolbar**   This toolbar enables you to precisely position elements on a page. It is discussed in more detail in Chapter 13.

- **Reporting toolbar**   FrontPage 2002 provides a large number of reports to help you manage your Web site and find errors. The Reports toolbar lets you choose the report you want to run and configure any parameters for the report. The Reports toolbar is discussed in more detail in Chapter 16.

- **Style toolbar**   The Style toolbar makes it easy to apply a style to text and modify the format of a style. Note that these styles will not be displayed correctly unless the reader's browser is fully compatible with *Cascading Style Sheets (CSS)*—and not many are.

- **Table toolbar**   Tables are important not only for the information they display, but also because they make it easy to align all sorts of elements on a Web page. The Table toolbar lets you perform just about anything you need to do with a table, including creating it, adding rows and columns, merging and splitting cells, changing the alignment of cell contents, and modifying the background color. For more detail on the Table toolbar—and tables—see Chapter 6.

- **Word Art toolbar**   Did you know you can make art out of words? You can take any text and change its orientation, color, size, and shape; and then use the results on a Web page. The Word Art toolbar, covered in Chapter 3, will help you get creative with text.

The Views Bar

The Views bar appears by default down the left side of the screen. From the Views bar, you can access the various FrontPage views. These views enable you to work on Web pages, work directly with files and folders, run reports, assemble the structure of your Web site and navigate it, view and work with hyperlinks, and assign and monitor tasks. To change the view, simply click the view you want to use. You can also choose the view you want from the top section of the View menu.

You can change the width of the Views bar by moving the mouse over the bar's right border, holding down the left mouse button, and dragging the border left or right. You can also hide the Views bar. To do so, right-click in the Views bar and pick Hide Views Bar from the shortcut menu. Alternatively, you can deselect Views Bar in the View menu. If the Views bar is hidden, select View | Views Bar to redisplay it.

NOTE   *You can change the size of the icons in the Views bar from the shortcut menu. Simply pick Small Icons or Large Icons to make your choice.*

The Main Window Area

The bulk of the FrontPage screen is taken up by the main window area. This is where you do your actual work, and the contents change depending on which view you are in. For example, if you are in Page view, the main window area is where you build your pages. If you are in Reports view, the output of the currently running report is displayed in this area.

The Folder List Bar

The Folder List bar is a navigation tool, optionally available in the Page, Navigation, and Hyperlink views, and always visible in the Folders view. The Folder List bar displays the folders and files that make up your Web site (except in the Folder view, where it displays the folders only). You can expand a folder that has files or subfolders by clicking on the "+" sign next to the folder name, much like Windows Explorer. To open any file and begin working with it, select the file in the Folder List bar and choose Open from the shortcut menu. Alternatively, you can just double-click the file. The file will open in whatever application is associated with the file type.

You can tell which files are currently open in the Page view by the icon displayed for the page in the Folder List. If the page is open, the Page icon is displayed with a small pencil overlaying the icon.

You can change the width of the Folder List bar by moving the mouse over its right border, holding down the left mouse button, and dragging the border left or right. You can also hide the Folder List bar. To do so, deselect Folder List in the View menu. If the Folder List bar is hidden, select View | Folder List to redisplay it.

NOTE *You cannot hide the Folder List while in Folder view; in that view, it is always displayed.*

The Navigation Pane

As will be discussed shortly, FrontPage provides the Navigation view to show you the structure of your Web site. However, as we'll see in Chapter 9, choosing the Navigation view from the Views bar displays the Navigation view in the main window area. As a result, you can't use the Navigation view to see both a page and the structure of the Web site at the same time. FrontPage provides another view of the Web site structure: the Navigation Pane (see Figure 1-3). Unlike the Navigation view, the Navigation Pane displays the structure as a tree. Other than that, though, the Navigation Pane functions pretty much the same way the Navigation view does. To access the Navigation Pane, choose View | Navigation Pane. Alternatively, if you are viewing the Folder List, click the Navigation tab at the bottom of the Folder List.

NOTE *To switch back to the Folder List from the Navigation Pane, click the Folder List tab.*

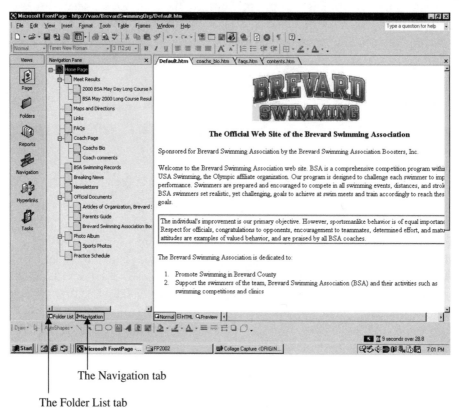

The Navigation tab

The Folder List tab

FIGURE 1-3   The Navigation Pane enables you to see both your Web pages and the structure of your Web site at the same time.

The Task Pane

The Task Pane (see Figure 1-4) provides easy access to three kinds of tasks: opening an existing Web page or creating a new Web page; working with the Office clipboard; and searching for specific files (all discussed in Chapter 2). The task is indicated by the Task Pane title, and you can switch tasks by clicking on the small arrow at the right end of the title bar and choosing the task you want from the drop-down list. You can also switch tasks by clicking on the left- or right-facing arrows at the left end of the title bar.

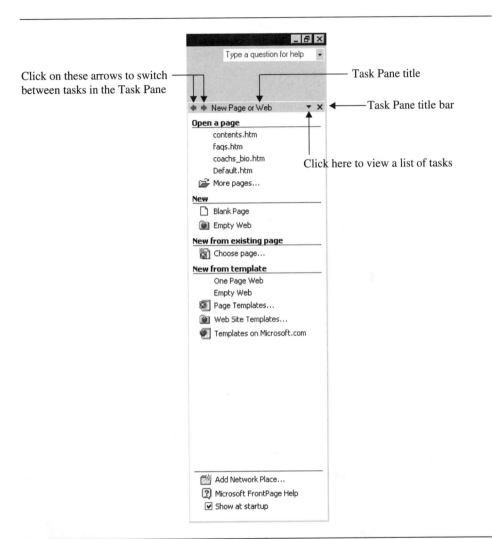

Click on these arrows to switch between tasks in the Task Pane

Task Pane title

Task Pane title bar

Click here to view a list of tasks

FIGURE 1-4   This version of the Task Pane provides the options you need to open or create a Web page.

The Task Pane is docked to the right edge of the screen by default. However, you can move the Task Pane by clicking and holding down the left mouse button on the title bar, and dragging the Task Pane away from the right edge. Once you have undocked the Task Pane, it turns into a free-floating window. You can drag this window to the left side of the screen and dock it at the left edge. You cannot dock the Task Pane at the top or bottom of the screen.

 *If you want the Task Pane to always appear when you start FrontPage, check the Show at Startup checkbox at the bottom of the Task Pane.*

Use Page View

The view where you'll probably spend most of your time in FrontPage is the Page view (see Figure 1-5). Page view is your document editor—it's where you build your Web pages, create and format text, add graphics, set up hyperlinks, and create forms and tables. In short, you add all the content to your Web site using the Page view.

Page view gives you three ways of looking at your Web page: Normal, HTML, and Preview. If you have multiple pages open, you can switch between the pages in any of these views either by selecting the page you want from the Window menu or by clicking on the page tab for the page you want.

Normal Page View

Figure 1-5 shows the Normal Page view. To switch to this view from any other view, click on the Normal tab at the bottom of the working area (visible in Figure 1-3). Normal Page view is where you actually build your Web pages, using all the tools we'll discuss in this book. While this view gives you a pretty good idea of what your page will look like, the layout is not exact, nor are elements such as DHTML and hyperlinks functional. Normal Page view is a *working* environment, not a testing environment.

FIGURE 1-5 Page view is where you create your Web pages.

 *Actually, you can follow hyperlinks in the Normal Page view. To do so,* CTRL-*click on the hyperlink.*

HTML Page View

As discussed in the Introduction, Web pages are largely made up of HTML code. When you use FrontPage as most people do—by adding and modifying text and graphics in the Normal Page view—FrontPage automatically generates the HTML code that makes up your page. The nice thing about FrontPage is that you don't have to know HTML. You don't even have to look at this programming code if you don't want to. Still, there are times when it can be helpful to work with a page's HTML source code. This is especially true if you know how to program HTML, and you want to add your own HTML code to the page. The HTML Page view (see Figure 1-6) enables you to view and even modify the defining code for an HTML page. To switch to this view from another view, click on the HTML tab at the bottom of the working area.

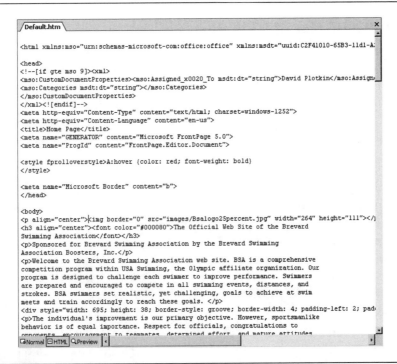

FIGURE 1-6   The HTML Page view is where you can see—and change—the HTML code for a page.

 *FrontPage makes it easy to locate a particular portion of a page in the HTML Page view. Simply highlight that portion of the page in Normal Page view, then switch to HTML Page view. The HTML code that defines the highlighted portion of the page will also be highlighted.*

Understand HTML Code

HTML is a coding language based on tags, which are commands enclosed in <brackets>. One tag turns a command on, and a matching tag—with a slash (/) in front of it—turns the command off. For example, to make text bold, HTML uses the command <b> to turn bolding on, and </b> to turn bolding off. Of course, writing the HTML code to define a complex structure such as a form, frame, or table can become quite tedious and prone to error. That's why you should generally let FrontPage do it for you. Nevertheless, if you want to modify the HTML code for your own special purposes, switch to the HTML Page view and make your changes. FrontPage will make sure the code you enter is valid (although its technique for correcting errors—which is simply to remove any erroneous tags—is not too informative).

Format the Display of HTML Code

You can customize the way the HTML Page view displays the HTML code. First of all, you can turn on color coding from the shortcut menu. With color coding turned on, different elements in the code are represented in different colors. For example, normal text is black, tags are blue, and components (you'll learn about these interesting creatures in Chapter 10) are depicted in gray. Without color coding, all the HTML code appears in black. To turn on color coding, right-click on the page and choose Color Coding.

You can also reformat the layout of the text in the HTML view to make it easier to read. To do so, choose Reformat HTML from the shortcut menu. Reformatting the HTML text places major tags (such as the <p> paragraph tag) on their own line of text.

You can further customize the HTML code display using the Page Options dialog box, discussed in Chapter 11.

Add Your Own HTML Code

If you are competent in HTML, you can add your own HTML code to the pages generated by FrontPage. To add HTML code to the HTML Page view, simply place the text cursor where you want to make your changes and begin typing in your code. You can edit the page much as you could with any word processor. If you make a syntax error in the code, FrontPage will try to correct it for you, adding tags as necessary to keep everything working. For example, many HTML tags must function in pairs, with an opening command and a closing command. If you add the opening command and forget the closing command, FrontPage will add it for you. Except for this syntax checking, FrontPage will not modify any HTML code you insert into the page.

You can also enter HTML directly in the Normal Page view. To do so, choose Insert | Web Component to display the Insert Web Component dialog box:

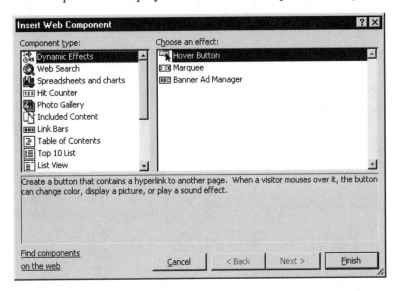

Select Advanced Controls from the Component type list on the left side of the dialog box, and pick HTML from the Choose a Control list on the right side of the dialog box. Then click the Finish button. FrontPage displays a dialog box for you to enter HTML:

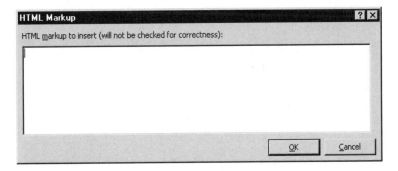

The code you enter by means of this dialog box is *not* checked for correctness, however, so be careful.

Preview Page View

The Preview Page view (see Figure 1-7) is where you can test some of your page functionality. For example, unlike Normal Page view, hyperlinks are "live" (just click on the hyperlink to navigate to the hyperlink's target) in Preview Page view, as are such features as DHTML effects. In addition, the layout is much more exact and gives you a better idea of what your Web page will look like on the Web. In fact, since FrontPage renders its pages using Internet Explorer 5, you'll see exactly what Web surfers will see if they, too, are using IE 5.

NOTE *Even in Preview Page view, certain features may not work on your local machine unless you have set up the Web site as a "server-based Web" (see Chapter 7). Such features include forms and most of the items in the Insert | Web Component menu. However, these features will work when you publish your Web site to a server running FrontPage extensions (see Chapter 17).*

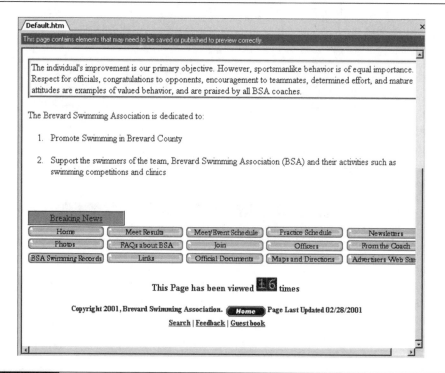

FIGURE 1-7 In the Preview Page view, you see almost exactly what Web surfers will see, and you can test many of your page features.

Make Use of Other Views

Although the Page view is where you'll spend most of your time, there are other views that are very important for managing your Web site. These views provide you with a way to see important aspects of the site, as well as run reports to identify potential problems. In addition, one of the views helps you plan the tasks involved in building and maintaining the site.

Examine Files with the Folders View

The Folders view (Figure 1-8) provides a view into your Web site that will be very comfortable for people used to dealing with files and folders. It exists for the benefit of those who wish to work with their Web site simply as a set of folders and files. To access the Folders view, click on the Folders icon in the Views bar, or choose View | Folders.

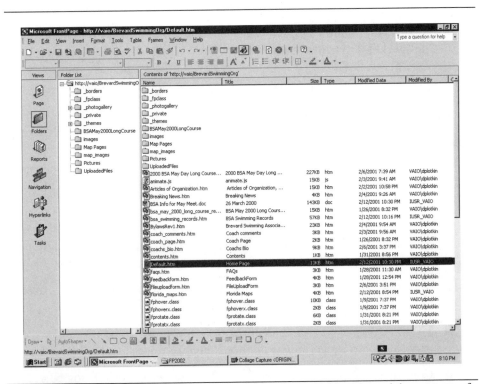

FIGURE 1-8 The Folders view shows the folders in the Folder List and the contents of the selected folder on the right.

Folders view offers both the Folder List (which you cannot turn off in this view) and the Contents pane. The Folder List is a collapsible list that shows you the folders contained in your Web site. You may wonder where some of the folders came from—for example, the _private folder. This is one of the folders created automatically by FrontPage when you create a Web site; you can see these folders in the Folder List, as well as any folders you create yourself.

The Contents pane displays both files and subfolders of the folder selected in the Folder List. Some of the subfolders may be *subwebs*—Web sites that are nested inside the current Web site. These are designated by a folder symbol with a globe superimposed on it.

Across the top of the Contents pane are several columns that label the information you can see. To shrink or expand the column width, move the mouse pointer to the border between two columns (it turns into a two-headed arrow when it's directly on the border), and drag the border left or right. The columns in the Contents pane are as follows:

- **Name** The actual name of the file or folder.

- **Title** This column shows the title by which a file is known in FrontPage. For an HTML document (Web page), this is the title you assign using the Page Properties dialog box. For other types of files (such as graphics) it is the full path to the file. This column is not populated for folders.

NOTE *When someone uses a Web browser to display a Web page, the title appears in the browser's title bar.*

- **Size** The size of the file in kilobytes (KB) or megabytes (MB). This column is not populated for folders.

- **Type** The document type, which is simply the last three letters (after the period) of the file name. For example, HTML files are labeled as .htm. This column is not populated for folders.

- **Modified Date** The date and time when the last modification was made to the file. This column is not populated for folders.

- **Modified By** The username of the person who made the last file modification. This column is not populated for folders.

- **Comments** The comments added in the Page Properties dialog box (Summary tab) for this file. This column is not populated for folders.

By default, Folders view does not display hidden files or folders. To show them, choose Tools | Web Settings and click on the Advanced tab in the Web Settings dialog box. Then check the Show Hidden Files And Folders checkbox.

The Folders view provides quite a number of ways of working with your files. The simplest way to make changes is to use the shortcut menu. Three different types of shortcut menu are available, depending on whether you right-click in an empty area, right-click a folder, or right-click a file.

If you right-click in an empty area of the Folders view, the following shortcut menu choices are available:

- **New | Page**   Adds a new page to the currently selected Web site or folder. Once the new page appears, you can open the Page Properties dialog box and give it a meaningful title.

- **New | Folder**   Adds a nested folder to the currently selected Web site or folder. Once the new folder appears, you can choose Rename from the shortcut menu for the folder and rename it whatever you want.

- **New | Document Library**   Enables you to create a library of documents. A document library is a folder that makes it easy to share documents with other team members working on your intranet. The folder (library) displays documents in a list that can be filtered and sorted. This option is only enabled if you installed the Office Web Server, a new collaboration tool packaged with Office XP. Use of the Document Library is not covered in this book.

- **New | List**   Enables you to create special, sharable lists. These lists include discussions, announcements (news and information), contacts, events, tasks, and custom lists. These lists are sharable by team members working on your intranet. This option is only enabled if you installed Office Web Server. Use of lists is not covered in this book.

- **New | Survey**   Enables you to create surveys for taking polls from your team members. You specify the questions and define how users enter their answers. This option is only enabled if you installed the Office Web Server. Use of surveys is not covered in this book.

- **Up One Level**   Only available in the Contents pane, when the current view is not the topmost level of the Web site. Choosing this option takes you up a level in the Web hierarchy, to the parent folder or Web site.

■ **Paste**   Pastes the contents of the clipboard at the selected location. This is only available if the contents of the clipboard are appropriate for pasting into the Folder List or Contents pane. For example, if you copy a Web page to the clipboard (by right-clicking on a Web page file and choosing Copy from the shortcut menu), you can paste the Web page into the Folders view. But if the contents of the clipboard are text you copied from a Word document (for example), the Paste option is unavailable because you can't paste text into the Folders view.

■ **Web Settings**   Only available in the Contents pane. Choosing this menu option displays the Web Settings dialog box.

If you right-click a file in the Folders view, the shortcut menu has the following options:

■ **Open**   Loads the page either into the page editor or into another editor you have already defined for the file type. See "Configure the Editors," later in this chapter, for more information on how to configure FrontPage to work with a different editor.

■ **Open With**   Loads the page into an editor that you select from the Open With dialog box.

■ **Preview in Browser**   Loads the page into your browser.

■ **Cut**   Removes the file from the display and places it on the clipboard, making it available to be pasted elsewhere. (This command is also available in the Edit menu.)

■ **Cópy**   Copies the file to the clipboard and makes it available to be pasted elsewhere. (This command is also available in the Edit menu.)

■ **Paste**   Pastes the file that is currently residing in the clipboard (as a result of using Cut or Copy) into the selected folder or Web site. If the folder or Web site already contains a file with the same name as the file you are pasting, FrontPage automatically renames the pasted file. (This command is also available in the Edit menu.)

■ **Rename**   Enables you to change the name of the file by typing a new name into the Folders view. Choosing Rename selects the existing name; you can then type in the new name. FrontPage recalculates any hyperlinks to a renamed file so that the hyperlinks are not broken. (As an alternative to using this shortcut menu option, you can also rename a file by clicking it, pausing, then clicking again.)

- **Delete**   Deletes the file from the Web site. However, hyperlinks that point to the deleted page from other pages remain in those other pages, and must be removed manually (the best way is by using the "Broken Hyperlinks" report, as detailed in Chapter 16). You can also delete a file by selecting it and pressing DELETE.

- **New | Page**   Available for folders only. This adds a new page to the currently selected folder.

- **New | Folder**   Available for folders only. This adds a nested folder to the currently selected folder.

- **Publish Selected Files**   Publishes the selected files to your Web site, as discussed in Chapter 17.

- **Don't Publish**   This option is a toggle—select it once to turn it on and select it again to turn it off. When this option is on, the file will *not* be included when you publish your Web site (as discussed in Chapter 17). This condition is indicated by a red "x" through the file's icon in the Content pane.

NOTE   *Selecting Don't Publish has the same effect as opening the file's Properties dialog box, clicking on the Workgroup tab, and checking the Exclude This File When Publishing The Rest Of The Web checkbox.*

- **Properties**   Opens the Properties dialog box for the selected file.

If you right-click a folder in the Folders view, the shortcut menu has the following options:

- **Convert to Web**   Available for folders only. This converts a folder to its own Web site, removing it from the Web site it was in before. Any files in the converted folder that you had placed in the parent Web site's Navigation view (see Chapter 9) remain available, and thus can be accessed from link bars that depend on the Navigation view. However, this folder is no longer considered part of the original Web site. Therefore, it won't be published along with the original Web site unless you specifically include subwebs (see Chapter 17). This also means that any new pages you subsequently add to the subweb (or existing subweb pages you had not added to the parent Web site Navigation view before converting the folder to a Web) are not available to be placed in the Navigation view of the parent Web site. As a result, you can't add these pages to link bars that depend on the Navigation view in the parent Web site.

■ **Convert to Folder** Available for subwebs only. Converts a subweb to a folder of the parent Web site. There are some things to keep in mind when converting a subweb to a folder. First, pages in the subweb will take on the "theme" of the parent Web site (see Chapter 5 for more on themes). Second, only people with access to the parent Web site will be able to see the pages in the new folder. Third, hyperlinks in link bars that depend on the Navigation view will be lost, and, finally, any tasks connected to pages in the subweb (see Chapter 16) are removed.

NOTE *Linkbar hyperlinks to the Web site home page and to the parent page are not lost when converting a subweb to a folder. That is because these links do not depend on the subweb's Navigation view—which is lost when you convert the subweb into a folder.*

■ **Cut** Removes the folder from the display and places it on the clipboard, making it available to be pasted elsewhere. (This command is also available in the Edit menu.)

■ **Copy** Copies the folder (and its contents) to the clipboard and makes it available to be pasted elsewhere. (This command is also available in the Edit menu.)

■ **Rename** Enables you to change the name of the folder by typing a new name into the Folders view. Choosing Rename selects the existing name; you can then type in the new name. FrontPage recalculates any hyperlinks to files in a renamed folder so that the hyperlinks are not broken. (As an alternative to using this shortcut menu option, you can also rename a file by clicking it, pausing, then clicking again.)

■ **Delete** Deletes the folder from the Web site. However, hyperlinks that point to the deleted pages (in the deleted folder) from other pages remain in those other pages, and must be removed manually (the best way is by using the "Broken Hyperlinks" report, as detailed in Chapter 16). You can also delete a folder by selecting it and pressing DELETE.

■ **Publish Selected Files** Publishes the selected folder to your Web site, as discussed in Chapter 17.

■ **Properties** Opens the Properties dialog box for the selected folder.

View Reports

The Reports view (see Figure 1-9) provides a series of reports that provide extremely useful information about your Web site. This view is accessible by clicking on the Reports icon in the Views bar, or by choosing View | Reports | Site Summary. The reports, which are discussed in considerable detail in Chapter 14, provide you with such information as internal and external hyperlinks, pages that load slowly, pages that contain broken or unverified hyperlinks, a list of uncompleted tasks, and old pages in the Web site. You can run reports by choosing the report you want from the View | Reports menu, picking the report from the Reporting toolbar, or clicking a line in the Site Summary report (to run the detailed report).

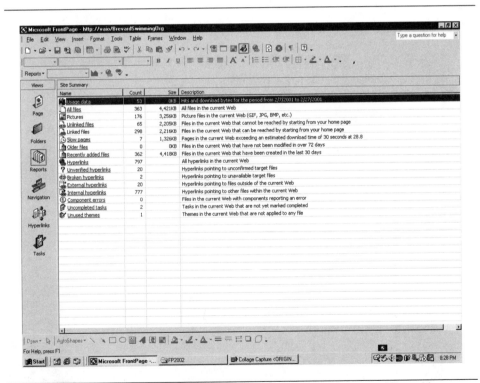

FIGURE 1-9   The Reports view provides important information you will need in managing your Web site.

Navigate the Structure of Your Web Site

You can create a navigation structure for your Web site by organizing your Web pages in Navigation view. The Navigation view (see Figure 1-10) provides a visual display of your Web site that makes it easy to make additions or reorganize it. To access the Navigation view, click on the Navigation icon in the Views bar, or choose View | Navigation. The purpose of the Navigation view is to show you the structure of your Web site—that is, to establish a hierarchy of pages and illustrate how the pages are connected. The connections are shown on pages in the Web site by means of *link bars* based on the Navigation view (see Chapter 9 for more on link bars). The lines in the main window of the Navigation view show which pages are connected by hyperlinks in the link bars.

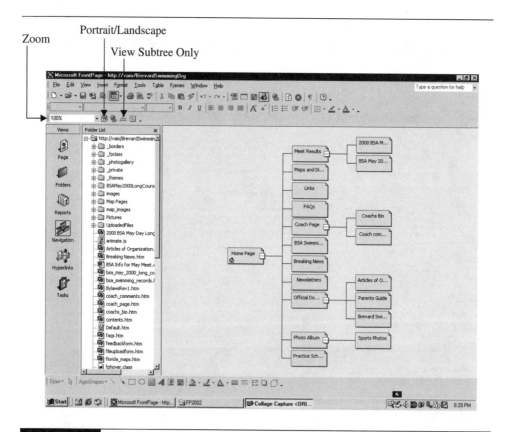

FIGURE 1-10   The Navigation view displays the structure of your Web site; the landscape mode is shown here (portrait is the default).

In the Navigation view main window, you can expand or collapse the page hierarchy. To expand subordinate pages, click the plus (+) sign of the parent page. To collapse the hierarchy and hide the subordinate pages, click the minus (–) sign of the parent page. You can also rotate the view from portrait to landscape mode and back. To do so, click the Portrait/Landscape button in the Navigation toolbar or the shortcut menu that appears when you right-click a blank area of the main window (that is, a nonpage area).

To zoom in (enlarge the picture) or zoom out (see more of the picture in the window), use the Zoom drop-down list in the Navigation toolbar. You can choose zoom levels from 25 percent to 150 percent, and fit the whole model in the window with the Zoom To Fit option. Zoom is also available in the shortcut menu that appears when you right-click a blank (nonpage) area of the main window.

If you want to focus on just one page and all its subordinate pages, click on the page you want and select View Subtree Only from the Navigation toolbar or the shortcut menu. This collapses (hides) the parents of the page you want, and displays a small up arrow (which looks just like the View Subtree Only button in the Navigation toolbar) at the top of the page symbol. To redisplay the rest of the Web site, click on the up arrow.

The shortcut menu you see when you right-click on a page in Navigation view also contains most of the same entries as the shortcut menu for pages in the Folders view. Some of these menu options work differently in Navigation View than they do in Folders view, however. The differences are noted in the following descriptions:

- **New | Page**   When you select New | Page, FrontPage creates a new page and attaches it to the selected page as a subordinate page.

- **New | Custom Link Bar**   Custom link bars (discussed in Chapter 9) are sets of hyperlinks you specify. Unlike link bars based on the Navigation view (sometimes called *Navigation bars*), custom link bars can contain any hyperlinks you wish, including external hyperlinks (hyperlinks to Web pages outside your Web site). These link bars can be placed on any page in your Web site and are useful for providing reusable sets of hyperlinks. Choosing New | Custom Link Bar starts the process for creating a custom link bar on the specified page.

- **Add Existing Page**   Enables you to add any file to the Navigation view as a subordinate (child) of the selected page. This option is most often used to add Web pages from outside your Web site to the Navigation view. To do so, specify an Internet URL on the Address line of the Insert Hyperlink dialog box, as shown in Figure 1-11. You can actually add *any* file to the Navigation view this way. For example, if you add a graphic file to the Navigation view, that file can appear in a Navigation bar, and clicking on the file's hyperlink in the Navigation bar will display the image.

NOTE   *As we'll see in Chapter 8, there is much more you can do with the Insert Hyperlink dialog box. For example, you can create a new document and add it to the Navigation view at the same time (choose Create New Document) or add an e-mail address to the Navigation view (choose E-mail Address). If someone clicks on the e-mail address hyperlink in a link bar, it automatically opens their e-mail application, ready for them to type in their message.*

- **Open**   Loads the page either into the page editor or into another editor you have already defined for the file type. See "Configure the Editors" later in this chapter for more information on how to configure FrontPage to work with a different editor.

- **Open With**   Loads the page into an editor you select from the Open With dialog box. This dialog box displays all editors you have previously associated with the file type .htm.

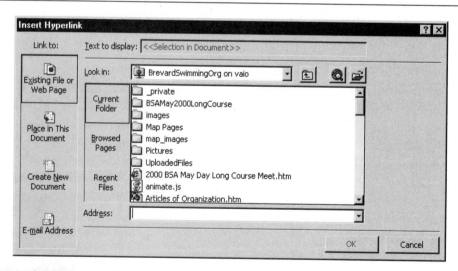

FIGURE 1-11   Choose a file from the list or type a filename in the Address line of the Insert Hyperlink dialog box.

- **Preview in Browser**   Opens the selected page in a browser so you can see how it looks.

- **Cut**   Removes the page from the display and places it on the clipboard, making it available to be pasted elsewhere. (This command is also available in the Edit menu.)

- **Copy**   Copies the page to the clipboard and makes it available to be pasted elsewhere. (This command is also available in the Edit menu.)

- **Paste**   When you paste a page in Navigation view, the page is pasted as a subordinate page to the selected page.

- **Rename**   Rename enables you to change the icon page title in the Navigation view. This icon page title is used to identify the page in link bars (see Chapter 9).

NOTE   *Rename does NOT change the filename the way it does in Folders view.*

- **Delete**   Displays choices for removing the page from the navigation structure only or actually deleting the page from the Web site.

- **View Subtree Only**   This option is only available when a page has a subtree of connected pages. If it does, you can toggle this option on to display just the selected page and its subtree of pages. Toggling this option off redisplays the entire Web site structure.

- **Included in Navigation Bars**   When toggled on, the page is included in the Web site's Navigation bars. When toggled off, the page does not appear in the Web site's Navigation bars.

- **Properties**   Opens the Properties dialog box for the file. If you want, you can change the icon page title using this dialog box, the same as using the Rename menu command.

A different shortcut menu appears when you right-click in a blank (nonpage) area of the main window. These menu options are

- **New | Top Page**   This menu option adds a box (page) to the Navigation view at the same level as the top box in the hierarchy (normally the Home Page of the Web site).

- **New | Custom Link Bar** Starts the process of creating a custom link bar. The custom link bar is not connected to any page, however, so it is of little use until you drag it within the Navigation view and connect it to a page (locating the custom link bar on that page).

- **Zoom** Opens a submenu in which you can choose the zoom (magnification) level. As with the Zoom option on the toolbar, you can choose various zoom levels between 150 percent and Size to Fit.

- **Portrait/Landscape** Choose this toggle to change the Navigation view from portrait to landscape and back.

- **Expand All** Expands all the collapsed subtrees in the Web site. This has the same effect as clicking all the plus (+) signs to expand individual subtrees.

- **Web Settings** Opens the Web Settings dialog box.

Use Hyperlinks View

Figure 1-12 shows the Hyperlinks view. This view shows the hyperlinks that connect the individual pages in the Web site. In other words, the Hyperlinks view shows you the Web site as a Web site, with the relationships between the pages clearly visible. To access the Hyperlinks view, click on the Hyperlink icon in the Views bar, or choose View | Hyperlinks. You can center the view on any page. To do so, right-click on a page in the Folder List or in the main Hyperlinks view, and choose Move To Center. Note that the Move To Center option is not available when you right-click on the page that is *already* in the center.

The shortcut menu displayed when you right-click in a blank area of the main window in Hyperlinks view offers the following commands for configuring how the Hyperlinks view works:

- **Show Page Titles** By default, the pages in the Hyperlinks view are labeled with their filenames. If you want them labeled with their titles instead, choose this option. When the checkmark appears alongside the menu command, the command is active; selecting it again turns the command off and redisplays the filenames.

- **Hyperlinks to Pictures** Normally, FrontPage does not show hyperlinks to pictures, which can clutter up the Hyperlinks view. However, if you would rather see these hyperlinks, toggle this command on. The linked images are shown with the Graphic icon.

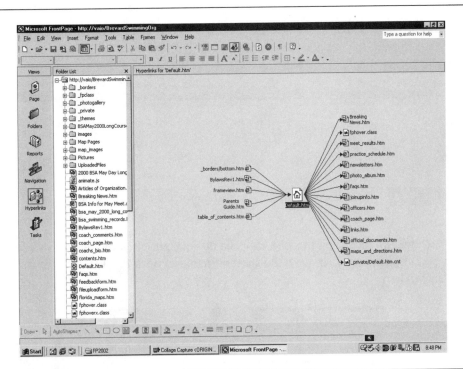

FIGURE 1-12   The Hyperlinks view shows you your Web site as a true Web site, with the hyperlinks between pages clearly delineated.

■ **Repeated Hyperlinks**   Pages often contain multiple links to another page. By default, FrontPage only shows one of these links to avoid cluttering up the Hyperlinks view. However, if you would like to see all instances of links between two pages, toggle this command on.

■ **Web Settings**   This command displays the Web Settings dialog box.

Manage Your Web Site with Task View

Tasks that are associated with a page are useful for launching that page and working on it. When you work on a page, you can even have FrontPage mark it as complete when you exit the page. With Task view, you can create tasks that may be associated either with particular pages or with general tasks, assign them to participants in the project, and check the progress of those tasks. To access the Task view, choose the Task icon in the Views bar, or choose View | Tasks. The Task view is shown in Figure 1-13.

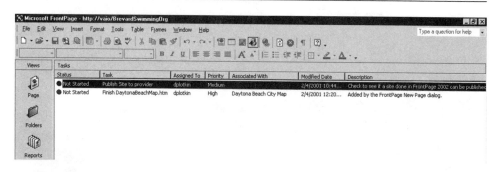

FIGURE 1-13 Task view is probably the most powerful of your Web management tools.

You can edit the properties of a task. To do so, right-click on the task in Task view and choose Edit Task from the shortcut menu to open the Task Details dialog box shown here.

You add a task by selecting Edit | Task | Add Task. If you have a Web page selected in Page, Folders, Navigation, or Hyperlinks view when you create the task, the task is automatically associated with the selected page. If no page is selected, the task is not associated with any page. You can also right-click in a blank area of the main window of the Task view and choose New Task from the shortcut menu. For any of these options, the New Task dialog box that appears looks identical to the Task Details dialog box above (except for the title bar).

The Task view contains several columns:

- **Status**   The Status column shows the status of each task in your Web site. There are three possible statuses: Not Started, In Progress, and Completed. You can change the status of a task in various ways, discussed in more detail in Chapter 16.

- **Task**   The Task column lists the names of the tasks themselves. You can change the name of the task by clicking on the name to select it and typing in your changes. Alternatively, you can edit the name of the task by opening the Task Details dialog box. To open the Task Details dialog box, double-click on the task, choose Edit Task from the shortcut menu, or select the task and choose File | Properties.

- **Assigned To**   This column enables you to enter the name, initials, or some other identifier for the person to whom the task is assigned. You can type whatever you want into this field in the Task Details dialog box; any previous entries are available in the drop-down list.

- **Priority**   This column lets you assign the priority of the task. Three values are possible: High, Medium, or Low. Choose one of the values in the Task Details dialog box.

- **Associated With**   This column shows the title of the page (in the FrontPage Web site) that the task belongs to. This column is populated only if you create a task with a page selected in Page view, Folders view, Navigation view, or Hyperlinks view. When a task is associated with a page, choosing Start Task from the shortcut menu opens the appropriate page in the Page view. You cannot add an Associated With link to a task you create manually.

- **Modified Date**   This column shows the date and time the task was last modified.

- **Description**   Put any information here that's worth noting.

Configure the Editors

When you first install FrontPage, it makes sure that "normal" Web file types are *associated* with an appropriate editor. For example, if you open a file in the Folders view whose filename ends with .htm, the file opens automatically in FrontPage. If you open a .doc file, the file opens automatically in Microsoft Word.

However, quite a few common file types you'll need to use to create a Web site do not have an editor associated with them in FrontPage. An example is a GIF or JPG graphical file type. By default, if you double-click a graphic in a Web page, FrontPage will display a dialog box that tells you no editor is associated with this file type. This can be quite inconvenient, because you'll have to close the page, open your graphics editor, load the image, modify it, save it, and reopen the page!

There is an easier way: Configure FrontPage to open the appropriate editor automatically when you double-click the file to open it. Here's how:

1. Choose Tools | Options to open the Options dialog box. Choose the Configure Editors tab to set up editors for additional file types.

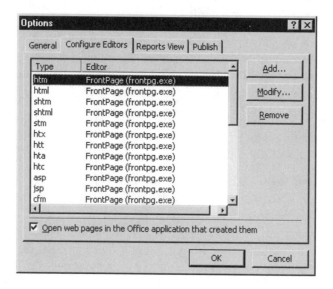

2. Choose the Add button to open the Add Editor Association dialog box, and fill in the information needed to identify the editor you want to use.

3. In the File Type field, type the filename ending that identifies the type of file you want to open in this editor. For example, enter **gif** for a GIF graphic file type.

4. Type the name of the editor in the Editor Name field. Type the name as you want it to appear in the Editor column of the Options dialog box.

5. In the Command field, enter the exact name of the program you want to run when you open this file type, including the path. Alternatively, you can click the Browse button, choose the program from the Browse dialog box, and then click Open.

6. Click OK to add the new editor.

7. Repeat steps 1–6 to add other editors, and click OK when you've finished.

NOTE *You can select an editor and click the Modify button to open the Add Editor Association dialog box to change the editor associated with a file type. Alternatively, you can delete an editor association by selecting the editor and clicking Remove.*

You can create Web pages in other Office applications. For example, you can create a word processing document in Word or a spreadsheet in Excel. If you then save the file as a Web page (see Chapter 18 for more information), you can incorporate the Web pages into your FrontPage Web site. However, by default, if you open a Web page in FrontPage that you created in another Office document, the page opens in the original Office application rather than in the FrontPage editor. If you don't like this behavior and would rather have all your Web page files open in the FrontPage editor, clear the Open Web Pages In The Office Application That Created Them checkbox.

TIP *If you have a Web page editor you prefer over FrontPage's editor, associate the .htm file type with this alternate editor.*

Work with Toolbars

As mentioned earlier in this chapter, toolbars are handy for getting at often-used commands. By default, FrontPage displays only two toolbars: the Standard toolbar and the Formatting toolbar. However, you can configure the FrontPage toolbars to make them more useful for you. You can turn toolbars off and on, hide buttons you don't use, add buttons to the toolbars, and even create your own toolbars that combine various commands. In addition, you can *dock*, or attach, toolbars to any edge of the window (by default, the Standard and Formatting toolbars are docked to the top of the window) or configure any toolbar as a *floating window*.

Configure the Toolbars

You can make quick changes to the toolbars—such as turning toolbars and buttons off and on, and relocating the toolbars—right from the FrontPage desktop.

Activate and Move Toolbars

To view a complete list of the available toolbars, right-click any toolbar to display the list of toolbars in the shortcut menu, as shown next. Toolbars with a checkmark next to them are visible; toolbars without the checkmark are currently not displayed. To make another toolbar visible, simply click next to the toolbar name to turn the toolbar on. Alternatively, to hide a visible toolbar, click next to a toolbar name to remove the checkmark.

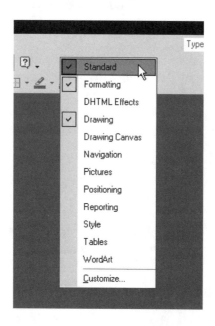

Toolbars can either float on the screen like a regular window or dock to the edge of the screen. If the toolbar is floating, you can resize it by dragging a corner or an edge. As you change the size, the buttons rearrange automatically to fit the toolbar's new size. Figure 1-14 shows the Positioning toolbar as a floating toolbar.

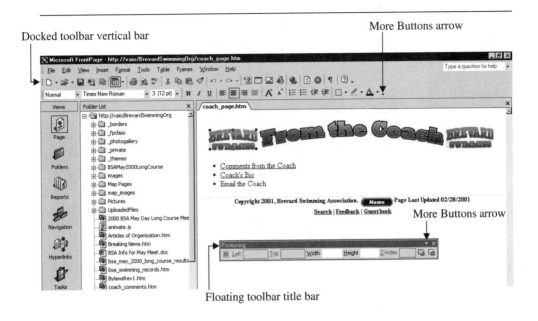

Docked toolbar vertical bar

More Buttons arrow

More Buttons arrow

Floating toolbar title bar

FIGURE 1-14   You can change the size of a floating toolbar, reposition it on the screen, or dock it to a screen edge.

To dock a floating toolbar to the edge of the screen, click the title bar at the top of the toolbar and drag the entire toolbar to the edge to which you want to dock it. You can also drag a docked toolbar back onto the screen, converting it to a floating toolbar. To do so, click the vertical bar at the left end of a horizontal toolbar or the horizontal bar at the top of a vertical toolbar. The mouse pointer becomes a four-headed arrow. Drag the toolbar onto the screen.

Finally, you can drag a toolbar alongside another toolbar, where it can coexist with that toolbar, as long as there is room on your screen. To do so, click on the bar at the left end (vertical) or top (horizontal) of the toolbar and drag the toolbar alongside another toolbar. In the following illustration, the Formatting toolbar is positioned alongside the Standard toolbar. Because there isn't room to display all the buttons, both the Standard toolbar and the Formatting toolbar display a small, double arrow pointing to the right. Clicking this double arrow displays a drop-down list that contains the rest of the buttons in the toolbar.

You can position the Standard and Formatting toolbars on the same line. Choose Customize from the Toolbar List to open the Customize dialog box, and click on the Options tab if it is not already showing. Then clear the Show Standard And Formatting Toolbars On Two Rows checkbox.

Adjust the Toolbar with the More Buttons Arrow

At the right end of each toolbar is the More Buttons arrow. You can see this button on the Standard and Formatting toolbars in Figure 1-14. Click this button, move the mouse over Add Or Remove Buttons, and then move the mouse over the name of the toolbar you want to modify. These actions display a complete list of buttons in the toolbar. Each displayed button has a checkmark visible; each undisplayed button lacks the checkmark, as shown in Figure 1-15. To make a button visible, simply click next to the button name to turn the button on. Alternatively, to hide a visible button, click next to the button name to remove the checkmark.

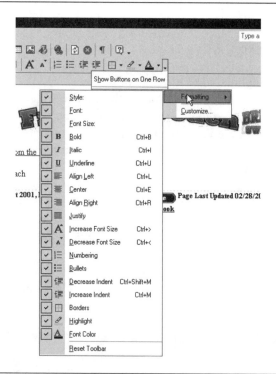

FIGURE 1-15   The buttons displayed with a checkmark when you click the More Buttons arrow are visible in the toolbar.

> **NOTE** *When you move the mouse over the selection Add Or Remove Buttons, the toolbar names that appear correspond to the toolbars that share that line. If only a single toolbar resides on the line (the normal case), then only the name of that single toolbar appears.*

If you want to reset the toolbar to the way it was when you installed FrontPage, choose Reset Toolbar at the bottom of the list of toolbar buttons.

> **TIP** *The More Buttons arrow provides another way to position the Standard toolbar and the Formatting toolbar. If these two toolbars currently reside on different lines, select Show Buttons On One Row to position the two toolbars on the same line. If they are on the same line choose Show Buttons On Two Rows to position the two toolbars on separate lines.*

Customize the Toolbars

FrontPage provides even more flexibility when it comes to toolbars. You can completely customize the appearance of the toolbars using the Customize dialog box. To open the Customize dialog box, choose Tools | Customize. Click on the Toolbars tab to view the tools for customizing toolbars.

> **SHORTCUT** *If you are already working with the Add or Remove Buttons list (as detailed in the last section), you can open the Customize dialog box by picking the Customize option at the bottom of the list.*

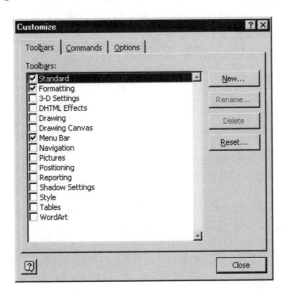

Add and Remove Toolbars

From the Toolbars tab, you can add and remove toolbars. This functionality duplicates what you can do with the toolbar shortcut menu, discussed earlier in the "Activate and Move Toolbars" section earlier in this chapter. To make a toolbar visible, check the checkbox alongside the toolbar name in the Customize dialog box. To hide the toolbar, clear the checkbox alongside the toolbar name.

Configure Buttons

When the Customize dialog box is open, you can rearrange the order of the buttons by dragging a button to a new location, either on the same toolbar or on any other visible toolbar. As shown here, as you drag the button, a black I-beam cursor displays where the button will be located if you release the mouse button.

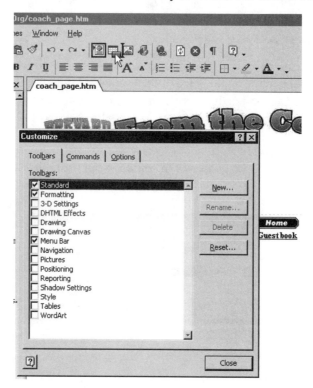

To copy the button rather than moving it, hold down the CTRL key while clicking and dragging the button.

You can delete a button from the toolbar by dragging it completely off the toolbar.

1

Each button also has a shortcut menu (see Figure 1-16) from which you can reset the button to its factory default, delete the button, change its name (by typing it in the Name field), and add a dividing line to the left of the button (horizontal toolbar) or above the button (vertical toolbar) by checking the Begin A Group option.

You can choose to display the button with a graphic, text, or both. Make the following selections from the shortcut menu:

- To display an image: Default Style

- To display only text: Text Only (Always)

- To display text and graphics: Image and Text

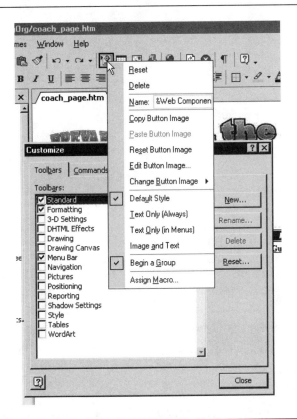

FIGURE 1-16   The shortcut menu for a button offers choices for changing how the button looks on the toolbar, as well as other properties of the button.

You can also change the button image by picking a new image from the images presented when you click on the Change Button Image option in the shortcut menu. You can even edit the button image directly, by choosing Edit Button Image from the shortcut menu to display the Button Editor, as shown below. To change the image, simply click on the color you want to use in the Colors section on the right side of the dialog box, and then click on a square in the Picture section to change that square to the selected color. You can also move the entire image by clicking on an arrow button in the Move section. When you are satisfied with the image, click OK. If you change your mind, click Cancel to leave the image the way it was.

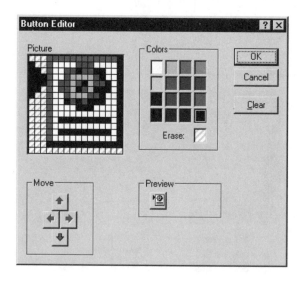

If you want to use a button image elsewhere, you can copy the button image to the clipboard by choosing Copy Button Image. To change a button image to the image you copied to the clipboard, simply choose Paste Button Image. And if you mess up the button image completely, you can reset it to the normal image for that button by choosing Reset Button Image.

Add Commands to the Toolbar

If you would like to add a button (command) to a toolbar, use the following steps:

1. Switch to the Commands tab of the Customize dialog box.

2. Choose the category of the command you want to add from the Categories list on the left side of the dialog box.

3. Choose the command itself from the Commands section on the right side.

4. Drag the command onto the toolbar, as shown in Figure 1-17. As with moving a toolbar button, the final location of the new button is displayed by a black I-beam cursor in the toolbar.

5. Use the button shortcut menu to configure the new button, including giving it an image.

Create a New Toolbar

To create a new toolbar from the Customize dialog box, switch to the Toolbars tab, and click the New button. Type the name of your new toolbar into the Toolbar Name field of the New Toolbar dialog box. FrontPage creates the new empty toolbar, and adds the toolbar to the list of available toolbars in the Customize dialog box, as shown in Figure 1-18.

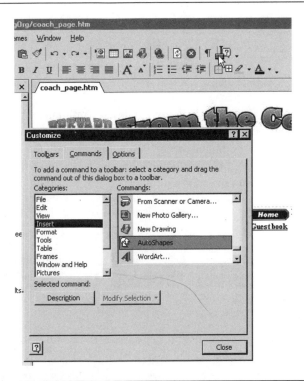

FIGURE 1-17   Choose a command and drag it onto a toolbar to add the command to that toolbar.

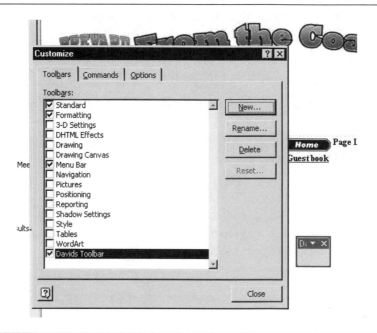

FIGURE 1-18   Your new, empty toolbar is now available—and is listed in the
Customize dialog box.

To add buttons to the new toolbar, switch to the Command tab of the Customize
dialog box, choose a category from the Category list, and pick a command from the
Commands list. Drag the command to the new toolbar to add the button to it. As
discussed earlier, you can configure the new buttons by right-clicking on the button
and making selections from the shortcut menu. Continue adding buttons until you
have the new toolbar looking just the way you want.

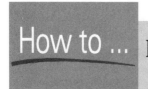 **Rename Custom Toolbars**

You can rename any of your custom toolbars from the Toolbars tab of the
Customize dialog box. Select the toolbar and click the Rename button. Then
type the new name into the Toolbar Name field of the Rename Toolbar dialog
box. Click OK to change the name. You cannot rename the standard toolbars.

Customize the Menus

You can customize the menus in FrontPage in the same ways you customize toolbars. Once the Customize dialog box is open, you can do the following:

- **Move an entire menu.** Click on the menu (such as File or View) and drag it to another position in the menu bar.

- **Reposition a menu item within the same menu.** Click on the menu, then select the menu item you want to move. Drag it up or down within the list of menu items.

- **Copy or Move a menu item to another menu.** Click on the menu to drop down the list of items. Click on the item you want to move and drag it over another menu. After a moment, the list of items under that menu will drop down and you can drag the menu item to its new location. To copy the menu item instead of moving it, hold down CTRL when clicking and dragging the menu item.

- **Set the properties of a menu or menu item.** To do so, right-click on the menu or menu item to display the shortcut menu. The options are virtually identical to those discussed previously for buttons.

- **Add a new item to a menu.** From the Commands tab of the Customize dialog box, pick the category and command, then drag the icon from the Commands list to the menu to which you want to add the command.

Chapter 2

Build a New Web Page

How to...

■ Create a new Web page

■ Add and format text and paragraphs

■ Check your content with the text-editing tools

■ Cut, copy, and paste multiple items

■ Search for text in your Web site

■ Save your Web page

Now that you have FrontPage configured the way you want and you understand the basics of navigating through the many available views, it's time to learn how to build Web pages. FrontPage provides many tools for creating Web pages. You can build a new Web page from scratch or use one of the many templates provided. You can also open existing files and import pages from another Web site.

Once you have a page created, you can add text to it, setting the font, style, effects, color, and other properties.

It's easy to add lists of text to your page and set the alignment and indent properties of paragraphs. With the spell checker, you can make sure you've spelled everything correctly (spelling errors look *so* unprofessional!), and you can use the thesaurus to ensure you've chosen just the right word.

Of course, FrontPage supports the normal Windows cut, copy, and paste operations, including using the Office clipboard to hold multiple items at one time. You can also search through the contents of your Web site to find a specific bit of text.

When you are working on a Web page, you should periodically save your work. You can create a Web page template so that it is easy to create new pages based on a common and look and feel.

Create a New Web Page

A Web site consists of many pages, so the first thing you need to learn how to do is create a Web page. Since you will normally be creating Web pages as part of ongoing Web site development, you should create a Web site to experiment with as we proceed. To create a new Web site, follow these steps:

2

1. Choose File | New | Page or Web. The Task Pane opens, displaying your choices for creating a new web page or a new web site.

If you have the Startup Task Pane option checked (choose Tools | Options and it is the first checkbox in the Startup section of the General tab), the Task Pane will appear automatically when you start a new Web site.

2. Choose Web Site Templates to open the Web Site Templates dialog box.

3. Specify the location on your hard drive where you want the new Web site located by typing the location into the Specify The Location Of The New Web field on the right side of the dialog box.

4. Double-click the Personal Web icon in the Web Site Templates dialog box.

5. FrontPage proceeds to create the new Web site, which takes a moment or two.

6. If you are presented with a new empty page, click the Close box in the upper-right corner of new_page_1.htm to close this page, as you won't be using it. You should then be looking at the default view of the screen, as shown in Figure 2-1.

As discussed in Chapter 1, you can create a new page from the shortcut menu in many of the available views. When you create a new page using the shortcut menu, the page is created immediately and displayed in the file listing. You do not get an opportunity to choose a page template or give the page a filename or title. While you can certainly edit the page properties and modify the filename and title, you can't choose a different template—you are stuck with the blank page "template."

You can create a new page using the shortcut menu in the following views:

■ **Page View**   From the Folder List only.

■ **Folder View**   From the Folder List or the Content Pane.

■ **Navigation View**   From the Folder List or by clicking on an existing page in the Content pane. If you create a page by clicking on an existing page in the Content pane, the new page is automatically a child of the selected page. Chapter 9 provides more details on creating new pages in Navigation view.

■ **Hyperlink View**   From the Folder List only.

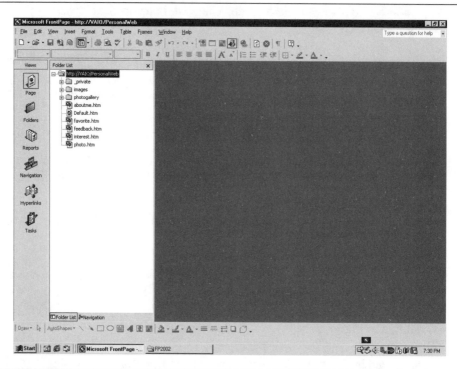

FIGURE 2-1   The default view of the FrontPage screen, ready to add pages.

Use General Templates to Create a Web Page

You can create a new page from the File menu in any view. This technique is the most flexible: You can select the page template (how the page looks) from a list of available templates, and name the page prior to creating it.

To create a new Web page from File menu, use the following steps:

1. Choose File | New | Page or Web. FrontPage displays the Task Pane.

2. In the New From Template section of the Task Pane, select Page Templates.

3. FrontPage opens the Page Templates dialog box and presents a set of common Web page templates, as shown here.

2

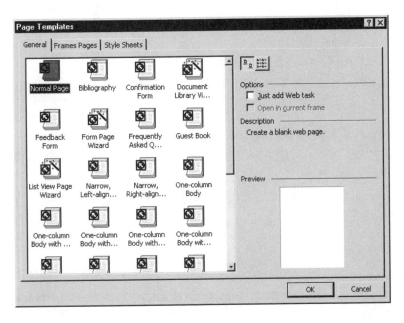

4. Select the template you want. As you select each template, a preview of the template appears in the Preview area in the lower-right corner and a textual description is displayed in the Description section on the right side of the dialog box.

SHORTCUT *To quickly create a Web page from a template, double-click on the template.*

5. If you want to add a style to your Web page, click the Style Sheets tab and pick a style. However, these styles depend on an advanced feature called Cascading Style Sheets (CSS), and only Netscape Navigator 4.5 (and later) and Internet Explorer 5 (and later) display them properly. In addition, each browser displays pages based on CSS quite differently, so it's difficult to predict how the page will look until you actually open it in the target browser.

NOTE *If you check the Just Add Web Task checkbox, FrontPage gives you a chance to name the page and select a title, then creates the page as well as a task to finish the page later. Creating a task to build a Web page is covered in Chapter 16.*

6. Click OK to create the new page (see Figure 2-2).

SHORTCUT *Want to take a quick look at your page in a browser? Choose File | Preview in Browser. If you have more than one browser installed, FrontPage will ask you which browser to open. Pick the browser from the list, and click Preview.*

7. Right-click anywhere on the page and choose Page Properties from the shortcut menu, or choose File | Properties. The Page Properties dialog box opens.

8. Enter a descriptive title for the page. Click OK to close the Page Properties dialog box.

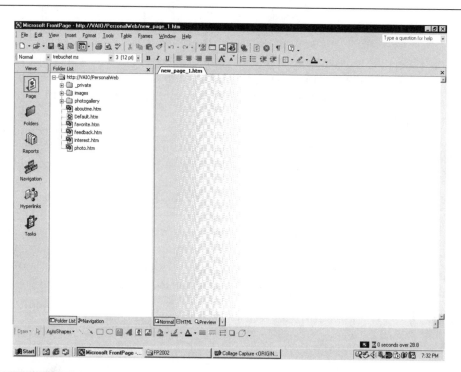

FIGURE 2-2   A newly created page in the Personal Web Site, ready to have a meaningful title assigned to it.

NOTE   *The page title appears in the title bar of Web browsers when displaying the page. It also appears in the Favorites or Bookmark list if viewers add the page to their list of favorites or bookmarks—so picking a good title is very important.*

9. Choose File | Save. The Save As dialog box opens. This box enables you to give your file a name as well as decide where it will be stored.

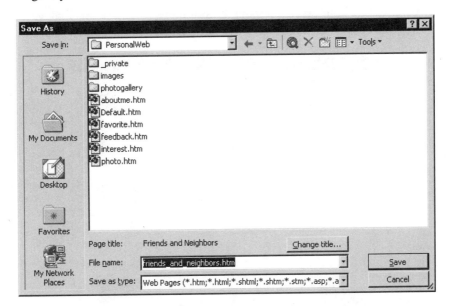

10. Enter the name of the file in the File Name field. If you wish to change the page title, click the Change Title button and enter the title in the Set Page Title dialog box that appears.

11. Click Save to save the page.

The default filename is the page title you gave the page, with spaces replaced by underscores. Choose a location to store your new file. The default location is in the Web site in which you are working, and that is usually a good choice. However, as with any other file dialog box in FrontPage, you can navigate to any location on your hard drive, network, or the Internet and place the file wherever you wish.

NOTE   *See "Save Your Web Page" later in this chapter for more information on saving a page to a variety of locations.*

Import Files and Folders

You can create Web pages by importing files and folders from other directories on your hard drive or network. Importing files and folders copies them and makes them part of your current Web site. You can also import files and folders from Internet Web sites.

To import files or folders from your hard drive or network, use the following steps:

1. Choose File | Import to open the Import dialog box. Use this dialog box to import files and folders from your hard drive, your network, or the Internet.

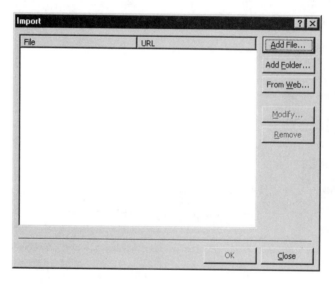

2. To add a file, click the Add File button. This opens a standard File Open dialog box, labeled Add File To Import List.

3. Choose a file from the list of files on your hard drive or network. The name of the file is displayed in the File Name field at the bottom of the dialog box.

SHORTCUT *Want to import multiple files from one folder? Hold down the CTRL key and click each of the files you want to import from that folder. This multiple-selection technique saves a lot of time. If you change your mind about one of the files, just click it again (with the CTRL key still held down).*

4. Choose Open to return to the Import dialog box. The file you chose is now listed, ready to be imported.

5. Continue adding files by repeating steps 2–4.

2

> **NOTE**
>
> *You can change the location within your Web site into which your file will be imported. Click the Modify button in the Import dialog box and use the resulting Edit URL dialog box to change the filename or path. For example, if you are importing a graphic file (such as a .jpg file), you can import the file into the images folder within your Web site by adding* **images/** *in front of the filename.*

6. To add a folder, click the Add Folder button to open the File Open dialog box (see Figure 2-3).

7. Navigate to the folder you want to import and choose it in the dialog box. Then click OK to add the folder and all its contents to the list in the Import dialog box.

8. Continue adding folders by repeating steps 6 and 7. When you are through, you'll have a list of files and folders to import. If you change your mind about a file or folder, simply select it in the Import dialog box and click the Remove button.

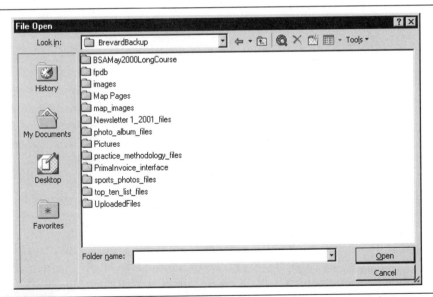

FIGURE 2-3   Use the File Open dialog box to find the folder you want to import.

9. Click OK to begin the process of importing. When the importing process is complete, you can view the new list of files in the Folders view.

To import files from the Web, make sure the Import dialog box is open (choose File | Import if it is not open), and proceed as follows:

1. Click the From Web button. FrontPage opens the Import Web Wizard. Fill in the location (a Web address known as a URL) for the page you want to import and click Next to proceed.

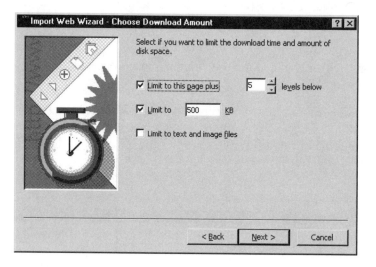

NOTE *Although the From A World Wide Web Site option is selected by default, you can choose the other radio button, From A Source Directory Of Files On A Local Computer Or Network. If you do, a Browse button appears, and the default value in the Location field changes to C:\ You can either type in a filename or click the Browse button to open the dialog box depicted in Figure 2-3. Then choose the desired folder, just as in the previous set of steps. You can also check the new Include Subfolders checkbox to import a folder and all its subfolders.*

2. Decide whether to limit the number of imported "levels" (hyperlinks) away from this page. If you choose to limit to five levels (the default), the page you chose and all the pages linked to that page, and all the pages linked to those pages, and so on for five levels, will be imported. So be careful what you choose!

> **TIP**   *To import just the specified page, change the limit to zero.*

3. Decide whether to place a limit on the amount of data to import. This is a good safeguard, especially if you don't really know how much data is in the pages linked to the page you are importing. By establishing a data limit, you can make sure you don't import too much.

4. Decide whether to limit your import to just text and graphics. If you *don't* limit the import to just text and graphics, you can import Java, JavaScript, ActiveX controls, and who knows what else!

5. Click Next to proceed, then click Finish to exit the Import Web Wizard and begin the import process. Unlike importing files and folders, you can't queue Web locations in the Import dialog box and import them all at once.

Create a New Page from an Existing Page

If you already have a Web page that you want to use as the starting point for a new Web page, FrontPage makes this task easy. To create a new Web page based on an existing Web page, use the following steps:

1. Choose File | New | Page or Web to display the Task Pane.

2. In the Task Pane, select Choose Page. This displays a standard File Open dialog box, labeled New From Existing Page.

3. If the page you want to use is not in the current Web site, choose the Web site or folder that contains the page from the Look In drop-down list.

4. Pick the page you want to use as the basis for the new page, and click the Create New button. A new page is created within your Web site based on the page you selected.

> **NOTE**   *The new page uses the theme (see Chapter 5 for more information on themes) from your current Web site.*

Add Text to a Web Page

Despite all the advances in Web page technology, a great deal of the information on a Web page is still text. FrontPage makes it easy to add text to a page in

Page view, which works much like a word processor. To start adding text, position the blinking text cursor where you want the text to appear and begin typing. To reposition the text cursor within existing text, just click at the new location or move the cursor using the arrow keys.

To replace existing text with new text, you must first select the existing text. There are several methods you can use to select text:

- **Click and drag with the mouse** You can select any block of text by holding down the left mouse key and dragging the pointer over it, then releasing the mouse key. The selected text will be highlighted.

- **Use the SHIFT key and arrow keys** Hold down the SHIFT key and use the arrow keys to move the text cursor. Everything between the original location of the text cursor and the new location will be highlighted (selected). If you use the LEFT and RIGHT ARROW keys, the text cursor moves one letter at a time. If you use the UP and DOWN ARROW keys, the cursor moves one line at a time.

- **Use the SHIFT, CTRL, and ARROW keys** Hold down SHIFT-CTRL while using the ARROW keys to move the text cursor. Using the LEFT and RIGHT ARROW keys selects the text one word at a time. Use the UP ARROW to select everything from the original location of the text cursor to the beginning of the paragraph. Use the DOWN ARROW to select everything from the original location of the text cursor to the end of the paragraph.

- **Use the SHIFT, CTRL, and HOME or END keys** Hold down SHIFT-CTRL and press the HOME key to select everything from the original location of the text cursor to the top of the page. Hold down the SHIFT-CTRL and press the END key to select everything from the original location of the text cursor to the end of the page.

Once you have selected the text you want to replace, simply begin typing. Your new text will replace the selected text.

Format Text

Of course, you are probably going to want to use a variety of text effects to make your Web page more exciting. After all, a page full of just plain text isn't very interesting. FrontPage lets you change the font, font style, effects (such as bold, italics, and underline), font size, and color. You can use the Formatting toolbar or bring up a special dialog box for modifying text.

Adjust the Text Style with the Formatting Toolbar

The Formatting toolbar is the quickest way to make changes to the style of your text. Not all of the tools on the Formatting toolbar apply to text; some of the tools apply to paragraphs, which will be covered in "Apply Paragraph Styles," later in this chapter. If you haven't moved the Formatting toolbar from its default location, it is the second toolbar at the top of the FrontPage screen (see Figure 2-4).

Change the Font

To change the font for the selected text, click the Font drop-down list to display a list of the fonts you have installed on your machine. You can pick a font from the list by clicking it. Before you change the font, however, consider this: Other people may not have the font you pick on their computers. If they don't have the selected font, your carefully crafted page will look different on their computers, because the browser will substitute a font they do have for the font you chose. Therefore, it's best to stick to common fonts, such as Arial or Times New Roman, which everyone has.

Change the Size

To change the size of the font, click the Font Size drop-down list to display a list of font sizes. These correspond to standard HTML font sizes and are the only ones you should use when constructing your Web pages. Pick the font size from the list by clicking it.

Apply Effects

To apply a bold, italic, or underline effect to the selected text, click one of the appropriate buttons.

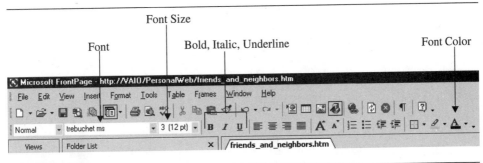

FIGURE 2-4   The Formatting toolbar provides a set of tools for formatting text and paragraphs.

Change the Text Color

The currently selected color is visible in the Font Color button. To apply this color, just click the Font Color button. Otherwise, to apply a different color to the selected text, use the following steps:

1. Click the small down arrow next to the Font Color button. FrontPage displays a list of some of the colors available for you to use (see Figure 2-5). The colors are broken into three sections: standard colors that should be available to anyone using a browser, theme colors if you are using a "theme" for your Web page (see Chapter 5), and any custom colors (More Colors) you have defined. Defining custom colors will be covered in the section "Choose More Colors," later in this chapter.

The theme colors are a matched set of colors specifically designed to work well together. If you have added a theme to your Web site, these colors are already in use in many places on the Web site.

2. If you see a color you like, click it in the list to choose the color.

3. If you want to choose a color that is not visible in the drop-down list, click the More Colors section at the bottom of the drop-down list. Then follow the instructions in "Choose More Colors," later in this chapter.

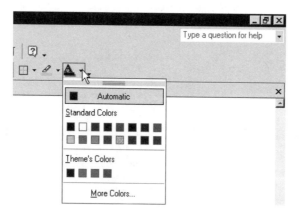

FIGURE 2-5 The Color drop-down list presents you with a list of some of the colors you can use.

Format Text with the Font Dialog Box

You can format your text from a single dialog box. To do so, select the text you want to format and choose Format | Font, or choose Font from the shortcut menu. FrontPage displays the Font dialog box.

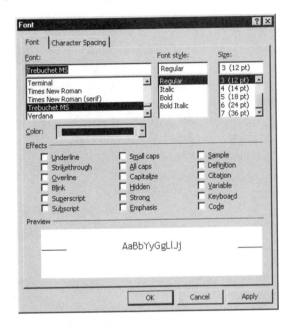

The Font dialog box consists of two tabs. The Font tab lets you make the same formatting choices as the Formatting toolbar. The Character Spacing tab enables you to control how letters are spaced and positioned in a line of text.

To apply text format using the Font tab, make your choices from the dialog box. As you make your choices, a preview of the changes to your text is shown in the Preview area of the dialog box.

■ **Font**   To change the font, choose from the scrolling list below the Font field in the upper-left corner of the dialog box.

■ **Font style**   To change the style, pick the combination of styles you want (bold, italic, or bold italic) from the Font Style list. Notice that the underline style is not available in this list; however, it is available in the Effects checkboxes at the bottom of the dialog box. To removed any styles, pick Regular from the Font Style list.

■ **Size**   To change the text size, pick the size you want from the list below the Size field in the upper-right corner of the dialog box.

■ **Color** To change the color, click the small down arrow at the right of the Color field. The resulting list of colors works identically to the Font Color button in the toolbar, described previously.

NOTE *The Automatic selection enables FrontPage to set the color based on its own rules for color. For example, choosing Automatic ensures that you do not end up with black text on a black background. Essentially, if you want to return a color to its normal default value, choose Automatic.*

■ **Effects** For special text effects, choose from the checkboxes in the Effects section at the bottom of the dialog box. Some of these effects you should recognize (such as underline), while others are holdovers from the early days of HTML. For example, Strong is the same as bold, and Emphasis is the same as italics.

TIP *Think long and hard before using the Blink effect. It calls attention to the text in a particularly annoying way. In addition, it doesn't work in Internet Explorer.*

The Character Spacing tab is shown here. It contains two types of adjustments—Spacing and Position—which enable you to set the spacing between letters and their position on the line.

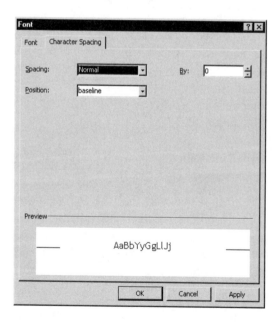

How to ... **Remove Character Formatting**

Once you have applied complex character formatting to text, it can be tedious to remove that formatting, turning off all the special effects, resetting the font, and so forth. The easiest way to remove the character formatting is to choose Format | Remove Formatting. For pages that do not use a theme, this returns the text to plain text with the default settings (Times New Roman, size 3, regular typeface, color black). However, if the page does use a theme, removing the formatting returns the text to the default font for that theme.

Spacing controls how far apart the letters are placed. To adjust the spacing, choose the type of spacing you want to perform: Expanded (letters farther apart) or Condensed (letters closer together). Then, use the By spinner to set the amount. Notice that you can set the Spacing drop-down list to Expanded, and then use the By spinner to set a negative value, giving you the same effect as using Condensed. You can do the same thing with Condensed—a negative value gives you expanded spacing. To remove all special spacing, select Normal from the Spacing drop-down list.

The Position drop-down list sets where the text appears relative to an imaginary line called the text baseline. If you chose a Position value of Raised, the text will appear above the text baseline. If you choose a Position value of Lowered, the text will appear below the text baseline. Set the amount by using the By spinner. Again, if you set a negative value, you get the opposite effect. For example, if you use a negative value in the By spinner when you have chosen Raised, you will get lowered text. To remove all special positioning, select Baseline from the Position drop-down list.

Work with Lists

When you need to present information in a structured way, lists are extremely useful. Lists help you communicate information in a concise and memorable way. You can use bulleted lists or numbered lists. Bulleted lists are better when there is no particular order to the list. Numbered lists help you represent the order of the information, such as performing a sequence of steps. They can also be used to rank things in order of importance. You can use graphics for the bullets in a bulleted list, and even create sublists when you need to break down one list item into smaller parts. Figure 2-6 shows examples of both a bulleted list and a numbered list, as well as the use of small pictures as bullets.

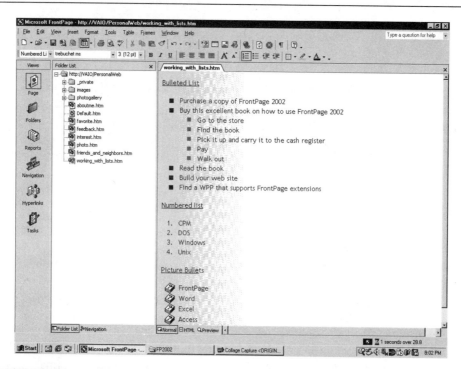

FIGURE 2-6   Both bulleted lists and numbered lists are useful in adding structure to the information on your Web page.

NOTE

When a Web page includes a theme, the default picture bullets are controlled by the theme, although you can pick another picture to use as the bullet (see Chapter 5 for more information on themes). In addition, you can't use plain bullets on a page with a theme. If you want to use plain bullets on that page, you'll have to remove the theme from the current page by choosing Format | Theme to open the Themes dialog box. Select the item (No Theme) from the list box of themes. Choose OK.

Create a Bulleted List

To create a plain bulleted list, use the following steps:

1. Place the text cursor where you want to start the list and choose Format | Bullets and Numbering. FrontPage opens the Bullets and Numbering dialog box. Click the Plain Bullets tab.

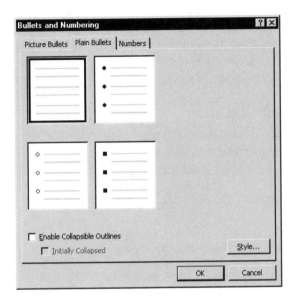

2. Choose the page icon that contains the bullet style you want.

3. Choose OK. The dialog box disappears and a bullet appears on the page.

4. Start typing your list, pressing ENTER at the end of each list item to move to the next line and create a bullet.

5. When you are done with the list, press ENTER twice to stop inserting bulleted items.

To insert a new item in the list, position the text cursor at the end of a line and press ENTER to add new line and bullet.

 *The quickest way to start a bulleted list is to choose Bulleted List from the Style drop-down list in the Formatting toolbar, or click the Bullets button in the same toolbar.*

Change the Bullet Style

If you decide you want to change the bullet style after you create the list, make sure the text cursor is somewhere in the list and choose Format | Bullets and Numbering (to display the Bullets and Numbering dialog box), or choose List Properties from the list's shortcut menu (to display the List Properties dialog box). Select the Plain Bullets tab and choose the page icon for the bullets you want to use. This technique for changing the bullet style works for sublists as well as the main list.

The above technique changes the bullet style for the entire list. If you are not using themes, you can change the bullet style for a single item in the list. To do so, choose List Items Properties from the shortcut menu for the item, then select the new bullet style from the List Item Properties dialog box.

Create Nesting Lists

You can create a sublist within a list to break down a bullet into more detail (see Figure 2-7). There are no limits to how deeply you can nest your lists, but the practical limit is three or four. After that, it gets pretty hard for the reader to keep track of the levels.

To create a sublist, use the following steps:

1. Place the text cursor at the end of a bulleted item in a list. Press the ENTER key to make a new bullet, but don't type anything.

2. Click the Increase Indent button twice. The first bullet of the nested list appears, indented under the parent list. By default, the nested list has a different style bullet than the parent, but you can change that if you wish, using the information in the last section.

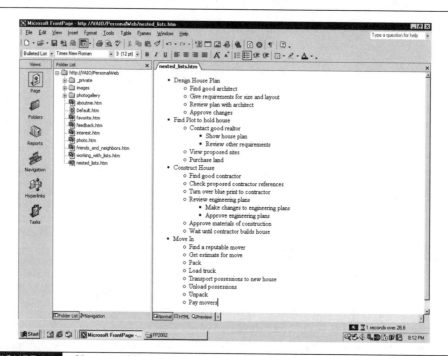

FIGURE 2-7   Use nested lists to provide more detail within a list.

2

3. Type the items in the nested list. Press the ENTER button at the end of each item to move to the next line and create the next bullet.

4. To end the nested list, press ENTER to get a bullet without any text. Press the Decrease Indent button twice. This creates a bullet in the parent list, no matter how deeply nested the sublist is.

You can promote a bullet to the parent list by placing the text cursor in the bulleted item and clicking the Decrease Indent button twice. To demote an item to the list nested below it, place the text cursor in the item and click the Increase Indent button twice.

Create a Numbered List

To create a numbered list, use the following steps:

1. Place the text cursor where you want to start the list and choose Format | Bullets and Numbering. FrontPage opens the Bullets and Numbering dialog box. Click the Numbers tab. Choose the numbering format for your numbered list.

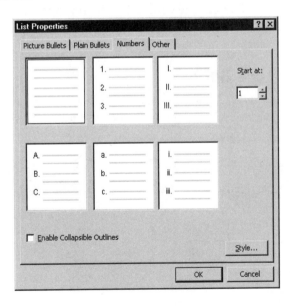

2. Click the page icon that contains the numbering format you want to use.

3. Choose the number with which to start the list from the Start At spinner.

4. Choose OK. The dialog box disappears and a number appears on the page.

5. Start typing your list, pressing ENTER at the end of each list item to move to the next line and create the next number in the list.

6. When you are done with the list, press ENTER twice to stop inserting numbered items.

 *The quickest way to start a numbered list is to choose Numbered List from the Style drop-down list in the Formatting toolbar, or click the Numbering button in the same toolbar.*

Change the Numbering Format

If you decide you want to change the numbering style after you create the list, make sure the text cursor is somewhere in the list and choose Format | Bullets and Numbering (to display the Bullets and Numbering dialog box), or choose List Properties from the list's shortcut menu (to display the List Properties dialog box). Select the Numbers tab, and choose the page icon for the numbering format you want to use. This technique for changing the numbering style works for sublists as well as the main list.

You can also change the numbering style for just a single item in the numbered list. To do so, click on the item and choose List Item Properties from the shortcut menu. In the List Item Properties dialog box, pick the page icon for the numbering format you want to use.

Specify a Picture Bullet

You can use pictures as the bullets in the bulleted list (see Figure 2-8). Don't overdo it—it is best to use simple graphics, such as those in the Buttons and Icons category of the Clip Art Gallery.

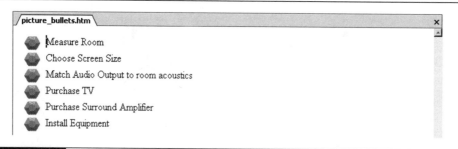

FIGURE 2-8 Using pictures as bullets can give your Web page some extra zip.

To create a bulleted list using pictures, use the following steps:

1. Choose Format | Bullets and Numbering, and click the Picture Bullets tab.

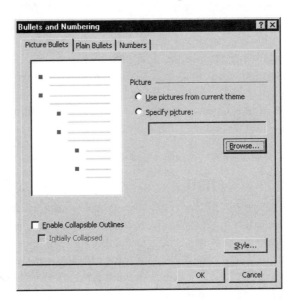

2. If you want to use the default picture bullet for the page's theme, choose the Use Pictures From Current Theme option. Otherwise, click the Specify Picture option.

3. You can type a path to a picture to use as a bullet, but you'll be better off clicking the Browse button to open the Select Picture dialog box.

4. Select a picture from the dialog box.

5. Choose OK in the Bullets and Numbering dialog box to select the picture. The dialog box closes and the first bullet appears.

6. Start typing your list, pressing ENTER at the end of each list item to move to the next line and create a bullet.

7. When you are done with the list, press ENTER twice to stop inserting bulleted items.

If the graphic you choose is not already saved within your Web site, FrontPage displays the Save Embedded Files dialog box when you save the Web page. Rename the image file to something intelligible and save it to your Web site.

Change the Bullet Picture

If you decide you want to change the picture used as a bullet after you create the list, make sure the text cursor is somewhere in the list, and choose Format | Bullets and Numbering (to display the Bullets and Numbering dialog box), or choose List Properties from the list's shortcut menu (to display the List Properties dialog box). Select the Pictures tab, and choose the new picture to use.

If you are not using themes, you can convert a single list item in a picture bullet list to a plain bullet. To do so, right-click on the list item you want to change, and choose List Item Properties from the shortcut menu. The resulting List Item Properties displays only the Plain Bullets tab; choose the page icon for the plain bullet you want to use.

Change the List Format

You can quickly change the list format—for example, converting a numbered list to a bulleted list. To do so, make sure the text cursor is somewhere in the list, and choose Format | Bullets and Numbering (to display the Bullets and Numbering dialog box), or choose List Properties from the list's shortcut menu (to display the List Properties dialog box). Select the tab for the type of bullets you want—for example, if you are converting a numbered list to a bulleted list, click on the Plain Bullets tab. Then pick the page icon for the type of bulleted list or numbered list you want. When you click OK, the entire list is converted to the new format.

 *If you want to convert the list to one of the standard HTML list styles (these appear in the Style drop-down list of the Formatting toolbar), click on the Other tab, and pick the list format from the List Style list box.*

Remove the List Format

You can turn off the numbers or bullets and return the numbered or bulleted list to plain text. To do this, make sure the text cursor is somewhere in a list, and then choose Format | Bullets and Numbering (to display the Bullets and Numbering dialog box), or choose List Properties from the shortcut menu (to display the List Properties dialog box). Then use one of the following techniques:

■ If the page does not use a theme, select the Plain Bullets tab and choose the page icon that does not contain any bullets.

■ In the Numbers tab, choose the upper-left rectangle, which displays no bullets.

■ In the Other tab, choose (Normal) from the List Style list box.

To quickly remove a bullet from a single line in a list, click anywhere in that line and then click the Bullets button in the Formatting toolbar (which deselects the button). This technique also works for numbered lists—just click the Numbers button in the Formatting toolbar instead.

Set Up a Collapsible Outline

If you've ever used Word or another word processor that supports outlining, you'll know how useful it is to be able to expand and collapse the outline to view it at different levels of detail. You can achieve the same effect with FrontPage—clicking a bullet or numbered list item that has a sublist opens that sublist, and clicking it again collapses the sublist.

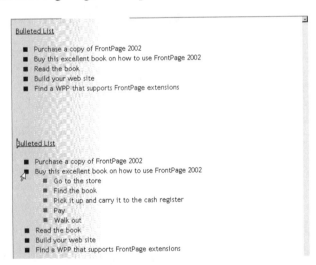

To create a collapsible outline, select a bulleted or numbered outline that contains one or more sublists. Right-click anywhere in the list and choose List Properties from the shortcut menu. Check the Enable Collapsible Outlines checkbox. If you want the outline to be collapsed when you first view it, check · the Initially Collapsed checkbox.

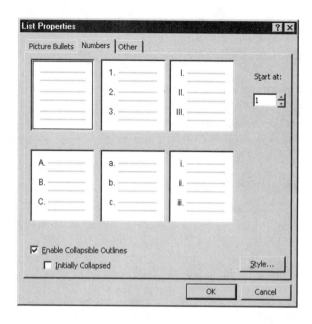

TIP
Since the finished Web page gives no indication that there is a collapsed sublist within a list, you should give your reader some clue. Two common methods include adding an ellipsis (…) to the end of the list item on which you can click to open a sublist, and changing the style of the bullet for that line.

NOTE
Since collapsible outlines use dynamic HTML (DHTML), these outlines will not work with browsers earlier than Netscape Navigator 4 and Internet Explorer 4. And they don't always work well with even the latest version of Netscape Navigator.

Clean Up Your Content with the Text Editing Tools

FrontPage provides text editing tools for spell checking your work (nothing says "amateur" like misspelled words), as well as finding and replacing words. There is also a thesaurus to help you find the right word.

Correct Spelling with the Spell Checker

A spell checker checks the spelling in your Web page. It is no substitute for careful proofreading, because if the misspelled word happens to also be a valid word, (such as misspelling "be" as "bee"), the spell checker won't complain about it—but you still look silly!

Configure the Spell Checker

Automatic spell checking is turned on by default. Misspellings are flagged with a red, wavy underline. If you find the red underlines distracting, you can turn them off. To do so, choose Tools | Page Options to display the Page Options dialog box. In the Spelling section of the General tab, you will find two checkboxes. To hide the red, wavy underlines, check the Hide Spelling Errors In All Documents checkbox. Clear this checkbox to redisplay the spelling errors, provided that automatic spell checking is enabled. To use automatic spell checking, check the Check Spelling As You Type checkbox. Clear this checkbox to turn off automatic spell checking. If you do clear this checkbox, you'll have to initiate spell checking manually (as discussed in the next section).

Spell Check Your Work

If you have automatic spell checking turned on and are not hiding the spelling errors, potentially misspelled words are flagged with a red, wavy underline. To correct the work, right-click the word to display the spelling shortcut menu (see Figure 2-9). You then have several choices:

- **Replace the word** If the spell checker has a suggested replacement for the word, it appears at the top of the shortcut menu. You can simply click the replacement to replace the word.

- **Ignore all occurrences of the word** If the word is spelled correctly but is not common enough for you to want to add to your spelling dictionary, select Ignore All. FrontPage will no longer flag this word as a misspelling anywhere in this Web site during this session.

FIGURE 2-9   The spelling shortcut menu appears when you right-click a misspelled word (indicated by the red, wavy underline).

■ **Add the word to your custom spelling dictionary**   If the word is spelled correctly and you want to add it to your custom spelling dictionary, click Add. The word is added to the dictionary and is not flagged as a misspelling in any Web site.

To manually initiate the spell checker, select Tools | Spelling. The Spelling dialog box appears, with the first potential misspelling already showing in the Not In Dictionary field. You have several options for correcting this misspelling.

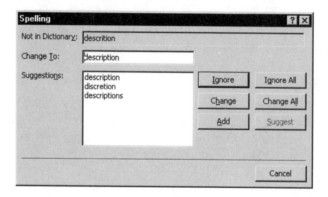

You can accept the suggested change that appears in the Change To field by clicking the Change button. If that is not the correct word, you can choose one of the alternate words in the Suggestions box and then click Change to accept that word instead (there are not always words in the Suggestions box). You can also click one of the other buttons in the dialog box:

■ **Ignore**   Bypasses this word, but continues to flag other spellings of the word as errors.

■ **Ignore All**   Bypasses this word and other instances of the word, and does not flag any of them as misspellings. You would use this button if the word is spelled correctly, but you don't want to add it to the spell checker's custom dictionary.

■ **Change All**   Changes this occurrence and all other occurrences of this word to the contents of the Change To field.

■ **Add**   Adds the new word to the custom dictionary. This word will no longer be flagged as an error in this or any other document.

■ **Suggest**   Select a word in the Suggestions box and click Suggest. This retrieves any other spelling suggestions from the dictionary.

Choosing Change, Change All, Ignore, or Ignore All immediately takes you to the next potential spelling error. This process continues until the page has been checked completely.

NOTE *If the "spelling" error is a repeated word—such as "cat cat"—the Change button turns into a Delete button, and all the other buttons are grayed out except the Ignore button. Click the Delete button to discard one of the occurrences of the repeated word. Alternatively, you can type a replacement word in the Change To field. If you do, the Delete button turns into a Change button, and you can proceed as described earlier.*

Pick the Right Word with the Thesaurus

If you are having trouble selecting the right word for your Web page, you can use FrontPage's thesaurus. A thesaurus provides you with a list of words that have a similar meaning to the selected word. This is especially handy when the same word appears over and over again in a sentence, which can read awkwardly.

To use the thesaurus, use the following steps:

1. Select the word that is giving you trouble. The easiest way is to just double-click the word.

2. Choose Tools | Thesaurus. The Thesaurus dialog box is displayed.

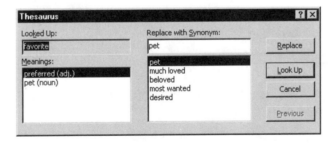

3. The Looked Up field contains the selected word. If the Meanings list box contains more than one suggestion, click the meaning that says what you want it to say. For example, when I chose "image" to look up, I was using it with the meaning "picture," rather than one of the other possible meanings, such as "perception" or "counterpart."

4. If you like the word that appears in the Replace With Synonym field, click Replace. If that word isn't right, you can choose any of the other synonyms in the list box on the right side of the Thesaurus dialog box. Then click Replace.

You can select any word from either list box and choose Look Up to bring up a new list of words to choose from. To return to the previous list, click the Previous button. Continue until you have found the word you want, then click Replace.

Find and Replace Text

To find occurrences of a word or text string, choose Edit | Find to display the Find and Replace dialog box. This features works just as in a word processor, enabling you to find the word you enter in the Find What field.

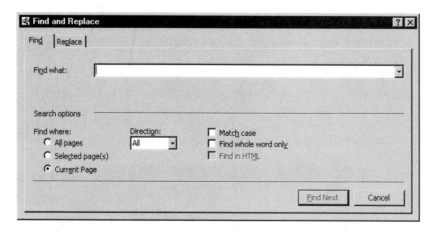

 *A list of words you recently searched for are available in the Find What drop-down list.*

You can set how the search progresses by using the options in the Search Options section of the dialog box. Your choices include searching the currently active page or all pages of the currently open Web site. If you are searching only in the current page, you can specify the search direction (all, up, or down) by choosing one of the Direction options. If you use the All option, the entire page will be searched. To ensure that the search is case-sensitive, check the Match Case checkbox. You might also want to check the Find Whole Word Only checkbox. If you don't, the text in the Find What field is found even when it is embedded inside a word (that is, "ward" would be found in the word "forward").

The Find In HTML checkbox is active only under the following circumstances:

■ You are searching only in the current page and have switched to the HTML tab of the page before beginning the search.

■ You selected the All Pages option or the Selected Pages option.

Checking this checkbox lets you search for text within the HTML code of the page. Such code could include tags or text that is not visible in the normal Page view.

Using Find In HTML is especially handy when you convert a page from another application to HTML. Often, such a conversion leads to a huge number of unnecessary tags, which can increase the file size considerably. You can find (and replace) such tags easily in HTML.

Once you have specified the search parameters (as detailed above), click the Find Next button (if you are searching in the current page) or the Find In Web button (if you are searching in All Page or in Selected Pages). FrontPage proceeds to find the selected text. If you are only searching in the current page, the found text is highlighted. You may need to move the Find dialog box out of the way to see the found text. If you are searching across multiple pages, the lower section of the Find and Replace dialog box displays a list of all pages where the text was found, as well as how many times the text was found on each page.

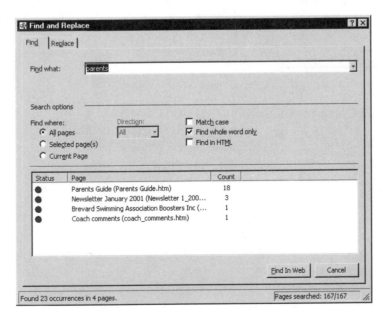

To view one of the pages in the list, double-click on the page. FrontPage displays the page, as well as the Find and Replace dialog box. To return to the list of found pages, simply click on the Back To List button that is now visible in the Find and Replace dialog box. To find the next occurrence of the text, click the Find Next button. If no more occurrences are on the current page, FrontPage queries you as to whether you want to move on to the next page in the list (click the Next Page button) or return to the original list of found pages (click the Back To List button) with the following dialog box:

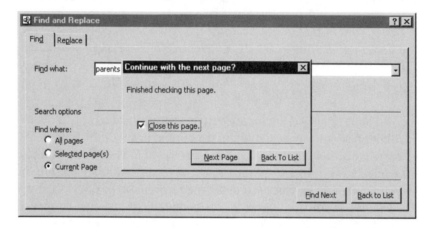

NOTE *You can edit the page you are viewing, even with the Find and Replace dialog box open on the screen. Additionally, once you have viewed one of the pages in the list (whether you change anything or not) the status of the page in the Find and Replace dialog box changes to Edited (the word "Edited" appears in the Status column).*

To search and replace a word or text string, choose Edit | Replace to open the Find and Replace dialog box with the Replace tab visible. The search options are identical to those discussed earlier in this section. Type the word or text string you want to find in the Find What field and the replacement text in the Replace With field.

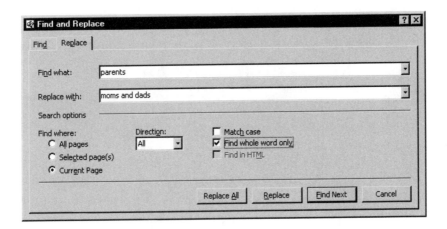

To find the first occurrence of the Find What string, click Find Next. If you want to replace this instance, click Replace. This performs the replacement and jumps to the next occurrence. If you decide you don't want to make the replacement for this instance, simply click Find Next to jump to the next instance.

You can automatically replace all occurrences of the string by choosing Replace All. However, FrontPage does not confirm the replacements, so be careful.

Using Replace All is useful if something that is mentioned frequently (such as a name or street address) changes. For example, if you move to a new address, you'd want to change all mentions of your old street address on the site.

Cut and Paste With the Office Clipboard

If you've been using Windows for a while, you are used to cutting, copying, and pasting a single item using the Windows clipboard. But all the applications in Microsoft Office provide access to the Office Clipboard—which works similarly to the standard Windows clipboard, but can hold 24 items at a time. This can be extremely handy if you have multiple items to paste into your web site. The contents of the Office Clipboard are stored in the clipboard option of the Task Pane. To view the contents of the Office Clipboard, choose Edit | Office Clipboard. Or you can choose View | Task Pane, and then select Clipboard from the list of Task Pane options available from the small down arrow near the right corner of the Task Pane.

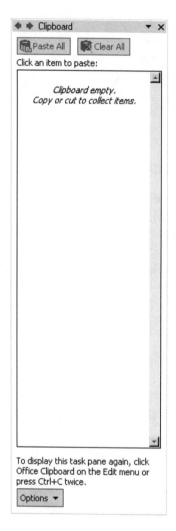

Once you have the Task Pane open to the clipboard option, using the Office Clipboard is very straightforward. To add an item to the Office Clipboard, select the item and cut (Edit | Cut) or copy (Edit | Copy) it. Each new item is added to the clipboard, along with a preview (if available) as shown in Figure 2-10.

2

Click to paste all Office Clipboard entries

Click to clear all Office Clipboard entries

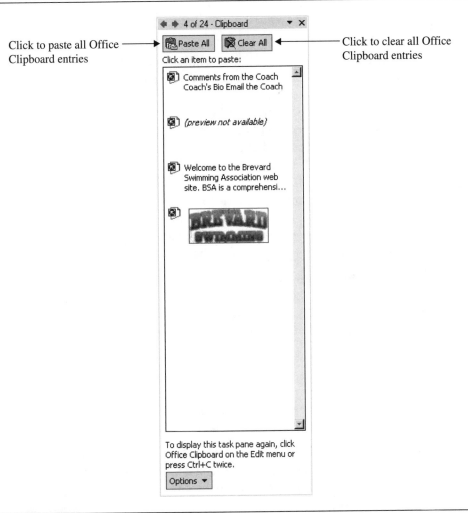

FIGURE 2-10   All your items are displayed in the Office Clipboard.

To paste one of the items in the Office Clipboard into a Web page, position the text cursor where you want to paste the item and move the mouse pointer over the item in the Office Clipboard. A rectangle appears around the selected item in the Office Clipboard. Click on the item to paste it. Or, you can click on the small down arrow at the right edge of the rectangle, and pick Paste from the drop-down list.

 *To delete the entry in the Office Clipboard, pick Delete from the drop-down list.*

You can paste all the items in the Office Clipboard by clicking on the Paste All button near the top of the Task Pane. You can also remove all the entries by clicking on the Clear All button.

You can configure how the Office Clipboard works from the selections under the Options button near the bottom of the Task Pane. All these options are toggles: click on the option to turn it on, and click on it again to turn it off. A checkmark next to the option indicates that the option is selected. The options are

- **Show Office Clipboard Automatically** Opens the Office Clipboard automatically once you have copied more than one item to the clipboard. That is, the clipboard does *not* open automatically when you add the first item to the clipboard, but *does* open when you copy the second item.

- **Collect Without Showing Office Clipboard** Once you have started the Office Clipboard, picking this option enables you to close the Office Clipboard/Task Pane and items you copy will continue to be added to the contents of the Office Clipboard.

- **Show Office Clipboard Icon On Taskbar** When the Office Clipboard is active, an icon appears in the tray at the right end of the taskbar. You can right-click on this icon to display a shortcut menu for setting the Office Clipboard options, clearing the contents, showing the Office Clipboard, and stopping the automatic collection of the items you cut or copy.

- **Show Status Near Taskbar When Copying** Each time you cut or copy while the Office Clipboard is active, a small window appears for a moment near the tray. This window shows how many items are currently in the Office Clipboard.

2

Paste the Way You Want

Normally, when you paste an item from the clipboard, it retains all its formatting, including its style, size, paragraph alignment, and other characteristics. However, there are times when all you want is the plain text, so that you can format it yourself without having to remove all the original formatting. "Paste the way you want" makes it quick and easy to choose either to keep all the original source formatting or to remove all formatting. To use this feature, paste an item just the way you would normally. The pasted item displays a small Paste Options icon.

The individual's improvement is our primary objective. However, sportsmanlike behavior is of equal importance. Respect for officials, congratulations to opponents, encouragement to teammates, determined effort, and mature attitudes are examples of valued behavior, and are praised by all BSA coaches.

Paste Options

Click on this icon and choose either Keep Source Formatting or Keep Text Only from the shortcut menu. You can go back and change your mind later if you wish.

 *If you don't want to see the Paste Options icon, select Tools | Page Options, switch to the General tab, and clear the Show Paste Options Buttons checkbox.*

Search with the Task Pane

You can search your computer's hard drives and your network to locate a file that contains information you are looking for. The search is done from the Task Pane, and you can select to do either a Basic Search (only a few options and quick to set up) or an Advanced Search. The Advanced Search is much more powerful, but also requires more effort to specify the search criteria.

The first step is to open the search version of the Task Pane, shown in Figure 2-11. The quickest way is to select File | Search. Or, if the Task Pane is already open on the screen, click on the small down arrow at the right end of Task Pane header to display the drop-down list. Select the Search option from the list.

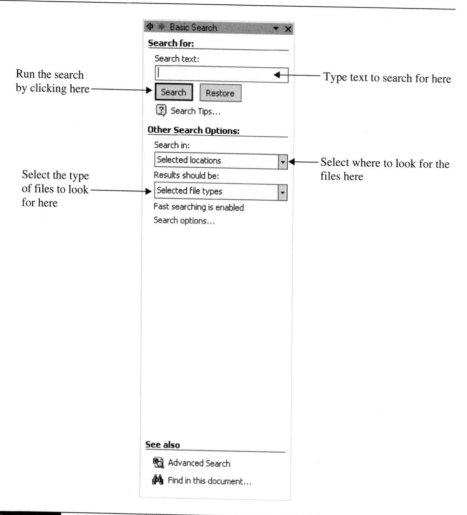

Run the search by clicking here ⟶

Type text to search for here ⟶

Select where to look for the files here ⟶

Select the type of files to look for here ⟶

FIGURE 2-11   The Basic Search version of the Task Pane. From here you can hunt down files that contain information you want quickly.

Build a Basic Search

To initiate a basic search, type the text you are looking for into the Search Text field. If you wish, you can set where the search hunts for results and the types of files it looks through by using the two drop-down lists in the Other Search Options section of the Task Pane.

2

Set the Search Locations

Click on the Search In drop-down list to specify where the search is to take place.

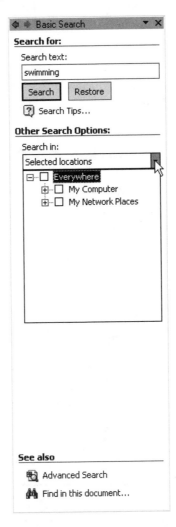

The contents of the drop-down list look much like the Folder List in Windows Explorer. Click on the plus sign (+) to expand a folder or drive and show the contents. All folders and drives are included in the search by default. To change whether a folder or drive is included in the search, click in the checkbox as follows:

■ Click once to deselect the folder or drive but leave the subfolders in the search.

■ Click twice to deselect the folder or drive *and* deselect all subfolders from the search.

■ Click three times to reselect the folder or drive but *not* include the subfolders in the search.

■ Finally, click four times to reselect the folder or drive *and* include all the subfolders (the default).

Set the Type of File

The FrontPage search can include any of the Office files, as well as Web pages. To set the types of files to include in the search, click on the Results Should Be drop-down list.

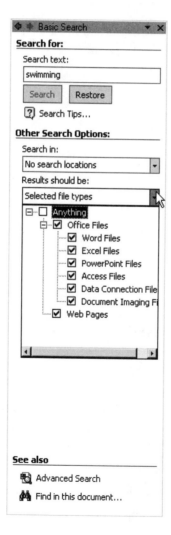

Select a checkbox to include the file type in the search, or clear the checkbox to exclude that type of file. Your list of available files may look different because the only files available in the list are those for the Office applications you installed. For example, if you didn't install PowerPoint or Excel, the PowerPoint Files entry and Excel Files entry would be missing from your list.

Run the Search

Once you have specified all the search parameters, run the search by clicking the Search button. The Task Pane switches to the Search Results version (see Figure 2-12),

FIGURE 2-12   All the files that meet your search criteria are listed in the Search Results version of the Task Pane.

and after a few moments, FrontPage lists all the files that match your search criteria. If you want to stop the search before it completes, click the Stop button.

If the number of results exceeds what can be shown in the Task Pane, you can click on the link at the bottom of the list to display the next batch of files. This link reads something like Next 20 Results (if there are 20 or more additional results). You can continue clicking on this link until you are viewing all the results in a scrolling list in the Search Results Task Pane.

NOTE   *To start a new search, click the Stop button (if it is visible) and then click the Modify button to return to the Search Task Pane. If the Stop button is not visible, simply click the Modify button.*

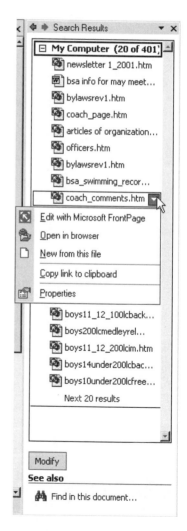

If you hover the mouse pointer over a file in the list, a ScreenTip appears that shows you the properties of the file, including the full path and when the file was last modified.

You can work with the individual files in the list of found files. As you pass the mouse pointer over each file, it is highlighted with a rectangle and a down arrow. Click on the down arrow, shown here at the right, to display your options for working with the file.

If the found file is a FrontPage Web page (.html file), the options enable you to edit the page in FrontPage, open it in a browser, create a new file based on the Web page, copy a link to the file to the clipboard, and view the properties of the file. If the file is a Web page but it was not created by FrontPage, you are offered the option to edit it in the application that originally created it instead: either Notepad or one of the Office applications (they are all capable of saving files to HTML). For any other type of Office file, you can edit the file in the associated application, create a new file based on the file, copy a link to the file to the clipboard, and view the properties of the file.

NOTE   *Some files (such as Access .adp files) do not provide the capability to create a new file from the original file. This is because the Office application does not have the capability to create this type of file, even though it might be able to edit it.*

Build an Advanced Search

If the capabilities of the Basic Search Task Pane don't allow you to narrow your search sufficiently, you can use the Advanced Search Task Pane. To access an Advanced Search, click the Advanced Search link near the bottom of the Basic Search Task Pane. This displays the Advanced Search Task Pane, as shown in Figure 2-13.

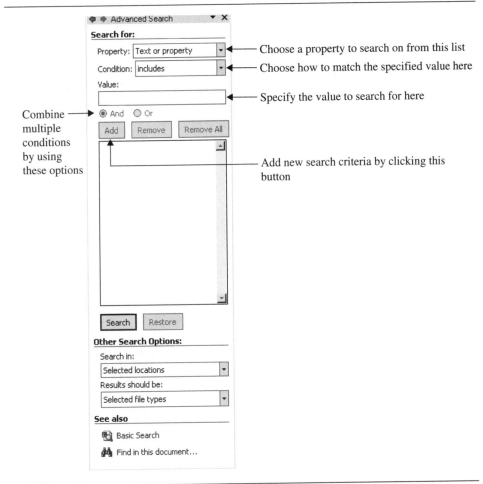

FIGURE 2-13   Use the Advanced Search Task Pane to specify exactly what you are looking for.

The Advanced Search Task Pane has the same options as the Basic Search Pane: The Search In drop-down list and Results Should Be drop-down list both appear near the bottom of the Task Pane. However, you can use the Property drop-down list and the Condition drop-down list along with the Value field to construct a search criterion. You can then combine multiple search criteria together to hunt down just about anything you want to find.

Create an Advanced Search Criterion

To build a search criterion, choose the property you want to search for from the Property drop-down list. There are no less than 32 choices of properties, including such things as the number of paragraphs, number of words, size, template, title, text, author, creation date, description, filename, and many more.

Once you have picked the property, type the value you want to look for into the Value field. Then pick how the value is related to the property by picking a value from the Condition drop-down list. The values available in the Condition drop-down depend on which Property you picked. For example, if you choose Author or Description as the property, the Condition list includes both Is (Exactly) and Includes. If you pick Creation Date, however, the Condition list includes On, On Or After, On Or Before, Today, Tomorrow, Yesterday, and many more.

Once you have specified the Property, Value, and Condition, you can add the search criterion to your list by clicking the Add button.

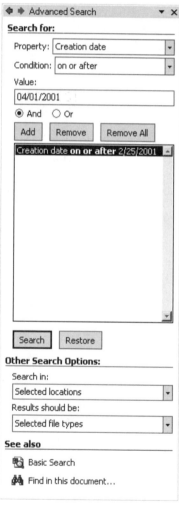

 You can remove a search criterion from the list by selecting the criterion and clicking the Remove button. The Remove All button empties out the list of search criteria.

*If you can't see the whole search criterion in the list, hover the mouse
pointer over the search criterion and a small window displays the search
criterion in its entirety.*

Combine Multiple Search Criteria

The Advanced Search Task Pane enables you to combine individual search
criteria together into a complex search specification. After you add the first
search criterion, construct the next search criterion as described in the previous
section. However, before clicking the Add button to add the criterion to the list,
choose either the And or the Or option.

These options specify the Boolean logic for which files match the search parameters. They work like this:

- **And option**   When two search criteria are combined with the And option, they must both be satisfied in order for the file to be part of the set of found files. For example, if the search criteria was *Creation date on or after 1/1/2001* AND *Number of Pages more than 10*, only files that met both these criteria would be returned in the list.

- **Or option**   When two search criteria are combined with the Or option, a file that satisfies *either one* of the criteria will be returned. For example, if the search criterion was *Creation date on or after 1/1/2001* OR *Number of Pages more than 10*, a file that met either one of these criteria would be returned.

Apply Paragraph Styles

FrontPage supports styles of text you can apply to a paragraph. The style you have seen the most of up to this point is Normal. However, if you click the Style drop-down at the left end of the Formatting toolbar, you'll see quite a few other styles available. To see how they work, place the text cursor in a paragraph and choose a style from the Style drop-down list. Table 2-1 summarizes the styles available for your use, and Figure 2-14 shows a screen with all the headings on it, along with Normal style text. It also shows a sample of a bulleted list and a numbered list.

Style	Description
Normal	Default text: 12 pt., left-aligned, one line of space before and after the paragraph.
Heading 1	Used for largest headings: 24-pt. bold, left-aligned, one line of space before and after the paragraph.
Heading 2	Used for medium-sized headings: 18-pt. bold, left-aligned, one line of space before and after the paragraph.
Heading 3	Next size smaller headings: 14-pt. bold, left-aligned, one line of space before and after the paragraph.

TABLE 2-1   The Styles in the Style List, Used to Format Paragraphs

Style	Description
Heading 4	An excellent choice for subheadings: 12-pt. bold, left-aligned, one line of space before and after the paragraph.
Heading 5	A good bold style, slightly smaller than Normal text: 10-pt. bold, left-aligned, one line of space before and after the paragraph.
Heading 6	A really tiny font, good for legalese, disclaimers, and other stuff you don't want people to read: 8-pt. bold, one line of space before and after the paragraph.
Address	A style designated for putting the Web page author's address on the page. This style is normally displayed in italics.
Formatted	A style designed to allow you to insert tabs and spaces and have them show up in the text. In Normal style, inserted tabs and spaces do not display either in the Web page or the browser. With Formatted style, however, these elements do display, making this style ideal for formatting that requires extra spaces or multiple levels of indent. However, Formatted style does *not* wrap—it appears as one long line. You have to force the wrap by inserting line breaks (press SHIFT-ENTER to add a line break).
Bulleted List	A format that places a bullet in front of each paragraph and the proper indenting for creating bulleted lists. You can replace the bullets with small pictures. Bulleted lists are discussed in much more detail in Chapter 3.
Numbered List	A format that places a number in front of each paragraph and the proper indenting for created numbered lists. Numbered lists are discussed in much more detail in Chapter 3.
Directory List	Visually, this style looks exactly like a bulleted list. This style is usually used for (what else?) directories of files.
Menu List	This style looks exactly like a bulleted list.
Defined Term/ Definition	These two styles are actually meant to be used together. The term being defined is entered first in Defined Term style. When you press ENTER, FrontPage automatically switches to the Definition style, which you use to provide the definition. After entering the definition, press ENTER again to switch back to the Defined Term style. Of course, you can use this pair of styles for any formatting that requires a heading/explanation style. Figure 2-15 shows an example of using these styles.

TABLE 2-1   The Styles in the Style List, Used to Format Paragraphs (continued)

NOTE   *"Pt." refers to "points." Points are a way of measuring the height of text—there are 72 points in an inch. For example, 10 pt. and 12 pt. are common text sizes.*

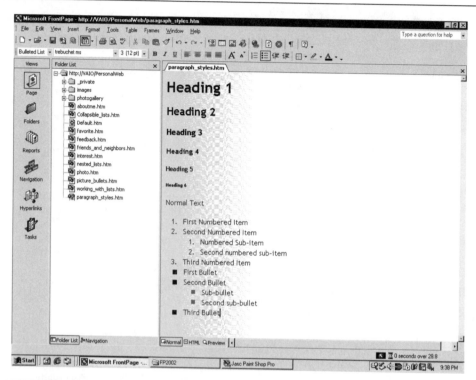

FIGURE 2-14 The heading styles and lists provide flexibility in how you format your text.

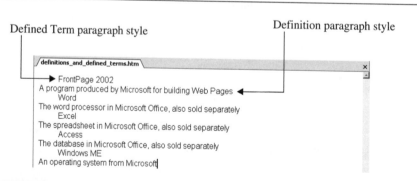

FIGURE 2-15 Use Defined Term/ Definition anywhere you need a heading and explanation style.

Format Paragraphs with the Paragraph Dialog Box

You can format the layout for a paragraph by choosing Format | Paragraph or selecting Paragraph from the shortcut menu. Either way, the Paragraph dialog box opens. In the Paragraph dialog box, you can set the alignment, indentation, and spacing. As you make changes to these settings, the sample text in the Preview area gives you an idea of what your text will look like.

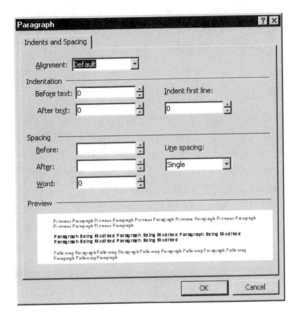

NOTE   *You can also set the alignment (left, right, center, or justify) from the alignment buttons in the Formatting toolbar.*

To set the layout of a paragraph, you can adjust the following settings:

- **Alignment**   Use the Alignment drop-down list to set the alignment of the paragraph to left, right, center, or justify (stretches across the screen from margin to margin unless the line ends with a return).

- **Indentation**   You can set three types of indentation. The Before Text spinner controls the left margin. The After Text spinner controls the right margin—that is, the distance from the right edge of the text to the right margin increases as you increase the After Text indent amount. The Indent First Line spinner increases the left indent for the first line of the paragraph only. This is handy if the style you use requires that the first line of a paragraph be indented.

NOTE _You can't indent the first line of a paragraph the way you would with a word processor, by pressing the TAB key. This is because both FrontPage and browsers ignore such extraneous tabs except in the Formatted Text style._

■ **Spacing** You can set four kinds of spacing. Before sets the amount of white space between this paragraph and the preceding paragraph. After sets the amount of white space between the paragraph and the following paragraph. Word increases the space between individual words. Finally, Line Spacing sets the spacing between lines of text in the paragraph to single, 1.5, or double-spaced.

Set Up Borders and Shading

FrontPage provides options for you to set the background color of a paragraph, or you can use a picture as a background for a paragraph. Additionally, you can place borders around one or more sides of a paragraph, choose a color for each border, and apply special effects to the borders. To set the borders and shading, place the text cursor in the paragraph you want to change and choose Format | Borders And Shading to display the Borders and Shading dialog box. Here you can establish the size, type, and color of borders and background for a paragraph. Any changes you make are visible in the Preview section on the right side of the dialog box.

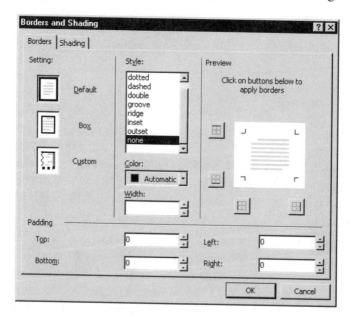

Configure the Borders

The first selection you will want to make is to establish the general type of border. In the Settings section, choose Default (for no border), Box (for a solid border all the way around), or Custom (for customized borders). Nothing actually changes when you choose Custom, but you can then proceed to click individual border buttons in the Preview section to turn specific borders on and off.

NOTE   *If you choose the Box option and then turn off one of the borders, the Settings selection automatically changes to Custom. Also, you can choose Default at any point to remove the borders, and choose Box at any time to place a solid border all the way around the paragraph.*

If you are using the Box setting, configuring the rest of the border parameters is fairly simple:

1. Choose the style you want from the Style list. Each style (such as dotted, dashed, groove, and so on) provides a different effect, and this effect is visible in the Preview area.

2. Choose a color from the Color drop-down list. This list looks similar to the Font Color tool. You can pick from the color palette, a theme color, your custom colors (if you've defined any), or you can choose More Colors to choose or set up a custom color.

3. Select the width for the border from the Width spinner. Notice that if you had not chosen the Box selection in the Settings section, changing the Width to a number higher than zero automatically chooses the Box selection.

4. In the Padding section, choose the amount of padding (blank space) between the border and the text. You can set the padding independently for the top, bottom, left, and right. A higher number provides more white space around the paragraph's text.

The Custom setting gets somewhat more complicated, because you can set the style, color, and width for *each* border. Here is how it works:

1. Turn on each border you want to use by clicking the buttons in the Preview section. When the button is shown as pressed, the border is present.

2. Set the style, color, and width as discussed above. Notice that the borders do *not* change their appearance in the Preview section.

3. Click a border button to apply the formatting you set in step 2 to that particular border. You'll see the change appear in the Preview area. If you want to turn the border off, you'll need to click the border button again, which removes the border.

Once you have created the border you want, there is a quick and easy way to adjust the size of the border—as well as the paragraph within the border. Simply click in the paragraph, and the border displays a set of sizing handles. Click on a handle and drag the border to adjust the size. If you try to drag either the left or right border past the edge of the paragraph's text, FrontPage adjusts the paragraph's width and height so that the text does not extend past the border. You cannot drag the top or bottom borders past the edge of the text.

You can also turn borders on and off using the Border tool in the Formatting toolbar. Click the small down arrow alongside the Border tool to display a list of border choices.

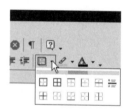

Click on the border option you want. For example, to establish a border around a paragraph, click on the Outside Borders tool in the list of border choices. These options are toggles: click on the option again to turn the border off.

Configure Shading

To configure the shading for a paragraph, click the Shading tab of the Borders and Shading dialog box.

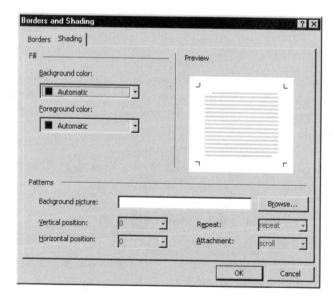

To set the background color for the paragraph, click the Background Color drop-down list. This action displays the standard color selection tool, where you can pick a color from the palette, one of the theme colors (if the page has a theme), or click More Colors to choose or create a custom color.

Choose a foreground color by clicking the Foreground Color drop-down list. The foreground color sets the color for the text in the paragraph, and overrides any text color you may have set.

If just having a background color isn't good enough for you, you can use a graphic image as the background for the paragraph. Be careful, though—many graphics are so busy that it is very difficult to read text against them. To assign a graphic as a background, use the following steps:

1. Type the name of the graphic into the Background Picture field. Alternatively, click the Browse button to open the Select Background Picture dialog box so you can choose a graphic.

2. Choose the vertical position for the graphic from the Vertical Position drop-down list. This is the vertical position (top, center, or bottom) of the graphic, relative to the paragraph. Note that if you choose a repeating graphic (see step 4), this is the vertical position where the repeating group starts.

3. Choose the horizontal position for the graphic from the Horizontal Position drop-down list. This is the horizontal position (left, center, or right) of the graphic, relative to the paragraph. Note that if you choose a repeating graphic (see step 4), this is the horizontal position where the repeating group starts.

4. Choose how you want the graphic to repeat by making a selection from the Repeat drop-down list. When you repeat a graphic, multiple copies of the graphic are placed edge to edge (called "tiling") to provide a background for the paragraph (see Figure 2-16). The choices are Repeat (repeats both horizontally and vertically), Repeat-x (repeats horizontally only), Repeat-y (repeats vertically only), and No Repeat.

5. Use the Attachment drop-down list to choose whether you want the background picture to scroll relative to the browser (choose Scroll) or to remain fixed while the browser scrolls (choose Fixed).

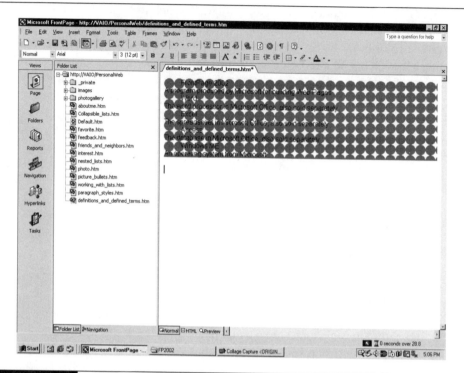

FIGURE 2-16 A tiled background for a paragraph can make your text very hard to read.

NOTE

As mentioned in steps 2 and 3, the tiling starts at the specified horizontal and vertical positions. Thus, for example, if you set both the Horizontal Position and Vertical Position to center and choose Repeat in the Repeat drop-down list, the tiled graphic will begin in the very middle of the paragraph and repeat to the right edge and the bottom edge. Additionally, the Attachment setting has no effect unless the graphic is large enough to fill the browser window or is tiled.

Choose More Colors

Any time you choose a color in FrontPage, you have the option of using any color your computer can display. However, the default color selection tool (shown earlier in Figure 2-5) does not display all those colors. To access additional colors, click the More Colors button at the bottom of the color tool. This opens the More Colors dialog box. Using this dialog box, you pick any color you want and save it to your collection of custom colors, making it easy to pick the same color again.

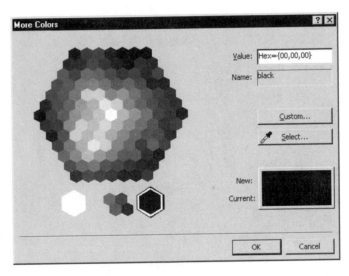

In the More Colors dialog box, you can pick one of the colors in the color wheel by clicking it. When you choose a new color, that color is shown in the New section of the rectangle in the lower-right corner of the dialog box. The hexadecimal (base 16) value for the color is shown in the Value field in the upper-right corner. If you know the hexadecimal value for a desired color, you can type it into this field.

NOTE *The hexadecimal values vary from 00,00,00 (white) to FF,FF,FF (black).*

Another way to choose a color is to click the Select button (the one with the eyedropper on it). When you do, your mouse pointer turns into an eyedropper. As you move the mouse pointer over the screen (including outside the dialog box), the New section of the rectangle shows the color under the pointer. When you see a color you want to use, simply click it. Thus, by using the Select button, you can choose any color you see. To help you remember what the eyedropper does, think about it "sucking up" a color.

If you still don't see a color you want to use, you can click the Custom button, which opens the Color dialog box. The Color dialog box enables you to pick any color your computer can display.

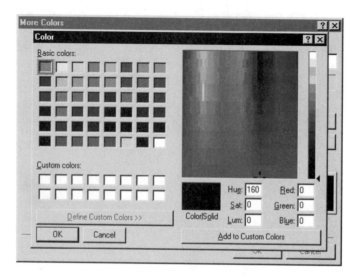

There are five ways to choose a color from the Color dialog box. They are

■ **Choose a basic color**   Choose one of the colored rectangles in the Basic Colors section of the dialog box. The color's numeric values are displayed using both the HSL and RGB systems. The values for HSL are displayed in the Hue, Sat (saturation), and Lum (luminance) fields, while the RGB values are displayed in the Red, Green, and Blue fields. When you have the color you want, click OK to return to the Web page.

■ **Pick an existing custom color**   Choose one of the colored rectangles in the Custom Colors section of the dialog box. As with basic colors, the color's values are displayed in the other fields in the dialog box. Click OK to return to the Web page.

■ **Pick a new custom color**   On the right side of the Color dialog box is a large square that displays every color your computer can display. To choose a color, click it in the square. Then select the brightness you want from the color slider at the far-right edge of the dialog box. When you have the color you want, click OK to return to the Web page.

- **Specify hue, saturation, and luminance**   If you know the values that define the color in the HSL system, you can type the values into the Hue, Sat, and Lum fields. Then click OK to return to the Web page.

- **Specify red, green, and blue**   If you know the values that define the color in the RGB system, you can type the values in the Red, Green, and Blue fields.

If you know you are going to want to add the selected color to your set of custom colors, click the square in the Custom Colors section of the dialog box *before* defining your color. After defining your color, click the Add To Custom Colors button. This changes the color of the square in the Custom Colors section to the defined color.

CAUTION   *It is important to click the square in the Custom Colors section before defining your color. If you define the color and then click the square, the color you defined will be replaced by the square's existing color.*

Save Your Web Page

Before you go very far in building a Web page, you'll need to know how to save the page so it is not lost if your machine locks up or a similar misfortune strikes. To save a Web page for the first time, choose File | Save. This opens the Save As dialog box. From here, you can choose to save the file in the current Web site on your hard drive (the most usual choice), in a different location on your hard drive or a network drive, or even on the Internet.

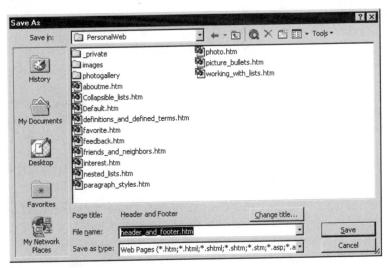

After the first time you save a Web page, choosing File | Save again simply saves the page under the same filename, so you won't see the Save As dialog box again. However, you can also save the page under a different filename (perhaps to clone the page and then change it). To do that, choose File | Save As.

The basic steps for saving a Web page to your hard drive or a network drive are as follows:

1. Use the Save In drop-down list (and perhaps the Up One Level button and New Folder button) to specify the folder in which to save the Web page file.

2. Enter the filename in the File Name field.

3. If you wish, change the page title by clicking the Change Title button alongside the page title at the bottom of the dialog box. Type the new title in the Set Page Title dialog box and click OK.

4. Click the Save button to save the file.

A variety of common destinations for saving files is listed down the left side of the Save As dialog box. The first four (History, My Documents, Desktop, and Favorites) represent folders on your machine. It's something of a mystery why you'd want to save your Web pages into one of these folders, but they are there if you want them. The last choice, Web Folders, is a new addition that is supported by all the applications in Office 2000. Web folders are a way to store files remotely. These Web folders can be located on your local machine, a network server, or even an Internet site. Web folders can be set up through My Computer, and creating a server-based Web site on your local machine creates a Web folder for it automatically.

NOTE *In Windows 2000, the Web Folders option is displayed as My Network Places. However, since Web folders are listed among the various network destinations, you can still use Web Folders in Windows 2000.*

Create Your Own Templates

If you find that you use a page that has a particular "look" to it over and over again, you may wish to create your own template that includes the main properties of the page. For example, you might have a page in which you have customized the colors, the background, and the font you use for the heading. Your page might also always have certain elements present, such as Navigation bars, a list that uses a special graphic for a bullet, and a timestamp. Rather than having to create this page from scratch each time (or customizing an existing FrontPage template), you can create and use your own template. This template is then available to you in the Page Templates dialog box when you choose Page Templates from the New Page or Web Task Pane.

To create a new template, first build the page you want to use as a template. Include as many of the common elements as possible so you won't have to do too much customizing later. Then use the following steps:

1. Choose File | Save As to open the Save As dialog box.

2. Click the small arrow at the right side of the Save As Type field and choose FrontPage Template (*.tem) from the drop-down list.

3. Enter the filename in the File Name field. Then click Save.

4. FrontPage displays the Save As Template dialog box. Here you can enter the descriptive parameters of your new template.

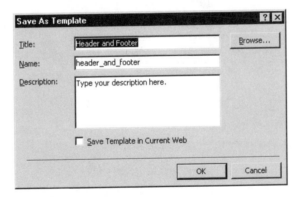

5. Enter the title of the template, the name, and a description. If you want the template saved only as part of the current Web site, check the Save Template In Current Web checkbox.

6. Click OK. If there are any graphics on the page, FrontPage displays the Save Embedded Files dialog box. This is because graphics associated with a template are saved in a different place than the graphics associated with a regular page in a Web site.

7. Click OK to save the embedded files to the destination suggested by FrontPage and create the template.

Once you have saved your new template, the template will be available in the General tab of the Page Templates dialog box (which appears when you create a new Web page). As you can see here, you can now choose your new template by its title, see a preview of it, and read the description.

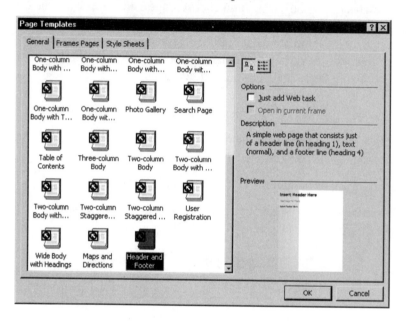

Chapter 3

Add Graphics and Sound to Your Web Page

How to...

- Add graphics to a Web page
- Customize your collection of clip art
- Change the properties of a picture
- Modify graphics using FrontPage's tools

You can communicate a lot of information with plain text, but pages that contain only unbroken text are boring! Adding graphics (within reason) adds interest to the page, as well as communicating graphic-based information. You can use prepackaged graphics, such as the clip art that comes with Microsoft Office, or add pictures and other graphics from files on your hard drive or the Internet. Once you have added graphics to your Web pages, you can change their size, how text wraps around them, and many other properties. You can even use tools built right into FrontPage to modify the graphics themselves.

Add Graphics to a Web Page

You can only go so far with text, even when you add fancy formatting to it. Sooner or later, you'll want to add graphics to your Web pages. You might want to emphasize a point with a graphic or animation, or publish photographs of your last family function. Whatever the reason, it's really not very hard to dress up your Web site with graphics.

Comprehend Graphic Formats

If you have been working with computers for a while, you probably know that there are a number of graphic formats. For a while, it seemed as if each new graphic application pioneered its own format. However, for the Internet, you'll want to use just two graphic formats: GIF (Graphics Interchange Format) and JPEG (Joint Photographic Experts Group). All graphics-capable browsers support these two formats and can display them without any help. Other graphics formats, such as PCX, BMP, and TIFF, can often be displayed by browsers using plug-in applications. However, since you can't guarantee that people who come to your site will have these additional applications, it is safest to stick with GIF and JPEG.

NOTE *There is another Web graphics format, PNG. However, this format is not widely supported, so it is best not to use it for now.*

The two graphic formats each have strengths and weaknesses, which make them useful for different purposes. GIF is quite compact and can handle up to 256 colors. It is great for line art and graphics that do not require continuous shading (such as you see in photographs). Further, most competent graphics editors allow you to reduce the number of colors in a GIF file, making the file smaller. JPEG files are slower to decompress (open onscreen) than GIF, but can support continuous shading and 16.7 million colors—making them a better choice for photographs. You can also adjust the amount of compression to reduce the size of a graphic at the expense of the quality. That is, the more file is compressed, the more the image quality is degraded.

Find Graphics

It isn't hard to find prebuilt graphics—FrontPage comes with a collection of more than 25,000 pieces of clip art, stored in the Clip Organizer. In addition, there are competent collections of clip art for sale on CD and DVD. Many of these collections have 100,000 or more graphics. On the Internet you can find many Web sites offering graphics you can download, although you have to be careful of violating copyrights. Many of the Web sites that feature clip art also specify the terms under which you can use that clip art on your site. Microsoft maintains a set of clip art at http://www.microsoft.com/clipgallerylive.

Store Graphics on Your Web Site

In general, it is best to include all graphics you use on your Web site within your current Web site file structure. While it is certainly possible to display graphics located elsewhere on your computer or network—or even located remotely on the Internet—you can't guarantee that the graphic will always be visible, especially since graphics outside your current Web site are not published to the hosting server when you publish the site.

FrontPage maintains a special folder called images within the file structure of your Web site. It is highly recommended that you store all your graphics in this folder. You can copy or import graphics files to the images folder before placing the graphics on a page, or (as discussed shortly) save copies of graphics located elsewhere into the images folder when you save the page.

Add Graphics from a File

You can add graphics to your Web page from two general locations: your hard drive/network drive or from the Internet.

Add an Image from Your Hard Drive

To add a graphic from your hard drive (or a network drive) to a Web page, use the following steps:

1. Choose Insert | Picture | From File. This displays the Picture dialog box (see Figure 3-1).

2. If the graphic you want is already present in the images folder, double-click the folder to open it and select the file you want. Otherwise, type the filename (complete with the path) in the File Name field, or use the Look In list to navigate to the file location and choose the file.

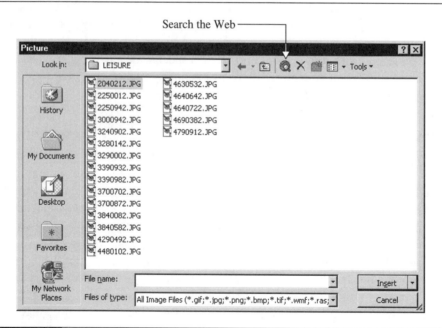

FIGURE 3-1 Select a graphic image in the Picture dialog box

3. Click Insert to place the graphic on the page, or choose Select from the graphic's shortcut menu.

Add an Image from the Internet

To add a graphic from the Internet to a Web page, use the following steps:

1. Choose Insert | Picture | From File. This displays the Picture dialog box (see Figure 3-1).

2. Click the Search the Web button (the third button to the right of the Look In field).

3. Your browser opens to the Web Search portion of MSN. From here you can search for a picture on the Internet, or specify a Web address that contains the picture you want to use.

4. Once you have navigated to the site that contains the picture you want, right-click on the picture and choose Save Picture As from the shortcut menu.

5. In the Save Picture dialog box, specify where you want to store the picture. Then click Save to save the picture to your hard drive.

NOTE   *Once you are done saving the picture to your hard drive, you can close the browser.*

6. Once you have the picture safely stored on your hard drive, use the instructions in the previous section to place the picture in a Web page.

Save Embedded Images

As mentioned earlier, it is best to keep images you are going to use in your Web site within the file structure of the Web site. If you placed image files from outside your current Web site file structure on a Web page, you are given the opportunity to copy those files into your Web site when you save the page. To do so, use the following steps:

1. Choose File | Save to save the Web page. This opens the Save Embedded Files dialog box. All files located outside your Web site file structure are

listed in the dialog box. Use the Save Embedded Files dialog box to copy image files to your current Web site.

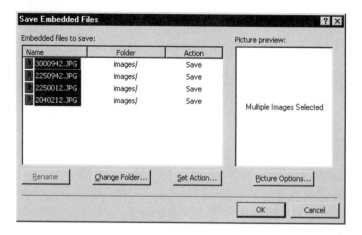

2. Choose a file by clicking it, and then choose Change Folder.

3. In the resulting Change Folder dialog box, navigate to the folder in which you want to save a copy of the graphic (the images folder is recommended). Open the folder by double-clicking it. The folder name appears in the Look In field at the top of the dialog box.

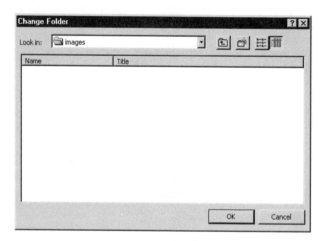

4. Choose OK. In the Save Embedded Files dialog box, the selected folder (images) appears in the Folder column. Click OK to save copies of the graphic files as well as the Web page.

> **NOTE** *You can select multiple files and change the folder for all selected files at one time. To select multiple files, CTRL-click each file you want.*

If you decide you don't want the image to be saved into the current Web site, you can prevent it. From the Save Embedded Files dialog box, select the file and click the Set Action button, then select the Don't Save option.

You can also specify some special options about the picture file by clicking on the Picture Options button. These options are discussed in "Insert Clip Art into Your Web Page," later in this chapter.

Insert Clip Art and Sound

When you installed FrontPage 2002, you had the option of installing the clip art. If you purchased FrontPage as part of the Microsoft Office suite, you get the Office clip art as well. These galleries include traditional clip art, icons, and buttons for Web pages, as well as videos, sound, and photographic images. You'll probably add clip art to your Web pages often, because the buttons and Web-related icons supplied as part of the gallery help dress up a Web page very nicely.

Insert Clip Art into Your Web Page

To add a picture from the clip art collection to your Web page, use the following steps:

1. Choose Insert | Picture | Clip Art or choose the Insert Clip Art tool in the Drawing toolbar. This opens the Insert Clip Art Task Pane (see Figure 3-2). This version of the Task Pane is identical to the Basic Search Task Pane discussed in the last chapter.

2. Use the Search In drop-down list to pick which of your clip art collections you want to search through. Choices include My Collections, Office Collection (if you installed FrontPage along with the rest of Microsoft Office) and Web Collections. Select the checkboxes for the collections in which you want to search.

> **NOTE** *The first time you try to use clip art or the More AutoShapes option in the Drawing toolbar (see Chapter 4), the Clip Organizer utility opens to catalog all the media on your drives (including clip art). Click the Now button to proceed to catalog the media. This utility automatically builds the collections mentioned in step 2. However, as discussed later in this chapter, you can add your own collections as well.*

FIGURE 3-2   Search for the clip art you want to use from the Insert Clip Art Task Pane.

3. Use the Results Should Be drop-down list to specify which types of media files you want to look for. The media files are grouped into Clip Art, Photographs, Movies, and Sound. Click the small plus (+) next to each type of group to expand the list and display the types of files included. You can select or clear the checkboxes for the individual file types if you wish.

4. Enter any keywords you want to search for in the Search Text field. You can search for multiple keywords by typing them into this field, separated with commas.

5. Click the Search button to locate any matching graphics. The graphics appear in the Task Pane.

6. Move the mouse over the piece of clip art you want to insert into your Web page and click the small down arrow that appears at the right side of the clip art's image.

7. Select Insert (the top selection in the shortcut menu) to add the clip art to your page. Or, you can click and drag the clip art onto the Web page.

> **TIP** *Another quick way to insert a piece of clip art is to double-click on it in the Insert Clip Art Task Pane. This automatically inserts the clip art at the location of the text cursor.*

When you save a page to which you've added clip art, you automatically see the Save Embedded Files dialog box so you can save a copy of the clip art to your Web site. The name of the clip art is generally something unintelligible (such as pe03254_.gif), so you'll want to use the Rename button in the Save Embedded Files dialog box to rename the clip art to something you'll recognize. Just click the Rename button, type the new name, and press ENTER. Then click OK to save the copy of the clip art to its new location with its new name.

Additionally, if the clip art is not in GIF or JPEG format, FrontPage will convert the clip to one of these formats automatically before displaying the Save Embedded Files dialog box. By default, FrontPage will convert the file to a GIF if it has 256 colors or fewer; otherwise, it converts it to a JPEG. However, you can override this choice by clicking the Picture Options button that appears in the Save Embedded Files dialog box when a file conversion is necessary. Doing so displays the Picture Options dialog box, where you can pick whether you want to use JPEG or GIF, and specify the options appropriate for each file type.

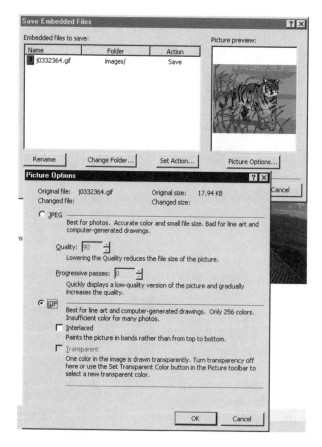

For a GIF file, these options are

- **Interlaced**   This option is a special way of saving GIF files. If you choose this option, the GIF is loaded into a browser in increments. The first increment is in low resolution, and each succeeding increment adds progressively higher resolution. Thus, the person viewing the Web page can get an idea what the image looks like before it has fully loaded, and perhaps choose not to wait for the full image to load. For large GIFs, it is considered good manners to create them as interlaced.

- **Transparent**   One of the ways to give your Web pages a more integrated appearance is to use transparent GIFs. A transparent GIF image lets the page background appear through one of the colors in the image (you can only set one color as transparent). Note that this option is available only if you have modified the GIF to actually *have* a transparent color, as discussed later in "Make Transparent Images."

For JPEG files, you can set the following options:

- **Quality**   JPEG stores files in a compressed format and is a "lossy" format—as the compression level increases, more and more information is left out of the file, leading to the degradation of the image. The amount of degradation is measured by the quality of the compression. A high quality (such as 99) leads to the lowest compression and the highest quality, while a low quality (such as 1) leads to the highest compression and the poorest quality. A good value for completed graphics is 75. However, if you still intend to edit the graphic, you'll want to store it with the highest quality; otherwise, the level of degradation increases each time you edit the graphic and save it.

- **Progressive Passes**   This option loads the image into the browser in increments. The first increment is in low resolution, and each succeeding increment adds progressively higher resolution. Thus, the person viewing the Web page can get an idea what the image looks like before it has fully loaded, and perhaps choose not to wait for the full image to load. A good number to use here is 4 or 5. For large JPEGs, it is considered good manners to create them with progressive passes.

Once you set the quality and save the image, you can't change the Quality setting again. Keep a backup copy so you can delete the current image, and reinsert it from the original file.

Customize the Microsoft Clip Organizer

Microsoft Office provides the Microsoft Clip Organizer utility to help you manage your graphics, sound, animation, and other types of media files. You can add your own collections of clip art to the Clip Organizer, add and remove clip art from a collection, edit the list of keywords (used for searching), and adjust the properties of a collection. The Clip Organizer collections are handy if you have a set of buttons or icons you use for many different Web sites. Instead of hunting them down on your hard drive each time, just add them to your Clip Art Gallery.

You can open the Microsoft Clip Organizer utility in two different ways. The first way is to click the Clip Organizer link in the See Also section near the bottom of the Insert Clip Art Task Pane. The other way is to click on the Start button and select Microsoft Office | Microsoft Office Tools | Microsoft Clip Organizer. Either way, the Microsoft Clip Organizer window appears (see Figure 3-3).

The Microsoft Clip Organizer's Task Pane (displayed at the left side of Figure 3-3) can be set to display either a hierarchical list of clip art collections (as shown next in Figure 3-3) or to search for clip art. The Search facility looks identical to the Insert

 **Insert Sound into Your Web Page**

You can add sound to a Web page from the Clip Organizer. If you do, the sound leaves no visible indicator on the page; it is added as the *background sound* for the page. Configuring the background sound is discussed in Chapter 5. To add a sound, use the same steps discussed earlier for inserting a piece of clip art, but make sure to include sound files in the search (check the Sounds checkbox in the Results Should Be drop-down list). You add a sound clip exactly the same way you add clip art.

View the list of collections
in the Task Pane

View the contents
of a collection here

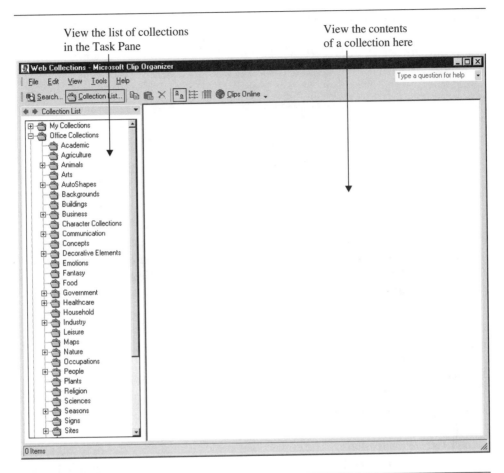

FIGURE 3-3 Use the Microsoft Clip Organizer to manage your collection of clip art. This view shows the Office Collections expanded so you can see some of the types of clip art included.

Clip Art Task Pane in FrontPage, discussed earlier in this chapter. To switch between these two Task Pane views, select the Search button or the Collection List button in the toolbar; choose either Search or Collection List from the View menu; or pick the view you want from the list under the small down arrow at the right end of the Task Pane header.

 You can undock the Task Pane in Clip Organizer if you wish. You do it just like undocking the Task Pane in FrontPage: click and drag the Task Pane header until the Task Pane turns into a free-floating window. You can redock the Task Pane at either the left or right side of the Clip Organizer window.

View the Collection List

When FrontPage (or some other Office application you happen to be using at the time) first catalogs the media on your hard drive, it creates three main categories—sets of clip art collections:

- **Office Collections**   The clip art that comes packaged with Microsoft Office is categorized under this category. Clicking on the plus (+) sign alongside the Office Collections entry displays the collections that make up Office Collections.

- **Web Collections**   This category is initially empty, but you can access Microsoft's Design Gallery Live to download clips into this category if you wish. To access the Design Gallery Live, click on the Clips Online link in the See Also section of the Insert Clip Art Task Pane in FrontPage. Alternatively, you can choose Tools | Clips Online in the Microsoft Clip Organizer.

- **My Collections**   All other media found on your disk are grouped into collections under the My Collections category. Unlike the Office Collections and Web Collections category (which are fixed), you can add, rename, and remove collections in the My Collections category. You can also change the structure of collections in this category. All of this is discussed later in this chapter, in the section "Modify the Collection List."

Catalog Your Clip Collection

As mentioned in the last section, the first time you try to use clip art in FrontPage or some other Office application, the Clip Organizer will display the Add Clips to Organizer dialog box and offer to catalog the media on your hard drive and create a set of collections for you.

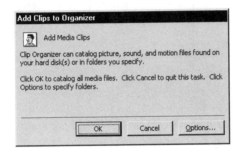

If you just click OK, the Clip Organizer will catalog your entire system, including all hard drives. If that is not what you want, you can click the Options button to open a list of drives and folders.

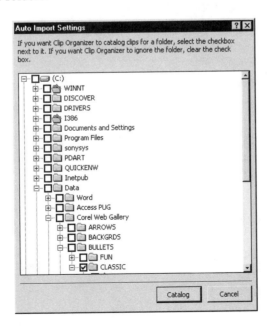

Check the checkboxes for the drives and folders you want cataloged, and clear the checkboxes for the drives and folders you want Clip Organizer to ignore.

 *Cataloging a large collection of media can take a long time! It is best not to interrupt the process while it is going on, as you run the risk of corrupting the media data file that stores the clip art collection information.*

You can instruct Clip Organizer to recatalog your system if you wish. You may wish to do this if you have recently added a large collection of media to your system, or if the media data file is hopelessly corrupted. To recatalog your system, choose File | Add Clips to Gallery | Automatically.

NOTE *If you find that clip art is not displaying thumbnails correctly, or operations (such as moving or copying clip art) do not seem to produce the results you expect, your media data file may be corrupted. Clip Organizer can sometimes detect this condition on its own, and warn you that the data file is corrupted. Before recataloging your system to rebuild the media data file, try choosing Tools | Compact. This menu option tries to remove corrupted data, reduce the size of the data file, and fix any other conditions that interfere with smooth operation of the Clip Organizer.*

Modify the Collection List

You can create a new collection, delete collections, rename them, and change the structure of the Collection list by moving or copying collections.

Add a New Collection

To add a new collection to your Clip Organizer, use the following steps:

1. Make sure the Collection List Task Pane is visible in Clip Organizer, and pick New Collection from the shortcut menu or choose File | New Collection. This displays the New Collection dialog box.

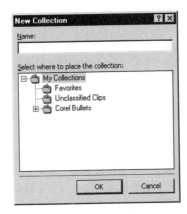

3

2. Type the name of the new collection into the Name field, and choose the location for the new collection in the lower portion of the dialog box.

3. Click OK to create the new collection.

Of course, when you create a new collection, it is empty. To specify the folders that contain media you want to be part of the collection, see the next section, "Modify the Collection Properties." To add individual pieces of clip art to a collection, see "Work with Clip Art" later in this chapter.

Modify the Collection Properties

You can modify the properties of your collections (as mentioned earlier, you can't change the Office Collections or the Web Collections). To do so, select the collection and choose Collection Properties from either the shortcut menu or the File menu. Clip Organizer opens the Collection Properties dialog box.

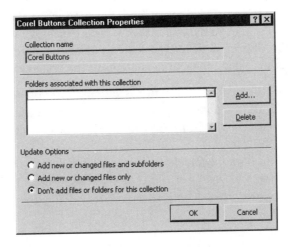

The Collection Properties dialog box enables you to change two properties about the selected collection. The first is the list of folders associated with this collection, and the other property is how you want the Clip Organizer to handle changes to the contents of these folders.

Change the Collection Folders

The folders displayed in the Folders Associated With This Collection list specify the contents of the collection. Any media contained in these folders are included in the list of media files that Clip Organizer displays in the main window when you select the collection from the Collection List Task Pane. To add more folders to this list (and expand the contents of the collection), click the Add button. This displays the standard File Open dialog box, labeled Add Directory To Collection Properties. Navigate to the folder you want to add, select the folder, and click the Add button. To delete a folder from the collection, select the folder and click the Delete button.

Modify the Update Options

The three radio buttons in the Update Options section of the Collection Properties dialog box specify how the contents of the collection will change if you add or remove media files to the folders included in the collection. The three options perform the following actions:

- **Add new or changed files and subfolders** Each time you access the collection, any changes to the files or subfolders in the included folders are cataloged and the contents of the collection are adjusted appropriately. Thus, if you add a new subfolder to a collection's folder, the contents of the subfolder are cataloged and the media files are added to the collection.

- **Add new or changed files only** Each time you access the collection, any changes to the files in the included folders are cataloged and the contents of the collection are adjusted. New subfolders are ignored—only changes to files in the folders impact the contents of the collection.

- **Don't add files or folders for this collection** If you add a new subfolder or new files, the contents of the collection are not adjusted. With this option, you will need to add files to the collection manually.

NOTE
Deleting files from the folders in a collection does not remove the files from the collection. However, the file is no longer available to be used, and the thumbnail is displayed with a small yellow x in the lower-right corner.

Rename a Collection

To rename a collection, select the collection you want to rename in the Collection list. Choose Rename from the shortcut menu or choose Edit | Rename Collection. You can also click on the collection, pause, and click on it again. Performing any of these actions makes the name of the collection editable; simply type the new name of the collection and press ENTER.

Delete a Collection

To delete a collection, select the collection you no longer need and choose Delete from the shortcut menu or choose Edit | Delete from Clip Organizer. Click Yes when prompted as to whether you really want to delete the collection.

Move a Collection

You can move a collection to a new location in the Collection list. To move a collection, select the collection you want to move and choose Move *Collection Name* To (where *Collection Name* is the name of the selected collection) from the shortcut menu or Edit | Move to Collection. This displays the Move To Collection dialog box.

Pick the parent collection (the one the moved collection is located in) and click OK. You can build a new collection to serve as the parent by clicking the New button and following the prompts.

You can also move a collection by clicking on the collection in the Collection List Task Pane and dragging the collection to its new location.

Copy a Collection

You can duplicate a collection by copying it to another collection. If you do, a new collection with the same name appears as a child of the collection you copied it to.

To copy a collection, select the collection you want to copy and choose Copy *Collection Name* To (where *Collection Name* is the name of the selected collection) from the shortcut menu or Edit | Copy to Collection. This displays the Copy To Collection dialog box.

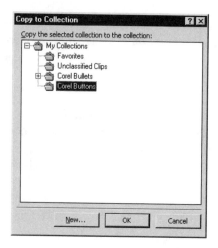

Pick the parent for the copied collection (the collection to which the copied collection will belong) and click OK. You can build a new collection to serve as the parent by clicking the New button and following the prompts.

You can also copy a collection by clicking on the collection in the Collection List Task Pane, holding down the CTRL key, and dragging the collection to its new location.

Work with Clip Art

The Clip Organizer refers to the contents of collections as "clip art" or "clips", despite the fact that the files may be sound or animation files. You can add and remove clips, copy or move them to another collection, and edit the keywords that the Search Task Pane (Clip Organizer) or the Insert Clip Art Task Pane (FrontPage) uses to find the clips.

You can perform most operations on multiple clips. To select multiple clips, select the first clip you want to work with, hold down the CTRL key, and click on the rest of the clips you want. Strangely, once you have selected a clip, you must release the CTRL key and click on the clip again to deselect it, removing it from the group of selected clips.

 Except for adding a clip, you can make changes to a clip from the shortcut menu. There are two ways to access the shortcut menu for a clip: the "normal way" (right-click on the clip) and by clicking on the down arrow that appears at the right edge of a clip when you move the mouse pointer over the clip.

3

Add New Clips to a Collection

To add a new piece of clip art to a collection in your gallery, use the following steps:

1. Choose the collection you want to add clips to in the Collection List Task Pane.

2. Select File | Add Clips to Gallery | On My Own. This displays a standard File Open dialog box, labeled Add Clips To Gallery.

3. Navigate to the file you want to add and select it. If you want a chance to change the collection to which you are adding the clip, click on the Add To button and choose the collection from the resulting list. Otherwise, just click the Add button to add the clip to the currently selected collection.

Delete Clips

If you decide you no longer want to include a clip in a collection, select the clip and choose one of the two delete options from either the shortcut menu or the Edit menu:

- **Delete From *Collection Name***   Use this menu item (where *Collection Name* is the name of the currently selected collection) to remove the clip from this collection only. It remains in any other collections, and the physical media file is *not* deleted.

- **Delete From Clip Organizer**   Use this menu item to remove the clip from the currently selected collection and any other collections in the Clip Organizer. The physical media file is *not* deleted.

Move Clips to Another Collection

To move clips to another collection, select the clips and choose Move To Collection from either the shortcut menu or the Edit menu. Pick the collection from the Move To Collection window that appears, and click OK. You can create a new collection for the clip(s) you are moving by clicking the New button in the Move To Collection window and following the prompts.

You can also move one or more clips by selecting them and dragging the clip(s) to the collection to which you want to move them in the Collection List Task Pane.

Copy Clips to Another Collection

To copy clips to another collection, select the clips and choose Copy To Collection from either the shortcut menu or the Edit menu. Pick the collection from the Copy To Collection window that appears, and click OK. You can create a new collection for the clip(s) you are copying by clicking the New button in the Copy To Collection window and following the prompts.

You can also copy one or more clips by selecting them, holding down the CTRL key, and dragging the clip(s) to the collection to which you want to add them in the Collection List Task Pane.

View Clip Properties

To view the properties of a clip—including file size, filename, and the keywords associated with the clip—select the clip and choose Preview/Properties from the shortcut menu or the View menu. This opens the Preview/Properties dialog box.

You can cycle through the clips in a collection by clicking on the > or < buttons below the preview image. You can also edit the list of keywords and the caption by clicking on the Edit Keywords button, as discussed in the next section.

Edit Clip Keywords

The keywords associated with a clip are used by the Search Task Pane in Clip Organizer and the Insert Clip Art Task Pane in FrontPage to locate clip art. Meaningful keywords are assigned to the clip art that ships with Microsoft Office, and as mentioned earlier, you cannot change the keywords for these clips. However, you can assign keywords to the clips in My Collections (and all the collections that belong to it). The default keywords assigned when the clips are added to a collection are not particularly meaningful, since Clip Organizer has no way to know what the graphic represents. It does assign keywords for the file type (such as jpg), the name of the collection(s) the clip art is present in, and the folder in which the file resides on your hard drive.

To modify the list of keywords, select the clip and choose Edit Keywords from the shortcut menu, or select Edit | Keywords. You can also click the Edit Keywords button in the Preview/Properties dialog box. Any way you go about it, FrontPage displays the Keywords dialog box, as shown in Figure 3-4.

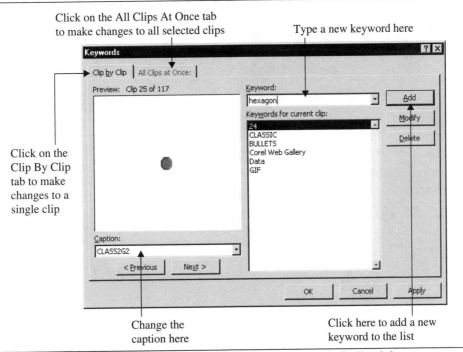

FIGURE 3-4   Add keywords to a piece of clip art to aid you in finding it later.

Here is what you can do in the Keywords dialog box:

- To add a new keyword to the list, type the keyword in the Keyword field and click the Add button.

- To change an existing keyword in the list, click on it so that it is visible in the Keyword field. Type in your changes and click the Modify button.

- To remove a keyword from the list, select it in the list and click on the Delete button.

- To change the caption for the clip, type the new text into the Caption field.

When you are done making your changes, click OK to close the Keywords dialog box. Alternatively, you can apply the changes without closing the dialog box by clicking the Apply button. You can also change to another clip in the collection by clicking on the <Previous or Next> buttons. If you don't apply your changes before moving to another clip, Clip Organizer will prompt you to do so.

If you select multiple clips before choosing to edit keywords, you can click on the All Clips At Once tab to show a slightly different version of the dialog box.

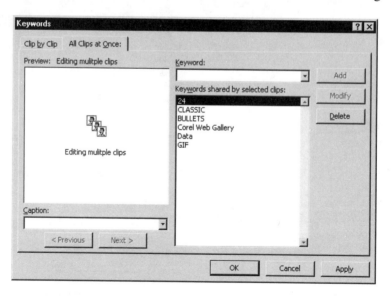

The list of displayed keywords includes only those that are common to all the selected clips and so the list may be empty even though the individual clips do have a list of keywords. Any additions, modifications, or deletions you make to keywords

3

will be applied to all selected clips. Further, if you change the caption from the All Clips At Once tab, the caption you enter will be applied to all selected clips—giving them the same caption (not sure why anyone would want to do that, but you can!).

Copy and Paste Clips into FrontPage

You can copy a clip directly from a collection in Clip Organizer and paste it into FrontPage (or any other Office application, for that matter). To do so, select the clip and choose Copy from either the shortcut menu or the Edit menu. Switch to FrontPage, open the page into which you want to paste the clip, and choose Edit | Paste. As with inserting a clip from the Insert Clip Art Task Pane (discussed earlier in this chapter), if the clip is not a GIF or JPEG, FrontPage will convert it for you before displaying the Save Embedded Files dialog box so you can save it into your Web site.

Add Horizontal Lines

You can use horizontal lines to break up sections on a Web page. To do so, choose Insert | Horizontal Line. This adds the line to the page (see Figure 3-5).

Provided you haven't assigned a theme to the page, you can adjust the properties of the horizontal line by right-clicking the line and choosing Horizontal Line Properties from the shortcut menu. This displays the Horizontal Line Properties dialog box. Here you can change the height, width, color, and alignment of the horizontal line.

From this dialog box, you can change the width of the line by typing a number in the Width field or by using the spinner. You can choose to set the width as either a percent of the window width (recommended) or in absolute pixels. You can also

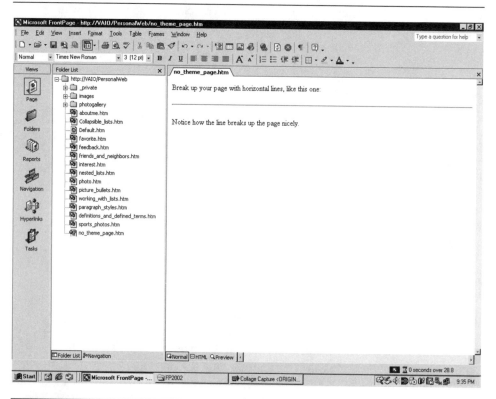

FIGURE 3-5 A horizontal line can break up page content.

set the height of the line using the Height spinner, although this quantity can only be set in pixels. Choose the alignment by selecting an option from the Alignment section of the dialog box, and choose the line color from the Color drop-down list. You can check the Solid Line (No Shading) checkbox, although this option seems to have no discernible effect on how the line looks.

Set the Picture Properties

Once you've placed an image on a Web page, you can modify many of the image properties. To do so, choose Picture Properties from the shortcut menu to open the Picture Properties dialog box (see Figure 3-6).

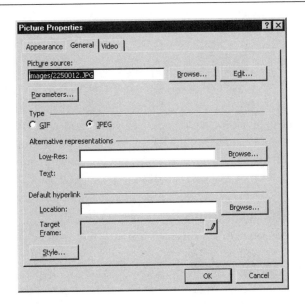

FIGURE 3-6   Use the Picture Properties dialog box to modify the properties of a graphic image. This shows the General tab, the most frequently used portion of this dialog box.

Set the General Properties

The General tab enables you to set the picture source, type, alternative representations, and default hyperlinks. The default hyperlinks portion of this dialog box will be discussed in Chapter 8.

Specify the Picture Source

The Picture Source field lets you change the image file that serves as the source for the picture. This field displays the full pathname to the file if the Web site is disk-based, or just the folder within the Web if the Web is server-based (as shown in Figure 3-6). To change the picture source, type a new path, or click the Browse button to select a picture file from the Picture dialog box. You can also edit the picture (provided you have associated an editor with this type of file) by clicking the Edit button.

Adjust the File Type

You can change the type of file and adjust how the file is saved in the Type section of the dialog box. The choices for file type are GIF and JPEG. To change the type of the file, choose one of the options in the Type section (the current type of file is indicated by the selected option). When you click OK, FrontPage will automatically convert the file. During the conversion, FrontPage displays the Save Embedded Files dialog box so you can name the new graphic file and choose where to save it. If you wish, you can click the Picture Options button to display the Picture Options dialog box. In this dialog box you can set the properties of the new graphic file, as discussed earlier in this chapter (see "Insert Clip Art into Your Web Page").

Alternative Representations

The Alternative Representations section of the dialog box enables you to specify (you guessed it) alternative representations for a graphic image. In the Text field, type a short phrase that describes the image. This text string is displayed when the page first loads, prior to loading the images. In addition, if you hover the mouse over the graphic while viewing the page in a browser, the contents of the Text field appear in a small window near the mouse pointer. In a browser configured to not display graphics, the text alternative representation is the *only* thing related to the graphic that is displayed (see Figure 3-7).

NOTE *In computer terms, a "string" is a sequence of typed characters.*

The Low-Res (low resolution) option is another way to give the viewer something to see while the full graphic loads. If you have specified the Low-Res option, the page initially loads into the browser just displaying the text and a low-resolution version of the graphic. Only after that does the browser go back and load the full graphic. To

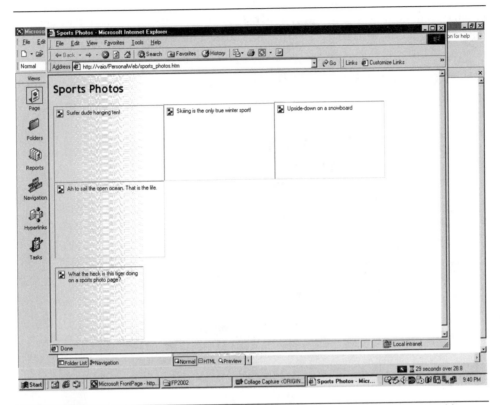

FIGURE 3-7   The text alternative representation is displayed instead of the graphic.

set up the Low-Res option, open the full graphic and use a graphic editor to create a version that loads faster (has a smaller file size). Common techniques for reducing file size include reducing the number of colors, cropping unimportant portions of the graphic, and reducing the physical dimensions of the graphic. Once you've created the low-resolution version, specify the filename in the Low-Res field.

Set the Appearance Properties

From the Appearance tab, you can set the layout and size of the graphic image.

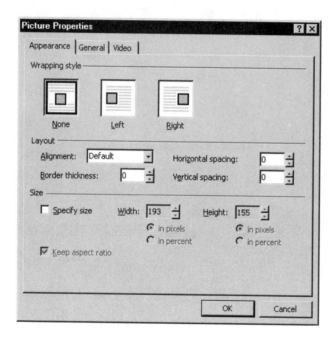

Set the Wrapping Style

If you place a graphic inside a block of text (by positioning the text cursor within the text block before inserting the graphic), the wrapping style is set to None. This means that the text does *not* wrap around the graphic. Instead, the text before the graphic is located above the picture, and the text after the graphic is located below the picture, as shown here:

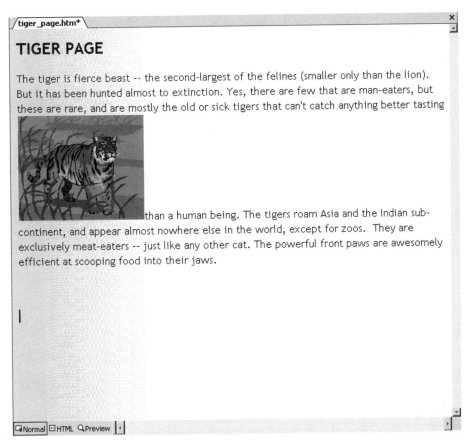

To change the wrapping style, select either the Left icon or the Right icon in the Wrapping Style section of the dialog box. If you choose Left, the graphic is located at the left margin, and the text flows to the right side of the image.

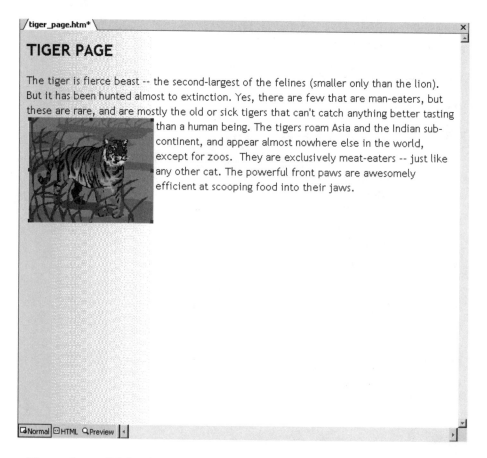

If you choose Right, the graphic is located at the right margin, and the text flows to the left side of the image.

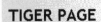

TIGER PAGE

The tiger is fierce beast -- the second-largest of the felines (smaller only than the lion). But it has been hunted almost to extinction. Yes, there are few that are man-eaters, but these are rare, and are mostly the old or sick tigers that can't catch anything better tasting than a human being. The tigers roam Asia and the Indian sub-continent, and appear almost nowhere else in the world, except for zoos. They are exclusively meat-eaters -- just like any other cat. The powerful front paws are awesomely efficient at scooping food into their jaws.

Normal HTML Preview

NOTE

Choosing Left or Right in the Wrapping Style section automatically sets the value of the Alignment drop-down list to Left or Right. Changing the value in the Alignment drop-down list to something other than Left or Right (for example, Top), automatically changes the wrapping style back to None.

Set the Spacing and Border Thickness

Using the settings in the Layout section of the dialog box, you can set the following:

- **Horizontal Spacing**   To set the amount of white space to the left and right between a graphic and any surrounding text or another graphic, use the Horizontal Spacing spinner. Higher numbers provide more white space.

- **Vertical Spacing**   To set the amount of white space above and below between a graphic and any surrounding text or another graphic, use the Vertical Spacing spinner. Higher numbers provide more white space.

- **Border Thickness**   If you want a black border around your graphic, set the thickness of that border with the Border Thickness spinner.

Align Graphics and Text

The Alignment drop-down list controls how adjacent text lines up with a graphic. From the Appearance tab, choose the value you want from the Alignment drop-down list. If you choose Top, Middle, or Bottom, a single line of text aligns with the top, middle, or bottom of the graphic, as shown in Figure 3-8.

You can make text adjacent to a graphic wrap around the graphic, with same effect as discussed in "Set the Wrapping Style," earlier in this chapter. To do so, use the following steps:

1. Click in the block of text that you want to wrap around a graphic.

2. Insert the image using the techniques discussed earlier.

3. Click the graphic and choose Picture Properties from the shortcut menu. When the Picture Properties dialog box appears, click the Appearance tab.

4. Choose Left or Right from the Alignment drop-down list. If you choose Left, the graphic is located at the left margin and the text flows to the right side of the image. If you choose Right, the graphic is located at the right margin and the text flows to the left side of the image. If you want to return the alignment to the default value (text does not wrap around the graphic), choose Default from the Alignment drop-down list.

5. Choose OK. The image moves to the appropriate margin and the text flows around it.

3

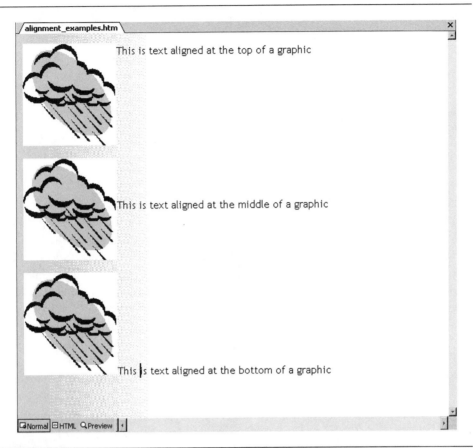

alignment_examples.htm

FIGURE 3-8   FrontPage enables you to align text with the top, middle, or bottom of an image.

NOTE   *If you simply want to center or right-align a graphic on the page, select the graphic and choose Format | Paragraph (or choose Paragraph from the shortcut menu). Then choose Center or Right from the Alignment drop-down list in the Paragraph dialog box. Alternatively, you can choose the Center or Align Right buttons in the Formatting toolbar.*

The rest of the choices in the Alignment list are less useful, as they don't seem to make any discernable difference to the text that wraps around the graphic when used. However, they are described in Table 3-1.

Option	Effect
Texttop	Aligns tallest text with the image top
Absmiddle	Aligns image with middle of current line
Absbottom	Aligns image with bottom of current line
Baseline	Aligns image with text baseline of current line

TABLE 3-1   Additional Alignments for Graphics and Text

Set the Size of the Graphic

In the Size section of the Appearance tab, you can specify the size of the graphic as well as choose to maintain the aspect ratio. To specify the size, check the Specify Size checkbox, and enter the size of the graphic by typing a quantity in the Width and Height fields, or by using the Width and Height spinners. You can specify the size of the graphic either in pixels (choose the In Pixels option) or as a percent of the browser window size (choose the In Percent option). If you choose to maintain the aspect ratio (the original ratio of the width to the height) by checking the Keep Aspect Ratio checkbox, changing either the Width or the Height automatically changes the other quantity.

TIP

You should maintain the aspect ratio of a graphic wherever possible. If you don't, the graphic can become so distorted that it is unrecognizable. This is especially true of thumbnails (small representations of images designed to give you an idea of what the larger image looks like).

NOTE

If you clear the Specify Size checkbox, the graphic returns to its original size.

You can also adjust the size of a graphic by clicking the graphic, and then clicking and dragging one of the square dots around the perimeter of the graphic (sizing handles), as shown here. If you click and drag a sizing handle in a corner of the graphic, the aspect ratio is automatically maintained; otherwise, you can stretch or shrink either the width or height of the graphic independently by using the top, bottom, or side sizing handles.

NOTE   *As we said earlier, reducing the size of a graphic is one way to make your images download faster. Unfortunately, merely resizing the appearance of the graphic does not enable the graphic to load faster, because the original graphic file is still just as large—it just looks smaller on the page. To make a graphic load faster, you must reduce the size of the file itself. Two ways to do this are cropping the graphic (removing unnecessary edges) or reducing the number of colors. Another way is to load the graphic into a graphic editor, and then use the editor's capabilities to reduce the image to the size you need and resave the file at that size.*

Incorporate Special Breaks to Coordinate Graphics and Text

Thus far, you've learned how to align a single line of text with the top, middle, or bottom of an image, as well as how to make text flow around an image that sits against the left or right margin. However, you may want to use multiple lines of text as a caption alongside an image and continue the balance of the text below the image. For example, look at Figure 3-9. There is a multiline caption, and the rest of the text should continue along the bottom border. However, since the text at the right of the

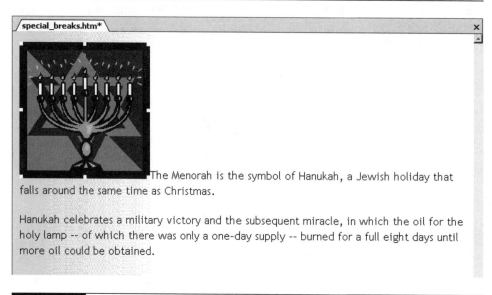

The Menorah is the symbol of Hanukah, a Jewish holiday that falls around the same time as Christmas.

Hanukah celebrates a military victory and the subsequent miracle, in which the oil for the holy lamp -- of which there was only a one-day supply -- burned for a full eight days until more oil could be obtained.

FIGURE 3-9   The image is positioned against the left margin, and the caption "spills off" the bottom of the image with its current Default alignment.

graphic is aligned to the bottom of the image, it falls below the image, looking awkward.

To fix this problem, use the following steps:

1. Change the picture alignment to Left. To do so, select Picture Properties from the image's shortcut menu, switch to the Appearance tab, and choose Left from the Alignment drop-down list.

2. Now both lines of the caption are positioned on the right edge of the graphic. However, any other lines you type also are positioned to the right of the image.

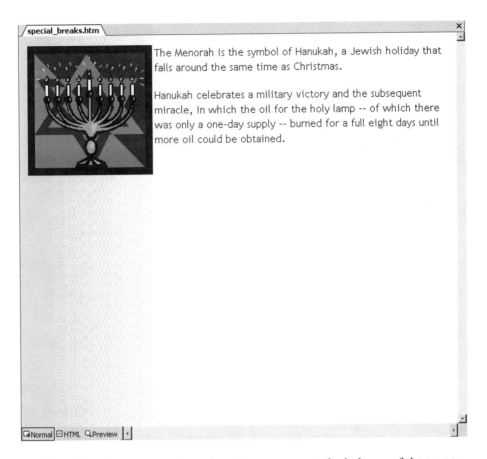

3. Position the cursor at the point where you want the balance of the text to be below the image, and choose Insert | Break to display the Break dialog box. Special line breaks give you control over the relationship between text and graphics.

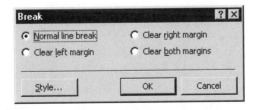

4. Choose the Clear Left Margin option and click OK. The balance of the text is moved below the graphic.

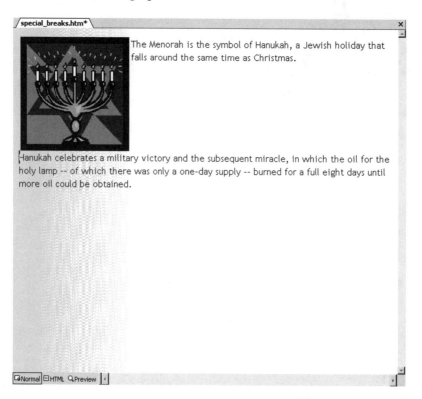

 If the graphic is aligned right, use Clear Right Margin in the Break dialog box instead. If you have two images of dissimilar size, one aligned left and the other aligned right, choose Clear Both Margins from the Break dialog box.

Modify an Image Using FrontPage's Graphics Tools

FrontPage includes a whole host of tools for modifying an image once you place it on a page. These tools are accessible from the Picture toolbar (see Figure 3-10), which appears automatically when you select a graphic. The Picture toolbar has 25 buttons to help you modify the graphic.

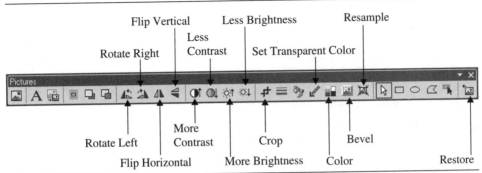

FIGURE 3-10   The Picture toolbar has 25 buttons that manipulate a graphic image.

If you make a change to a graphic image and save the page, you will see the Save Embedded Files dialog box so you can provide a filename for the changed version of the graphic if you wish and save the changed version without affecting the original. However, *every* graphic in your Web site that referred to the original image will now automatically refer to the new, changed image file. If that is not what you want, you'll have to select each graphic and redirect it to the original unchanged version using the Picture Source field in the General tab of the Picture Properties dialog box.

TIP   *To avoid having to do all this redirection, you can create a copy of the image and place the copy on the Web page before changing it. The easiest way to do this is to select the image file in the Folder List, choose Copy from the shortcut menu, then paste the copy back into the images folder (if that is where you keep your images). Rename the copy (choose Rename from the shortcut menu), and place the copied image you want to change on the Web page. Now, when you change the image and give it a new name, the references to the original image are unaffected.*

Flip and Rotate a Graphic

You can rotate an image 90 degrees clockwise or counterclockwise by using the Rotate Right and Rotate Left buttons in the Picture toolbar. You can also reverse the image left to right using the Flip Vertical button, and reverse the image top to bottom by using the Flip Horizontal button.

Adjust the Brightness and Contrast

There are four buttons on the Picture toolbar that adjust contrast and brightness. To increase the contrast, click the More Contrast button; to decrease the contrast, click the Less Contrast button. To add brightness to the image, click the More Brightness button; to decrease the brightness, click the Less Brightness button. Each time you click a button, it applies the intended effect again to incrementally add or decrease contrast or brightness.

Crop an Image

You can crop an image—cut out a rectangular area of the image to use. This is handy if the image (usually a photograph) has unneeded areas around the borders and you haven't removed those areas using an image editing tool.

To crop an image, select the Crop tool. A dashed cropping rectangle appears on the image (see Figure 3-11). Click the sizing handles to adjust the size of the cropping rectangle until only the desired portion of the graphic is included in the rectangle. Click the Crop button again, and the image is cropped.

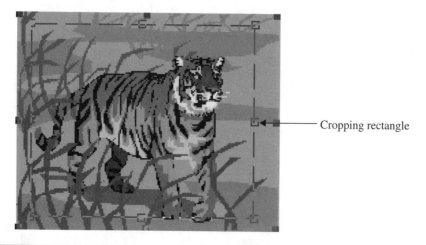

Cropping rectangle

FIGURE 3-11   Use the cropping rectangle to show where the new edges of a graphic will be.

Make Transparent Images

When you add an image to a page that has a background color other than the background color of the image, the effect is somewhat jarring. To achieve an integrated effect when you add an image to a page, you may wish to use a transparent image. A transparent image allows the page to show through parts of the image. So, for example, you could change the predominant background color of the image to be transparent so it will look much more like it belongs on the page. You can see the difference in Figure 3-12. You can only choose one color to be transparent, and this effect only works on GIFs.

To make a color transparent, select the graphic and click the Set Transparent Color button. Move the mouse cursor (which now looks like the eraser end of a pencil) to the color you want to make transparent, and click. All places in the graphic that are drawn in the color become transparent (invisible).

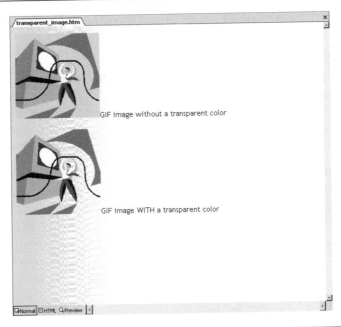

FIGURE 3-12   A transparent GIF (the lower image) harmonizes with the page much better than the one above it, which contains all opaque colors.

If you change your mind about using a transparent color, click the Set Transparent Color button again, and click on the color you previously chose to be transparent in the image. Alternatively, you can choose a different color to be the transparent color by clicking on a different color in the image. The previously transparent color is restored to its original color, and all places in the graphic that are drawn in the newly selected color become transparent.

Adjust the Color Options

The Color button in the Pictures toolbar displays a shortcut menu when you click on it. Although there are four options in this menu (Automatic, Grayscale, Black & White, and Wash Out), only two of them (Grayscale and Wash Out) are active when you are working with clip art.

Convert an Image to Grayscale

The Grayscale option converts the image to shades of gray. Selecting the Grayscale option again returns the image to its original colors.

Use the Wash Out Option

The Wash Out option washes out the image by 50 percent. This has the effect of reducing the color intensity. Unlike the Grayscale option, selecting Wash Out again does not reverse the effect, nor does it wash the image out further. The only way to return to the original image is to use Edit | Undo.

Bevel the Image Borders

Bevel creates a beveled outline around the image. This beveling is done using white and gray, so it shows up best on a background color other than white or gray.

Make an Image Larger or Smaller with Resample

If you need to make an image larger or smaller, the Resample tool is very useful. To use it, select the image and use the sizing handles to adjust the size. Then click the Resample button.

Restore the Image with the Restore Button

If you change an image and decide you don't like the way it looks, you can simply reinsert the original image from its file—provided you haven't saved the image yet. To restore the image, simply click the image and then click the Restore button. In addition to removing any other changes you have made, the image is returned to its original size, overriding any resizing.

3

Chapter 4

Add Shapes and Photos

How to...

- Create drawings in a Web page using AutoShapes
- Modify the properties of the shapes and the shapes they reside in
- Add Photos to your Web site using the Photo Gallery facility
- Create graphics with Office's WordArt tool

Sometimes, it is not enough to just paste a piece of clip art into a page in your Web site. Using the Drawing toolbar and AutoShapes, you can create your own drawing. After you add the shapes to the drawing, you can change their size, color, fill, line style, and other properties.

In addition, with the advent of inexpensive scanners and reasonably priced digital cameras, digitized pictures are becoming more and more common and accessible. With FrontPage, you can create a photo gallery right in your Web site. You can choose from a variety of gallery styles, add captions to your pictures, and adjust the display size.

You can also create art from text—stretching and coloring the text in all sorts of imaginative ways by using the WordArt tool.

Create Shapes with the Drawing Tools

The tools available from the Drawing toolbar are useful for creating drawings that use shapes (such as rectangles, stars, arrows, etc.), lines, and text blocks to create an image. These types of images are effective for drawing flowcharts, organization charts, simple maps, and similar diagrams. You can adjust the size, line style, line color, fill color, stacking order, text font, and many other properties of the shapes to get the effect you want.

 The placement and display of the drawing and its associated shapes depend on Cascading Style Sheets (CSS) and Extensible Markup Language (XML). CSS and XML are not widely supported even by the most modern browsers, so your drawing may not display properly (or at all) in versions of Netscape Navigator earlier than 6.0, or Internet Explorer earlier than version 5.0.

> **NOTE**   *The shapes available from the Drawing toolbar are called "vector shapes." This means that, unlike bitmaps (such as GIF or JPEG images), you can resize these shapes as much and as often as you wish, and their quality will never degrade.*

Create a Drawing

The first step in creating a diagram is to insert a drawing—an area on the page where you are going to place your shapes. To do so, choose Insert | Picture | New Drawing. A rectangular area appears where you will build your diagram, as shown in Figure 4-1.

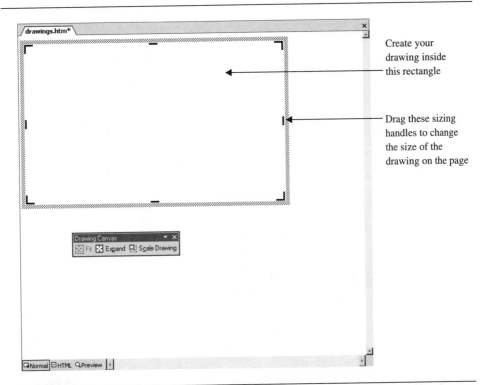

Create your drawing inside this rectangle

Drag these sizing handles to change the size of the drawing on the page

FIGURE 4-1   Add shapes, lines, and text blocks to the drawing area, denoted by the rectangular area.

NOTE   *Strictly speaking, you don't have to create a new drawing before adding shapes to a page. You can simply start adding shapes, lines, and text blocks to the page. However, there are advantages to creating the shapes inside a drawing. You can apply a consistent background to the entire drawing, resize the drawing and all the shapes contained in it, and attach a hyperlink to the drawing (see Chapter 8). And, you can easily wrap text around the entire drawing, just as we did with clip art in the last chapter.*

You can easily resize the diagram in the Web page by clicking and dragging the sizing handles located around the edges of the drawing. However, once you have added shapes to a drawing, you cannot drag the edges of the drawing past a shape (which would leave the shape outside the boundaries of the drawing). For example,

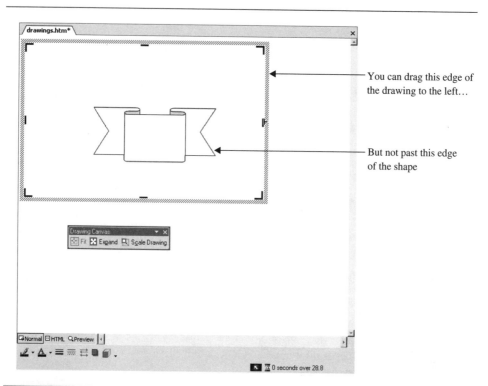

FIGURE 4-2   A shape inside a drawing limits how you resize the drawing.

look at Figure 4-2. You can click on the sizing handle in the middle of the right edge and drag it to the left. But, you can't drag it past the right edge of the shape.

Add Shapes to the Drawing

Once you've created the drawing, its time to add content to it. The Drawing toolbar (see Figure 4-3) provides the tools to add and format shapes as well as format the drawing itself.

To add one of the simple shapes (line, arrow, rectangle, or oval) from the Drawing toolbar to a drawing, use the following steps:

1. Click on the tool for the shape you want to use.

2. Move the mouse pointer to the spot where you want the upper-left corner of the shape (or the beginning of a line or arrow).

3. Hold down the left mouse button and drag the mouse pointer to the lower-right corner of the shape (or the end of the line or arrow). Release the left button and the shape is added to the drawing.

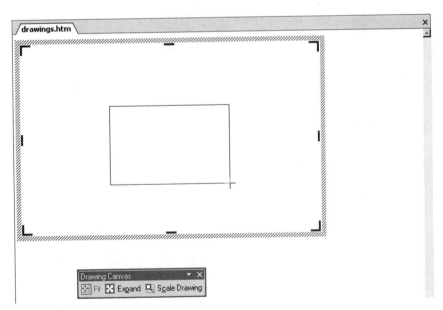

You are not limited to the simple shapes on the Drawing toolbar. You can also use AutoShapes: more complex shapes that are useful for drawing flowcharts and

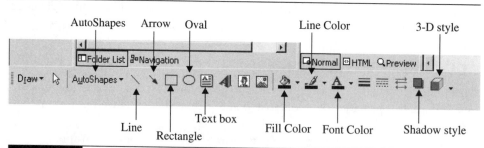

FIGURE 4-3   The Drawing toolbar provides the shapes with which to construct your drawing.

other types of diagrams. To access the AutoShapes, click on the AutoShapes entry in the Drawing toolbar. This displays the AutoShapes pop-up menu.

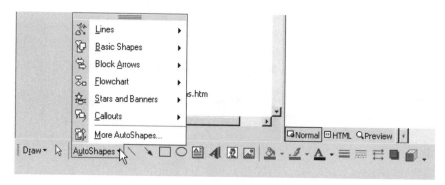

The shapes in the AutoShapes pop-up menu are grouped into categories, such as Lines, Basic Shapes, Block Arrows, Flowchart, Stars and Banners, and Callouts. To select a shape from one of these categories, move the mouse pointer over the category name to display a fly-out menu of the available shapes.

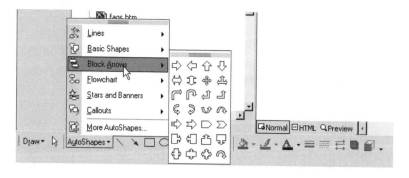

Click on the shape and add it to the drawing just as you would with one of the toolbar shapes discussed previously.

You can treat any graphic as an AutoShape if you have added the graphic to a collection in the Clip Organizer. To add a graphic as an AutoShape, choose More AutoShapes from the AutoShapes pop-up menu. This opens the Insert Clip Art Task Pane, from which you can search through your media files, as described in Chapter 3 (see the "Insert Clip Art into Your Web Page" section).

4

NOTE   *If you've never cataloged the media on your system using Clip Organizer (as described in Chapter 3), choosing More AutoShapes will prompt you to do so.*

FrontPage also provides the AutoShapes toolbar.

To make this toolbar visible, you can either select it from the toolbars menu (right-click in the toolbar area at the top of the screen to view the menu) or choose Insert | Picture | AutoShapes. Once the toolbar is visible, click on one of the icons to display a list of the shapes, and pick the shape from the resulting drop-down list.

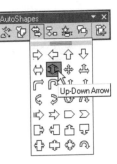

NOTE   *Each of the drop-down lists in the AutoShapes toolbar has a title bar (visible in the last illustration). You can click this title bar and drag to create a floating menu that remains visible until you close it by clicking the "x" in the upper-right corner.*

Add Text Boxes to the Drawing

A block of text can provide descriptive information in a drawing. To add a text box, click on the Text Box tool in the Drawing toolbar, and click and drag in the drawing to define the boundaries of the text box.

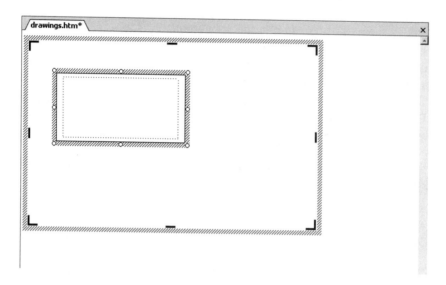

Type the text you want into the text box. Once you are done, you select any of the text and use the text formatting tools discussed in Chapter 2 to change the font, size, style, effects, and color of the text.

You aren't limited to placing text in text boxes. In fact, except for lines and arrows, you can add text to any shape. To do so, click on the shape and choose Add Text from the shortcut menu. Proceed to type in the text you want and format it as described in Chapter 2.

NOTE *Once you've added text to a shape—even if you later removed all the text—the shortcut menu changes from Add Text to Edit Text. You can choose Edit Text from the shortcut menu, or just click inside the shape. The text edit cursor appears, and you can type in your text.*

You can set the font color by clicking on the small down arrow to the right of the Font Color tool in the Drawing toolbar. This opens a pop-up menu.

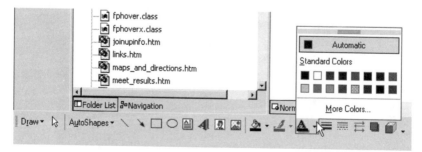

Choose a color or click on More Colors to open the More Colors dialog box, described in Chapter 2 (see the "Change the Text Color" section). You can click and drag the title bar of the pop-up menu to "tear off" the menu and make it constantly available in a small window.

Move and Size Shapes

You can modify the position and size of shapes (including text boxes) using nothing but your mouse. To move a shape, click inside the shape (the mouse turns into a cross) and drag the shape to its new position.

4

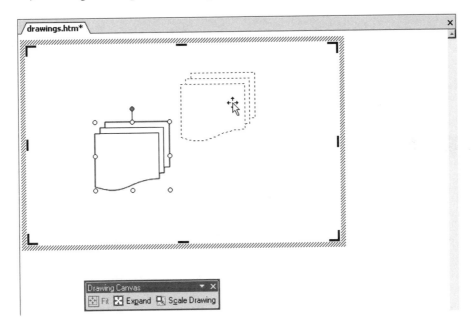

To resize a shape, click on one of the sizing handles, as shown in Figure 4-4. For closed shapes, sizing handles look like small hollow circles around the outside of a shape. For lines and arrows, there is a sizing handle at each end of the line.

Some of the more complex shapes—such as many of the block arrows—have shaping handles. These look like small yellow diamonds and are visible (although not in color) in Figure 4-4. Clicking and dragging a shaping handle changes the proportions of the shape. For example, dragging the handle at the bottom of the block arrowhead changes the width and height of the arrowhead.

Finally, you can rotate any shape except a line or arrow. The rotation handle appears as a small green circle initially above the shape. To rotate the shape, click on the rotation handle (the mouse pointer turns into a circular arrow) and drag the rotation handle.

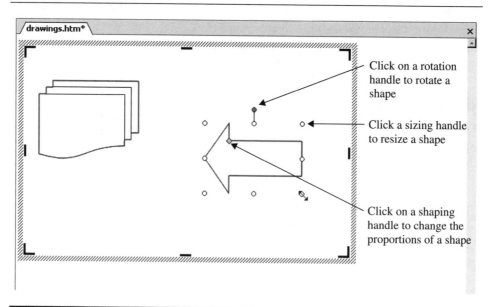

Click on a rotation handle to rotate a shape

Click a sizing handle to resize a shape

Click on a shaping handle to change the proportions of a shape

FIGURE 4-4   Click and drag shape handles to change the shape.

Modify the Drawing and Shape Properties

When you first create a drawing and add shapes to it, it is rather plain. That might be exactly what you want—after all, too many special effects often get in the way of the "message." There is, however, much more that you can do with the drawing and shapes. You can add fill color, adjust the line style, resize and reposition the drawing and shapes, adjust the layout, and even substitute alternative text for the drawing or shapes.

To adjust the properties of the drawing or a shape, right-click anywhere within the item and choose one of these items from the shortcut menu:

- Format Drawing Canvas (for a drawing)
- Format AutoShape (for any shape except a line or arrow)
- AutoShape (for a line or arrow)
- Format Text Box (for a text box)

You can also select Format | Drawing Canvas, Format | AutoShape, or Format | Text Box (depending on what type of item is selected). Whichever of these options you choose, a formatting dialog box opens. The dialog box is called Format Drawing Canvas for a drawing, Format AutoShapes for any other shape (including lines and arrows), or Format Text Box for a text box. Other than the title, the dialog boxes are almost identical, although certain options are not available for certain shapes. For example, you won't be able to apply a fill color to a line or arrow. Figure 4-5 shows the Format Drawing Canvas dialog box.

NOTE *Once you have specified the properties for the drawing or a shape, you can have FrontPage create new drawings and shapes with the same set of properties. To do so, check the Default For New Objects checkbox in the Colors and Line tab of the Format Drawing Canvas dialog box.*

Format the Fill Color

You can specify the details of the drawing, text box, or AutoShape background fill from the Colors and Lines tab (see Figure 4-5). To do so, click on the Color drop-down list.

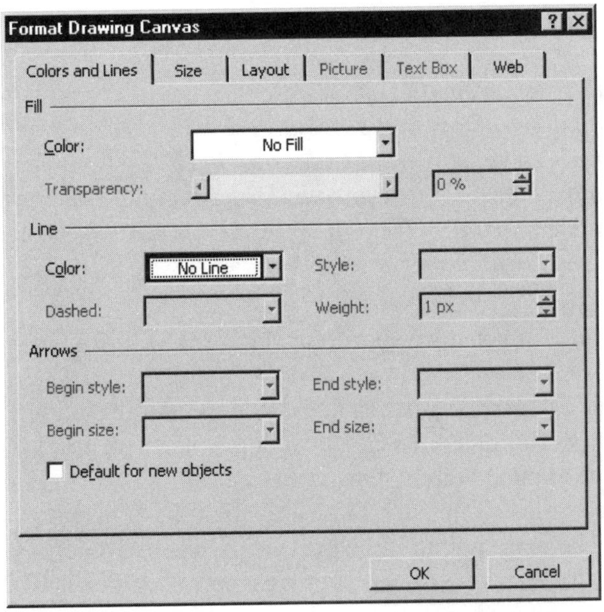

FIGURE 4-5   Use the Format Drawing Canvas dialog box to adjust the properties of the drawing and shapes.

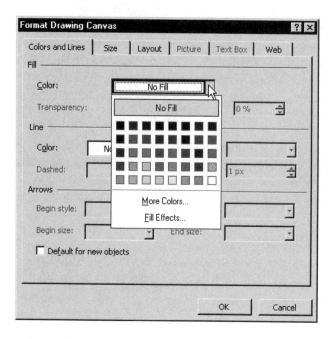

To pick one of the displayed colors for the fill color, click on that color in the center section of the drop-down list.

NOTE *You can access a similar set of options in a pop-up menu by clicking on the small down arrow to the right of the Fill Color tool in the Drawing toolbar. Clicking on the Fill Color tool itself resets the fill color to the Automatic color (as determined by FrontPage). If you wish, you can click on the title bar of the pop-up menu and tear off the menu to make it constantly available in a small window.*

To remove any fill you have specified, choose No Fill from the Color drop-down list.

To pick a fill color that is *not* displayed in the Color drop-down list, click the More Colors entry. This opens the Colors dialog box, which has two tabs: Standard and Custom. The Standard tab is show in Figure 4-6.

To pick one of the colors in the Standard tab of the Colors dialog box, simply choose it with the mouse pointer. The previously selected color is displayed in the lower portion of the rectangle in the lower-right corner of the dialog box. The newly selected color is displayed in the upper portion of the rectangle.

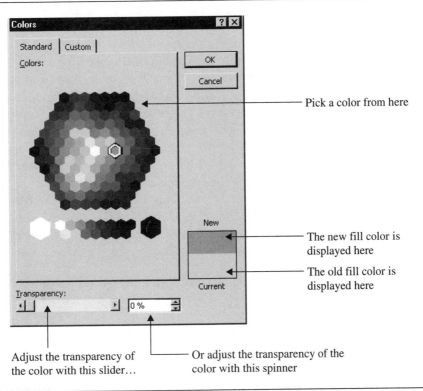

Pick a color from here

The new fill color is displayed here

The old fill color is displayed here

Adjust the transparency of the color with this slider...

Or adjust the transparency of the color with this spinner

FIGURE 4-6   Pick one of the many available colors in the Standard tab of the Colors dialog box to use as a fill color for an item.

You can specify the transparency of the fill color using the Transparency slider or the Transparency spinner, both located in the lower portion of the Standard tab of the Colors dialog box. A transparency of 0% means that the color is totally opaque—nothing located in back of the item (more on this in a moment) will show through. As you increase the transparency of the color, the shade of the selected color progressively lightens, and more of what is behind the item shows through the color. At a transparency of 100%, the fill color is invisible and the background shows through like you had not applied a fill color.

You can also set the transparency of the fill color using the Transparency slider or the Transparency spinner in the Colors and Lines tab, visible in Figure 4-6.

NOTE   *Under normal circumstances, there will be nothing "behind" an item (drawing or shape) to show through, no matter how transparent you make the background color. That is because text wraps around these items, and other graphics (e.g., clip art) are positioned somewhere outside or alongside the drawing or shape. But, as you'll learn in Chapter 13, you can use a concept called "absolute positioning" to essentially move an item—including a drawing or shape—anywhere on a page, and have the rest of the elements on the page ignore the item. If you use absolute positioning for the item and drag the item on top of other items on the page, those items will show through if the fill color is at least partially transparent. To try this, select the drawing, choose Format Drawing Canvas from the shortcut menu, click on the Layout tab, choose Absolute from the Positioning Style section, and click OK. Then drag the drawing on top of text or other items in the page, and they will show through (provided that the fill color is at least partially transparent).*

If the color you want to use is not available from the Standard tab of the Colors dialog box, you can switch to the Custom tab (shown in Figure 4-7) and pick a color from there.

You have several options for picking a fill color from the Custom tab. First, you can simply click on a color in the large color box in the center of the dialog box and adjust the intensity of the color by dragging the left arrow up or down the intensity bar. As with the Standard tab, FrontPage displays the new fill color in the upper portion of the rectangle in the lower-right corner, and you can set the transparency of the color with the Transparency slider or the Transparency spinner.

There is another option for choosing a color from the Custom tab: choose the color model you want to use from the Color Model drop-down list and type in the values that specify the color into the three fields below the Color Model drop-down list. The two color models are

- **RGB**   In the RGB (red-green-blue) color model, you specify how much of each of these colors you want in the fill color. When you use the RGB color model, the three fields are labeled Red, Green, and Blue. You can specify a value of 0 to 255 for each of these fields. A value of zero for all three fields yields a color of black, and value of 255 for each field yields a value of white.

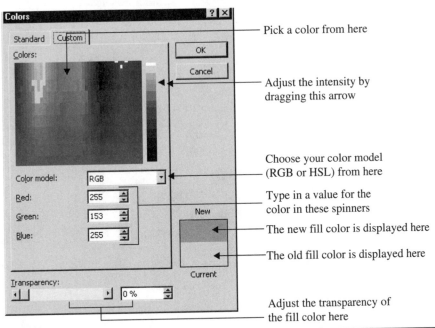

FIGURE 4-7   Pick any color your computer can display from the Custom tab of the Colors dialog box.

■ **HSL**   In the HSL (Hue-Saturation-Luminance) color model, you specify the color (hue), the intensity of the color (saturation), and the brightness (luminance). When you use the HSL color model, the three fields are labeled Hue, Sat, and Lum. As with the RGB model, you can specify a value of 0 through 255 for each of the fields. A value of zero for all three fields yields a color of black, and value of 255 for each field yields a value of white.

Format the Fill Effects

The last option on the Fill Color drop-down list is Fill Effects. Using Fill Effects, FrontPage enables you to really "dress up" a background—applying gradients, textures, colored patterns, and even a graphic. Choosing Fill Effects opens the Fill Effects dialog box.

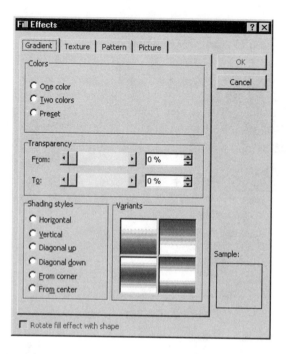

Use a Gradient Fill Effect   The Gradient tab enables you to set the background to a graduated fill. The options are

- **Colors**   Choose the option for the number of colors present in the background gradient from the radio buttons in the Colors section. Once you have made a selection, the dialog box changes to provide drop-down lists for picking the color(s) you want to use. Figure 4-8 shows the result when you choose the Two Colors option. If you choose One Color, the gradient varies from one intensity of the selected color to another. Select the color from the Color 1 drop-down list, and the overall intensity of the fill from the slider beneath the color (Dark to Light). If you choose Two Colors, the gradient varies from the first color to the second. Select the two colors from the Color 1 and Color 2 drop-down lists. The Color 1 and Color 2 drop-down lists enable you to either pick a standard color or choose More Colors to open the Colors dialog box, which contains the Standard tab and Custom tab, as discussed in the last section. If you choose the Preset option, you select from a set of built-in gradient schemes in the Preset Colors drop-down list that appears alongside the color options.

- **Transparency**   Use the two sliders or two spinners in the Transparency section to set the transparency of the fill color. The transparency will vary across the gradient from the value in the first slider or spinner to the value in the second slider or spinner.

- **Shading Styles And Variants**   Pick one of the options in the Shading Styles section to display from 2 to 4 variations of that shading style in the Variants section. For example, picking the Horizontal shading style displays four variants, all of which vary from top to bottom. Pick the variation you want from the Variants section.

NOTE   *When checked, the Rotate Fill Effect With Shape checkbox rotates the gradient fill when you rotate the filled shape. This option is not available for drawing background fills.*

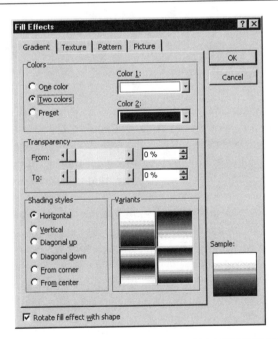

FIGURE 4-8   Picking a color option in the Colors section displays one or more drop-down lists for choosing the color you want.

Use a Texture Fill Effect You can fill the background with a prebuilt texture.

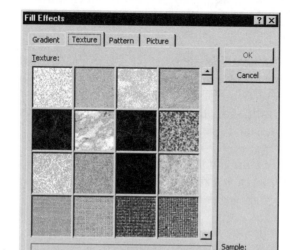

To do so, pick the texture you want from the Texture tab of the Fill Effects dialog box. If the texture you want is not available from the list, you can click the Other Texture button to open a standard File Open dialog box labeled Select Texture. You can choose a graphic in any of the graphic formats available. If the selected graphic is smaller than the drawing, it will be tiled to fill the drawing.

NOTE *Unlike clip art, FrontPage does not prompt you to save the image file within your Web site. However, don't worry about that—the image is saved automatically in a special folder within your Web site.*

Use a Pattern Fill The Pattern tab of the Fill Effects dialog box enables you to pick one of 48 different patterns and choose the foreground color and background color for the pattern fill.

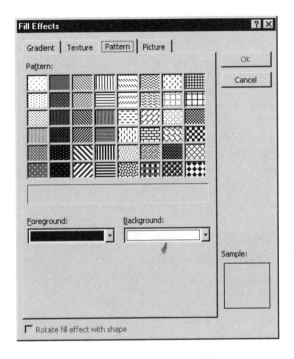

The foreground color is the color of the fill itself, while the background color is the color that appears behind the fill pattern. A sample of your selection is displayed in the Sample rectangle in the lower-right corner. Both the Background and Foreground color drop-down lists enable you to either pick a standard color or choose More Colors to open the Colors dialog box.

Use a Picture Fill   To use any image as a background fill, choose the Picture tab. Pick a picture by clicking on the Select Picture button and choosing the image (any recognized graphic format) from the resulting Select Picture dialog box. Click Insert to close the Select Picture dialog box and insert the image as the background. Any picture you select will be stretched to fill the entire area of the drawing. The Lock Picture Aspect Ratio checkbox controls how the picture is displayed: If you check this checkbox, FrontPage preserves the aspect ratio of the picture (ratio of the height to width). This may result in only a portion of the picture being displayed. If you clear this checkbox, the entire picture is displayed as the background; however, if the aspect ratio of the drawing is different from the aspect ratio of the picture, the picture will be distorted in either the height or the width to fill the drawing.

As with textures, any picture you use as a background is saved automatically into a special folder in your Web site.

Format Lines

You can set the properties of a drawing's borders, a line or arrow, or the outline of a shape (including a text box). To do so, use the tools in the Line section of the Colors and Lines tab. You can set the color and pattern of the line, as well as the style and weight (thickness).

To set the line color, click on the Color drop-down list.

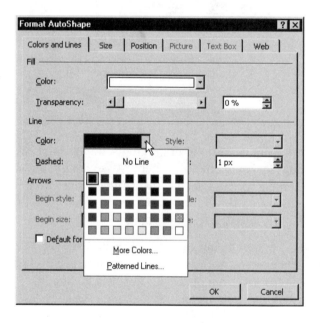

You can choose a color from the set of available colors, click on More Colors to open the Colors dialog box (described previously), or choose Patterned Lines to display a set of patterns to use for the line. The patterns, as well as the Foreground and Background drop-down lists (for choosing the foreground and background colors), work identically to the choices described in the "Use a Pattern Fill" section earlier in this chapter.

NOTE

You can access a similar set of options in a pop-up menu by clicking on the small down arrow to the right of the Line Color tool in the Drawing toolbar. Clicking on the Line Color tool itself resets the line color to the Automatic color (as determined by FrontPage). If you wish, you can click on the title bar of the pop-up menu and tear off the menu to make it constantly available in a small window.

To choose a type of dashed line for the border, click on the Dashed drop-down list.

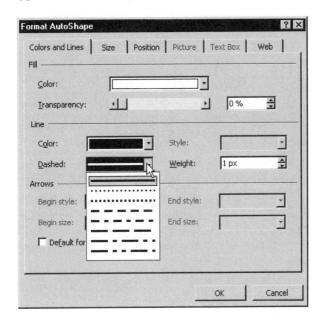

Pick a dashed line from the list. Note that if you had previously chosen a patterned line from the Color drop-down list, choosing one of the dashed lines overrides this choice. You can also pick a dashed line by clicking on the Dash Style tool in the Drawing toolbar and choosing the dashed line you want from the pop-up menu.

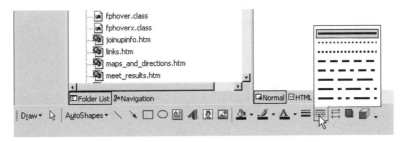

For lines and arrows, you can pick a line style from the Style drop-down list.

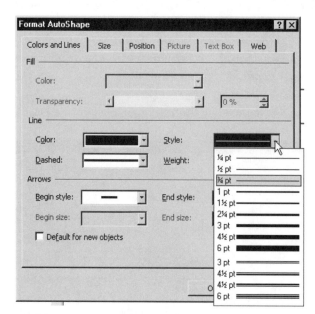

Styles include a variety of line thicknesses, as well as double and triple lines. You can choose a line style by clicking on the Line Style tool in the Drawing toolbar or the Pictures toolbar and choosing the line style you want from the pop-up menu.

You can also specify a line thickness by using the Weight spinner. If you change the line thickness with the Weight spinner, however, it overrides the choice you made in the Style drop-down list.

Format Arrows

The Format Arrows section of the Colors and Lines tab is only available for lines and arrows. You can set the style and size of arrowheads at both ends of a line using these options. To do so, click on either the Begin Style or End Style drop-down list to display your arrowhead style options.

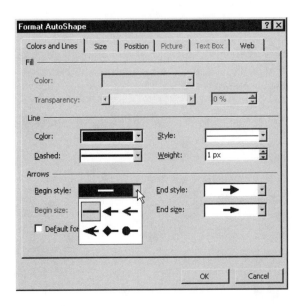

Pick the style you want and then click on the Begin Size or the End Size drop-down list to pick the size of the arrowhead. You can also pick from a variety of common arrow styles by clicking on the Arrow Style tool in the Drawing toolbar and picking the arrow style you want from the pop-up menu.

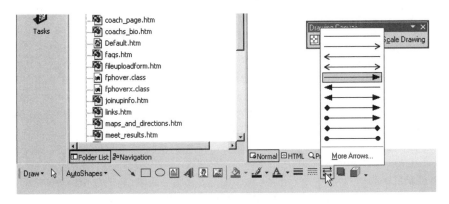

Format the Size

Although the easiest way to adjust the size of an item is to click and drag the sizing handles, you can also adjust it using the Size tab of the Format Drawing Canvas (or Format AutoShape) dialog box.

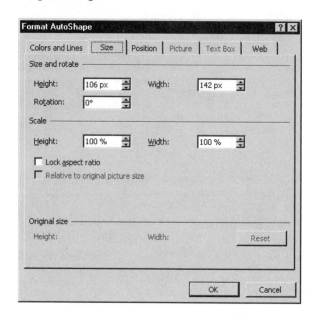

You can adjust the size of the drawing (in pixels) using the Height and Width spinners in the Size And Rotate section of the dialog box. You can also set the rotation angle using the Rotation spinner (not available for drawings and text boxes).

To scale the drawing (in percent), adjust the Height and Width spinners in the Scale section of the dialog box. When you scale a drawing, it not only changes the size of the drawing but scales the size of all shapes within the drawing as well.

Checking the Lock Aspect Ratio checkbox ensures that adjusting one dimension (either height or width) automatically adjusts the other dimension so that the ratio of height to width remains the same as it was prior to adjusting the size.

Format the Position

The easiest way to position a shape within a drawing is to click and drag it. However, you can also position it using the Position tab of the Format AutoShape dialog box.

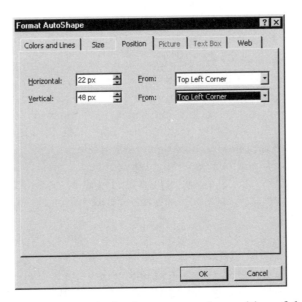

Use the Horizontal and Vertical spinners to set the position of the shape in pixels. You can set the position relative to either the top-left corner or the center of the drawing. Choose the option you want from the From drop-down list for both Horizontal and Vertical positions.

Format the Layout

You can adjust how text wraps around the drawing and the positioning style using the Layout tab.

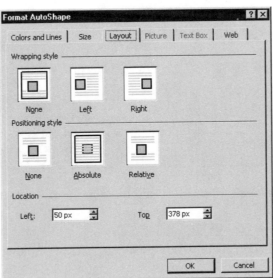

This tab is only available for drawings and for shapes that are *not* located within drawings.

Choose the wrapping style (None, Left, or Right) by selecting the icon in the Wrapping Style section of the dialog box. Text wraps around the entire drawing or shape in the same way as it wraps around graphics you insert into a page (see the "Set the Wrapping Style" section in Chapter 3). Choose the Positioning style (None, Absolute, or Relative) by selecting the icon in the Positioning Style section of the dialog box. Positioning will be discussed in chapter 13.

For a shape that is not located within a drawing, you can position the shape on the page using the Left and Top spinners in the Location section of the dialog box. These spinners locate the shape in pixels relative to the (can you guess?) top-left corner of the page.

Format the Text Box

You can specify the margin between text and the outline of shapes for text boxes and for any shape into which you have inserted text. To do so, click on the Text Box tab.

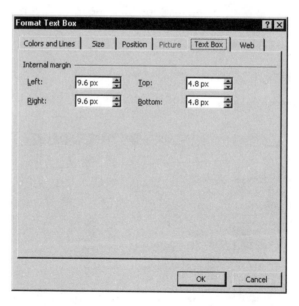

Set the margins (Left, Right, Top, and Bottom) in pixels from the spinners.

Specify Alternative Text

As mentioned earlier, many browsers are not capable of displaying a drawing or shape due to the advanced technology used to create them. For browsers that can't display the drawing or shape, it is advisable to display some text that explains what the drawing was showing or the purpose of the shape. To specify alternative text, select the Web tab and type text into the Alternative Text field.

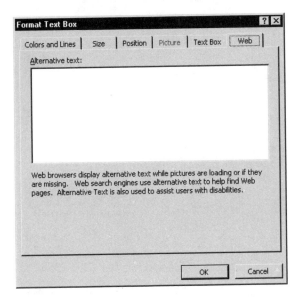

Add and Format Shadows

You can apply shadows to any drawing or shape—even a line. However, some of the shadow options are not available for all shapes. To apply a shadow, select the drawing or shape and click on the Shadow Style tool in the Drawing toolbar to open the pop-up menu.

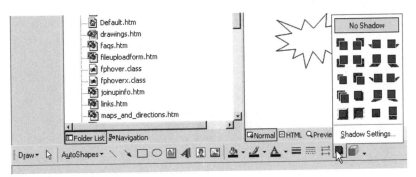

Pick the style of shadow you want, and the shadow appears alongside the selected drawing or shape. To remove a shadow, pick No Shadow from the Shadow Style tool.

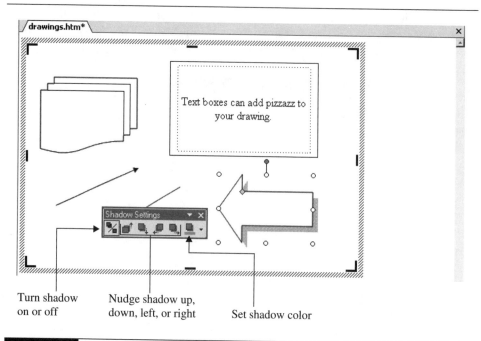

Turn shadow
on or off

Nudge shadow up,
down, left, or right

Set shadow color

FIGURE 4-9   The Shadow Settings toolbar lets you move a shadow and adjust the color.

Once you have created a shadow, you can make changes to it via the Shadow Settings toolbar (shown in Figure 4-9). To display the Shadow Settings toolbar, click on Shadow Settings in the Shadow Style pop-up menu.

If the shadow is not exactly where you want it, you can "nudge" it in a given direction by clicking on the appropriate tool in the Shadow Settings toolbar. To change the color of the shadow, click the small down arrow alongside the Shadow Color tool to display a pop-up menu.

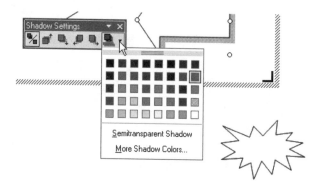

From the pop-up menu you can choose from the predefined selection of colors, click on More Shadow Colors to display the Colors dialog box (discussed previously), or select a semitransparent shadow. Just like transparent fill colors, anything behind a semitransparent shadow shows through the shadow.

Apply 3-D Effects

You can apply 3-D effects to any drawing or shape. To apply a 3-D effect, select the drawing or shape and click on the 3-D Style tool in the Drawing toolbar to open the pop-up menu.

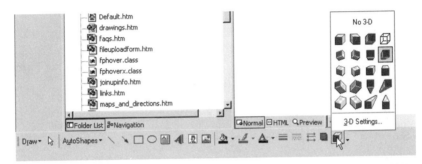

Pick the 3-D style you want and the shape takes on the selected 3-D style. To remove a 3-D effect, pick No 3-D from the 3-D Style tool.

Once you have added a 3-D effect to a shape, you can make changes to it via the 3-D Settings toolbar (shown in Figure 4-10). To display the 3-D Settings toolbar, click on 3-D Settings in the 3-D Style pop-up menu.

Tilt the 3-D Effect   You can tilt a drawing or shape's 3-D effect up, down, left, or right in small increments by clicking on the appropriate Tilt tool in the 3-D settings toolbar.

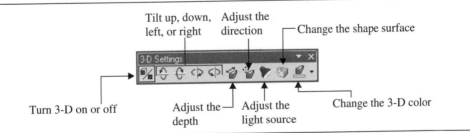

FIGURE 4-10   Use the tools in the 3-D Settings toolbar to make changes to the 3-D style applied to a shape.

Adjust the 3-D Effect Depth To adjust the depth (how far "back" a 3-D effect extends), click on the Depth tool in the 3-D Settings toolbar to display a pop-up menu.

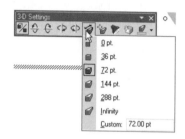

Pick the depth you want from the values in the list, or enter a value by clicking in the Custom field and typing the desired depth.

To adjust the direction in which the 3-D effect extends, click on the Direction tool in the 3-D Settings toolbar to display a pop-up menu.

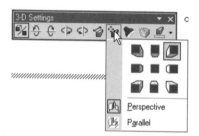

Choose the direction from the nine available choices, and choose whether you want the 3-D effect to use perspective or parallel. With perspective, the 3-D effect appears to converge on a vanishing point; with parallel, the 3-D effect does not converge, and instead, the edges of the effect are parallel to each other. The difference between these two effects is shown in Figure 4-11.

Adjust the Lighting You can set the direction and intensity of the light that shines on the 3-D effect, which changes the brightness of the sides of the effect. To adjust the lighting, click on the Lighting tool to display a pop-up menu.

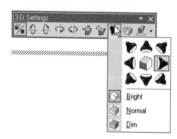

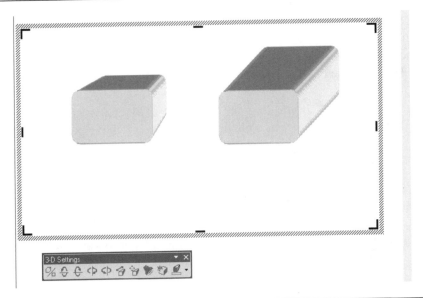

4

FIGURE 4-11   The difference between 3-D effects that use perspective (on the left) and parallel (on the right)

Pick the lighting direction from the top portion of the pop-up menu, and the lighting intensity (Bright, Normal, or Dim) from the three choices at the bottom.

Adjust the Material   You can select the 3-D effect material (Wire Frame, Matte, Plastic, or Metal) from the pop-up list that appears when you click on the Material tool. These "materials" vary the reflectiveness of 3-D effect, with metal being the most reflective.

Adjust the Color   To change the color of the 3-D effect, click the small down arrow alongside the 3-D Color tool to display a pop-up menu. From the pop-up menu you can choose from the predefined selection of colors, or click on More Shadow Colors to display the Colors dialog box (discussed previously).

Work with Multiple Shapes

You can select multiple shapes and work with them at the same time. This can be very handy for moving related shapes, applying consistent colors and line styles, and adding or formatting multiple shadows or 3-D effects.

There are two ways to select multiple shapes. The first way is to drag a rectangle around the shapes with the mouse pointer. All shapes that are fully contained within the rectangle are highlighted (selected). The other way to select multiple shapes is to click on the first shape, hold down the CTRL key, and click on the rest of the shapes. Clicking on a selected shape with the CTRL key still held down deselects that shape.

Once you've selected multiple shapes, you can work with them just like a single shape. Here is some of what you can do:

- **Move shapes** If you drag one of the shapes to reposition it, all the selected shapes move as well, maintaining their relative positions.

- **Size shapes** If you click on the sizing handles and resize one of the selected shapes, all the selected shapes resize proportionally.

- **Rotate shapes** If you click on a rotation handle and rotate one of the selected shapes, all the selected shapes rotate the same amount.

- **Apply formatting options** Any formatting options you choose from the Format AutoShape dialog box or the Drawing toolbar are applied to all the selected shapes.

Group Shapes

As you have probably figured out, it is possible to use a number of simple shapes to create a more complicated shape. For example, you could combine a set of rectangles, the heart AutoShape from Basic Shapes, and a few text blocks into an image that looks like a deck of cards. Once you have gone to all this trouble, you might want to work with this multitude of shapes as a single shape. Working with the image as a single shape makes it easier to copy and paste it, add a shadow to the overall shape, and size or move it without inadvertently leaving out one of the shapes and messing up your carefully crafted image.

To group a set of shapes into a single shape, select all the shapes using the techniques discussed previously. Choose Grouping | Group from the shortcut menu, or Group from the Draw menu at the left end of the Drawing toolbar. FrontPage creates a single shape from the selected shapes. Figure 4-12 shows the "before" and "after" views of creating a single shape from a set of multiple shapes. Notice that the after view has only a single set of sizing handles.

If you need to ungroup a set of shapes after you grouped them, simply select the shape and choose Grouping | Ungroup from the shortcut menu or Ungroup from the Draw menu.

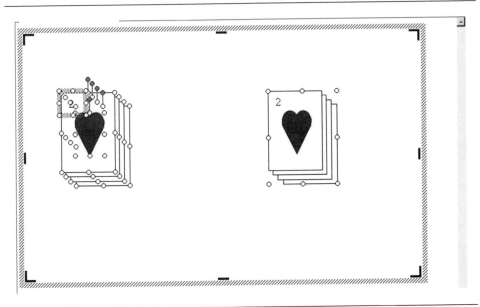

FIGURE 4-12   Before grouping multiple shapes (left) and after grouping them (right)

NOTE *You can group images that are themselves formed by grouping other images. For example, you could create two groups, each consisting originally of three AutoShapes. You can then group these two images into a single image. If you ungroup this final image, the result will be the two images you had before grouping them into the final image. To return to the original AutoShapes that formed the two images, you'll have to individually ungroup both of the two images. This type of intermediate grouping can be very helpful in building up complex diagrams.*

Set the Stacking Order

Each time you place a shape in a drawing, FrontPage places that shape in a new layer. As long as none of the shapes overlap, you will never notice this layering effect. However, if you decide to place two shapes in positions where they overlap, one of the shapes hides the other.

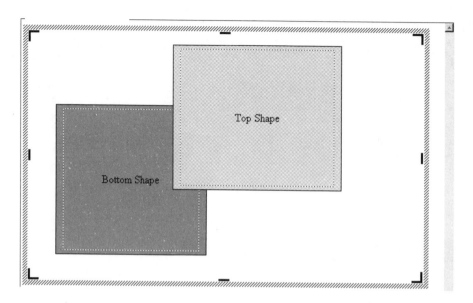

Which of the shapes ends up on top depends on the order in which you placed them in the drawing. The first shape is on the lowest layer—the bottom of the stacking order, so to speak. The next shape is on the next higher layer, and so on. If you arrange these two shapes so that they overlap, the second shape will hide part (or all) of the first shape. You are not stuck with this order, however: You can change the stacking order of the shapes. To change the stacking order of a shape, click on the shape and choose one of the four options in the Order menu item in either the shortcut menu or the Drawing menu:

- **Bring To Front**   Changes the stacking order of the shape so that it is on the top layer—in front of all the other shapes.

- **Send To Back**   Changes the stacking order of the shape so that it is on the bottom layer—in back of all the other shapes.

- **Bring Forward**   Brings the shape one layer towards the front. For example, if the shape was on layer 3, it is now on layer 4, and the shape that was formerly on layer 4 is now on layer 3.

- **Send Backward**   Sends the shape one layer towards the back.

NOTE   *The Pictures toolbar also contains the Send Backward and Bring Forward tools.*

Use Nudge and Snap To Position Shapes

The Nudge command gives you still another way to move your shapes. Nudge does just what the name indicates—gives the shapes a little push in the desired direction (up, down, left, or right). When you click Nudge in the Drawing menu, select the nudge direction from the submenu that appears.

The Snap options in the Drawing menu control how shapes behave when you reposition them by dragging. The two options are

- **Snap To Grid**   When you use Snap To Grid, you can move the shapes in very fine increments, positioning anywhere you want.

- **Snap To Shapes**   When you use Snap To Shape, the shape moves in increments as you drag it—that is, it doesn't move smoothly and there are only certain positions where you can position the shape.

Align and Shapes

It can be difficult to line up shapes on a drawing by eye. Fortunately, the Drawing menu provides some help. Once you select multiple shapes, you can choose to align them either horizontally or vertically using the six options in the Align Or Distribute submenu.

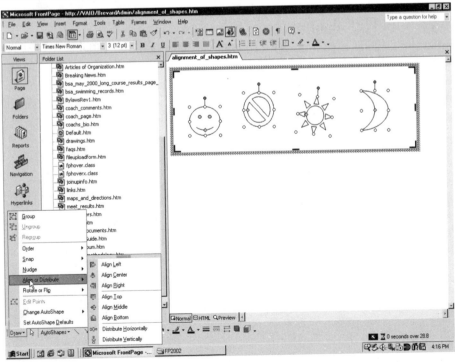

The alignment options are

- **Align Left**   Aligns the left edges of all selected shapes.
- **Align Center**   Aligns the vertical centerlines of all selected shapes.
- **Align Right**   Aligns the right edges of all selected shapes.
- **Align Top**   Aligns the tops of all selected shapes.
- **Align Middle**   Aligns the horizontal centerlines of all selected shapes.
- **Align Bottom**   Aligns the bottoms of all selected shapes.

You can also distribute three or more selected shapes evenly either horizontally or vertically using the last two options in the Align Or Distribute submenu. When you distribute shapes horizontally, FrontPage evenly distributes all the selected shapes along a horizontal line. The leftmost shape defines the left end of the horizontal distribution line, while the rightmost shape defines the right end of the line. Distributing shapes vertically is similar, except that the shapes are evenly distributed along a vertical line, with the topmost and bottommost shapes defining the ends of the vertical distribution line.

Rotate and Flip Shapes

Earlier in this chapter we discussed rotating a shape using the rotation handle. You can also rotate shapes by selecting them and choosing Rotate Or Flip | Free Rotate. This action places four green dots at the corners of the selected shape, and turns the mouse cursor into a rotation tool. Simply place the mouse cursor over one of the green dots and move the cursor to rotate the shape.

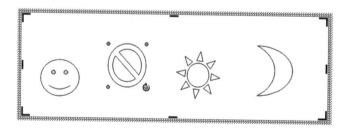

You can also rotate and flip shapes as follows:

- **Rotate Left**   This action rotates the shape 90 degrees left (counterclockwise). Choose Rotate Or Flip | Rotate Left from the Draw menu, or click on the Rotate Left tool in the Pictures toolbar.

- **Rotate Right**   This action rotates the shape 90 degrees right (clockwise). Choose Rotate Or Flip | Rotate Right from the Draw menu, or click on the Rotate Right tool in the Pictures toolbar.

- **Flip Horizontal**   This action flips the shape horizontally (see Figure 4-13). Choose Rotate Or Flip | Flip Horizontal, or click on the Flip Horizontal tool in the Pictures toolbar.

- **Flip Vertical**   This action flips the shape vertically (around a horizontal axis). Choose Rotate Or Flip | Flip Vertical, or click on the Flip Vertical tool in the Pictures toolbar.

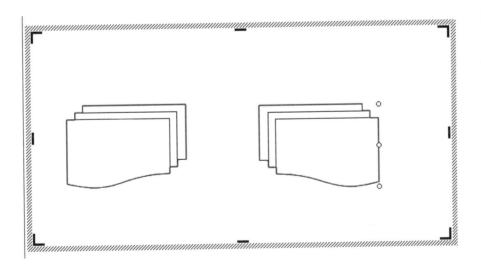

FIGURE 4-13   A shape before flipping it horizontally (on the left) and afterwards (on the right)

Modify the Drawing Canvas

You can modify the drawing as a whole using the Drawing Canvas toolbar (see Figure 4-14).

The three tools work as follows:

- ■ **Fit**   Clicking on this tool resizes the diagram to be just big enough to contain the shapes you have placed in the drawing.

- ■ **Expand**   Clicking on this tool enlarges the drawing evenly on each edge. Any shapes contained in the drawing are repositioned so that they remain in the same relative position.

- ■ **Scale Drawing**   When you click and drag the sizing handles around the edges of a drawing, you can adjust the size of the drawing. However, this action does not affect the size of shapes contained in the drawing. However, if you choose the Scale Drawing tool first, the drawing handles change from dark lines to small hollow dots. If you click and drag these sizing handles, the drawing *and the shapes contained within it* are all resized proportionally. For example, here is a drawing containing a few shapes before resizing:

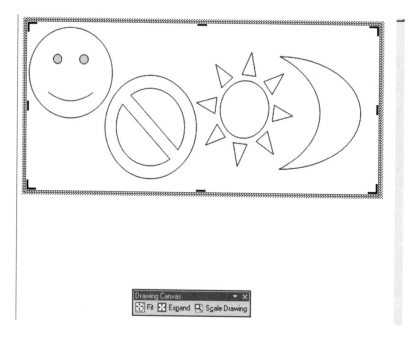

Expand Drawing

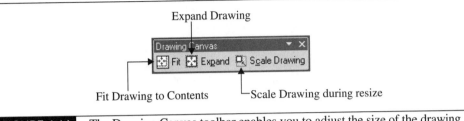

Fit Drawing to Contents   Scale Drawing during resize

FIGURE 4-14   The Drawing Canvas toolbar enables you to adjust the size of the drawing.

Here is the same drawing after resizing with the Scale Drawing tool active:

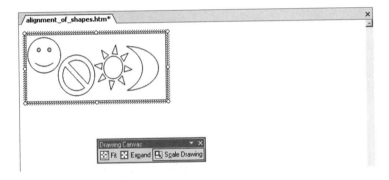

Add Photos to Your Web Site with the Photo Gallery

With the advent of digital cameras and inexpensive flat-plate scanners, it has become fast and easy to create digital photographs or convert photographs into digital form. One interesting use for digital photos is to post them on your Web site, where friends and family can view and download them. Unfortunately, displaying a set of full-size photos on a Web page can make the page take a long time to display in a browser. And, it can be a lot of effort to add and format textual descriptions for the photos. One solution to displaying full-size photos is to display "thumbnails"—reduced-size versions of the photos that give the reader some idea of what the photo looks like. Ideally, you would link the thumbnail to the full-size photo so that the reader could click on the thumbnail to view the photo. Earlier versions of FrontPage helped you with the process of creating thumbnails and linking with the AutoThumbnail function (which is still available in the current version). But you were still left with doing a lot of manual work to set up a gallery of photos.

The new version of FrontPage provides a tool to automate most of the process of creating a photo gallery—called, appropriately enough, "Photo Gallery" (see Figure 4-15 for a sample). Using the Photo Gallery, you can create a custom layout of photographs, generate the thumbnails, link them to the full-size images, and add textual descriptions that are visible in the gallery. You can also easily modify individual thumbnails and text.

Create a Photo Gallery

To create a photo gallery, choose Insert | Picture | New Photo Gallery. This displays the Photo Gallery Properties dialog box.

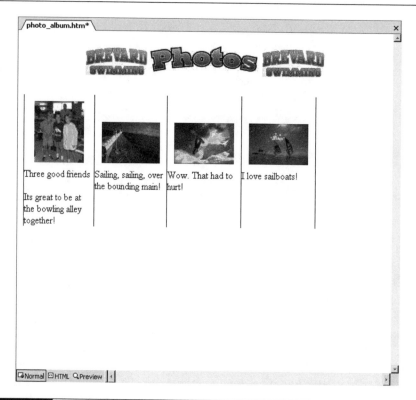

FIGURE 4-15   Display your digital photos in FrontPage's Photo Gallery

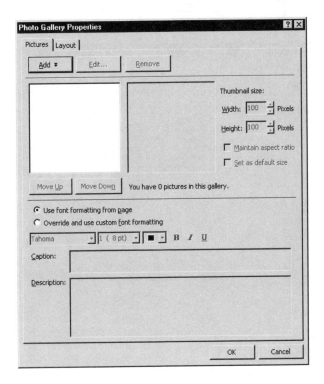

The first step is to add pictures to the gallery. To do so, click the Add button and pick one of the two options:

- **Pictures From Files**   Displays the File Open dialog box, from which you can pick one or more files on your hard drive or network.

- **Pictures From Scanner Or Camera**   Retrieve pictures using your scanner or camera. The device must be connected to your computer when you choose this option, at which point FrontPage walks you through the process of moving the digitized picture from the scanner or camera to your computer.

Once you have created a list of pictures for the photo gallery (see Figure 4-16), you can customize how each picture and caption is displayed in the gallery.

List of pictures in the gallery

See a preview of the selected picture here

Set the size of the thumbnail here

Rearrange the order of the pictures using these buttons

Adjust the font, color, and style of the text here

Add a caption for the picture here

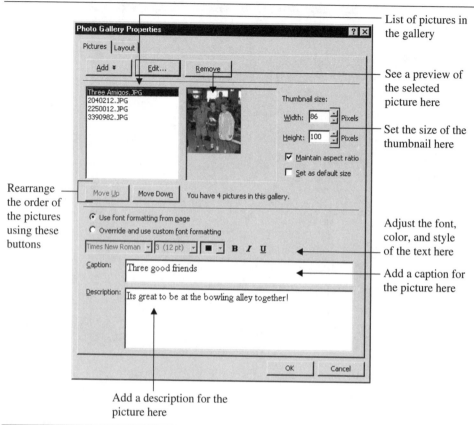

Add a description for the picture here

FIGURE 4-16   Work with the pictures in the gallery using the Photo Gallery Properties dialog box.

NOTE

You can also create a Photo Gallery by choosing Insert | Web Components and picking the Photo Gallery option from the Insert Web Component dialog box. Pick one of the available layouts from the dialog box (these are the same as the layout options discussed below), and click Finish to display the Photo Gallery Properties dialog box.

FrontPage displays the photos in the gallery in the same order as the list. To change the order of the pictures, select a picture in the list and click Move Up (moves the picture higher in the list) or Move Down (moves the picture lower in the list).

You can see a thumbnail preview of the currently selected picture in the square to the right of the picture list. You can also set the thumbnail size (in pixels) using the Width and Height spinners. If you check the Maintain Aspect Ratio checkbox, adjusting either dimension automatically adjusts the other dimension to maintain the original ratio of height to width and display the thumbnail without distortion. If you have a set of pictures that are all the same size, you may want to set up a thumbnail size you like and check the Set As Default Size checkbox so that each picture will have that thumbnail size as the default.

Each picture has two text fields: the caption and the description. Where the caption and description are displayed depends on the layout you pick for the photo gallery (more on this shortly). For example, in the Horizontal layout, the caption (normally fairly brief) is displayed immediately below the thumbnail in the photo gallery and the description is displayed underneath the caption. In the Montage layout, however, the caption appears only when you hover the pointer over a picture, and the description is not displayed at all. To create a caption and description, just type the text you want into the Caption and Description fields. You can change the font, size, color, and effects (Bold, Italic, or Underline) using the text tools immediately above the Caption field.

The last step in setting up a photo gallery is to choose a layout for your thumbnails. To do so, click on the Layout tab in the Photo Gallery Properties dialog box.

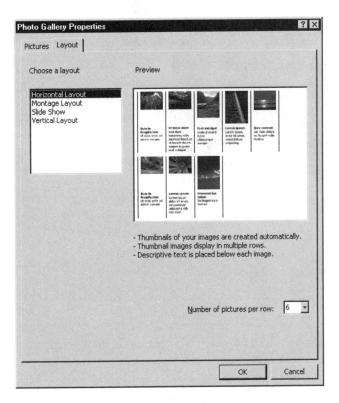

Choose a layout from the list in the left window, and view the preview in the Preview window. A textual description of the layout is provided below the Preview window. For some layouts, you can also pick the number of pictures per row from the Number Of Pictures Per Row drop-down list.

The most useful part of the textual description is the explanation of how the caption and description are displayed in that layout. This explanation keeps you from having to go back and change the layout later to get the caption and description to your liking.

Once you are done setting up the photo gallery, click OK to create the gallery. If the pictures you chose are stored outside your Web site, FrontPage will offer to copy them to your Web site. As always, this is highly recommended.

Edit Pictures in the Photo Gallery

The Photo Gallery Properties dialog box enables you to do a limited amount of editing on individual pictures. To edit a picture, select the picture in the list and click the Edit button to open the Edit Picture dialog box.

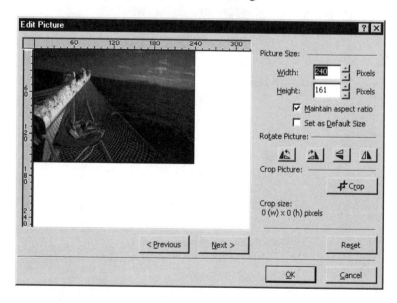

This dialog box shows a larger version of the picture than the thumbnail in the Photo Gallery Properties dialog box. You can cycle through the other pictures in the gallery using the Next and Previous buttons.

> **NOTE** *You can return the picture to the condition it was in when you opened the Edit Picture dialog box by clicking the Reset button.*

Here are the editing operations you can carry out:

■ **Change the width and height** If you want to change the size of the picture, you can do so using the Width and Height spinners. It is advisable to leave the Maintain Aspect Ratio checkbox checked so that the picture is not distorted as you adjust the dimensions. You can also check the Set As Default Size checkbox to set this size as the default for the other pictures in the gallery. Realize, however, that FrontPage resizes the rest of the pictures the moment you click OK to close the Edit Picture dialog box.

> **CAUTION** *It is* not *a good idea to increase the size of small picture. When you do this, the pixels in the picture all get larger, and you can see the blockiness (called "pixelation").*

■ **Rotate or flip the picture** As with AutoShapes (discussed earlier in this chapter), you can rotate a picture left (counterclockwise) or right (clockwise), and flip it vertically or horizontally using the buttons in the Rotate Picture section of the dialog box.

How to ... **Crop a Picture**

Pictures often contain extraneous material that detracts from the main subject, or just increases the file size of the picture (and thus the download time) without adding anything interesting to it. The Edit Picture dialog box enables you to "crop out" the unnecessary parts of the picture. To do so, use the following steps:

1. Click the Crop button. This places a cropping rectangle in the large preview of the picture.

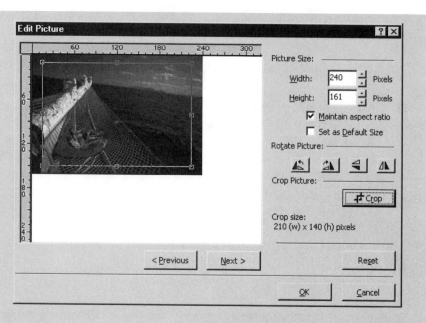

2. Use the mouse pointer to adjust the cropping rectangle. You can either click and drag a new rectangle, or click on a sizing handle and drag to resize the rectangle. The cropped size is indicated just below the Crop button.

3. Click the Crop button again. The Edit Picture dialog box crops the picture to the desired dimensions. Click OK to save the results. FrontPage saves the cropped picture and regenerates the thumbnail preview for the photo gallery.

CAUTION   *FrontPage saves the cropped picture by the same name as the original, overwriting the original picture file. If you don't want to lose the uncropped picture, make sure to make a copy of it before cropping it.*

Create Graphics with WordArt

WordArt is a utility that enables you to turn plain text into fancy graphics. WordArt is especially suited for building Web sites, where you'd like to dress up your text a little. To create a WordArt graphic use the following steps:

1. Choose Insert | Picture | WordArt or click the WordArt button in the Drawing toolbar. This opens the WordArt Gallery dialog box.

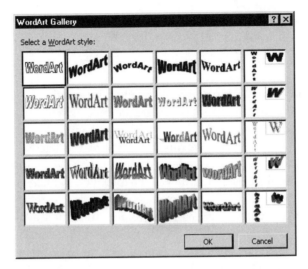

2. Pick the basic style you want to use, and click OK. This opens the Edit WordArt Text dialog box.

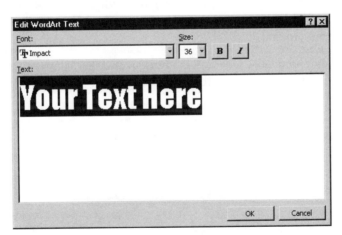

3. Type in the text you want to create your WordArt from and choose the font and size from the drop-down lists. If you want the text to be bold or italics, click the button(s) alongside the Font Size drop-down list. Click OK. FrontPage creates the WordArt and displays it on the screen.

You can change the WordArt graphic by clicking and dragging the sizing handles or using the rotation handle to rotate the image. WordArt has a special Adjust Shape handle. It looks like a yellow diamond and is located just below the middle of the WordArt graphic. Clicking and dragging this handle tilts the WordArt text left or right, similar to applying italics to text.

The WordArt toolbar (see Figure 4-17) enables you to make other changes to the WordArt image.

Use the following tools in the WordArt toolbar to modify a WordArt graphic:

- **Edit Text**   To change the text from which the WordArt image is constructed, click the Edit Text tool to reopen the Edit WordArt Text dialog box (discussed previously).

- **WordArt Gallery**   To change the basic style of the WordArt image, click the WordArt Gallery tool to reopen the WordArt Gallery dialog box, also discussed previously.

- **Format WordArt**   Clicking the Format WordArt tool opens the (you guessed it) Format WordArt dialog box. This dialog box is identical to the

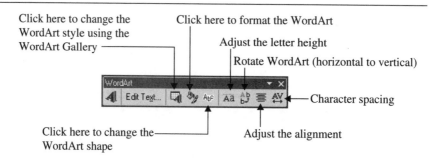

FIGURE 4-17   Use the WordArt toolbar to adjust the properties of a WordArt graphic.

Format AutoShapes dialog box discussed earlier in this chapter. From this dialog box, you can specify the fill and line properties (Colors and Lines tab); size (in pixels) and rotation angle (Size tab); wrapping style and positioning style (Layout tab); and alternative text (Web tab). You can also access this dialog box by selecting Format WordArt from the WordArt shortcut menu.

■ **WordArt Shape**   You configure the WordArt image to take on an overall shape, such as a wave, arch, oval, banner, fade, and many others. Experiment with these shapes—it is fun! To change the shape, click on WordArt Shape tool and pick the shape you want from the menu.

■ **WordArt Same Letter Heights**   By default, letters in the WordArt image are different heights: uppercase letters are taller than lowercase letters, an "h" is taller than an "e", and so on. However, you can specify that all letters are the same height by clicking on the WordArt Same Letter Heights tool. This tool is a toggle—click it once to specify the letters to be the same height, click it again to return the letters to different heights. This illustration shows the same WordArt shape with letters in different heights (left) and the same height (right).

■ **WordArt Vertical Text**   Use this toggle tool to switch the orientation of the WordArt image text between horizontal and vertical (shown here):

■ **WordArt Alignment**   Change the alignment of the WordArt image *within the space allocated to the image* by clicking the WordArt Alignment tool and selecting one of the alignment options (Left Align, Center, Right Align, Word Justify, and Stretch Justify). Word Justify fills the allocated area by adding space between words, whereas Stretch Justify fills the allocated area by adding space between letters.

NOTE   *Using WordArt Alignment is very different from the paragraph alignment options available in the Formatting toolbar or Paragraph dialog box. The paragraph alignment options align the WordArt shape on the page. Thus, clicking Align Left on the Formatting toolbar moves the WordArt shape to the left border of the page. However, choosing Center from the WordArt Alignment tool in the WordArt toolbar centers the image within the allocated space—even though that space is still left-aligned on the page.*

■ **WordArt Character Spacing**   You can set the spacing between letters in the WordArt image using the WordArt Character Spacing tool. To do so, click on the tool to display the options available in a drop-down menu.

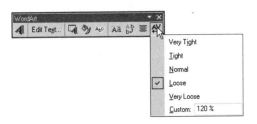

The options vary from Very Tight (letters very close together) to Very Loose (letters relatively far apart). Or, you can set a custom distance by typing a number into the Custom field at the bottom of the drop-down menu. This illustration shows the difference between Very Tight spacing (on the left) and Very Loose spacing (on the right).

NOTE *When you set the character spacing, the overall width (for horizontal WordArt) or height (for vertical WordArt) does not change. For tight spacing, the letters actually get wider so that they appear to be packed more tightly. For loose spacing, the letters become more narrow, leaving more space between them.*

Chapter 5

Format the Page

How to...

- Set page background and colors
- Set page margins
- Set up workgroup properties
- Apply themes to pages and sites
- Modify theme characteristics
- Add banners, comments, dates, and times to a page

Now that you've learned how to create a page and add text, graphics, and some fancy effects, you need to learn how to apply formatting that applies to the page as a whole. This formatting includes specifying the page background, applying "themes" (coordinated sets of colors and bullets), setting margins, and managing pages with the workgroup tools.

Set Page Properties

You can set many properties for your Web pages using the Page Properties dialog box.

To open the Page Properties dialog box, right-click anywhere on the page and choose Page Properties from the shortcut menu. Alternatively, you choose File |

Properties. The Page Properties dialog box has several tabs, and we'll cover most of them in this chapter. Some page properties (such as the Default Target Frame) will be deferred for discussion in later chapters.

Set the General Properties

From the General tab, you can change the title of the page by typing it in the Title field. You can also add a background sound to play when the reader first enters the page. To add a background sound, type the path to the sound file in the Location field of the Background Sound section, or click the Browse button to open the Background Sound dialog box and pick the sound file. Then click OK to pick the sound and return to the Page Properties dialog box. Choose the number of times you want to repeat the sound from the Loop spinner. You can choose to loop forever by checking the Forever checkbox, but this can become very annoying!

Specify the Background

The Background tab of the Page Properties dialog box (see Figure 5-1) is only available if the page does not have a theme assigned to it. When a page does have a theme, the Background tab is missing.

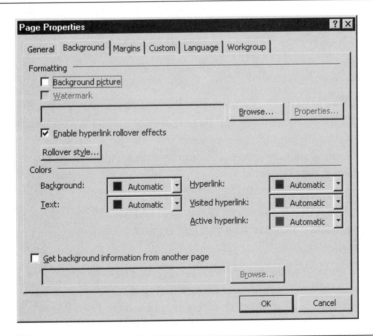

FIGURE 5-1   Use the Background tab to specify how the page background will look on pages that do not use themes.

Assign Background and Text Colors

To use a single color for the page background, click the Background drop-down list in the Colors section of the Background tab. This displays the standard Color tool, covered in Chapter 2. Choose the color you want to use from the Color tool. You can also pick a default color for all the text on the page from the Text drop-down list. This text color can be overridden by assigning colors to specific text on the page.

Assign Hyperlink Colors

You can assign colors to the three types of hyperlinks: Hyperlink (a hyperlink you have not visited), Visited Hyperlink (hyperlinks that you have visited), and Active Hyperlink (the currently selected hyperlink). Be sure to choose distinct colors for these different types of hyperlinks, as most people (including me) use the color cues to remember whether they have been to the hyperlink's destination. Clicking any of these drop-down lists displays the standard Color tool.

Assign a Background Picture

If you wish, you can use a picture as the background for the page. Remember that a busy picture will make the page exceedingly hard to read, so you should pick a simple picture, such as a subdued texture.

To add a background picture, use the following steps:

1. Check the Background Picture checkbox.

2. If you want to use the Watermark feature, check the Watermark checkbox. Normally, when you scroll a page that contains a background picture, the picture scrolls too. However, when you use the Watermark feature, the background picture remains stationary—that is, the page scrolls over the background picture.

NOTE   *You can only see the effect of the watermark in Preview mode. The normal Page mode always scrolls the background picture.*

3. Type the path to the background picture, or click the Browse button to open the Select Background Picture dialog box (see Figure 5-2). Choose a background picture and click Open to return to the Page Properties dialog box.

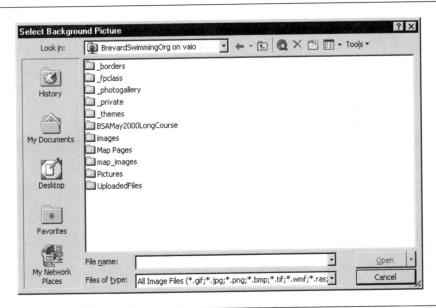

FIGURE 5-2   Use the Select Background Picture dialog box to choose a graphic to use as a background for the page.

4. Choose OK to close the Page Properties dialog box and display the Web page with the background picture (see Figure 5-3).

5. When you save the Web page, you'll see the Save Embedded Files dialog box if the background picture is not part of the current Web site. Save the images into your Web site, as discussed in Chapter 3.

You can also set the background for a page using the background information from another page. This is very handy if you have a page you've set up with the background the way you want it, and you want to apply that background to all the pages in your Web site. In addition, if you change the background of the source page (the page from which the others get their background information), the change is applied to all the pages. To obtain the background information from another page, check the Get Background Information From Another Page checkbox. Enter the filename for the page that will serve as the source page, or click the Browse button to open the Current Web dialog box, which displays all

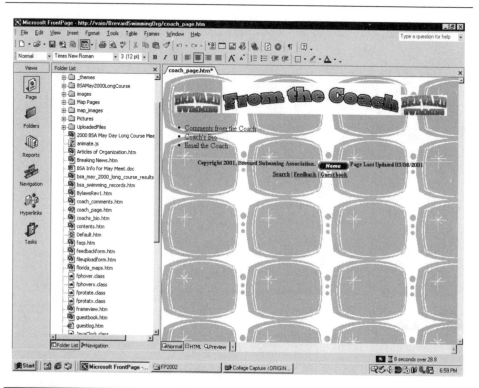

FIGURE 5-3   A page with a background picture can add pizzazz—as long as you don't overdo it!

the pages in the current Web site. Choose the page and click OK to return to the Page Properties dialog box. The background from the source Web page is now visible on your new Web page.

Enable Hyperlink Rollover Effects

A rather neat effect is hyperlink rollovers (see Figure 5-4). If you have these enabled and you move your mouse pointer over a hyperlink, the properties of the hyperlink change to call attention to the hyperlink. You have quite a bit of control over these effects.

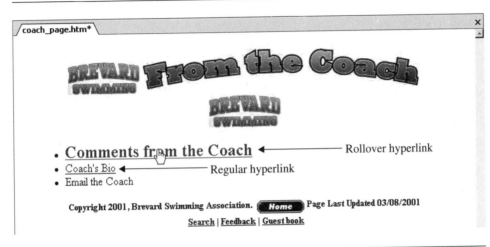

FIGURE 5-4   With hyperlink rollover effects, a hyperlink can really call attention to itself.

To activate hyperlink rollover effects, check the Enable Hyperlink Rollover Effects checkbox in the Background tab of the Page Properties dialog box. Then click the Rollover Style button to open the Font dialog box, as shown here:

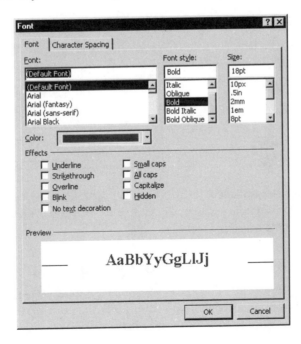

All the text options discussed in Chapter 2 are available, including changing the font, color, size, style, and effects. You can also switch to the Character Spacing tab to adjust the spacing (Normal, Expanded, or Condensed) and position (Subscript, Superscript, etc.).

When you have the effect set up just the way you want, click OK in the Font dialog box. Click OK in the Page Properties dialog box and switch to Preview to see the hyperlink rollover effect in action.

Set Up Page Margins

You can set the top and left margins of the page from the Margins tab of the Page Properties dialog box.

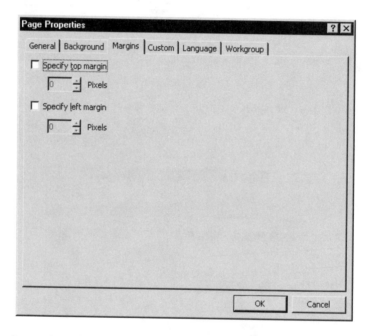

To set the top margin, check the Specify Top Margin checkbox and set the margin (in pixels) using the spinner. To set the left margin, use the same technique with the Specify Left Margin checkbox.

Manage Your Pages with Workgroup Properties

FrontPage provides some powerful tools for managing the construction of your Web site. These tools are especially useful if more than one person is participating in the construction, because you can categorize the Web pages, assign them to individuals, and set their review and publishing status. All these tasks can be completed from the Workgroup tab of the Page Properties dialog box (see Figure 5-5). Many of the properties you set here can be adjusted using FrontPage's reports (see Chapter 16).

Work with Categories

When creating a Web site with a workgroup, you can use categories to classify Web pages. Sample categories include Business, Competition, Goals/Objectives, In Process, and Waiting. Using such categories, you can assign not only what part of your business or project the Web page belongs in, but also the current state of the page. You can assign multiple categories to a page, and create new categories if the categories supplied with FrontPage don't meet your needs. The current categories assigned to a page are visible in the Item(s) Belong To These Categories field (this field can't be edited—it is for display only).

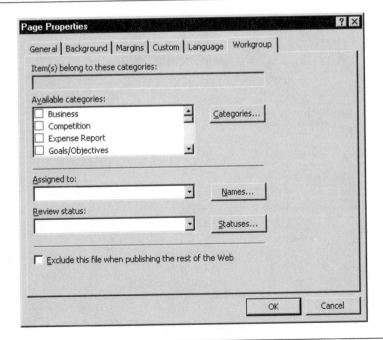

FIGURE 5-5   Coordinate workgroup activities related to a page from the Workgroup tab of the Page Properties dialog box.

To assign a page to a category, check the category's checkbox in the Available Categories list box. To remove a category from a page, clear the checkbox.

You can adjust the list of categories by clicking the Categories button to display the Master Category List dialog box (see Figure 5-6).

From this dialog box, you can do the following:

- **Remove a category** If you are not going to use a category, you can select it in the list box and click the Delete button. The category disappears from the Master Category List and is also removed from the list for any pages that were assigned to it.

- **Add a category** To add a new category, type the new category in the New Category field. Then click the Add button to add the category to the list. This category will now be available in the Available Categories list box for all pages.

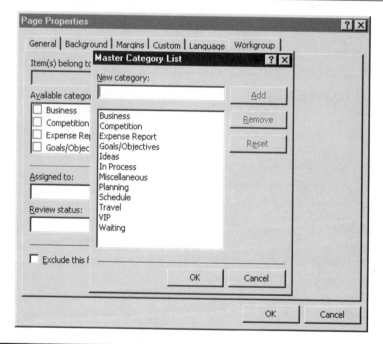

FIGURE 5-6 Adjust the categories you use to classify your Web pages.

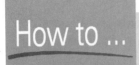

Add Responsibilities

You can assign Web pages to someone, making it his or her responsibility to create or enhance the Web page. Realize, however, that you can type anyone's name (or anything else, for that matter) as the responsible party, and FrontPage does not validate the entry.

To assign a page to someone, you can choose a name from the Assigned To drop-down list or type a name into the field. New names you type into the list are not automatically added to the list of available names. You won't be able to choose this new name from the drop-down list for another Web page unless you add the name to the list of names. To add names to the drop-down list (making them available on any page), click the Names button to open the Usernames Master List dialog box. This dialog box looks like the Master Category List dialog box (see Figure 5-6). To add a name, type the name into the New Username field and click the Add button. To remove a name, select the name in the list box and click the Delete button.

Set the Review Status

If you have developed a methodology for creating Web pages, a page may go through several stages of review, including management approval, legal, and marketing review. To keep track of the current status of a Web page, you can use the Review Status drop-down list. To record the current status, either choose the status from the drop-down list or type in a status. Like the Assigned To list (see the previous section), new statuses you type into the list are not automatically added to the list of available statuses. You won't be able to choose this new status from the drop-down list for another Web page unless you add the status to the list of statuses.

To add a new status to the list of statuses available in the Review Status drop-down list, click the Statuses button. This opens the Review Status Master List dialog box. This dialog box looks like the Master Category List dialog box (see Figure 5-6). To add a status, type the status into the New Review Status field and click the Add button. To remove a status, select the status in the list box and click the Delete button.

5

Set the Publish Status

A page has one of two publishing statuses: Publish or Don't Publish. If you set the status to Publish, the page will be published to your site's Web host server the next time you use FrontPage to publish your Web site. Conversely, if you set the status to Don't Publish, the page will not be published to the host server. This feature can be handy when you just need to publish a few changed pages.

To change the publishing status to Don't Publish, check the Exclude This File When Publishing The Rest Of The Web checkbox. Clear this checkbox to return the page publishing status to Publish. When the status is set to Don't Publish, the page appears in the Folder List with a small red x on its icon.

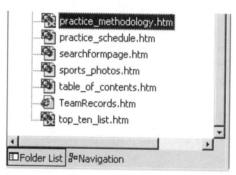

NOTE   *You can also adjust the publishing status directly in the Folder List. To do so, right-click on a page and select Don't Publish from the shortcut menu. This menu item is a toggle: if it is already checked, selecting it again will return the page to Publish status.*

Work with Themes

A theme is a collection of properties you can apply to selected pages or to your whole Web site. These properties include a coordinated palette of colors, button styles, bullet styles, page background properties (graphic, color, rollover effect), and text styles. The purpose of a theme is to give a consistent look to your site. To pick a theme for your page or site, use the Themes dialog box, shown in Figure 5-7.

Apply Themes to Pages or a Site

To apply a theme to a page or a site, you can open the Themes dialog box using any of the following options:

- From Reports or Tasks view, select Format | Theme. The All Pages option is the only one available.

- From Hyperlinks or Navigation view, select a page, then choose Format | Theme. The default selection is the Selected Page(s) option, but you can choose All Pages to apply the theme to all pages in the Web site.

- From the Folders view, select one or more pages (only the Folders view enables you to pick multiple pages). Choose Format | Theme. The default selection is the Selected Page(s) option, but you can choose All Pages to apply the theme to all pages in the Web site.

Once you've opened the Themes dialog box, you can pick a theme from the list of themes on the left side of the dialog box. Clicking a theme displays a sample of the theme in the Sample Of Theme area (the large window that dominates the dialog box). Once you've got a theme you like, click OK to apply the theme to the site or the selected pages (depending on the option chosen in the Apply Theme To section in the upper-left corner of the dialog box).

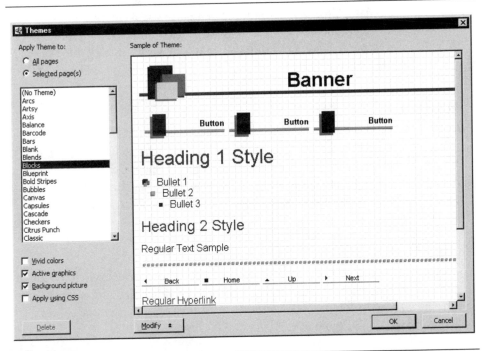

FIGURE 5-7   The Themes dialog box shows you a preview of what a theme looks like, as well as providing the tools for customizing a theme.

Set Theme Options

You can modify some of the options associated with a theme using the four checkboxes in the lower-left corner of the Themes dialog box. The available options are

- **Vivid Colors**   Provides a brighter set of theme colors.

- **Active Graphics**   Converts the buttons and bullets into Dynamic HTML elements that support DHTML formatting (discussed in Chapter 13).

- **Background Picture**   Some themes include both a background color and a background graphic. Themes only use one of these options at a time, and those themes that include both either use the background graphic or the color as the default. By checking the Background Picture checkbox, you can override the color default and use the background picture instead. By clearing the checkbox, you can override the background picture default and use the color instead.

- **Apply Using CSS**   Establishes the theme using the Cascading Style Sheet standard. This gives you more standardized code, but older browsers cannot handle CSS, and those that do may not all handle it the same way, leading to Web pages that look substantially different in different browsers.

Modify the Properties of a Theme

FrontPage provides many themes, and one may be perfect for you to use just the way it is. If you want to modify a theme to make it more to your liking, however, FrontPage provides all the tools you need. To modify a theme, open the Themes dialog box and click the Modify button. This reduces the size of the Sample Of Theme area and provides three more buttons: Colors, Graphics, and Text (as shown in Figure 5-8).

Modify Theme Colors

To modify the theme's colors, click the Colors button to open the Modify Theme dialog box (see Figure 5-9). This dialog box contains three different methods for modifying a theme's colors. Each method has its own tab. The first tab, Color Schemes, is visible in Figure 5-9.

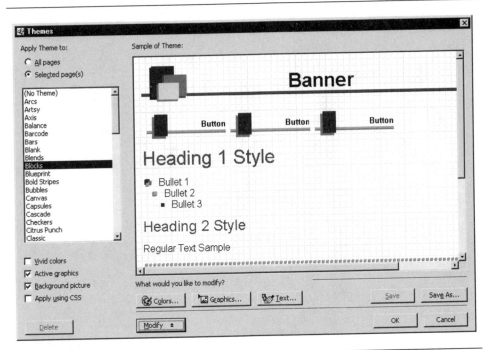

FIGURE 5-8   The three new buttons at the bottom of the Themes dialog box provide tools for modifying a theme.

The Color Schemes tab enables you to choose a color scheme from another theme. To do so, choose the name of the theme whose color scheme you want to use from the list of themes on the left side of the dialog box. Click the Vivid Colors option to use a richer color set. The Sample Of Theme area shows you how your choice will look. Choosing an already-defined color scheme is useful in giving you a starting point for making further color modifications. You can also create a theme that combines a color scheme from one theme with custom graphics and text specifications.

The Color Wheel tab (see Figure 5-10) contains a color wheel from which you can choose a specific color. However, note that selecting a color in the color wheel actually changes all the colors in the scheme, not just one color. To make a color

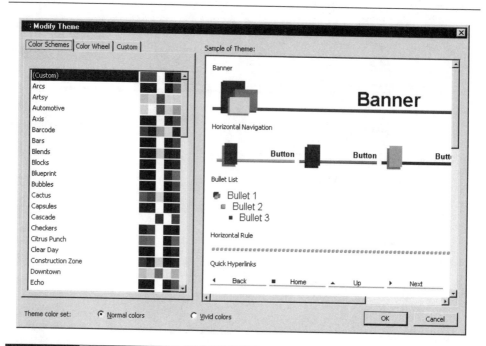

Use the Modify Theme window to change the colors of a theme.

selection, either click anywhere in the color wheel, or click the tiny round cursor in the color wheel and drag it to the color you want to use. Adjust the brightness of the color set using the Brightness slider. Once again, the Sample Of Theme area shows what your selection of colors will look like.

The last tab, Custom (see Figure 5-11), enables you to select individual colors for each element in the theme. To do so, choose the item whose color you want to modify from the Item drop-down list. Then click the Color drop-down list to display the standard Color tool. Pick the color you want from the available colors or click More Colors to open the More Colors dialog box and pick any color your

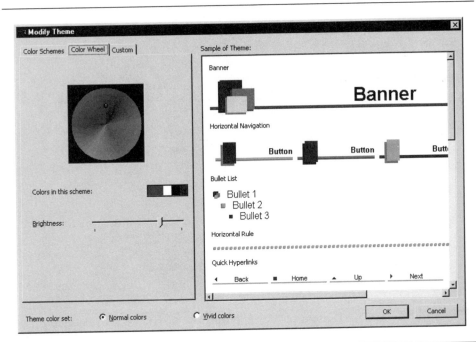

FIGURE 5-10   Use the Color Wheel tab to choose a set of colors and their brightness.

computer can display. Continue choosing items and assigning colors until you have a set of colors you are happy with.

Modify Theme Graphics

You can change the graphics assigned to any element of a theme. You can change the background graphic, the graphics assigned to bullets, hyperlinks, buttons, and so on. If the element also includes text (as banners and many navigation buttons do), you can also change the text characteristics. Click the Graphics button in the main Themes dialog box to open the Modify Theme dialog box (see Figure 5-12).

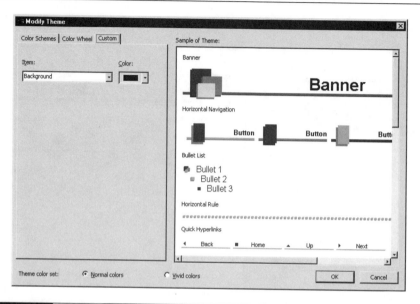

FIGURE 5-11   Use the Custom tab to define individual colors for each element in a theme.

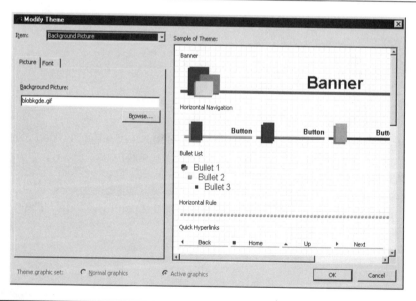

FIGURE 5-12   Modify the graphics and text for any element in the theme using the Modify Theme dialog box.

To change a graphic element, use the following steps:

1. Choose the element you want to change from the Item menu at the top of the dialog box. As soon as you choose an element, the Sample Of Theme portion of the window adjusts to display that element.

2. In the Picture tab, specify the graphic you want to use for the element. Some elements (such as many of the buttons and bullets) use multiple graphics. With buttons, for example, there are usually three graphics: the graphic used for the "normal" picture, individual graphics used for the "selected" picture, and the "hovered" picture (used when you move the mouse pointer over the button). If the element does use multiple graphics, you can specify all the graphics in the Picture tab. Use the Browse button alongside each Picture field to open the Open File dialog box and choose an image to use.

3. If the selected element includes a text component, switch to the Font tab.

4. Choose a Font from the list of fonts on the left side of the Font tab. If the selected element uses multiple fonts (for example, one for each of the button states discussed in step 2), the list of fonts is displayed in the Font

field, separated by commas. You can customize your list by selecting your own desired fonts. Be sure to use the same number of fonts as were initially displayed in the Font field.

5. Choose a style, size, horizontal alignment, and vertical alignment from the appropriate drop-down lists.

Modify Theme Text

The last modification you can make is to change the text characteristics of theme elements that do not have a graphic associated with them. These include the body text and all the headings. To make changes to these text-only elements, click the Text button in the main Themes dialog box. This displays still another version of the Modify Theme dialog box (see Figure 5-13).

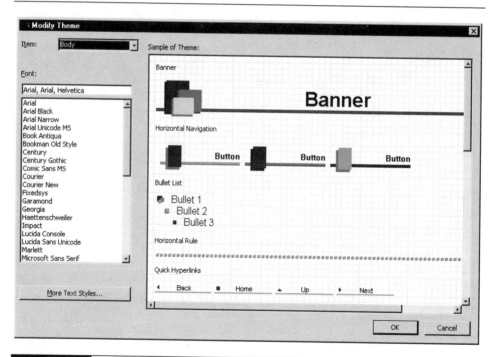

FIGURE 5-13 Modify the characteristics of text-only elements of a theme.

Choose the element you want to change from the Item drop-down list.
Then choose the font you want to use from the list of fonts located just below
the Font field.

Save Your Theme Changes

Two other buttons also appear in the main Themes dialog box: Save and Save
As. Use the Save button to save your changes to the currently selected theme,
overwriting the theme. The Save As button saves your changes to a new theme
(this is much safer). When you select the Save As button, you must enter a new
name for the theme in the Save Theme dialog box that appears. Clicking OK in the
Save Theme dialog box saves your theme under its new name, and the new theme
is then available in the list of themes.

5

Add Page-Based Elements

You can customize your Web page further by adding a page banner, comments,
and a timestamp. You can also set up the transition used to make the page appear
when the reader opens the page in a browser (called a page transition).

Title Your Page with a Page Banner

A page banner is a special header for a page. It always appears at the top of the
page, and can consist of either just text or text and a graphic. However, if you
do choose to include a graphic in the page banner, you can't pick the graphic
yourself—you can only use the banner graphic for the page's theme. If the page
does not include a theme, you can't use a graphic in the page banner.

TIP
*If you want to include a graphic banner on a page that does not have
a theme, and the banner is the* only *thing on the page you want to have
associated with a graphic image, create a small empty graphic using any
graphics tool, and call it empty.jpg. Create a theme that associates every
graphic element except the banner with empty.jpg. Create the graphic you
want to use for the banner, and associate the banner with that graphic.
You can also create a separate theme for each page for which you want
a new banner and modify the banner graphic used.*

To create a page banner, choose Insert | Web Component, and choose Included
Content from the Component Type list on the left side of the Web Component

dialog box. Then pick Page Banner from the content list on the right side of the dialog box.

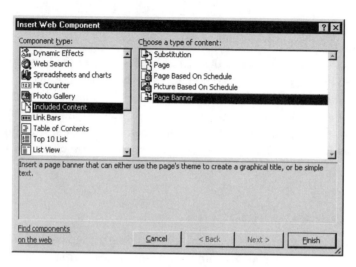

Click Finish to close the Insert Web Component dialog box and open the Page Banner Properties dialog box.

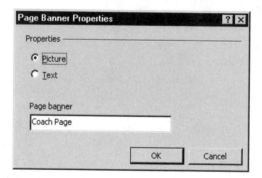

Choose either the Picture or Text option, and fill in the text of the page banner in the Page Banner text field. This text appears regardless of which option you picked. Click OK to create the page banner.

The text field is only available if you have added the page to the Navigation view. Also, the default text that appears in the Page Banner Properties dialog box is the page's title in the Navigation view. If you change the text, you are also changing the page title in the Navigation view.

Once you create the page banner, you can change its properties by right-clicking it and choosing Page Banner Properties from the shortcut menu. More importantly, you can also choose Font or Paragraph from either the shortcut menu or the Format menu to change the font, size, style, effects, and alignment of the page banner. You can also use the tools in the Formatting toolbar.

NOTE *Unlike normal text, you can't select and change the font or paragraph properties of only a portion of the page banner—your changes apply to all the text in the banner.*

5

Add Comments

If you have ever taken any programming classes, one of the first things you learned was to add comments to your code so someone else could figure out what you have done. Comments are also helpful in reminding you what *you* did and why you did it. The same is true of Web pages.

FrontPage enables you to add comments to your Web pages, as shown in Figure 5-14. Comments are a special kind of text. You can see them in the normal Page view in FrontPage, but they don't display in a Web browser or in the preview Page view.

CAUTION *Your comments are visible if a reader views the HTML source for your page. So word your comments carefully to avoid embarrassing yourself!*

FIGURE 5-14   Add comments to your Web pages to help you remember what you did.

To add comments to your Web page, choose Insert | Comment. This opens the simple Comment dialog box, where you can enter the text of the comment. When you close the Comment dialog box, the comment is inserted into the Web page at the text cursor location.

To change the text of a comment after you have added it to the Web page, right-click the comment and choose Comment Properties from the shortcut menu. The Comment dialog box appears again, with the existing text of the comment already present. Make any changes to the text and click OK. You can change the Font and Paragraph properties by selecting the text of the Comment and choosing Font or Paragraph from either the comment's shortcut menu or the Format menu, or by using the tools in the Formatting toolbar. Your changes apply to all the text in the comment—as with the page banner, you can't change just a portion of the text in the comment.

TIP   *Although you can set the font color of a comment, FrontPage overrides any changes you make to this one property and always displays comments in the default purple. However, if you are really determined to change the comment color, you can. Select the comment and switch to the HTML view. At the beginning of the highlighted line of HTML that defines the comment, you'll see something like "webbot bot = PurpleText". Change PurpleText to some other color, such as "RedText", and the color of the comment will change!*

Add a Date and Time

When you are building many Web pages, it is very handy to be able to keep track of the last time a page was modified. It can also be helpful to people viewing your Web page to have this information. You have the option of inserting just a date, just a time, or a date and time. You can also decide whether the date/time should reflect when the page was last edited or when the page was last automatically updated.

To add a date and time to a page, choose Insert | Date and Time to display the Date and Time Properties dialog box.

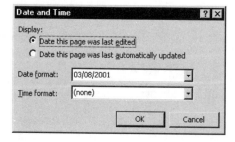

Make the following selections from the Date and Time Properties dialog box:

■ **Date format**   Select (None) from the Date Format drop-down list to suppress the date. Otherwise, choose the format of the date you want to display from this drop-down list. Formats available include a variety of orders for the month, day, and year, both two- and four-place years, and formats that include spelling out the day of the week and month name.

■ **Time format**   Select (None) from the Time Format drop-down list to suppress the time. Otherwise, choose the format of the time you want to display from this drop-down list. Formats available include both A.M./P.M. and 24-hour formats, varying degrees of precision, and the ability to show the difference between local time and Greenwich mean time (the formats that include TZ, for time zone).

You can change the font and paragraph properties by selecting the date/time and choosing Font or Paragraph from either the Date/Time's shortcut menu or the Format menu, or by using the tools in the Formatting toolbar. Your changes apply to all the text in the date/time—as with the page banner, you can't change just a portion of the text in the date/time.

Transition Between Pages

If you've worked with Microsoft PowerPoint, you are probably familiar with page transitions—special effects that take place as a PowerPoint slide is displayed or exited. Such effects go by names such as wipes, fade ins, blinds, and so on. You can use page transition effects with FrontPage Web pages as well. In addition, you can apply a transition effect when the user enters or leaves the site.

Open Page view in the page to which you want to attach page transitions. Choose Format | Page Transition to display the Page Transitions dialog box.

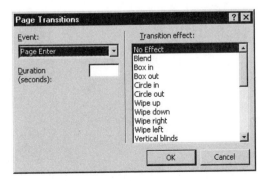

From the Page Transitions dialog box, make the following selections:

- **Event**   From the Event drop-down list, choose when the selected transition will occur. Your choices are to have the transition occur when the page is entered, when the page is exited, when the site is entered, and when the site is exited. There can, of course, be only one type of transition for the Site Entered and Site Exited choices.

- **Duration (seconds)**   You can vary how long the transition effect goes on. It's a good idea to keep the transitions short (if you use them at all—I don't) because they can quickly become annoying when the person just wants to see the page. Enter the duration in seconds. You can include a decimal point (for example, 4.5 seconds).

- **Transition effect**   Select the transition effect you want from the Transition Effect list box.

You can set page transitions for multiple events on a page. Simply go back and select a different event from the Event drop-down list and specify the other quantities.

NOTE   *To preview the transition, switch to the Preview page mode.*

Chapter 6

Work with Tables

How to...

- Insert a table
- Draw a table
- Add, delete, and modify rows and columns
- Split a table
- Modify cells
- Set table properties
- Fill a table with data
- Convert text to tables and tables to text
- Build tables using Word and Excel

Tables are exceedingly useful tools when building a Web page. With tables, it is easy to line up items on the page in rows and columns, giving the page the layout you want. Many two-column and three-column lists on Web pages are actually contained in a table. You may not realize this because the outlines of the table can be made invisible. Tables are also very useful for aligning images on a page.

Understand Basic Table Concepts

FrontPage tables are similar to tables in other Microsoft Office applications. For example, if you have ever worked with tables in Microsoft Word, you are already familiar with many of the features of FrontPage tables, although FrontPage tables give you many more configuration options. In fact, as you'll see later in this chapter, it is easy to convert a Word table into a FrontPage table.

The basic premise of tables is that they arrange information into rows and columns (see Figure 6-1). The intersection of each row and column is referred to as a *cell,* much like the cells in a spreadsheet. You can place any information you want into a cell—text, graphics, hyperlinks, and even another table.

Insert a Table

The simplest way to add a table to a Web page is to insert it (you can also draw a table, covered in the next section). There are two ways to insert a table: from the Standard toolbar and from the Table menu.

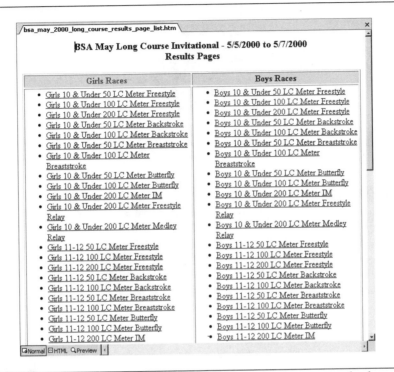

| FIGURE 6-1 | A table makes it easy to arrange information into rows and columns. |

Insert a Table from the Standard Toolbar

To insert a table from the Standard toolbar, click the Insert Table button. FrontPage displays a small worksheet from which you can choose the number of rows and columns you want in your table. Drag the mouse pointer over the worksheet. As you do, the status line at the bottom of the worksheet tells you how many rows and columns will be present when you release the left mouse button to create the table (see Figure 6-2).

You aren't limited to choosing a table that is the initial size of the worksheet. If you drag the mouse pointer past the initial boundaries of the worksheet, the worksheet will grow to add more rows or columns.

Once you release the left mouse button, the table appears.

After you create a table—or anytime the text cursor is located within the boundaries of a table—FrontPage displays the Table toolbar (see Figure 6-3).

FIGURE 6-2 Move the mouse pointer over the worksheet that appears when you click the Insert Table button to specify the size of the table you want.

This toolbar contains a set of tools for modifying table properties, which will be discussed throughout this section.

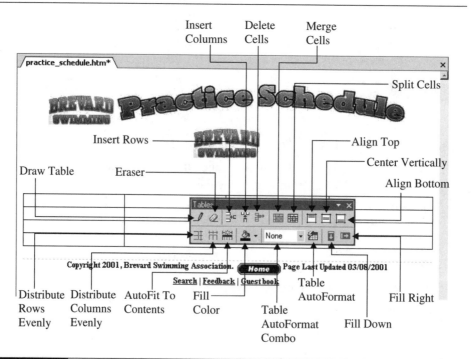

FIGURE 6-3 Use the tools in the Tables toolbar to quickly modify the properties and contents of a table.

NOTE   *If the Tables toolbar does not appear when the cursor is within a table, choose View | Toolbars | Tables to turn the Tables toolbar on.*

Insert a Table from the Table Menu

To insert a table into a Web page using the Table menu, choose Table | Insert | Table. This displays the Insert Table dialog box.

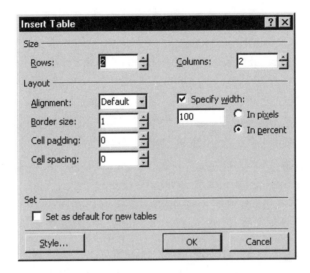

Use the fields in the Insert Table dialog box to configure the table as follows:

- **Specify the number of rows**   Use the Rows spinner to set the number of rows in the table. You can also type the number of rows into this field.

- **Specify the number of columns**   Use the Columns spinner to set the number of columns in the table. You can also type the number of columns into this field.

- **Set the table alignment**   Use the Alignment drop-down list to specify whether you want the table against the left margin, the right margin, or centered on the page. Note that if you specify the width of the table to be 100 percent of the page width, the table alignment setting doesn't really change anything.

- **Set the border size**   Use the Border Size spinner to set the thickness of the table border and cell borders in pixels. A value of 0 specifies no border.

You can override the cell border width by setting up borders for individual cells, as discussed later in this chapter (in the "Modify the Border Colors and Background" section).

> NOTE
> *If you choose a border size of 0, the table and cells are outlined in dotted lines in the normal Page view so you can tell where the table is. However, these outlines are not visible in the Preview mode or when viewed with a browser.*

- **Set the cell padding** Use the Cell Padding spinner to specify the amount of white space (in pixels) you want between the cell's contents and the inside edge of the cell boundary. You can override this quantity on a cell-by-cell basis.

- **Set the cell spacing** Use the Cell Spacing spinner to specify the amount of white space (in pixels) you want between cells.

- **Set the width of the table** If you want to specify the width of the table, check the Specify Width checkbox. You can set the width in either pixels or in percent by choosing the appropriate option. Type the width into the Specify Width text field.

> TIP
> *Be careful about specifying the width of the table in pixels. If the reader has a browser set to a lower resolution than yours—which renders objects larger than a high-resolution display—the table could spill off the side of the screen, forcing the reader to scroll back and forth to see the table contents. It is much better to set the table width in percent, as the browser will then scale the table so that no horizontal scrolling is necessary (assuming you don't set the table width to a value greater than 100 percent).*

When you are done setting the table's initial properties, click the OK button to create the table.

Draw a Table

You can also draw a table, first drawing in the outlines and then subdividing the table into rows, columns, and cells. To draw a table, choose Table | Draw Table, or select the Draw Table tool from the Table toolbar. The mouse cursor turns into a pencil, and you are ready to draw the table.

To draw a table, use the following steps:

1. Hold down the left mouse button and drag the drawing tool diagonally across the page to create a rectangle that is about the size of the table you want. When you release the mouse button, FrontPage creates the table border with a default thickness of 1 pixel. The table consists of one large cell.

2. Drag the drawing tool horizontally or vertically within the table border to create new cells, columns, and rows. As you draw, a dotted line indicates where the new cell border is going to be (see Figure 6-4).

3. You can adjust the size of a cell by moving the pointer on top of the cell border until it becomes a double-headed arrow. Drag the border to adjust the size of the cell. This technique works for table borders as well.

If you need to erase a border (to delete the boundary between cells), choose the Eraser tool from the Table toolbar. Click and drag the Eraser tool across a border until the border turns red to indicate it is selected. Release the mouse button and the border disappears. The table borders cannot be erased this way—you won't be able to select these borders with the Eraser tool.

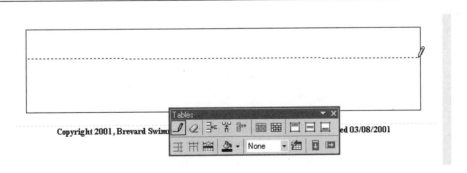

FIGURE 6-4   A dotted line indicates where the cell boundary is going to be when you release the left mouse button.

Split a Table into Multiple Tables

You may find that you need to split one table into two (or more). For example, someone may provide a table of calendar events for the whole year. However, when you publish this calendar table on your Web site, you might wish to insert the month as a text line for the events for that month. FrontPage makes it easy to split a table. To do so, click in any cell of the table just below where you want the split to be. Choose Table | Split Table. The table splits into two parts: All rows above the cell containing the text cursor become one table, and all rows from the cell containing the text cursor on down become another table. FrontPage even inserts a text line between the two newly formed tables, as shown in Figure 6-5.

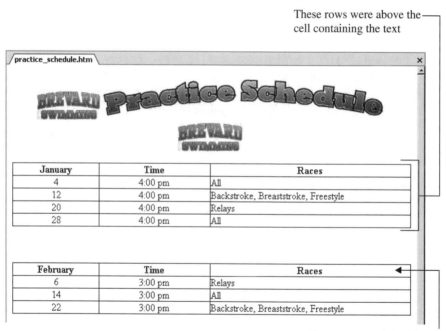

These rows were above the cell containing the text

The text cursor is in this cell

FIGURE 6-5   The result of splitting a table: two tables and a text line between them

Add Content to Cells

As mentioned earlier, you can populate the cells of a table with almost anything you can put on a page. As you insert content, the cell will resize to hold the content.

To add text to a cell, place the text cursor in the cell and begin typing. The text wraps around when it reaches the cell margin, and it will push the bottom of the row down to make room if necessary. You can add text and paragraph formatting just as you would with any other block of text: creating bulleted and numbered lists; adjusting font, size, style, effects, and color; and setting the alignment of the paragraph. To move quickly from one cell to another, press the TAB key.

To insert images or any other page element, click in the cell and use the appropriate menu to insert the item. For example, to insert a clip art image, choose Insert | Picture | Clip Art and follow the normal procedures to insert a piece of clip art.

You can add another table to a cell as well. To do so, click in the cell and choose Table | Insert | Table. You can't draw a table within a cell—you must insert it.

TIP *When you insert a table into the cell of another table, and specify the table width in percent, the percentage refers to the width of the containing cell. For example, if you specify the table width to be 100 percent, the new table will fill the entire width of the cell that the new table is contained in.*

You can fill the cells in a table with specified content by using the Fill Right and Fill Down functions. To use the Fill Right function, use the following steps:

1. Add content (text, graphics, etc.) into one or more cells in a column.

2. Select the cells containing the contents you want to duplicate and all the cells to the right of these cells you want to fill with this content.

3. Select Table | Fill | Right or click the Fill Right tool in the Tables toolbar. The selected cells are filled with the content, as shown in Figure 6-6.

Fill Down works similarly, except that you add your content to one or more cells in a row, then duplicate that content to cells below them in columns by selecting Table | Fill | Down or by selecting the Fill Down tool in the Tables toolbar.

These cells now contain
the duplicated contents

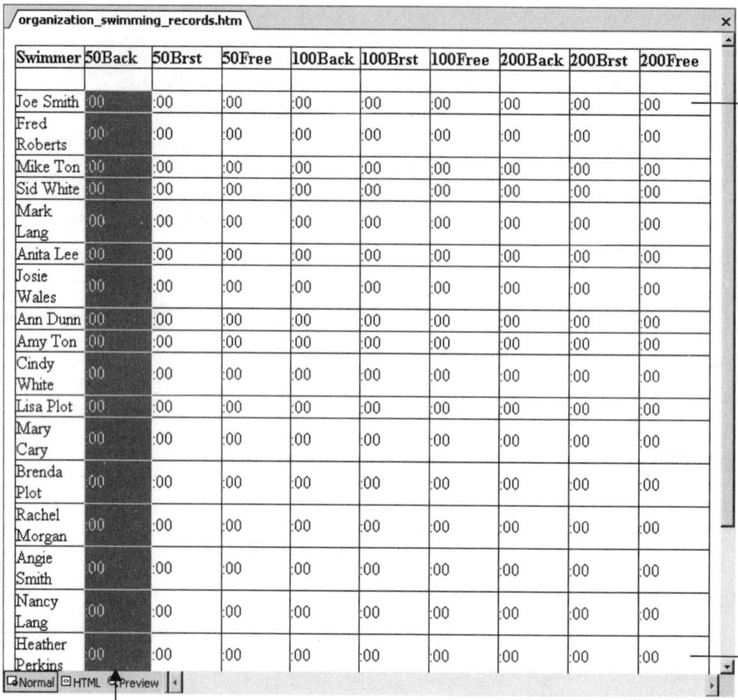

Swimmer	50Back	50Brst	50Free	100Back	100Brst	100Free	200Back	200Brst	200Free
Joe Smith	:00	:00	:00	:00	:00	:00	:00	:00	:00
Fred Roberts	:00	:00	:00	:00	:00	:00	:00	:00	:00
Mike Ton	:00	:00	:00	:00	:00	:00	:00	:00	:00
Sid White	:00	:00	:00	:00	:00	:00	:00	:00	:00
Mark Lang	:00	:00	:00	:00	:00	:00	:00	:00	:00
Anita Lee	:00	:00	:00	:00	:00	:00	:00	:00	:00
Josie Wales	:00	:00	:00	:00	:00	:00	:00	:00	:00
Ann Dunn	:00	:00	:00	:00	:00	:00	:00	:00	:00
Amy Ton	:00	:00	:00	:00	:00	:00	:00	:00	:00
Cindy White	:00	:00	:00	:00	:00	:00	:00	:00	:00
Lisa Plot	:00	:00	:00	:00	:00	:00	:00	:00	:00
Mary Cary	:00	:00	:00	:00	:00	:00	:00	:00	:00
Brenda Plot	:00	:00	:00	:00	:00	:00	:00	:00	:00
Rachel Morgan	:00	:00	:00	:00	:00	:00	:00	:00	:00
Angie Smith	:00	:00	:00	:00	:00	:00	:00	:00	:00
Nancy Lang	:00	:00	:00	:00	:00	:00	:00	:00	:00
Heather Perkins	:00	:00	:00	:00	:00	:00	:00	:00	:00

organization_swimming_records.htm

Normal HTML Preview

These cells contain the content to be duplicated
(filled) in the cells to their right

FIGURE 6-6   Fill cells with content automatically using Fill Right.

Select Parts of a Table

FrontPage provides quite a few tools for modifying the layout of a table. However, before you can use most of these layout tools, you need to know how to select individual cells, entire rows and columns, and the table as a whole. Here is how you select portions of a table:

- To select a single cell, click in the cell and choose Table | Select | Cell. The selected cell turns black to show that it is selected (see Figure 6-7).

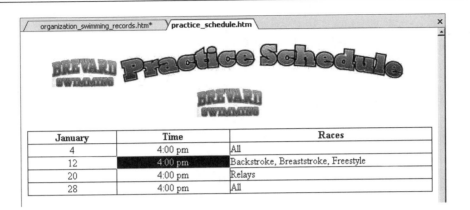

FIGURE 6-7   Selecting a part of a table (here, a single cell) turns the selected part black to indicate it is selected.

- To select multiple adjacent cells, click in a cell and drag the mouse pointer over the adjacent cells. As you do, all the selected cells turn black to show that they are selected.

- To select a column, move the mouse pointer over the top of the column until it becomes a down arrow and click to select the column. Alternatively, click any cell in the column and choose Table | Select | Column.

- To select a row, move the mouse pointer to the left end of the row until it becomes a right-facing arrow and click to select the row. Alternatively, click any cell in the row and choose Table | Select | Row.

- To select the entire table, click any cell in the table and choose Table | Select | Table.

To delete a table, select the entire table and press the DELETE key.

Work with Rows and Columns

You aren't limited to the number of rows and columns you specified when you first created the table. FrontPage makes it easy to add or remove both rows and columns from your table.

 *You can add rows to a table as you are typing text into the table. To do so, simply press the TAB key (the same key you use to move from one cell to the next) when the text cursor is in the cell at the lower-right corner of the table. FrontPage adds another row, and you can keep entering your text.*

Add Rows and Columns

If you don't get the table exactly the right size, you can add rows and columns to the table:

- To insert a single row above the currently selected cell or row, click the cell (or select the row) and choose Insert Row from the cell's shortcut menu, or click the Insert Row button in the Table toolbar.

- To insert a single column to the left of the currently selected cell or column, click the cell (or select the column) and choose Insert Column from the cell's shortcut menu or click the Insert Column button in the Table toolbar.

- To control the position and number of added rows and columns, choose Table | Insert | Rows Or Columns. This displays the Insert Rows Or Columns dialog box.

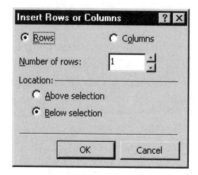

Choose the option you want (Rows or Columns) and then use the spinner to select the number of rows or columns you want inserted. Use the options in the Location section to determine whether you want the insertion done Above Selection or Below Selection.

 *Need a quick way to insert multiple rows or columns into the table? Select multiple rows or columns by clicking and dragging to highlight them. Then choose the Insert Column or Insert Row command from the shortcut menu. For example, if you select three columns and then choose Insert Column, three new columns will be inserted to the left of the leftmost selected column.*

Size Rows and Columns

You can change the size of a row or column easily. To change the size of a column, move the mouse pointer over the left or right edge of the column until it becomes a double-headed arrow. Click and drag the border. As you do, a dashed line appears to show you where the border will be when you release the mouse button (see Figure 6-8).

Changing the size of a row works just the same way. Move your mouse pointer over the top or bottom of the row until it becomes a double-headed arrow. Click and drag the border. As you do, a dashed line appears to show you where the border will be when you release the mouse button.

Distribute Rows and Columns Evenly

You can select multiple adjacent columns or rows and quickly give them an even distribution—that is, make all the selected columns or rows the same size. To

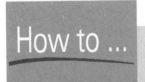 ## Delete Cells, Rows, and Columns

To delete one or more cells, select the cells you want to delete and select Table | Delete Cells, or choose Delete Cells from the cell's shortcut menu. Alternatively, you can click the Delete Cells button in the Table toolbar.

To delete a row or column, select the row or column and select Table | Delete Cells, or choose Delete Cells from the cell's shortcut menu. Alternatively, you can click the Delete Cells button in the Table toolbar.

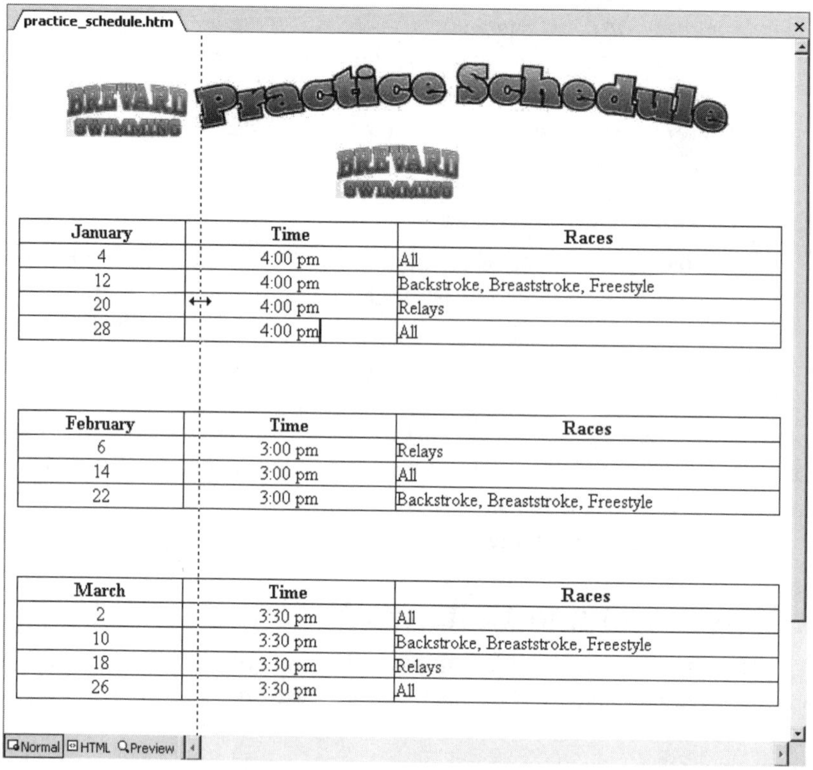

FIGURE 6-8   A dashed line shows where the border of the resized column will be.

provide an even distribution of columns, select the columns and choose either the Distribute Columns Evenly button in the Table toolbar, or the Distribute Columns Evenly menu option in the shortcut menu or the Table menu. For rows, the Table toolbar button is called Distribute Rows Evenly, as is the menu option in the shortcut menu and the Table menu.

Work with Cells

You can modify a table structure by working directly with the cells. Unlike a spreadsheet, tables do not have to be even sets of rows and columns. You can remove cells, merge multiple cells into a single cell, and even stretch a cell across multiple columns and rows. In short, you are free to arrange your table pretty much any way you please.

Split and Merge Cells

If you find that a regular rectangular grid of cells doesn't meet your needs, you can split and merge cells to get the exact table layout you want. To split a cell, click in the cell and choose Split Cells from either the shortcut menu or the Table menu. Alternatively, you can choose the Split Cells button in the Table toolbar. FrontPage will then display the Split Cells dialog box.

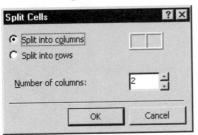

In the Split Cells dialog box, choose whether to split the cells into columns or into rows by picking the appropriate option. Use the Number Of Columns spinner (which becomes the Number Of Rows spinner if you picked the Split Into Rows option) to set the number of rows or columns to split the cell into. Data in the original cell is preserved. If you split a cell into columns, the original data is placed in the leftmost cell. If you split a cell into rows, the original data is placed in the uppermost cell. Figure 6-9 shows a table that contains split cells. The cell in the lower-left corner has been split into columns, and the cell in the upper-right corner has been split into rows.

You can merge multiple adjacent cells into a single cell. To do so, select the cells you want to merge by clicking and dragging to highlight the cells. Choose the Merge Cells button in the Table toolbar. Data in all the cells is preserved and moved into the merged cell. The contents of each of the original cells is placed on its own line in the merged cell.

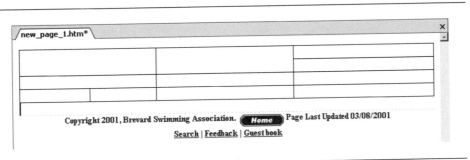

FIGURE 6-9   The lower-left cell has been split into columns; the upper-right cell has been split into rows.

Add Cells to the Table

You can easily insert more cells into an existing table. To do so, select Table | Insert | Cell. Exactly where the new cell is inserted depends on the contents of the selected cell. If the selected cell is empty or the text cursor is at the left end of the data in the cell, the new cell is added to the left of the current cell. If the text cursor is at the right end of the data in the cell, the new cell is added to the right of the current cell.

Adjust Cell Size with AutoFit

Once you have placed the content into your table, you may find that some cells are too large for their content and some cells may even be empty. This can result in a table that is too large and takes up more space on the Web page than it needs to. To rectify this situation, click in any cell in the table and choose Table | AutoFit To Contents, or click the AutoFit To Contents button in the Table toolbar. The table shrinks to the minimum size necessary to contain the contents (see Figure 6-10).

Set Cell Properties

You can customize the way a cell looks and acts from a single integrated dialog box. With the Cell Properties dialog box (see Figure 6-11), you can align the contents of the cell, customize the border and background, and set the size of the cell. To display the Cell Properties dialog box, select one or more cells and choose Cell Properties from the shortcut menu or choose Table | Table Properties | Cell.

January	Time	Races
4	4:00 pm	All
12	4:00 pm	Backstroke, Breaststroke, Freestyle
20	4:00 pm	Relays
28	4:00 pm	All

February	Time	Races
6	3:00 pm	Relays
14	3:00 pm	All
22	3:00 pm	Backstroke, Breaststroke, Freestyle

FIGURE 6-10   Using the AutoFit function shrinks the table to the minimum size necessary to hold its contents (the top table was shrunk).

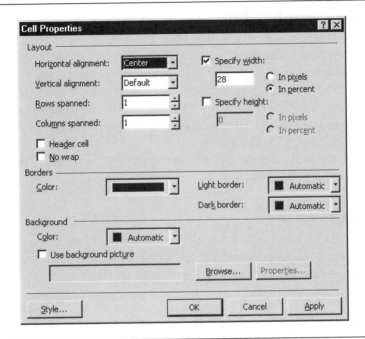

FIGURE 6-11   Set the cell properties from this comprehensive dialog box.

Align the Cell Contents

Depending on what you put into a cell, you may wish to change the alignment of the contents. For example, images usually look best when they are centered, whereas text (except for column headings) usually looks best when it is left-aligned. You can set the alignment of cell contents using the Horizontal Alignment and Vertical Alignment drop-down lists in the Cell Properties dialog box. You can change the vertical alignment using the Align Top, Center Vertically, or Align Bottom buttons in the Table toolbar.

NOTE
You can also set the horizontal alignment of a cell's contents using the Formatting toolbar or the Paragraph dialog box. To open the Paragraph dialog box, select the cell's contents and choose Format | Paragraph. The value you choose from the Alignment drop-down list in the Paragraph dialog box overrides any alignment selections you make in the Cell Properties dialog box or the Formatting toolbar.

Span Rows and Columns

You can force a cell to stretch across more than one column or row. This is called *spanning*. The effect is similar to merging cells into a larger cell. The difference is that when you span a cell, the cells it spans across are pushed down or sideways, as if you had inserted cells. You can then delete these cells if you wish. In Figure 6-12, the large cell in the center of the table was created by spanning a cell across two columns and two rows. The cells that were pushed out of the way are clearly visible at the right edge of the table.

To set the cell span, use the Rows Spanned and Columns Spanned spinners in the Cell Properties dialog box.

Add Header Cells

Many tables have column headers that tell you what kind of data is in each column. Some tables also have row headers. A quick way to emphasize these header cells is to select them and check the Header Cell checkbox. This adds bold formatting and centers the contents of the cell.

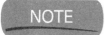 *If you set the horizontal alignment for a cell using the Paragraph Properties dialog box, the alignment settings you specified override the center alignment that usually results from checking the Header Cell checkbox.*

Specify the Minimum Cell Width

You can set the minimum cell width in the Cell Properties dialog box by checking the Specify Width checkbox and entering a value in the field. Specify whether the entered value is in pixels or percent—as mentioned earlier, percent is usually the better choice to allow for different browser resolutions. By default, the columns in

January	Time	Races		
4	4:00 pm	All		
12		4:00 pm	Backstroke, Breaststroke, Freestyle	
20			4:00 pm	Relays
28	4:00 pm	All		

FIGURE 6-12   Cell spanning enables you to create large cells that cross multiple rows and columns.

a table are split evenly in size; if you create a four-column table, each one will be sized at 25 percent of the total width.

Adjusting the minimum cell width is a tricky business. If you adjust the minimum width of a single cell in a column of cells, you may not see any change. For example, if you reduced the minimum width in our four-column example to 15 percent, the column width would not change because the other cells in the column are still "holding" the column width at 25 percent. Only after changing the minimum width of all the cells in the column would you see the column shrink. Also, if you set the width of some columns so that very little room is left over, the other columns in the table will shrink as much as possible, but will not shrink past the minimum width where they can display their contents.

There is another bit of strangeness associated with minimum column widths as well. You can set the sum of the minimum widths of columns to be more than 100 percent, and FrontPage is perfectly happy with this situation. For example, you could set all the columns in our four-column example to be 75 percent of the total width. If you do this, FrontPage scales the first cell to be as close as possible to the specified width, shrinking the other cells (if necessary) for this to occur. As noted previously, however, FrontPage won't shrink the cells past the point where they can't display their contents.

Suppress Word Wrap

Word wrap is a feature used in word processors and other text-based programs. It automatically breaks a line of text when it reaches the margin or border of a text area, and "wraps" it around to the next line. Checking the No Wrap checkbox turns off word wrap in the cell. Be careful when you turn off word wrap, as it is hard to predict what a nonwrapped cell will do to the table layout in a browser, especially if the browser is running at a lower resolution than you used when you designed the table.

Modify the Border Colors and Background

You can specify the border colors of a cell using the Borders section of the Cell Properties dialog box. To set a single color for the cell border, click the Color drop-down list and choose a color from the standard color tool. If you want a two-color border scheme, pick one color from the Light Border drop-down list and another from the Dark Border drop-down list. With a two-color scheme, FrontPage uses the light border color for the right and bottom borders, and the dark color for the left and top borders.

If you check the Show Both Cells And Table Borders checkbox (in the Table Properties dialog box, discussed later in this chapter), each cell has a border that is independent of the border of the adjacent cells. That is, the border line for one cell does not overlap the border line for the adjacent cell, as shown here:

January	Time	Races
4	4:00 pm	All
12	4:00 pm	Backstroke, Breaststroke, Freestyle
20	4:00 pm	Relays
28	4:00 pm	All

Thus, you can set the colors of each cell's borders independently and you'll be able to see the borders for each cell. However, if you clear the Show Both Cells And Table Borders checkbox, each cell shares borders with its neighbors. If you set the color of the cell borders to different values for adjacent cells, you get a conflict. Basically, when this happens, a cell controls the color of its right and bottom border. Since, for example, the cell to the left controls *its* right (and bottom) borders, the left border of the selected cell is actually controlled by the border color for the cell to its left.

You can also set a color or use a graphic as the background for the cell. To choose a background color, click the Color drop-down list in the Background section of the Cell Properties dialog box. As usual, pick the color you want from the Standard Color tool.

To add a background picture to the cell, check the Use Background Picture checkbox. Type the path to the graphic to use as the background, or use the Browse button to pick the graphic. If this looks familiar, it should—it is the exact same technique discussed in Chapter 5 to add a background graphic to a page.

NOTE *If the graphic is too large to fit into the cell, only as much of the graphic as will fit in the cell is displayed. However, the visitor to your Web site will have to wait for the graphic to load even if he or she can only see a small part of the graphic. Therefore, it is better to pick a small graphic that fits inside the cell.*

Set Table Properties

As with cells, you can set a variety of properties for the table as a whole. To do so, choose Table | Table Properties | Table, or right-click in the table and choose

Table Properties from the shortcut menu. Either way, FrontPage displays the Table Properties dialog box.

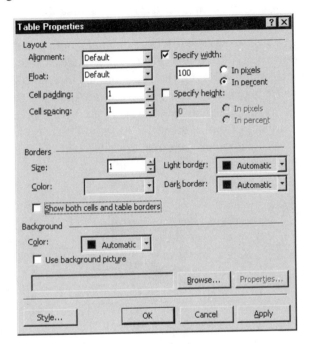

6

Some of the table properties—such as alignment, cell padding, cell spacing, and border size—were discussed earlier when we were initially creating the table. You can adjust these properties in the Table Properties dialog box. The Float drop-down list determines which edge of the page the table floats (is positioned) against. The default value is for the table to position against the left edge of the page.

The Border color options work identically to those for a single cell, except that when you set the border colors for a table, the colors are used for the main table border as well as the default for all cells. Any border colors you set for individual cells override the table border colors. For example, if you choose blue for your table border, all cell borders will also be blue unless you specify otherwise for individual cells. The background color and picture settings also work identically for a table as they do for a cell.

Finally, the fields and options in the Specify Width and Specify Height sections apply to the table as a whole rather than to individual cells.

AutoFormat a Table

It can be a lot of work to set up an attractively designed table. You may have to specify the colors for borders and backgrounds, as well as fonts and colors for headings and other cells. FrontPage offers a potential solution to doing all this work manually, however: AutoFormat. FrontPage includes a set of predefined formats that you can apply to tables. The AutoFormats include specifications for borders, shading, font, color, and even whether to AutoFit the cells to their contents. Once you have applied an AutoFormat, you can use it "as is" or as the starting point for further customization.

There are two ways to apply AutoFormat to a table. The quickest (and simplest) way is to pick the format you want from the Table AutoFormat Combo tool in the Tables toolbar. This drop-down list is shown here:

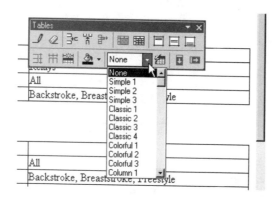

Of course, there are drawbacks to using the Table AutoFormat Combo tool—you don't get to see a preview of the format you are applying, and you don't get to customize which parts of the format you want to apply (you do get to specify this using the other Table AutoFormat options). Still, once you know the formats (they are the same ones that are available using the other Table AutoFormat options), the Table AutoFormat tool is quick and easy to use.

To preview and customize a Table AutoFormat before applying it to a table, choose Table | Table AutoFormat or select the Table AutoFormat tool from the Tables toolbar. This displays the Table AutoFormat dialog box.

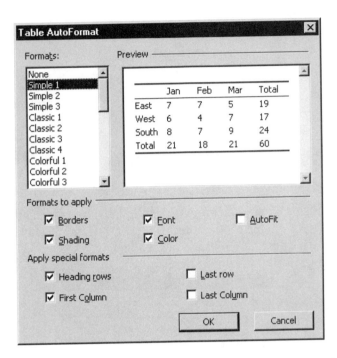

Pick the format you want from the Formats list, and view the preview of that format in the Preview area on the right side of the dialog box. Check or clear the checkboxes to specify which portions of the format to apply to the table in the Formats To Apply section and the Apply Special Formats section of the dialog box. For example, if don't want the table to have a border, clear the Borders checkbox. As you make these selections, you can preview the effect of the change in the Preview area.

Add a Table Caption

A table caption is essentially a title for the table. To add a table caption, click anywhere in the table and choose Table | Insert | Caption. A blank line is inserted at the top of the table, with a blinking text cursor. You can then type the text of the caption (see Figure 6-13). If you wish, you can use all the text and paragraph formatting tools discussed previously to customize the caption text. You can also insert graphics into the caption by choosing Insert | Picture and selecting the picture the usual way.

March Practice Schedule		
March	Time	Races
2	3:30 pm	All
10	3:30 pm	Backstroke, Breaststroke, Freestyle
18	3:30 pm	Relays
26	3:30 pm	All

FIGURE 6-13   You can use a table caption to provide a title for a table.

To change the position of the caption, right-click the caption and choose
Caption Properties from the shortcut menu, or choose Table | Table Properties |
Caption. This opens the Caption Properties dialog box.

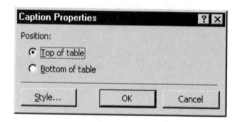

In this dialog box, choose the option you want for the position of the caption:
Top Of Table or Bottom Of Table.

Convert Text to Tables

FrontPage provides a feature to convert plain text into a table. This can be very handy
if you want to display data as a table that is already on a Web page. For example,
you could export the contents of a company address book in a comma-delimited
(separated) format, insert the file into a Web page, and then convert the text into a
table of company contacts.

To convert text into a table, select the text you want to convert, and choose Table |
Convert | Text To Table. This displays the Convert Text To Table dialog box.

Choose the option that corresponds to how you want to separate the text:

6

- **Paragraphs** This option creates a single-column table, with each paragraph in its own row (and in its own cell).

- **Tabs, commas, or other** If your text is delimited by tabs, commas, or some other character, choose one of these options. If you choose the Other option, enter the delimiter character into the text field. Each piece of delimited text is placed in its own cell (column). FrontPage creates a new row in the table each time it encounters a new paragraph. Figure 6-14 shows both the original comma-delimited text (each line is a paragraph) and the table it would become. Notice that the original text does not include spaces after the commas. Normally, of course, the table replaces the text; you are not left with both when you are done.

- **None (text in single cell)** Choosing this option places all the selected text into a single-cell table.

Convert Tables to Text

If the data you have is already in a table, you can convert it back to regular text. To do so, click anywhere in the table and choose Table | Convert | Table To Text. Each cell in the table is converted into a separate line of text on the page.

Head Coach, John Hughes, hughesj@flnet.com

President, Joel Dodds, 321-555-3656, jmldodds@flnet.com

Vice President, Leslie Berens, 321-555-2599, JCBerens@flnet.com

Treasurer, Trudy DAmico, 321-555-8385, OneFastSwimmer@flnet.com

Secretary, Brenda Plotkin, 321-555-0148, BFlatPlot@flnet.com

Head Coach	John Hughes		hughesj@flnet.com
President	Joel Dodds	321-555-3656	jmldodds@flnet.com
Vice President	Leslie Berens	321-555-2599	JCBerens@flnet.com
Treasurer	Trudy DAmico	321-555-8385	OneFastSwimmer@flnet.com
Secretary	Brenda Plotkin	321-555-0148	BFlatPlot@flnet.com

FIGURE 6-14   The comma-delimited text converts cleanly into a table.

Create a Table from a Word Table

If you are more comfortable working in a word processor such as Microsoft Word, you may wish to create the table in Word and then add it to a FrontPage Web page. To do so, simply select the entire table in Word and copy it to the clipboard (choose Edit | Copy, or press CTRL-C). Switch to FrontPage and paste the table into the Web page (choose Edit | Paste, or press CTRL-V).

Create a Table from an Excel Spreadsheet

If you are familiar with entering content into a spreadsheet such as Microsoft Excel, you may wish to enter your data into a grid of cells in Excel, and then convert the cells into a FrontPage table. Realize that you can only create a regular rectangular grid of cells this way. To create a table from a grid of Excel cells, select the cells in Excel and copy them to the clipboard (choose Edit | Copy, or press CTRL-C). Switch to FrontPage and paste the table into the Web page (choose Edit | Paste, or press CTRL-V). Most of the formatting you can apply to a cell in Excel is transferred to FrontPage. However, some effects—such as a background fill pattern—are not preserved, so view the results in FrontPage carefully and reapply any lost formatting you want.

Part II

Build Web Sites

Chapter 7

Build an Initial Web Site

How to…

- Create a new Web site
- Import an existing Web site
- Open an existing Web site
- Delete a Web site

Up to now, you've only built individual Web pages. However, to post your pages on the Internet, you need to know how to create a complete Web site—the entire collection of pages, images, documents, and any other files needed. Fortunately, FrontPage provides you with tools to help you build Web sites. Using FrontPage's predefined Web site styles, you can easily create the framework for a personal Web site, corporate Web site, or even a complex, special-purpose site such as a discussion group Web. You can import existing Web sites from a hard drive or the Internet, which is very convenient if someone else created a Web site you now want to maintain in FrontPage. You can also decide how and where you want to store your new Web site.

Once you have created the framework of your Web site, you can use the tools you've already learned to create the Web pages.

Understand Disk-Based and Server-Based Web Sites

This version of FrontPage does not require, and does not include, a personal Web server such as Microsoft's Personal Web Server or Internet Information Server (IIS). When you use FrontPage to create a new Web site, you can simply specify a physical directory on your hard drive to store all the files needed to later publish your Web site to the Internet (see Chapter 17 for more information on publishing a Web site). A Web site set up this way is called a disk-based Web site. Overall, this technique is simple and works fairly well.

However, there is a drawback to creating a disk-based Web site. Certain features of FrontPage Web sites cannot be tested using a disk-based Web site. These features include forms (see Chapter 10), many components (see Chapter 12), Dynamic HTML effects (see Chapter 13), and any other features that need the FrontPage extensions to work. In order to test these features on a disk-based Web site, you must publish your Web site (see Chapter 17) to a Web server running FrontPage extensions, and test them on the remote Web server. Of course, if you find errors, you'll have to fix them and then republish your site to the remote server to test them again. If you have a sizable Web site, this cycle can take a long time.

The alternative is to set up a Web server on your local machine by installing the Microsoft Personal Web Server (PWS) or IIS. When you create a new Web site, you can choose to "locate" it on the server provided on your computer by PWS or IIS (you can also choose to locate it in a directory on your hard drive, as before). Doing so creates a server-based Web site. The PWS or IIS URL is usually called http://default, although you can rename it if you wish. Thus, if you create a Web site called myweb, its full address on your computer is http://default/myweb if you use a server-based Web site. To test all the Web site's features, access your server-based Web site with a browser by using the Web site's URL (for example, http://default/myweb). You can use a browser to navigate through the entire Web site on your local machine. However, realize that your response time will be much better on your local machine than what you'll get once you access the Web site on the Internet!

Whether you have PWS or IIS available depends on which Microsoft Windows operating system you are using. Additionally, the version of FrontPage extensions you can use also depends on your operating system, as detailed in the next two sections.

Using PWS with Windows 98

Microsoft Personal Web Server (PWS) was supplied with Windows 98 (both the original and SE), but it is not supplied with Windows ME (although it runs under Windows ME). Thus, if you are running Windows ME, you'll have to try and locate a Windows 98 CD to install PWS, as detailed in Appendix C.

Once you have PWS installed and running in Windows 98, SE, or ME, you'll need to install the FrontPage Server extensions, also detailed in Appendix C. Unfortunately, you can't install the latest version (FrontPage 2002 extensions), as these don't work with PWS. You *can* install FrontPage 2000 extensions, but again, you'll have to locate them—probably on an Office 2000 CD. While many features of FrontPage 2002 do work with the FrontPage 2000 Extensions, not all of them do. For example, Link Bars, the Upload File form component, top 10 list components, and usage reports all require the most advanced version of FrontPage extensions.

Using IIS with Windows 2000

A much better answer is available to you if you are running Windows 2000. You can install Microsoft Internet Information Server (IIS) 5.0 to provide a local server. You can also load FrontPage 2002 extensions, built into the Office Web Server (OWS) software included on the Office CD. With both the Office Web Server and latest FrontPage extensions, you can test all the features of FrontPage 2002.

Windows 2000 Professional comes with a single-user version of IIS, while Windows 2000 Server comes with a multiple-user version. Either version is capable of having the FrontPage extensions installed and powering a server-based FrontPage Web site.

 The examples in the screen shots in this book mostly use IIS server-based Web sites, because testing a server-based Web site is so much easier.

Create a Web Site

To create a new Web site, choose File | New | Page or Web. This opens the New Page Or Web Task Pane.

From the New Page Or Web Task Pane, you have several options: create a new empty Web site, create a Web site based on templates you have used recently, or create a new Web site based on the FrontPage built-in templates.

To create a new Web site using one of the built-in FrontPage Web site templates, use the following steps:

1. In the New From Templates section of the Task Pane, choose Web Site Templates. The Web Site Templates dialog box opens to show you a variety of templates you can use to create your new Web site (see Figure 7-1).

NOTE *If you choose Empty Web from the New section of the Task Pane, or one of the recently used templates from the New From Template section, the Web Site Templates dialog box opens with that template already selected.*

7

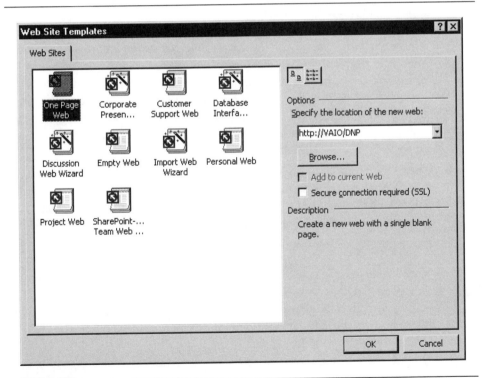

FIGURE 7-1 Use the templates in the New dialog box to pick the type of Web site you want to create.

2. Pick one of the templates. Each template you click displays a description of the template's purpose in the Description area at the lower-right corner of the New dialog box.

NOTE *If the Web site already exists and you just need to import it into FrontPage, pick the Import Web Wizard. For more on using this useful wizard, see "Import an Existing Web Site" later in this chapter.*

3. Specify where you want the Web site to be located by using the Specify The Location Of The New Web field. For a disk-based Web site, the default location is *C:\My Documents\My Webs*. You will probably want to create a subdirectory for each new disk-based Web site you create. If you installed Microsoft Personal Web Server or IIS, you will also have the option of picking http://default (or whatever the server URL is called on your machine). To specify the location of the new Web site, you'll need to add to this path, because you can't create a Web site directly in http://default. For example, you can locate the Web site in http://default/myweb.

NOTE *You can actually specify a URL on the Internet as the location to create your Web site, if you wish. However, I don't recommend this approach, because you will need to be connected to the Internet at all times when you want to work on the Web site, and you won't have a copy of the Web site on your local machine. In addition, you'll most likely need to log in to the remote server every time you want to make changes to the site.*

4. Click OK. FrontPage creates the structure of your new Web site, including the folders it needs to work properly. It also creates the new home page and any other pages that are part of the chosen template (unless you chose the Empty Web template). Figure 7-2 shows the Folder List displaying the pages that are part of the Personal Web Site template.

NOTE *The "home page" is the title of the page that someone first sees when navigating to your site. The filename chosen by FrontPage varies depending on whether you chose to create a disk-based site or a server-based site. The file is called index.htm for a disk-based site, and default.htm for a server-based site.*

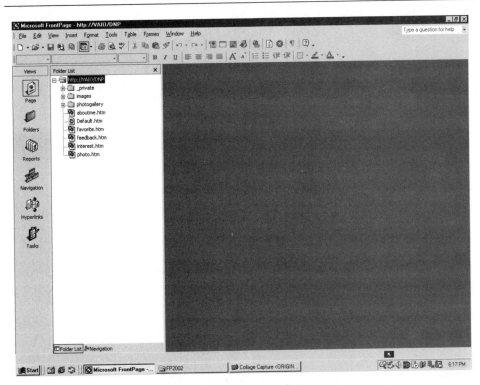

FIGURE 7-2   FrontPage automatically creates any new pages that are part of the chosen template.

Import an Existing Web Site

Occasionally, you will need to bring a Web site that has already been created into FrontPage. You might run into this situation if you take over the maintenance of an existing site, for example. The site might be disk-based or residing on a network hard drive, or it might be an operating Web site on the Internet. FrontPage makes it easy to import a site using the Import Web Wizard.

To import a Web site into FrontPage from a hard drive or network drive, use the following steps:

1. Choose File | New | Page or Web to open the New Page or Web Task Pane. Choose Web Site Templates to open the Web Site Templates dialog box.

2. Specify the location of the new Web site on your hard drive (disk-based Web site) or on your local Web server (server-based Web site).

3. Click the Import Web Wizard icon.

4. Click OK. FrontPage creates the initial Web site structure and then starts the Import Web Wizard.

5. Choose the first option from the two options available (From A Source Directory Of Files On A Local Computer Or Network, as shown in Figure 7-3).

6. In the Location field, enter the path to the files that comprise the Web site. You can use the Browse button to open a dialog box in which you can pick the folder. If the folder contains subfolders you need to include, check the Include Subfolders checkbox.

7. Click the Next button. The next dialog box shows you a list of all the files that will be included in the imported Web site (see Figure 7-4). If you want to exclude a file, select the file and then click the Exclude button. This action removes the file from the list.

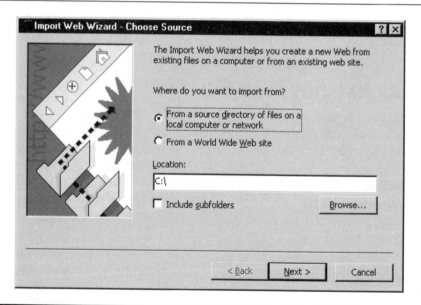

FIGURE 7-3   Use the Import Web Wizard to import a Web site.

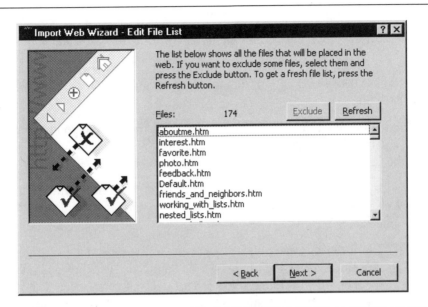

FIGURE 7-4   Select any files you don't want to import and click the Exclude button.

NOTE *If you change your mind about excluding a file, press the Refresh button. However, this places all excluded files back on the list.*

8. Click Next. The Import Web Wizard displays the Finish box. Read and enjoy Microsoft's heartfelt congratulations on completing this oh-so-difficult set of tasks. Then click the Finish button.

9. FrontPage imports the Web site, updates the hyperlinks, and presents you with the finished Web site. This process can take a few minutes for a complex Web site, so be patient.

To import an existing Web site from an Internet site, you must be connected to the Internet. Use the following steps:

1. Choose File | New | Page or Web to open the New Page or Web Task Pane. Choose Web Site Templates to open the Web Site Templates dialog box.

2. Specify the location of the new Web site either on your hard drive (disk-based Web site) or in terms of your local Web server (server-based Web site).

3. Click the Import Web Wizard icon.

4. Click OK. FrontPage creates the initial Web site structure and then starts the Import Web Wizard.

5. Choose the second option from the two available (From A World Wide Web Site).

6. In the Location field, enter the Internet URL from which you want to import the site. If the site requires a Secure Sockets connection, check the Secure Connection Required (SSL) checkbox.

7. Click Next. In the Choose Download Amount panel of the Import Web Wizard (see Figure 7-5), you can limit what you download. Your options are

- **Limit to this page plus** If you want to limit the levels of pages you download, check the Limit To This Page Plus checkbox and set the number of levels in the spinner. The levels of pages refers to how many levels of hyperlinks you want to download, starting with the home page of the imported site. For example, if you choose to download two levels, the following pages will be downloaded: the home page, all the pages hyperlinked to the home page, and all pages hyperlinked to those pages.

- **Limit to** If you want to limit the total amount you download (measured in kilobytes), check the Limit To checkbox and enter the number of kilobytes (KB) in the text field.

- **Limit to text and image files** Finally, if you just want to download text and image files (leaving out JavaScript, Java, and other components), check the Limit To Text And Image Files checkbox.

8. Click Next, and then click Finish. The import begins and proceeds until either the entire Web site has been imported or the limits you set in step 7 (if any) are reached.

NOTE *If the Web site you are importing was created with FrontPage, you may get a warning that the theme of the imported Web site will be replaced by the theme of your new Web site. Just click Yes to continue with the import process. If you click No, the import process stops.*

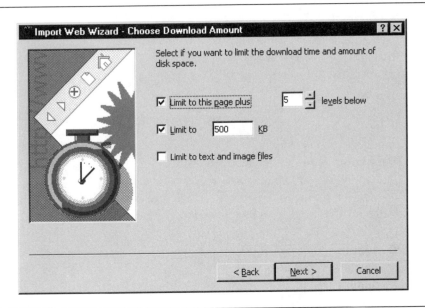

FIGURE 7-5   Limit the amount you want to download from an Internet Web site during the import.

When the import process has completed, FrontPage presents you with the imported Web site. If you limited the amount of information (either in kilobytes or the number of page levels) included in the import, the resulting Web site is likely to be incomplete, missing graphics, pages, and components. If you want to retrieve the missing information, you'll need to reimport the Web site, allowing either more data or more page levels—or not putting any limits on the download.

A partially imported Web may have problems with the following elements:

■ **Graphics**   If a graphic was not downloaded, it cannot be displayed on a page. Missing graphics are displayed as a small, red "x".

■ **Components**   Special effects and features may be nonfunctional because the component is missing from the Web site. If the component is called by the Web page's HTML, you will get an error when you open the page or try to trigger the effect.

- **Hyperlinked Web pages**   If you click on a hyperlink that links to a missing page, you will get an error because the page is not available to display.

- **JavaScripts**   Features implemented via missing JavaScripts will not function.

- **Themes**   Themes will not display properly if the images that make up the theme have not been imported.

- **Databases**   If you either send the results of a form to a database (see Chapter 19) or retrieve database contents from a form (see Chapter 20), the forms will not function. You will get an error if you try to open a database results form or send form results to a missing database.

- **Forms**   If a form uses either a missing confirmation or error form, you will get an error when you submit the results of the form.

Open an Existing Web Site

There are quite a few ways to open a Web site once you have created it. First of all, you can choose File | Recent Webs to see a list of recently opened Web sites. Click one of these Web sites or simply type the number of the Web site as it appears on the list (see Figure 7-6).

Another way to open a Web site is to choose File | Open Web. This opens the Open Web dialog box, from which you can pick the Web site you want to open.

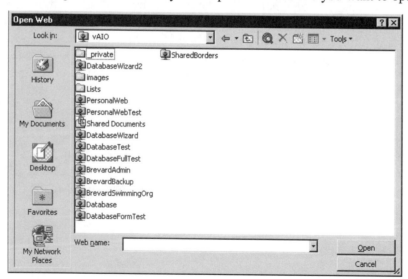

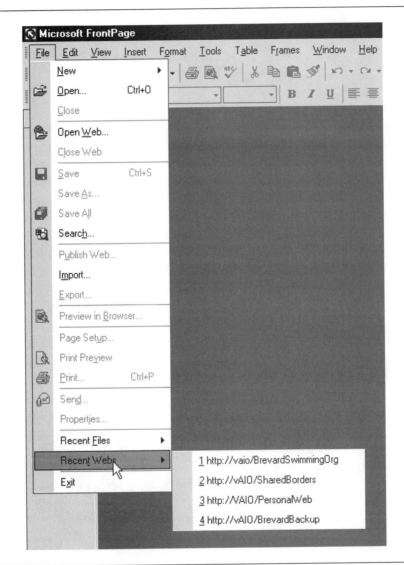

FIGURE 7-6   Pick one of your recently opened Web sites from the File menu.

Open a Disk-Based Web Site

In the Web Name field, enter the name of the folder that contains the Web site you want to open. If you are opening a disk-based Web site, you'll enter a folder on your hard drive or a network drive. To enter the folder name, you can type it into

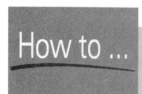 **Pick a Location from the Look In Field**

The Look In field at the top of the Open Web dialog box enables you to specify where you want to look for the Web site. Choices in the Look In field include all your hard drives and network drives, Web folders (more on this shortly), or FTP sites you define to store your Web site files on another computer. (See Chapter 17 for more information on setting up and accessing FTP sites with FrontPage.) You can also click the Search the Web button (the small globe with a magnifying glass) to open your browser and look for a Web page on the Internet. This URL of the Web page may come in handy later.

The column on the left side of the Open Web dialog box also lets you navigate easily to often-used destinations, such as a list of folders you have worked with (History), the My Documents folder, the Desktop, your Favorites list, and Web Folders.

> **NOTE**   *The entry Web Folders does not appear in Windows 2000. Instead, the last entry on the left is My Network Places. If you select My Network Places, a list of Web folders appears in the main area of the dialog box.*

If you frequently work with a particular Web site (either a disk-based Web site or a server-based Web site), you can add it to your list of favorites so you can access it quickly. To do so, navigate to the Web site (as described in the next section) and choose Tools | Add To Favorites. From then on, you can choose this Web site by clicking the Favorites icon in the Open Web dialog box and picking the Web site from the main area of the dialog box.

the Web Name field or choose the folder from the large area in the center of the dialog box. For example, in Figure 7-7, I have selected a disk-based Web site located in C:\inetpub\wwwroot\PersonalWebTest. Click Open to open the disk-based Web site.

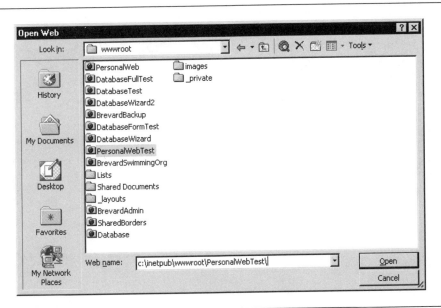

FIGURE 7-7   Specify the folder that contains your disk-based Web site.

Open a Server-Based Web Site

If you are opening a server-based Web site, click the Web Folders selection in the left column or pick Web Folders in the Look In field. Remember, in Windows 2000 you would choose My Network Places instead. Since FrontPage creates a Web folder automatically for each new server-based Web site you create, choosing Web Folders (or My Network Places) lists all your server-based Web sites (see Figure 7-8). Click one of the Web folders to place the folder name in the Web Name field. Then click Open to open the Web site.

NOTE   *Remember, to open a server-based site on your local machine, you must have installed Microsoft Personal Web Server (PWS) or IIS.*

If you choose the "root" Web site for your server-based Web sites (http://default or whatever you named your root Web site, as shown in Figure 7-8) and then

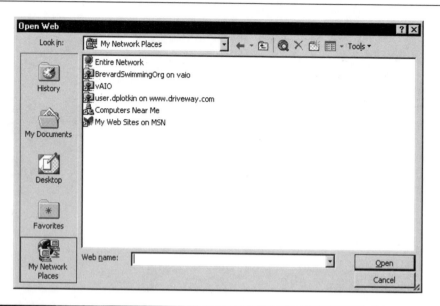

FIGURE 7-8   Look in Web Folders or My Network Places to see a list of your server-based Web sites.

choose Open, FrontPage opens the root Web site (see Figure 7-9). You can't do much with the root Web site directly, but the Folder List does show you all your server-based Web sites. To open one of these server-based Web sites, double-click it in the Folder List. The server-based Web site opens in a new FrontPage window.

This trick also works for any folder on your hard drive—once you open the folder, the Folder List displays a list of folders and files that are inside the selected folder. Any folders whose contents represent a FrontPage Web site are displayed with a small globe overlaying the Folder icon. Double-clicking one of these folders opens the Web site in a new FrontPage window.

NOTE   *You can enter a full URL for an Internet site in the Folder Name field. If you do, FrontPage will try to open the site directly from the Internet. However, this usually doesn't work because most servers have some security that doesn't permit opening their Web pages for writing (which is what you are requesting).*

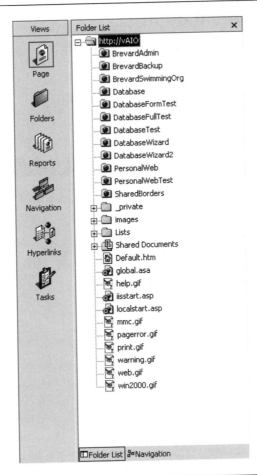

FIGURE 7-9   Opening the root Web site (if you have installed PWS or IIS) shows you a
list of all your server-based Web sites.

TIP

*You can have FrontPage automatically open the last Web site you worked
with. This is handy if you frequently work on one Web site. To set this
option, choose Tools | Options and check the Open Last Web
Automatically When FrontPage Starts checkbox.*

Delete an Existing Web Site

If you no longer want to use a Web site, you can delete it and recover the space. To delete a Web site, open the site and make sure the Folder List is visible. Click the top line of the Folder List—the line that contains either the full pathname to the folder that contains the Web site (disk-based) or the full URL of the Web site (server-based). Press the DELETE key, or choose Edit | Delete. FrontPage confirms the deletion with the Confirm Delete dialog box.

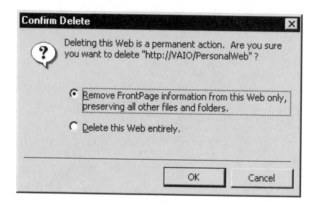

If you want to preserve the files and folders that make up the Web site, but you no longer want FrontPage to recognize this folder or URL as a FrontPage Web site, choose the first option. You may wish to keep the files on your hard drive for a while in case you find you need to reuse a Web page file or image from the deleted site. However, this Web site won't clutter up your list of active Web sites. If you want to delete the Web site completely (including all the files and folders), choose the second option (Delete This Web Entirely). This frees up the space on your hard drive.

Chapter 8

Build Hyperlinks

How to...

- Add text hyperlinks to pages in your Web site
- Add text hyperlinks to Internet pages
- Create graphic hyperlinks
- Define bookmarks and create hyperlinks to bookmarks
- Build image map hyperlinks
- Verify and recalculate hyperlinks

Virtually every Web site has more than one page in it. If it didn't, it wouldn't be very interesting! In order to navigate from one page to another—and to various points within pages—you must use hyperlinks. In essence, hyperlinks are the glue that holds a Web site together.

Understand and Use Hyperlinks

Hyperlinks let you navigate the Internet easily. Unless special permission is needed, you can access almost any page on the Internet by specifying its full URL in your browser. However, how could you possibly know the location of every page you want to visit? You can't, and with hyperlinks you don't have to. Once you reach the main page of a site, it can provide hyperlinks to other pages of interest. Simply by clicking one of these links, you can view the page without knowing its URL. Thus, hyperlinks are one of the most important elements of Web pages (besides content, of course).

What Are Hyperlinks?

There are three main kinds of hyperlinks. They are

- **Internal hyperlinks**   Hyperlinks that point to destinations contained within your own Web site.
- **External hyperlinks**   Hyperlinks that point to destinations on another Web site.
- **Bookmarks**   Hyperlinks that point to a specific place on a page on your Web site. If you are familiar with Microsoft Word, you have seen bookmarks in action.

A hyperlink always has two points of interest: the hyperlink itself and the destination of the link. The destination is where you end up when you click the hyperlink. The most common destination of a hyperlink is another Web page—either inside or outside your Web site. However, the destination of a hyperlink can be almost anything, including images, audio or video clips, programs, etc.

The hyperlink itself is attached to either a piece of text (sometimes referred to as *hypertext*) or a graphic (such as a button). In fact, you can attach multiple hyperlinks to a single image by creating an *image map*. We'll explore how to do that later in this chapter.

Someone browsing your site needs to have a clue where the hyperlinks are on a page, so they know where to click to trigger a hyperlink. Text-based hyperlinks are displayed in a browser underlined in blue unless the reader has already navigated to the destination of the hyperlink, in which case the hyperlink text is shown in purple. In addition, moving the mouse pointer over hypertext or a graphic that contains hyperlinks changes the mouse pointer into a pointing hand (see Figure 8-1).

NOTE *The hyperlink colors displayed on your page may be different if you change the default hyperlink colors in the Background tab of the Page Properties dialog box.*

TIP *When building a Web page, don't use blue underlined text in your normal (nonhyperlink) content. Since most people are used to associating blue underlined text with hyperlinks, this will cause confusion.*

In addition to the automatic ways of clueing people in to the presence of a hyperlink, you can add your own effects. For example, in Chapter 5, you saw how you can add rollover effects to "flag" a hyperlink's presence. You can also add Dynamic HTML effects (discussed in Chapter 13) or use the "hover button" component to call attention to a hyperlink (discussed in Chapter 12).

Copyright 2001, Brevard Swimming Association. (Home) Page Last Updated 03/08/2001
Search | Feedback | Guestbook

FIGURE 8-1 When you move the mouse pointer over a hyperlink, the shape changes to a pointing hand.

Add Text Hyperlinks to Pages in Your Web Site

The most common hyperlink you'll build while constructing your Web site is a link to another page on your Web site. You can either create a link to a page that already exists or create the hyperlink and the page it links to at the same time.

Create Text Links to Existing Pages in Your Web Site

To create a link to an existing page in your Web site, use the following steps:

1. In Page view, select the text that will be used as the hyperlink. If the text doesn't already exist, type it into the page and then select it.

You should make the hyperlink text descriptive of the destination. For example, a hyperlink that returns to your home page could say "Return to Home Page".

2. Right-click the selected text and choose Hyperlink from the shortcut menu. Alternatively, click the Hyperlink button in the Standard toolbar or choose Insert | Hyperlink. The Insert Hyperlink dialog box opens (as shown in Figure 8-2).

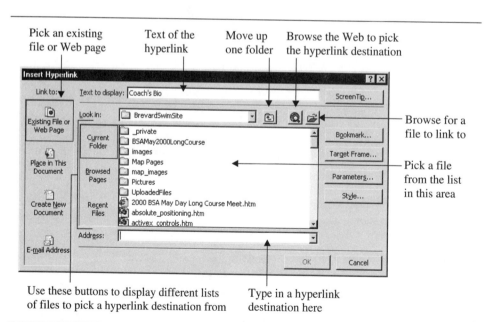

FIGURE 8-2 Specify the destination of your new hyperlink with the Insert Hyperlink dialog box.

NOTE *The Text To Display field at the top of the Insert Hyperlink dialog box shows the text you selected in step 1. You can change the hyperlink text by making changes in this field.*

3. Create the hyperlink in one of the following three ways:

■ Click the Existing File Or Web Page button and select a page in your current Web site from the list of files in the Insert Hyperlink dialog box.

■ Click the Folders button (labeled Browse For File) to open the Link To File dialog box and navigate to a page that is stored on your hard drive or network drive. Click the file to which you want to link.

■ Use the Address field to type the exact path to the file to which you want to link.

When the page to which you want to link appears in the Address field, click OK to create the link. You'll know the link was created because the text is now blue and underlined—unless you have changed the hyperlink default colors, or the theme you are using overrides the color and effect for hyperlinked text.

You can also create a hyperlink using the Folder List or the Navigation Pane. To do so, open the page that you want to add a hyperlink to in the Page view. From either the Folder List or the Navigation Pane, drag the page to which you want to link into the open page.

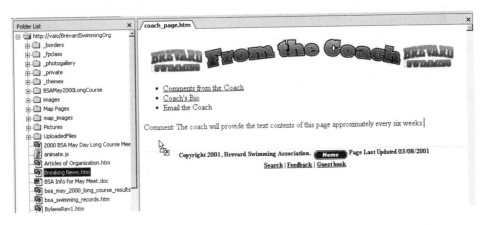

The hyperlinked page title is used as the text of the new hyperlink, but you can change that if you wish by modifying the Text To Display field in the Edit Hyperlink dialog box.

You can test your hyperlink in Page view, either in normal or preview. In normal Page view, hold down the CTRL key and click the hyperlink to switch to the destination page. In preview Page view, simply click the hyperlink to navigate to the destination page.

Create Text Links to New Pages in Your Web Site

If you want to create hyperlinks as you build your Web site—and perhaps determine the need for new pages as you create hyperlinks—you can create the link and the page at the same time.

To create hyperlinks in this way, use the following steps:

1. In Page view, select the text that will be used as the hyperlink. If the text doesn't already exist, type it into the page and then select it.

2. Right-click the selected text and choose Hyperlink from the shortcut menu. Alternatively, click the Hyperlink button in the Standard toolbar, or choose Insert | Hyperlink. The Insert Hyperlink dialog box opens.

3. Click the Create New Document button in the list of buttons at the left edge of the dialog box. FrontPage displays a new version of the Insert Hyperlink dialog box.

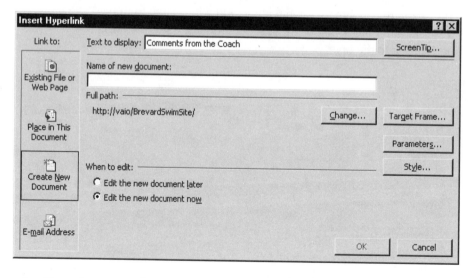

4. Enter the name of the new document in the (can you guess!) Name Of New Document field.

5. In the When To Edit section, choose when you want to edit the new document:

- ■ **Edit the new document later**   When you complete the creation of the page and hyperlink, the new page is created but you are still viewing the page into which you inserted the hyperlink.

- ■ **Edit the new document now**   When you complete the creation of the page and hyperlink, the new page is displayed, ready for editing.

6. Click OK to create the new page and hyperlink. The new page is a blank Web page—you do not have the opportunity to pick from the Web Page templates if you create a page in this manner.

When you create and name the new page, the hyperlink automatically adjusts to point to the new page with the name you gave it.

Create Links to Other Files

Although the most "normal" destination for a hyperlink is a Web page either within or outside your Web site, you are not limited to hyperlinking to Web pages. You can link to any file, including graphic files (JPG or GIF), documents (such as a Word or Excel document), and even program files. The Link To File dialog box includes a Files Of Type drop-down list near the bottom.

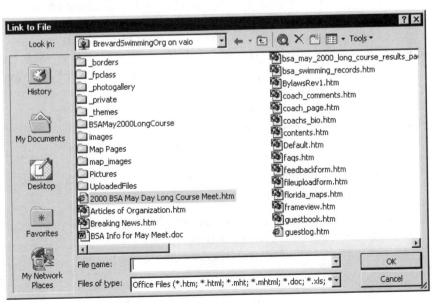

These files include all the different Microsoft Office applications documents and templates, and all the common Internet files (HTM, HTML, etc.), as well as the recognized Web graphics formats (JPG and GIF).

If you build a link to one of these file types and then use the preview Page mode to test the link, the result will depend on how you have your computer configured. For example, if you have the Office application (such as Word or Excel) installed on your computer, the linked item will open in FrontPage (or within your browser if you preview it in the browser). So, if you click on a link to a Word document, the document opens within FrontPage or within your browser. You can even edit the document if you are using Internet Explorer. However, if you choose a file type that is *not* a recognized document file for an application installed on your computer (for example, a program file such as WinWord.exe), clicking on the link opens a dialog box that enables you to pick a destination on your hard drive or network and download the file to your computer.

Create Links to External Web Sites

It is only a little more involved to create a hyperlink to another Web site on the Internet. This can be quite handy. Instead of duplicating someone else's content on your Web site (which wastes space and could get you in big trouble for copyright violation), you can simply provide a link to the information on another Web site. An advantage to this approach is that if the information is updated on the destination page, you'll be pointing to the most up-to-date information. However, if the destination site changes its structure and the linked page disappears (or the filename changes), your link will be broken—and your viewers will get the dreaded HTTP 404 (file not found) error. Thus, if you link to external Web sites you'll want to test these links periodically. An easy way to verify all your hyperlinks is to use the report designed exactly for this purpose. This report (and many other useful reports) is discussed in Chapter 16.

To create a link to an external Web site, you must be connected to the Internet. Use the following steps:

1. In Page view, select the text that will be used as the hyperlink. If the text doesn't already exist, type it into the page and then select it.

2. Right-click the selected text and choose Hyperlink from the shortcut menu. Alternatively, click the Hyperlink button in the Standard toolbar, or choose Insert | Hyperlink. The Insert Hyperlink dialog box opens.

3. Click the middle button in the row of buttons adjacent to the Look In field. It is labeled Browse The Web. This action opens your browser.

NOTE
If you know the exact URL of the page or file you want to link to, you can skip the rest of the steps and just enter it in the Address field. Make sure that the entire URL is entered, including the http:// portion.

4. Use the standard browser techniques to navigate to the page to which you want to link. Once you have reached the page, return to FrontPage.

5. The Insert Hyperlink dialog box now shows the site in the Address field. Click OK to create a hyperlink to this site.

Reformatting Hyperlinks

Under normal circumstances, hyperlinks are displayed in a blue, underlined font. With this new version of FrontPage, however, you can modify the font properties of a hyperlink, applying virtually any font, color, size, and effect you want. To do so, simply select the hyperlink text and make your modifications as described in Chapter 2 in the "Format Text" section.

CAUTION
FrontPage uses Cascading Style Sheets (CSS) to make the modifications to the hyperlinked text format. As mentioned earlier, many browsers don't display CSS properly—if at all. So, unless you have a really good reason to change the style of the hyperlinked text, it is best to leave it alone.

8

How to ... **Change the ScreenTip**

One of the downsides to using graphics as hyperlinks is that the reader may have trouble figuring out where the hyperlink goes. For example, a person who is new to the Internet may not realize that a graphic of a mailbox is actually a hyperlink they can use to send an e-mail. However, you have the option of including a *ScreenTip* for both text and graphic hyperlinks. A ScreenTip is small text flag that appears when you hover the mouse pointer over a hyperlink.

Copyright 2001, Brevard Swimming Association. (Home) Page Last Updated 03/09/2001

Search | Feedback | Guest Click here to return to the home page

To specify a ScreenTip, click the ScreenTip button—visible near the top of the Insert Hyperlink dialog box. This opens the Set Hyperlink ScreenTip dialog box.

Enter the text of your ScreenTip and click OK.

Build a Graphic Hyperlink

When building hyperlinks, you aren't limited to just using text—you can use a graphic as a hyperlink as well. The technique is identical to setting up a text hyperlink, except that you select the graphic (instead of text) prior to defining the hyperlink. However, unlike a text hyperlink, a graphic gives no indication that it represents a hyperlink unless you move the mouse pointer over the graphic.

When you define a graphic hyperlink, you have an alternate method of defining the destination of the hyperlink. To use this alternate method, right-click the graphic and choose Picture Properties from the shortcut menu, then switch to the General tab.

To specify the hyperlink destination, type it into the Location field, or click the Browse button to open the Edit Hyperlink dialog box and select the hyperlink as discussed earlier. Click OK to close the Picture Properties dialog box and add the hyperlink to the picture.

Create and Link to Bookmarks

Standard hyperlinks take you from page to page or from Web site to Web site. Bookmarks allow you to jump to a specific location within a Web page.

What Are Bookmarks?

As with hyperlinks, linking with bookmarks requires two things: the hyperlink itself and the destination of the link. A *bookmark* is the destination. It is a special placeholder you can place on a Web page. Bookmarks are most useful when you create a long scrolling page that contains a lot of information arranged in a structured fashion. Thus, typical uses for bookmarks include a table of contents or alphabetical toolbar at the top of a long page. You might also create links throughout a long page that instantly return you to the top of the page.

To link using bookmarks, you must set up both the link and the bookmark.

Create Bookmarks

Before you can link to a bookmark, you must create the bookmark, using the following steps:

1. In Page view, select the text or graphic you want to link to. As with hyperlinks, you can select any text (including a single letter, word, or line) or a graphic. Headings or subheadings on the page are prime candidates for bookmarks because you often want to jump straight to a heading.

2. Select Insert | Bookmark. The Bookmark dialog box opens.

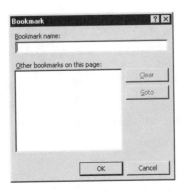

3. Give the bookmark a name in the Bookmark Name field. The name should be short but meaningful, since you'll need to recognize the bookmark name when you build the hyperlink that links to it.

4. Click OK to close the Bookmark dialog box and create the bookmark.

In normal Page view, the bookmark appears with a dashed underline (see Figure 8-3). However, the bookmark is invisible in preview Page view or in a browser.

NOTE *You can create a bookmark without first designating text or a graphic as the bookmark. If you do, the bookmark is created at the cursor position. The location of the bookmark is designated on the page by a small flag that shows the dashed underline. This flag is not visible in preview Page view or in a browser.*

You can jump directly to a bookmark on a page within FrontPage. This can be handy to navigate quickly to a particular section on a page so you can modify that section. To jump to a bookmark, choose Insert | Bookmark to open the Bookmark dialog box. In the Other Bookmarks On This Page text box, pick the bookmark to which you want to jump. Click the Goto button to jump to the bookmark.

January 2001 Newsletter

LANELINE NEWS
BREVARD SWIMMING ASSOCIATION
January – 2001 Published for Brevard Swimming Association by the BSA Boosters, Inc.

FIGURE 8-3   A bookmark is visible in normal Page view as a dashed underline.

Edit and Delete Bookmarks

If you want to change the name of a bookmark, right-click the bookmark and choose Bookmark Properties from the shortcut menu to open the Bookmark dialog box. To change the name of the bookmark, simply type the new name into the Bookmark Name field and click OK. FrontPage reconfigures any hyperlinks that use this bookmark as a destination to reflect the new bookmark name.

To delete a bookmark, choose the bookmark from the Other Bookmarks On This Page text box and click the Clear button. The bookmark is deleted and the dashed underline disappears from the page. However, note that any hyperlinks that used this bookmark as a destination are *not* automatically modified, and will now be nonfunctional because they point to a nonexistent bookmark. You will need to locate and repair these broken hyperlinks.

Link to Bookmarks

Once you've built a bookmark, you can create a link to it. Although the normal use of bookmarks is to link to them from the same page on which the bookmark is located, you can actually link to a bookmark from any page—it is just another hyperlink destination. Thus, creating a link to a bookmark is very similar to creating any other hyperlink. Use the following steps:

1. In Page view, select the text that will be used as the hyperlink. If the text doesn't already exist, type it into the page and then select it.

2. Right-click the selected text and choose Hyperlink from the shortcut menu. Alternatively, click the Hyperlink button in the Standard toolbar, or choose Insert | Hyperlink. The Insert Hyperlink dialog box opens.

3. To link to a bookmark in the current page, click the Place In This Document button to display a list of bookmarks for the document:

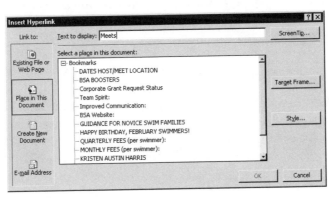

8

4. Choose the bookmark and click OK. This creates the hyperlink to the bookmark on the Web page.

If you want to create a hyperlink to a bookmark on a *different* Web page, first create the hyperlink to the page as detailed in "Create Text Links to Existing Pages in Your Web Site," earlier in this chapter. With the Insert Hyperlink dialog box still open, click the Bookmark button to open the Select Place In Document dialog box:

Pick the bookmark from the list of bookmarks in the dialog box and click OK to create the hyperlink to the bookmark on the Web page.

*HTML provides an automatic bookmark called "top." This bookmark takes you back to the top of the current page, even if you didn't define a bookmark there. This is handy when you have a long page. You can provide one or more hyperlinks that take the reader back to the top of the page. You might want to word this hyperlink "Back to Top." To use this automatic bookmark, create a hyperlink that points to the current page. Then, click at the end of the current page name in the Address field (such as Default.htm), and type **#top**.*

E-Mail from a Hyperlink

Have you ever seen a hyperlink in a Web page that says something like "Click here to send an e-mail"? When you clicked such a link, your e-mail program opened, ready for you to compose your e-mail. The e-mail address was probably already filled in, and the subject might have been filled in as well!

You can easily create this sort of hyperlink in your Web site. This type of link is called a "mailto" link because the HTML keyword that appears in the hyperlink is "mailto," rather than the http:// keyword that indicates the target of the hyperlink is a location (either a Web page or a bookmark).

To create a mailto link, use the following steps:

1. In Page view, select the text that will be used as the hyperlink. If the text doesn't already exist, type it into the page and then select it.

2. Right-click the selected text and choose Hyperlink from the shortcut menu. Alternatively, click the Hyperlink button in the Standard toolbar, or choose Insert | Hyperlink. The Insert Hyperlink dialog box opens.

3. Click the E-Mail Address button to open a new version of the Insert Hyperlink dialog box:

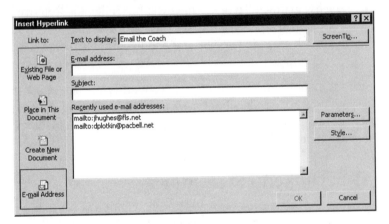

4. Enter the e-mail address in the E-mail Address field of the dialog box. As you begin to type the e-mail address, FrontPage automatically fills in the necessary "mailto" keyword.

5. If you wish, you can specify the subject of the e-mail as well by typing it into the Subject field.

6. Click OK to close the Insert Hyperlink dialog box and create the e-mail hyperlink.

When viewers click on the hyperlink in a browser, their e-mail application will open automatically. The e-mail address you specified (and the subject, if you defined one) will be filled in automatically.

Modify and Delete Hyperlinks

As you modify your site, you may find that you need to revise a hyperlink. For example, you may decide that you no longer need a hyperlink, but you want to keep the text or graphic that the hyperlink is attached to. Or you may want to redefine the destination page of a hyperlink. To make this sort of change, use one of the methods discussed previously to open the Edit Hyperlink dialog box (the simplest way is to right-click the hyperlink and choose Hyperlink Properties from the shortcut menu). From this dialog box, you can do the following:

- **Modify the hyperlink destination**   To change the destination page of a hyperlink, reselect the page using the previously discussed techniques. You can link to any of the destinations mentioned earlier, including Web pages within your site and external Web pages.

- **Delete the hyperlink**   To delete the hyperlink, click the Remove Hyperlink button to clear the contents of the Address field, and then click OK. The hyperlink is deleted, and the blue text and underline (if it was a text-based hyperlink) disappear.

- **Modify the bookmark destination**   To modify the bookmark that a hyperlink links to, or add a bookmark to a link, pick a bookmark from the list of bookmarks you can display by clicking on the Place In This Document button.

Create Hyperlinked Text Buttons

Buttons are one of the most effective ways to call attention to a hyperlink. However, since a button is a graphic, you must either find a graphic you want to use (granted, that isn't too hard) or create a graphic yourself. If you just want to create a "button-like" effect in FrontPage using the text and paragraph formatting tools, you can do so, although you are limited to one "button" on each line. Use the following steps:

1. Create the hyperlinked text, as described previously. Make sure the text is the only text on the line.

2. Select all the hyperlinked text and select Format | Borders and Shading. This opens the Borders and Shading dialog box.

3. From the Borders tab, choose the style of border you want for your "button." Effective borders include the Ridge, Inset, and Outset styles with a border setting of Box (borders on all sides of the text).

4. From the Shading tab, choose a background color from the Background Color drop-down list. Typically, light colors work best.

5. Click OK to make the border and shading selections and return to the Web page. The hyperlinked text now shows the border and shading selections you made. However, the border and shading extends over the whole line—which makes for a rather strange-looking button. We'll correct that now.

6. Click on the sizing handles around located around the edges of the border.

7. Drag the sizing handles to adjust the width and height of the border until it looks the way you want. You now have text that looks like a button (see Figure 8-4).

Build Image Maps

Up to this point, you've created hyperlinks attached to a block of text or a single graphic. It is also possible to attach multiple hyperlinks to an image. Clicking a particular part of the graphic links to one destination, while clicking another part of the graphic sends you somewhere different. Welcome to the world of image maps.

What Is an Image Map?

An image map is a graphic that contains one or more hyperlinks within its boundaries. To define an image map, you specify the graphic as well as one or more hotspots. A hotspot is a bounded area within the graphic to which you can attach a hyperlink. Since an image map graphic can contain multiple hotspots, and

FIGURE 8-4   It's just text, but it looks like a button.

each hotspot can be attached to a hyperlink, the overall image map can contain multiple hyperlinks.

Image maps can be very handy in any situation where a particular area of an image needs to have meaning. For example, if you were running a travel site, you could place a graphic of the state of Florida on your Web page. Clicking different areas of the state (such as cities, national parks, and so on) could provide information about that area.

Add a Graphic to the Page

The first step in building an image map is to add the graphic to the page. There is really nothing special about the graphic at this point, so you can add the graphic just as detailed in Chapter 3, in the section "Add Graphics from a File." To insert a picture from a file, choose Insert | Picture | From File. To insert clip art, choose Insert | Picture | Clip Art. Then follow the resulting dialog boxes to choose the graphic.

Once you add the graphic to the page and select it, FrontPage makes the Pictures toolbar available. If you don't see it, you may have turned it off. To reenable the Pictures toolbar, right-click on any toolbar to display a list of toolbars and click on Pictures in the list. By default, the Pictures toolbar appears at the bottom of the screen, but as with any other toolbar, you can drag it off the bottom and position it as a window or dock it against a different edge of the screen. Some of the tools in the Pictures toolbar (see Figure 8-5) are designed especially for creating hotspots for image maps, and we'll cover those tools in the next few sections.

Create Hotspots Using Text in a GIF

If you just need a rectangular hotspot (either with or without a text label), the easiest way to create it is to use the Text tool in the Pictures toolbar. This technique only works for GIF graphics. If you try to use the Text tool for a JPEG, FrontPage will automatically convert it to a GIF, warning you beforehand that this

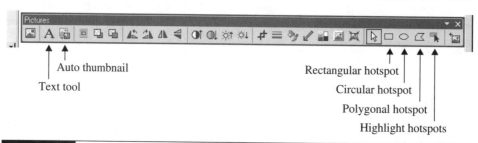

FIGURE 8-5   Use the special tools in the Pictures toolbar to define hotspots.

conversion may cause the number of colors to decrease. To create a hotspot using the Text tool, use the following steps:

1. Click the Text tool in the Pictures toolbar. A small, rectangular hotspot appears in the selected GIF.

2. Type any text you want in the hotspot (see Figure 8-6).

3. Select the hotspot by clicking in the graphic outside the hotspot, then clicking in the hotspot again. When the hotspot is selected, you'll be able to see the sizing handles.

4. Click inside the hotspot and drag it to where you want it. This location must be within the bounds of the graphic. If you want to resize the hotspot, click one of the sizing handles and drag the rectangle to the size you want. To edit the text, click within the text to provide the text cursor and edit the text using standard techniques.

Once you have created the hotspot with the Text tool, you can attach a hyperlink to it. To do so, right-click the hotspot and choose either Picture Hotspot

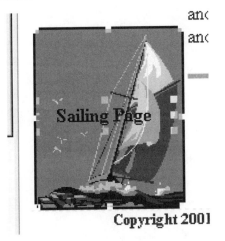

an<
an<

Sailing Page

Copyright 2001

FIGURE 8-6   Use the Text tool to add a hotspot with text to a GIF.

8

Properties or Hyperlink from the shortcut menu (or choose Insert | Hyperlink). This opens the Insert Hyperlink dialog box. Create a hyperlink for the hotspot just as you would any other hyperlink.

Create Hotspots Using the Pictures Toolbar Tools

The rest of the hotspot tools in the Pictures toolbar work somewhat differently from the Text tool. For one thing, you can add a hotspot to a JPEG without converting it to a GIF. In addition, the moment you draw the hotspot on the graphic, the Insert Hyperlink dialog box appears. Therefore, you must have the hyperlink's destination created—and the address at hand—prior to creating the hotspot, because if you click Cancel in the Insert Hyperlink dialog box, the hotspot is not created.

To create a hotspot using one of the Pictures toolbar tools, click the tool shape you want to use. If you choose the Circular or Rectangular tool, click and drag

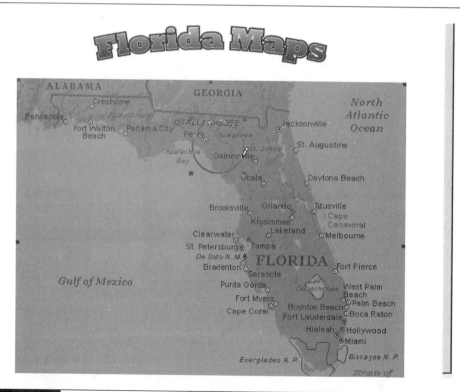

FIGURE 8-7   Click and drag with the Circular Hotspot tool to create a hotspot in an image.

inside the outline of the graphic to create the shape (Figure 8-7 shows this using the Circular Hotspot tool).

The moment you release the mouse button, the Insert Hyperlink dialog box appears. Select the hyperlink as usual, and click OK to close the dialog box and create the hyperlink. Once the hotspot is created, you can click in it to select it (the sizing handles appear), and drag it to a new location or resize it by dragging one of the sizing handles. You can also right-click a hotspot and choose Picture Hotspot Properties or Hyperlink from the shortcut menu to open the Edit Hyperlink dialog box and change the hyperlink.

The Polygonal Hotspot tool is often used to outline a particular area of a graphic. For instance, you could use it if you wanted to outline a Florida county on the graphic in Figure 8-7. To create the hotspot with Polygonal Hotspot tool, click where you want the hotspot to start. Continue clicking around the outline of the area you want highlighted. To complete the hotspot, click the start of the outline again. At this point, the Insert Hyperlink dialog box opens and you can proceed to define the hyperlink, as described above.

NOTE   *When editing the shape of the polygonal hotspot, you can adjust the shape by dragging any of the sizing handles. The sizing handles appear at each of the spots you clicked to originally create the shape.*

Sometimes it is helpful to see just the hotspots in a graphic. To hide the graphic in which the hotspots are embedded, click the Highlight Hotspots button in the Pictures toolbar. This shows the outline of all the hotspots (see Figure 8-8). You can select a

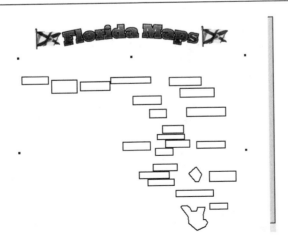

FIGURE 8-8   Click the Highlight Hotspot button to see just the hotspots in an image map.

hotspot (it turns black), or double-click the hotspot to open the Edit Hyperlink dialog box. However, you can't resize or move the hotspots in this view.

Create an Auto Thumbnail for an Image

If you've ever waited for a page full of images (especially photographs) to load in your browser, you know it can take a while! Many people may give up and go elsewhere if your page takes too long to load. One common trick to shorten the download time for a Web page is to use thumbnails. A thumbnail is a reduced version of an image. This reduced version (which loads much faster than the full image) gives the reader an idea of what the full image will look like. If you attach a hyperlink to the thumbnail and attach the hyperlink destination to the full image, the reader can click the thumbnail to view the full image.

You can configure how FrontPage creates the auto thumbnail by choosing Tools | Page Options and clicking the Auto Thumbnail tab.

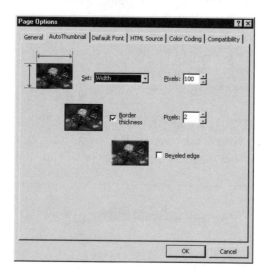

From this dialog box, you can configure the following properties of an auto thumbnail:

- **Size** Bigger thumbnails give a better idea of what the image is, but also lead to bigger files. To set the size of the thumbnail, choose the dimensions from the Set drop-down list. Choices include Width, Height, Longest Side, and Shortest Side. Set the value for the selected dimension by using the adjacent Pixels spinner. You can specify the size for more than one of these dimensions, but only one of the dimensions—the last dimension you set—has any effect on the thumbnail size.

■ **Border Thickness**   If you want the thumbnail to have a border, check the Border Thickness checkbox. Set the thickness of the border in the adjacent Pixels spinner.

■ **Beveled Edge**   If you want the thumbnail to have a beveled edge, check the Beveled Edge checkbox.

NOTE   *The changes you make to the Auto Thumbnail properties apply to subsequently created thumbnails. Existing thumbnails don't change.*

FrontPage makes it very easy to use hyperlinked thumbnails. To do so, use the following steps:

1. Create a Web page that contains the photos you want to display, in the order you want to display them. Save the page, and allow FrontPage to copy any images into the Image directory of the current Web site.

2. Click an image, and choose the Auto Thumbnail button in the Pictures toolbar.

3. FrontPage automatically creates a reduced version (thumbnail) of the graphic, and replaces the full version with the thumbnail (see Figure 8-9). The thumbnail is actually a hyperlink to the full version of the graphic.

4. Switch to Preview and click one of the thumbnails. The page is replaced by a page containing the full version of the graphic.

5. Switch back to normal Page view, and save the page (File | Save). FrontPage provides the Save Embedded Files dialog box so you can save the automatically created thumbnail images.

6. Click OK to save the thumbnail images and finish saving the page.

Recalculate Hyperlinks

Hyperlinks are very important to a Web site because they let you navigate the site easily. However, FrontPage also uses hyperlinks in some of the special-purpose Web pages and components it can create for you. These include the table of contents component (see Chapter 12) and shared borders (see Chapter 9). Because

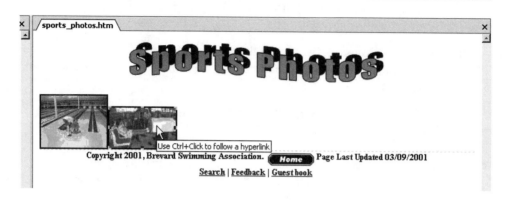

FIGURE 8-9 With Auto Thumbnail, FrontPage creates a thumbnail version of a graphic and adds a hyperlink to the full version.

of this, it is important to keep FrontPage's internal "map" of hyperlinks complete and up-to-date. Thus, you should periodically recalculate the hyperlinks. To do so, choose Tools | Recalculate Hyperlinks. Click OK in the dialog box that warns you that the process can take a few minutes, and wait for the process to finish. Once it is done, your table of contents, shared borders, and other automatically maintained hyperlinks will be complete and accurate.

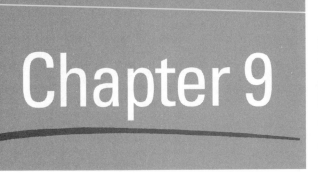

Chapter 9

Build Shared Borders and Link Bars

How to...

- Add and customize shared borders
- Work with the Navigation view
- Create custom link bars to link to any Web page
- Create link bars based on the Navigation view

FrontPage includes a special tool called shared borders. As you will see, shared borders enable you to give a Web site a consistent look and feel, as well as use hyperlinks efficiently. With shared borders, you have the option of having FrontPage maintain sets of hyperlinks between pages (called link bars) automatically, saving you quite a bit of work.

You can also create custom link bars—reusable sets of hyperlinks that can include links to any Web page.

Understand and Use Shared Borders

When you create a Web site, it is important that your pages look like they were well planned and designed to work together. We've already discussed one tool that can help you achieve this effect: themes. Shared borders (coupled with link bars) is another tool that can help your site have a consistent look and feel.

What Are Shared Borders?

A shared border is an area of the page that is the same on each Web page on which it appears (see Figure 9-1). Thus, you can add text and graphics to a shared border, and that text and graphics will appear on each page. A shared border can be turned on or off for a page, but cannot be customized to look different on one or more pages of the Web site. As you can probably guess from the name, the shared borders are located around the borders of the page, and you can activate the top, left, right, or bottom shared borders.

Shared borders are most powerful when used with link bars based on the navigation structure (covered in more detail later in this chapter). In essence, these link bars are automatically maintained hyperlinks that make it easy to find your way around the Web site. You can create a structure of your Web site (like an organization chart) using the Navigation view (also covered later in this chapter),

Top shared border   Right shared border

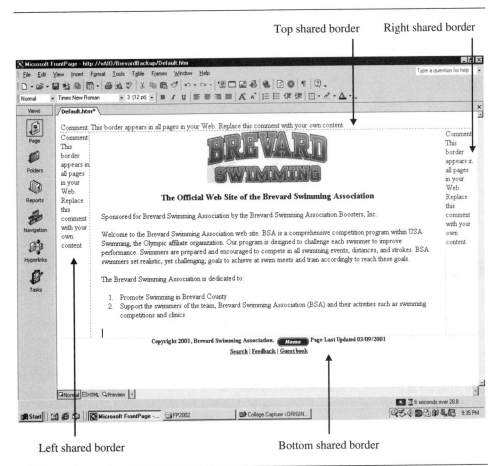

Left shared border   Bottom shared border

FIGURE 9-1   Shared borders allow you to place the same content on each page
of your Web site.

and FrontPage will automatically construct the appropriate hyperlinks in the link
bar based on the navigation structure.

Add Shared Borders to a Site

To add shared borders to a site, choose Format | Shared Borders to open the
Shared Borders dialog box (shown in Figure 9-2).

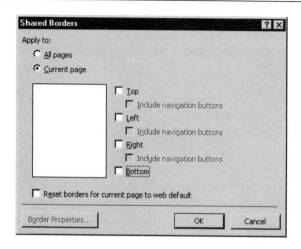

FIGURE 9-2   Use the Shared Borders dialog box to specify which borders to display.

To add any of the shared borders to the page, click in the Top, Left, Right, or Bottom checkboxes. To determine how much of the Web site to apply the shared borders to, pick one of the options at the top of the dialog box. The All Pages option applies this set of shared borders to all the pages in the Web site. The Current Page option applies this set of shared borders only to the current page. Thus, you can set up the entire site to use Top and Left shared borders by picking the All Pages option. You can then open individual pages and turn on additional shared borders or turn off existing shared borders and pick the Current Page option to change only that page.

Add Color and Images to Shared Borders

FrontPage enables you to set the background color or use a picture for the background of a shared border. To do so, right-click in a shared border and pick Border Properties from the shortcut menu. This displays the Border Properties dialog box.

If you have more than one shared border active, pick the shared border you want to customize from the Border drop-down list. To add a background color, check the Color checkbox, and pick the color from the Color drop-down list.

To add a picture to the background, check the Picture checkbox and either type in the filename (including the full path) for the picture or click the Browse button and choose the picture from the file dialog box that appears.

> **NOTE**   *You can only pick a background picture from the current Web site. The file dialog box used for picking the picture file does not allow you to navigate to another location on your hard drive. Therefore, you'll need to import the background picture into your current Web site before you can add it to the shared border as a background.*

Customize Shared Borders Content

You can place virtually any page element in a shared border—graphics, text, components (where appropriate), and even hyperlinks. Anything you place in the shared border shows up on every page that includes the shared border. In general, you add items to a shared border just as you would to any other portion of the page. You can format text using all the same font and paragraph formatting tools.

> **TIP**   *One very handy use of the bottom shared border is to put copyright and revision information there.*

Page banners work a little differently, however. When you add a page banner to the top shared border, it automatically takes the name of the page as it is displayed in Navigation view (covered later in this chapter). Thus, page banners are *not* the same on every page.

Enable Navigation Buttons

Navigation buttons (see Figure 9-3) give readers hyperlinks they can click to navigate their way through your Web site. Depending on the theme, these hyperlinks can show up as text links or buttons. The set of navigation buttons are actually a special form of link bar, discussed later in this chapter. This Navigation bar provides buttons on each page that reflect the structure of your Web site, and can give readers easy ways to navigate "down" to subordinate pages or "up" to the parent page—and even make a quick jump back to the home page. The really nice thing about the Navigation bar is that FrontPage keeps track of it, and as the reader browses from

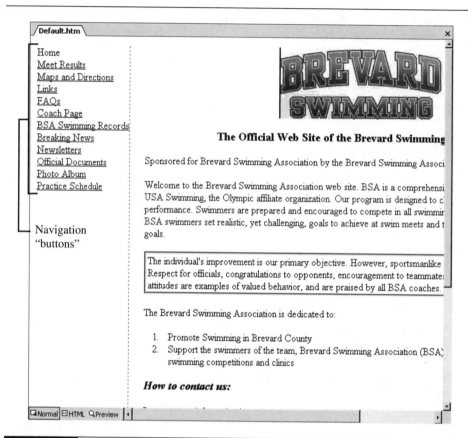

FIGURE 9-3 Navigation buttons give your readers an easy way to navigate through the structure of your Web site.

one page to the next, FrontPage makes sure that the navigation buttons on the current page reflect the structure of the Web site. And, if you change the structure of your Web site, FrontPage will make sure the Navigation bar reflects the structure change as well. You'll see how to create the structure of your Web site in the next section.

You can add a Navigation bar containing the navigation buttons to either the top or left shared borders, or both. Use the Shared Borders dialog box (see Figure 9-2) to turn on the navigation buttons. To place a set of navigation buttons in the top shared border, check the Include Navigation Buttons checkbox right below the Top checkbox. To place a set of navigation buttons in the left shared border, check the Include Navigation Buttons checkbox right below the Left checkbox. The Include Navigation Buttons checkbox is only available if the All Pages option is selected in the Shared Borders dialog box.

NOTE *If you enable navigation buttons on a page that is not included in the Navigation view (structure of the Web site), the buttons will not be visible in the shared border. Instead, a note will prompt you to add the page to the Navigation view.*

Work with the Navigation View

To build meaningful Navigation bars and make sense of their properties (which we will discuss shortly), you need to tell FrontPage the structure of your Web site. You can think of the structure of your Web site as being similar to an organization chart. At the top of the chart is the home page (CEO), and successive levels of pages (departments) fall below that. Once you specify this organization structure, FrontPage will be able to create and maintain your Navigation bars.

You set up the structure of your Web site using the Navigation view (see Figure 9-4). To open the Navigation view, click the Navigation icon in the Views bar or

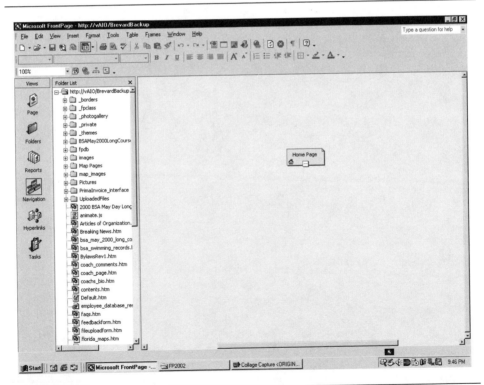

FIGURE 9-4   Use Navigation view to build the structure of your Web site.

choose View | Navigation. The Folder List displays all the pages in your Web site, and the large area to the right is where you'll build your Web site's "organization chart." Initially this area contains only the home page, which is normally the top layer of your Web structure.

Build the Web Structure

To begin building the structure of your Web site, use the following steps:

1. From the second level of the Web site, drag a page from the Folder List into the main window. As you do, a connector appears between the home page and the dragged page (see Figure 9-5). Position the page below the home page and release the mouse button.

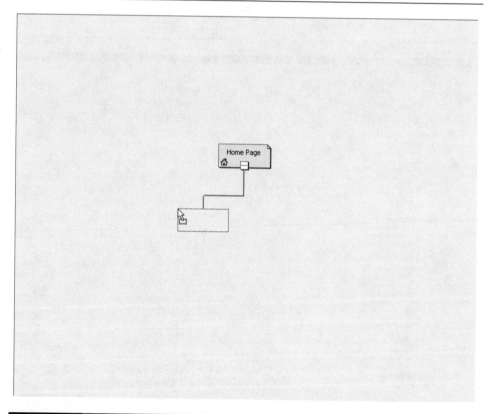

FIGURE 9-5   The connector shows you which page the dragged page will be connected to.

2. Continue dragging pages into the main window. As you move a page close to a page already in the window, the connector will connect to that page. By maneuvering the pages in the main window, you can build your Web site structure's second level, third level, and so forth. When it is done, you might have something like that shown in Figure 9-6. This structure is turned 90 degrees so that more of it is visible.

You can rearrange the structure easily. For example, if you want to change the order of pages connected to a common parent page, just drag one of the pages horizontally, and release it where you want it. The other pages will move out of the way to make room for the relocated page. You can also change the parent of a page. To do so, start dragging the page until the connector disconnects from the current parent. Continue to move the page close to the intended parent until the connector connects to the appropriate parent.

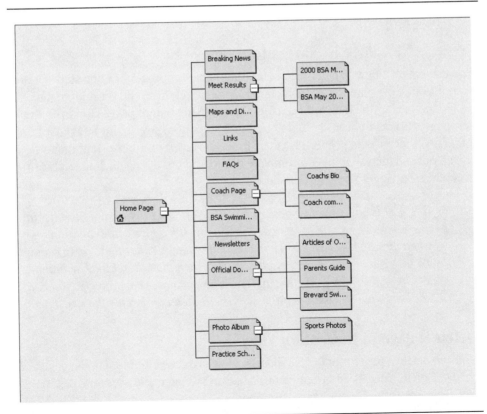

FIGURE 9-6   A complete Web site structure might look something like this.

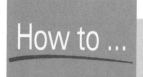

Exclude Pages from Navigation Bars

At times, it may be appropriate to place a page in the navigation structure, but *not* include it as a hyperlink in the Navigation bar. A good example might be the confirmation page for a form—since the reader should only reach the confirmation page after submitting the form. To exclude a page from the Navigation bar, right-click the page and deselect the Included In Navigation Bars option. There is also a button for this purpose in the Navigation bar. FrontPage excludes the selected page and any subordinate pages, and changes their icons to gray to indicate their state.

Create a New Page in Navigation View

You can create a new page and connect it to its parent page all in one step. To do so, right-click the parent page and choose New | Page from the shortcut menu. FrontPage creates the new page and attaches it to the parent page. However, the new page has not yet been created as a file—it does not show up in the Folder List, nor can you access its properties (the Properties entry in the shortcut menu is grayed out and unavailable). To complete the creation of the page, double-click it in Navigation view to open it in Page view.

> **TIP**   *It is best to give the new page a meaningful name before double-clicking it to open it. The name of the page is used as the default title and filename when the page is created, so a meaningful name is better than "new_page_1". To give the page a name, click it, pause, then click it again. The name becomes selected, and you can type a new name. Alternatively, you can choose Rename from the page's shortcut menu and enter the new name.*

Delete a Page in Navigation View

You can delete a page from the Navigation view. To do so, right-click the page and choose Delete from the shortcut menu, or select the page and press the DELETE key. This opens the Delete Page dialog box.

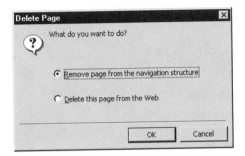

The Delete Page dialog box gives you two options: to remove the page from all the Navigation bars (and thus from the main window of the Navigation view), or to delete the page from the Web site altogether. Choose the option you want and click OK.

Customize the Navigation View

You can customize how the Navigation view looks. Here are the available options:

- **Zoom in and out**   You can change the zoom level to zoom in and see more details, or zoom out and see more of the overall diagram. To change the zoom level, use the Zoom drop-down list in the Navigation bar to set the zoom you want. Alternatively, you can right-click a blank area of the Navigation view main window and pick Zoom from the shortcut menu.

- **Expand and collapse subtrees**   You can collapse the view of subordinate pages by clicking the minus sign (-) on a page. To reexpand the subtree, click the plus sign (+) that replaced the minus sign when you collapsed the subtree. You can also choose to view just a page and its subtree (see Figure 9-7) by right-clicking the page and choosing View Subtree Only in the shortcut menu, or by clicking the View Subtree Only button in the Navigation bar. To return to viewing the whole tree, click on the View Subtree Only button once again— either in the Navigation bar or just above the page at the top of the subtree.

- **Switch between portrait and landscape**   Sometimes, you can see more of your Web structure by viewing it laid out from left to right, rather than top to bottom. To switch between portrait and landscape modes, click the Portrait/Landscape button in the Navigation bar. You can also right-click in an empty area of the main window and choose Portrait/Landscape from the shortcut menu.

9

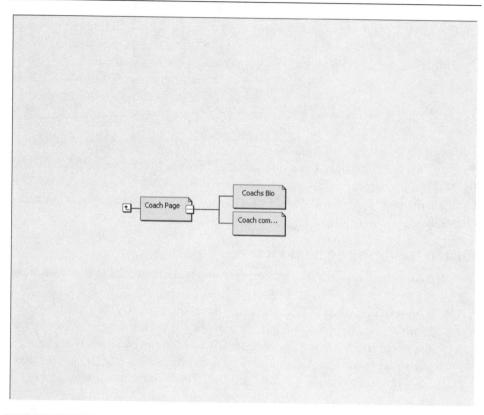

FIGURE 9-7 Focus on one page and its subtree by viewing only that part of the structure.

Rename Pages in Navigation View

The icon names you see in Navigation view are very important and just a little confusing. These names are *not* the same thing as either the filename or the title of the page, although the icon name is initially set to the same value as the page's title. The icon's title is important not only because it is the only visible label in Navigation view, but also because this title is what FrontPage uses for the page banner of a page. In addition, it is the hypertext or button label that FrontPage uses for any references to this page in a Navigation bar. For example, let's say you create a page with a filename of MyPage.htm and title (in Page Properties) of MyPage. You then change the icon name to Silly Page. The page banner or any hypertext or button in a Navigation bar whose hyperlinked destination is this page will use Silly Page as the hypertext or button label.

There are two ways to rename the icon in Navigation view. First of all, you can click the icon, pause, and then click again. This selects the icon name and makes it editable. Just type the new name. The second way is to right-click the icon and choose Rename from the shortcut menu. This action makes the name editable.

You can also change the page title from the Navigation view. To do so, right-click the icon and choose Properties from the shortcut menu. This opens the Properties dialog box where you can enter a new page title in the Title field.

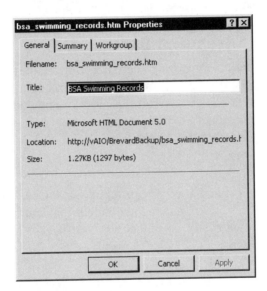

Add Existing Pages in Navigation View

To add an existing Web page to the Web site structure in Navigation view, right-click on a page in the Navigation view and choose Add Existing Page from the shortcut menu. This opens the Insert Hyperlink dialog box. From this dialog box, you can choose an existing page in the Web site. But, as you learned in Chapter 8, you can also choose an address on the Internet, create a new document and hyperlink to it, and insert an e-mail address link. In fact, about the only type of hyperlink you *can't* insert is a bookmark.

Link with Link Bars

Link bars are aids to navigating both your Web site and the Internet. There are two types of link bars. The first has already been mentioned: Navigation bars are based on the structure of your Web site. Once you specify how you want the link bar configured, FrontPage will automatically maintain Navigation bars for you, modifying them as necessary when you change the structure of the Web site. In addition, the Navigation bar on a particular page reflects where that page is in the structure of the Web site. Navigation bars are discussed in the next section.

The other type of link bar is a "custom link bar." Essentially, a custom link bar is a reusable set of hyperlinks. You construct a custom link bar by specifying the set of hyperlinks to be included in it. Once built, you can place the custom link bar in any Web page—and even embed it in a shared border so that it appears on every page. Custom link bars are discussed later in this chapter.

Navigate with Navigation Bars

Navigation bars are easy to create and configure, and are one of FrontPage's best ease-of-use features. Before Navigation bars, it was up to you to rebuild sets of hyperlinks if you restructured your Web site. With Navigation bars, you can concentrate on content and let FrontPage worry about the "housekeeping" of navigating the structure of your Web site.

Create a Navigation Bar

You can create a Navigation bar several different ways. One of those ways was covered earlier in this chapter: checking the Include Navigation Buttons checkbox in the Shared Border dialog box. The other way you can create a Navigation bar is to use the following steps:

1. Choose Insert | Navigation to open the Insert Web Component dialog box with the Link Bars option already selected in the Component Type list.

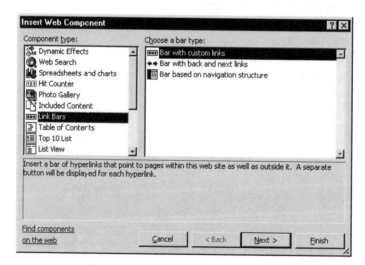

2. In the Choose A Bar Type window, click on Bar Based On Navigation Structure. Then click the Next button to proceed.

 You can also choose Insert | Web Component, pick Link Bars from the Component Type list, and then click on Bar Based On Navigation Structure in the Choose A Bar Type window.

3. The next dialog box displays a list of styles for the navigation buttons. Choose one of the styles in the Choose A Bar Style and click Next to proceed. If you choose the Use Page's Theme option (the first one in the list), the button styles will change if you change the page theme.

4. From the next dialog box, pick either a horizontal or vertical orientation for the navigation buttons and click Finish to proceed.

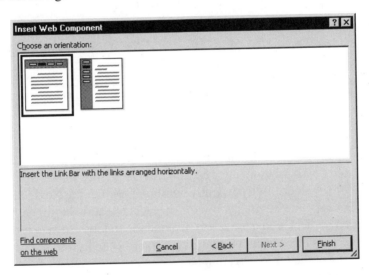

5. FrontPage opens the Link Bar Properties dialog box so you can configure the Navigation bar's hyperlinks (see Figure 9-8). The next section details how to set which hyperlinks are displayed in a Navigation bar.

Configure a Navigation Bar

You can configure a Navigation bar to specify exactly what hyperlinks it is to display, as well as set how the Navigation bar displays those links.

To set up which levels of your Web structure a Navigation bar is going to link to, you can adjust the link bar properties when you first build the Navigation bar or by

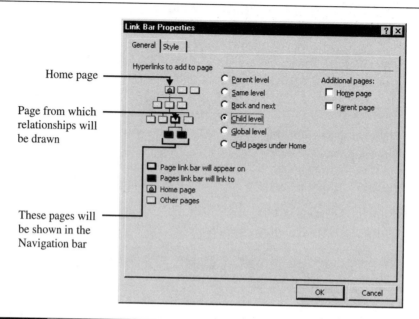

Home page

Page from which relationships will be drawn

These pages will be shown in the Navigation bar

FIGURE 9-8   Use the Link Bar Properties dialog box to set which hyperlinks to display and how to display them.

modifying the properties later. To modify the properties of an existing Navigation bar, switch to Page view, right-click in a Navigation bar, and choose Link Bar Properties from the shortcut menu. The Link Bar Properties dialog box appears (see Figure 9-8). You can independently configure each of the Navigation bars on your page. For example, if you choose to place a Navigation bar in both the top and left shared borders, you can set up each one separately. However, the top Navigation bar has the same configuration on every page in which it appears. This is also true of the left Navigation bar.

The Link Bar Properties dialog box shows you a representation of the general structure of a Web site. The purpose of this structure is to show you which related pages will have hyperlinks in the Navigation bar. As you make selections from the options in the Hyperlinks To Add To Page section, pages that will be hyperlinked are represented by a blue rectangle. The page from which the relationships are drawn is represented by the rectangle with the blue border.

You have many options about what pages you want hyperlinked in the Navigation bar. You can link to the Parent Level (up one level), pages on the Same Level, the Child Level (down one level), only to the Global Level (pages at the same level as the home page) of the Web, and only the pages just beneath the home page (Child

Pages Under Home). You can also just use buttons that navigate back to the previous page you visited and (once you have used the Back button) forward to the page you just stepped back from (Back And Next). In addition, you can add links to both the home page and the parent page.

> **TIP** *Use the two available shared border Navigation bars for different purposes. For example, use the left Navigation bar for child pages, and the top Navigation bar for the same level or parent level (whichever makes more sense in your Web site).*

You can adjust the style of the Navigation bar at any time by clicking on the Style tab in the Link Bar Properties dialog box.

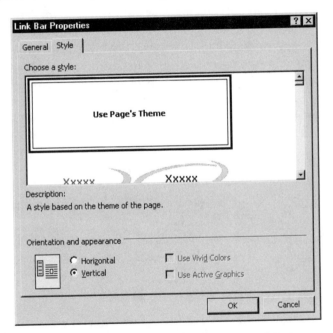

Pick either the Horizontal or Vertical option to change the orientation of the navigation buttons. You can also choose Use Vivid Colors or Use Active Graphics to brighten and animate the navigation buttons—just as you could with themes (see Chapter 5).

Insert a Navigation Bar Without Shared Borders

You can use Navigation bars even when you don't have shared borders on a page. To do so, place the text cursor where you want to add the Navigation bar and choose Insert | Navigation, then pick the Bar Based On Navigation Structure, just as you did before. This opens the Link Bar Properties dialog box. Pick the options you want and click OK to create the new Navigation bar. You can move the Navigation bar around just like a block of text. However, since this Navigation bar is not in a shared border, it does not automatically appear on the other pages of the Web site. Unlike Navigation bars placed in shared borders, you can uniquely configure the Navigation bar on each page. For example, the left Navigation bar on one page could show child pages, while the left Navigation bar on another page could show parent pages.

Insert a Navigation Bar with Existing Shared Borders

Although it doesn't happen very often, you may wish to insert Navigation bars when you already have shared borders on the page—even when some of those shared borders already include a Navigation bar. One reason would be to add a Navigation bar to the right or bottom shared borders, which you cannot otherwise configure to include a Navigation bar with the Shared Borders dialog box. Another reason would be if you want to include two Navigation bars in a shared border. For example, the "normal" Navigation bar in the top shared border might be configured to display pages at the same level in the Web site. You could add a second Navigation bar that displays child pages. The Corporate Presence Wizard (a wizard for building a corporate Web site) uses this trick.

NOTE   *Remember, since the Navigation bar is in a shared border, it will appear on every page of the Web site that displays the shared border.*

To add a Navigation bar to a shared border, click in the shared border and create a Navigation bar as previously discussed.

Build a Link Bar with Custom Links

Custom link bars are new with this version of FrontPage. A custom link bar, shown next, enables you to create a set of hyperlinks that you can use over and over. Thus, if you have a standard set of hyperlinks to Web sites that you want available on many pages, create a custom link bar and just include it on those pages. In fact, if you place the custom link bar in a shared border, the link bar will be available on every page that includes the shared border. Custom link bars don't *look* much different from Navigation bars—but they are very useful because you can include hyperlinks to pages outside of your Web site as well as pages in your Web site.

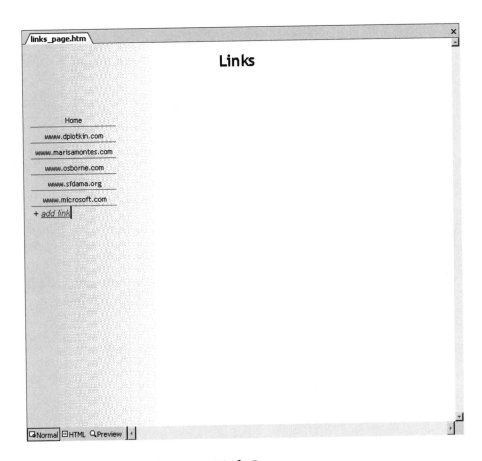

Create and Insert a Custom Link Bar

To create a custom link bar, use the following steps:

1. Choose Insert | Navigation to open the Insert Web Component dialog box with the Link Bars option selected in the Component Type list.

2. Choose Bar With Custom Links from the options in the Choose A Bar Type list on the right side of the dialog box. Click Next to proceed.

3. Pick a style for the buttons in the custom link bar from the list of available styles. Click Next to proceed.

4. Choose either Horizontal or Vertical as the orientation for the buttons in the custom link bar. Click Finish.

5. FrontPage opens the Link Bar Properties dialog box. If you have not yet created any custom link bars, the first thing you'll see is the Create New Link Bar dialog box.

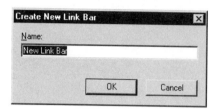

NOTE *The Link Bar Properties dialog box associated with custom link bars is very different from the Navigation bar's Link Bar Properties dialog box.*

6. Type in a name for the custom link bar and click OK. This action closes the Create New Link Bar dialog box and makes the Link Bar Properties dialog box available.

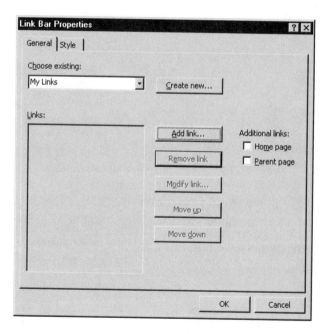

7. Click the Add Link button to open the Add To Link Bar dialog box where you can define the link (see Figure 9-9).

Browse the Web   Browse for File

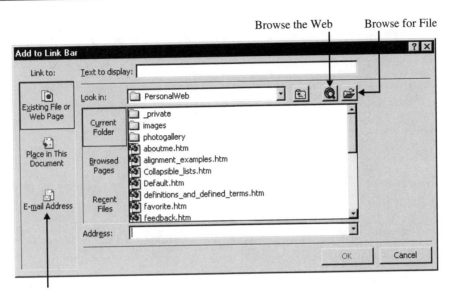

Specify an e-mail link

FIGURE 9-9   Use the Add To Link Bar dialog box to pick the destination of the links in the custom link bar.

8. Use any of the techniques for specifying a hyperlink discussed in Chapter 8 to specify a link. Briefly, these include the following:

■ Specify links in the current Web site. Choose the Current Folder button and pick a file. You cannot, however, pick a bookmark on the current page.

■ Browse the Web for hyperlinks. Click on the Browse the Web button, which looks like a small globe with a magnifying glass. It is located in the center of the three buttons alongside the Look In drop-down list.

■ Include an e-mail address. Click on the E-mail Address button and fill in the e-mail address and subject.

■ Browse for a file on your hard drive or network. Click on the Browse For File button, which looks like a small open folder. It is located at the right end of the three buttons alongside the Look In drop-down list. This opens the Link To File dialog box where you can pick the file to link to. Pick the file and click OK to return to the Add To Link Bar dialog box.

9. Type the text to display on the button in the Text To Display field.

10. Click OK to return to the Link Bar Properties dialog box.

11. Repeat steps 8 and 9 to continue adding links to the custom link bar.

12. If you want to include the home page or the parent page (for the page on which the custom link bar is shown), check the Home Page checkbox or the Parent Page checkbox.

13. Click OK to create the custom link bar and add it to the page.

In addition to adding a link, you can perform the following operations from the Link Bar Properties dialog box:

- **Remove link**   Click the Remove Link button to delete the selected hyperlink.

- **Modify link**   To change the address for the link or the text to display, click the Modify Link button to open the Modify Link dialog box. Other than the title, it is identical to the Add To Link Bar dialog box.

- **Move up or move down**   The links are displayed in the order in which they appear in the list. To rearrange the order, click on a link and click either Move Up or Move Down.

- **Configure additional links**   To add the Web site home page or the parent page to the custom link bar, check the Home Page checkbox or the Parent Page checkbox. Unlike the rest of the links in the custom link bar (which are the same no matter what page you place the link bar in), the parent page will change to show the parent page (if any exists for the current page).

- **Change the style**   If you change your mind about the style of the buttons, you can click on the Style tab and pick a different style.

Once you have created your first custom link bar, the Link Bar Properties dialog box appears immediately when you click the Finish button in step 4 (earlier). To create another new custom link bar, click the Create New button, type in the name of the link bar in the Create New Link Bar dialog box, and click OK. Then add links as preivously described. To simply insert an existing link bar into a Web page, pick the link bar from the Choose Existing drop-down list in the Link Bar Properties dialog box and click OK.

TIP

Want to place your custom link bar on every page in your Web site? Piece of cake—just add a shared border to the pages in the Web site and add the custom link bar to the shared border!

Modify Custom Link Bar Properties

Once you have built a custom link bar and added it to a page, you aren't stuck with it. To modify the custom link bar, simply right-click on it and choose Link Bar Properties from the shortcut menu. This reopens the Link Bar Properties dialog box, where you can change any of the properties of the link bar, including changing the style, adding and removing links, rearranging the link order, and configuring additional links.

NOTE

One thing you can't change from the Link Bar Properties dialog box is the orientation of the link bar. To change the orientation (for example, to go from a horizontal link bar to a vertical link bar), you'll have to remove the link bar from the page and then reinsert it.

If you just want to quickly add another link to a custom link bar, all you have to do is click on the Add Link hyperlink at the right end (for horizontal link bars) or the bottom (vertical link bars). Clicking on the Add Link hyperlink opens the Add To Link Bar dialog box (see Figure 9-9), where you specify the additional link.

To delete a custom link bar altogether, select the link bar and press the DELETE button.

Work with Custom Link Bars in Navigation View

Any custom link bars you build show up as separate structures in the Navigation Pane or the Navigation view, as shown in Figure 9-10. In this figure, you can see the hierarchical Web site structure as well as the two custom link bars.

You can make the following modifications to the custom link bar in the Navigation Pane or the Navigation view:

- **Move a page from the Web site structure to the custom link bar** You can remove a Web page from the navigation structure (and thus from any Navigation bars you have created) and into a custom link bar. To do so, click and drag the Web page from the navigation structure to the custom link bar. As you do, a shadowed line and rectangle indicate where the page will be located in the custom link bar when you release the mouse button.

9

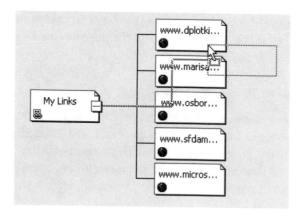

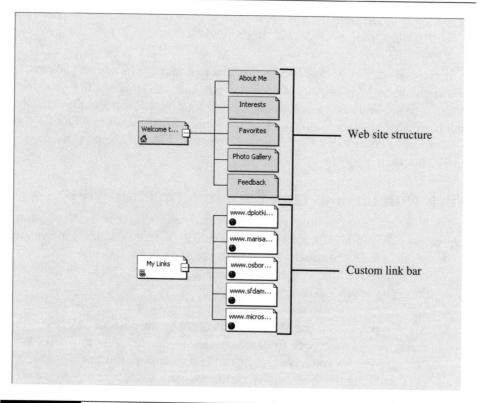

FIGURE 9-10   The Navigation view displays the custom link bars as well as the Web site structure.

- **Rearrange the order of the links in the custom link bar** You can rearrange the order of the links in a custom link bar. To do so, click and drag the link to its new position in the link bar. As you do, a shadowed line and rectangle indicate where the page will be located when you release the mouse button.

- **Add an existing page to the custom link bar** To add an existing Web page to a custom link bar, right-click on the link bar name and choose Add Existing Page from the shortcut menu. This opens the Insert Hyperlink dialog box. From this dialog box, you can choose an existing page in the Web site. But, as you learned in Chapter 8, you can also choose an address on the Internet, create a new document and hyperlink to it, and insert an e-mail address link. In fact, about the only type of hyperlink you *can't* insert is a bookmark.

- **Remove a link from the custom link bar** To remove a link from the custom link bar, click on the link and press the DELETE key or choose Delete from the shortcut menu.

- **Rename a link in the custom link bar** Renaming a link in the custom link bar changes the displayed text for the link when you add the link bar to a Web page. It also changes the displayed text for the link on any pages where you have already used the link bar. To change the name of the link in the link bar, right-click on the link and choose Rename from the shortcut menu. Or, click on the link, pause, and then click again. Either way, the link name becomes editable and you can type in the new name.

- **Add a new blank page to a custom link bar** To create a new blank page and add it to a custom link bar all in one operation, right-click the link bar name and choose New | Page. A new blank Web page is created and added to the custom link bar.

- **Create a new, empty link bar** To create a new, empty custom link bar, right-click in a blank area of the Navigation view and choose New | Link Bar from the shortcut menu. You can then add links to the empty link bar using any of the techniques discussed previously.

CAUTION *While you can select a custom link bar and copy it (Edit | Copy or choose Copy from the shortcut menu), this doesn't seem to do anything useful— you can't paste the link bar into a page.*

9

Chapter 10

Collect Data with Forms

How to...

- Add forms with the Form Page Wizard

- Create a custom form

- Set up the form results destination

- Add and configure form fields

- Add a search form

- Build forms with the form templates: confirmation, feedback, guest book, and user registration

So far, you've learned quite a bit about building a Web site. However, all the Web pages you've learned to build and the capabilities you have learned to implement have one major limitation: the readers can look, but there is no mechanism for them to provide you with feedback or input. Forms change all that. If you add forms to your Web site, your reader can send you information in a format you specify.

If forms are so powerful, why aren't there more of them on the Internet? The short answer is that forms are hard to implement—or they were, until FrontPage came along. Before FrontPage (and the FrontPage server extensions), creating and getting feedback from forms involved writing Common Gateway Interface (CGI) scripts to process the data on the form. In addition to writing the scripts, you had to install the scripts on the Web server—something that many hosting companies would not allow.

With FrontPage (and a Web server running FrontPage server extensions), you can quickly build and customize forms and specify where you want the results to go—and you're done. No writing scripts, and no installing those scripts on a server. Of course, analyzing the data submitted by the readers may be no easy matter—but that is not an issue you can solve with FrontPage!

What Are Forms?

A *form* is a special section of a Web page (see Figure 10-1). A form can be a stand-alone Web page, or it can be added to an existing page with other page elements. Within the form, you can place text and fields to collect data from the reader. Forms support many different kinds of fields—text boxes, drop-down lists, radio buttons, and so on. Later in this chapter, you'll see how you can add and customize fields in a form and even apply validation rules to the data. A form must include at least one button (usually labeled "Submit") that sends the information to the Web server. Most forms also include a button that clears the contents of the form, enabling the reader to start over.

As a Web designer, you can use forms for many purposes. You can collect readers' opinions on your business or Web site, provide a place for customer complaints or (hopefully!) praise, or enable a reader to subscribe to a newsletter. FrontPage even has a special form for searching the contents of your Web site.

Since forms gather information from a reader that you usually want to keep, the form must have a way of forwarding the reader's input (the form's *results*) to you. FrontPage enables you to send form results to a text or HTML file that you can look at with a browser or download to your computer. If you send the results to a text file, you can format the results so they can be easily loaded into a spreadsheet or database. You can even have FrontPage send you an e-mail with the results.

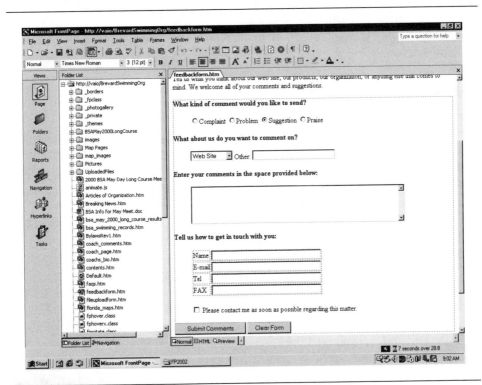

FIGURE 10-1   Use a form to gather input and return the input to you.

NOTE *You can send the form results to a database for further analysis. For more information on this useful feature of FrontPage, see Chapter 19.*

FrontPage provides three different ways to create forms: the Form Page Wizard, customized forms, and form templates. Of course, once you finish using the Form Page Wizard or a form template, you can use the customizing tools to add fields, modify text, rearrange the form, and so forth.

Build a Form with the Form Page Wizard

FrontPage's Form Page Wizard enables you to create a form quickly and easily. It automates much of the grunt work involved in laying out a form and provides you with some pretty good formatting.

To start the Form Page Wizard, choose File | New | Page to display the New Page or Web Task Pane. Then click on Page Templates to open the Page Templates dialog box. Select the Form Page Wizard and click OK. The first dialog box of the Form Page Wizard appears. Since no input is needed for the first dialog box, choose Next to proceed.

Add Questions to the Form

The next dialog box in the Form Page Wizard (see Figure 10-2) lets you add questions to your form. Each question you add requires you to specify various details about the question. Once you complete setting up the question, it will be listed in the text box below the Add button. At any time, you can select a question and either change it by clicking the Modify button or get rid of it by clicking the Remove button.

The questions appear on the finished form in the order in which they are listed in the Form Page Wizard. To change the order of the questions, click a question and click the Move Up or Move Down button.

To add a question, click the Add button. This displays a comprehensive scrolling list of questions you can add to your form. General question categories, such as Contact Information, Account Information, and Product Information, enable you to easily add a whole group of data elements to your form. Pick the question from the list and read the description in the Description field. If you wish, you can customize the text of the question by typing your text into the Edit The Prompt For This Question field. Click Next to move to the next Form Page Wizard dialog box.

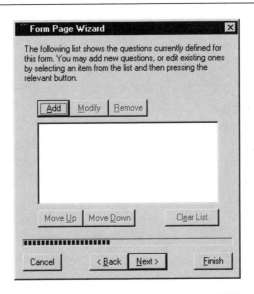

FIGURE 10-2   Click the Add button to add a question to your form.

Specify the Fields to Capture

The next dialog box you see (an example is shown in Figure 10-3) lists the fields you might want to include as part of the question. This list of fields is different for each question (that is, the list of fields for providing contact information is different from the list of fields for providing product information). Nevertheless, the format of the dialog box is the same: To add a field to the form, check the field's checkbox. For certain fields (such as the Name field in Figure 10-3), you may also have options on how to display the requested information.

Click Next to return to the first dialog box, where you can continue adding questions. Once you are done adding questions in the first dialog box, click the Next button to proceed to the presentation options.

Add Your Own Questions

If none of the "canned" questions (such as providing personal data) meet your needs, the Form Page Wizard provides some very general questions you can customize. Once you pick one of these general questions, you can configure the question using different options. In addition to the options listed here, you must specify the text of the question and the name of the variable that stores the information.

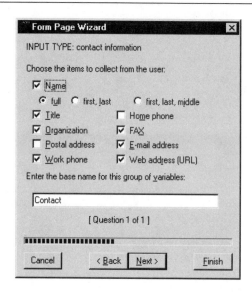

FIGURE 10-3   Specify which fields to ask the reader to provide.

    The variable name is used to reference the entered information in confirmation forms and results files (both discussed later in this chapter), and to provide the default names for database fields (see Chapter 18).

To get at the general questions, scroll down the list of questions. Near the bottom, you find such options as:

- **One of several options**   This is a question that has a small number of possible answers. The reader can pick only one option. For this question, you specify the list of possible answers, and whether you want these answers presented as radio buttons, a drop-down menu, or a list.

- **Any of several options**   This is a question that has a small number of possible answers, and the reader can pick more than one of the options using checkboxes. For this question, you specify the list of possible answers, and whether you want these answers presented in multiple columns.

- **Boolean**   This is a question that can be answered yes/no or true/false. For this question, you specify whether you want the answers presented as yes/no radio buttons, true/false radio buttons, or a checkbox.

- **Date**   This question asks the user to provide a date. You can specify the format of the date entered.

- **Time**   This question asks the user to provide a time. You can specify the format of the time entered.

- **Range**   This question asks the user to rate something on a five-level scale. For this question, you can specify whether you want the scale to be numeric (1–5), bad to good (and three intermediate values), or disagree strongly to agree strongly (with three intermediate values). You also can choose whether to use the midrange value as the default value, and whether to use a drop-down menu instead of the default radio buttons.

- **Number**   This question asks the user to enter a number. You can set the maximum length allowed.

- **String**   This question asks the user to enter a text string. You can set the maximum length allowed.

- **Paragraph**   This question asks the user to enter one or more lines of text in a multiline text box.

Specify the Presentation Options

The next Form Page Wizard dialog box lets you specify how you want the data presented on the form.

You can format the questions with the following options:

- As normal paragraphs

- As a numbered list

- As a bulleted list

- As a definition list

If your form is very long, you can choose to have FrontPage provide a table of contents. The table of contents appears at the top of the page. Clicking one of the questions jumps you right to that question on the page.

A recommended option is Use Tables To Align Form Fields. This makes sure that the fields line up and look ordered on the form. The table border is invisible, so the reader doesn't see the table. For more information about using tables, see Chapter 6.

Save the Results

The last Form Page Wizard dialog box lets you choose how the data entered in the form will be saved.

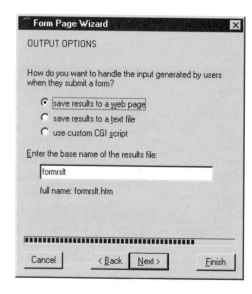

You have the following options:

- **Save results to a web page**   This option creates an HTML file in your Web site. Each time a reader clicks on the Submit button at the bottom of the form, the set of paired values of the field name and the data (value) entered by the reader are saved to the Web page. The Web page file is given the name you specify in the Enter The Base Name Of The Results File field, appended with the appropriate extension (for example, .txt for a text file, .htm for a HTML file).

- **Save results to a text file**   This option creates a text file in your Web site, and saves the data the same way as described in the previous bullet. A text file can be handy when you want to export the results to a database or a spreadsheet.

- **Use custom CGI script**   This option tells FrontPage that a CGI script (which you must write) is responsible for accepting the data and producing the results file.

Finish Up with the Form Page Wizard

Click Next, and then click Finish to create the new form (see Figure 10-4).

You need to do some customizing to the form before you save it. Here is what you need to change:

- The heading at the top of the page reads "New Page 1" (or something similar). You'll want to give the form page a more informative heading.

- Just below the heading is a line that reads "This is an explanation of the purpose of the form." Delete the text and replace with your explanation of what your form is for.

- The author name and copyright information are at the bottom of the page. You need to replace the placeholder text (for example, "Author information goes here") with your name and any copyright information you want on the form (including changing the default copyright year of 1999).

- Right-click the page and choose Page Properties from the shortcut menu. Change the page title to something meaningful.

- Finally, save the page and give it a meaningful filename. Unlike saving most other Web pages, choosing File | Save the first time you save does *not* give you the opportunity to name this page. If you use File | Save, the page

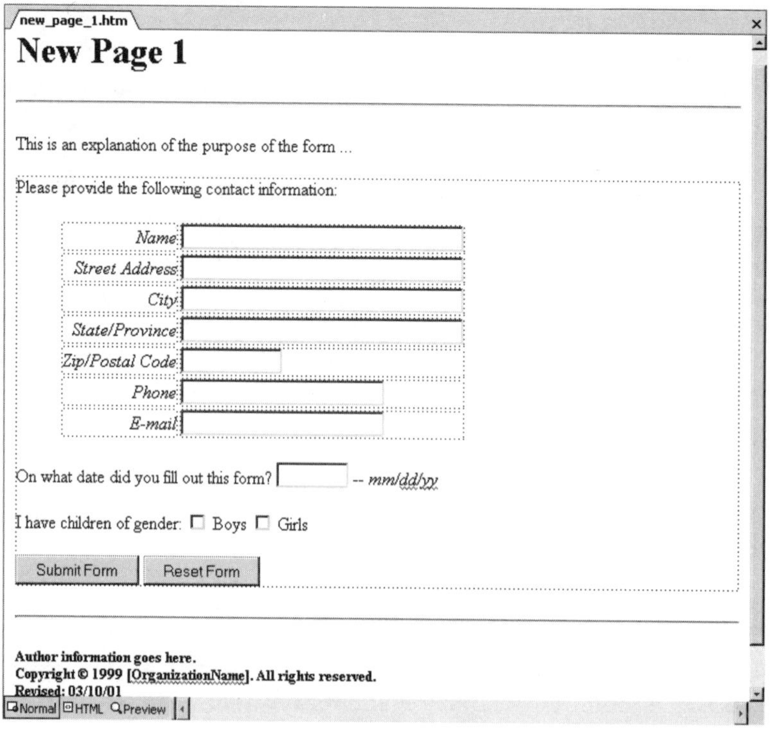

FIGURE 10-4 You still need to customize some items on the "finished" form.

will automatically be named something like new_page_1.htm. Instead, choose File | Save As, and provide the page name you want in the Save As dialog box.

Another oddity of pages generated by the Form Page Wizard is that shared borders do *not* appear, even though the Shared Borders option is actually on (choose Shared Borders from the shortcut menu for the page to see this). To force the shared borders to show, check the Reset Borders For Current Page To Web Default checkbox in the Shared Borders dialog box. Also, FrontPage does *not* apply a theme to the form, although you can add one if you want. To do so, choose Theme from the form's shortcut menu, and choose the theme for the page.

NOTE *The default theme for the rest of the site appears at the top of the list on the left side of the Theme dialog box, making it easy to find.*

View the Form Page Results

As people begin filling out your form and pressing the Submit button, you'll need to know where to go to look at the results. If you specified that the information should be saved as a Web page, you'll see a new Web page in your Folder List. You can open this page in a browser. If you specified that the information should be saved as a text file, you'll see the text file in your Folder List. You can view the text file with any application capable of opening such a file, such as Notepad or a word processor.

> **NOTE** *If you look for your results file (either a Web page or a text file) immediately after creating your form, you won't see it. FrontPage creates the file automatically the first time someone fills out the form and submits the results.*

Build Custom Forms

The forms generated by the Form Page Wizard are pretty good, but they may not meet your needs, especially if you want to format your forms very differently from the options offered. You can customize a generated form using any of the techniques discussed in this section. However, you may just want to build a completely custom form.

> **NOTE** *If you inspect any form page, you'll see a dashed line surrounding the section containing the form. This dashed line identifies the form boundary. Insert any new fields inside this boundary. Inserting a form field outside the boundary actually creates a new form if you checked the Automatically Enclose Form Fields Within A Form checkbox in the General tab of the Page Options dialog box. Since form fields outside of a form are pretty useless, there is really no reason to clear this checkbox (it is checked by default).*

Create the Form

To create a custom form, use the following steps:

1. Open or create the page on which you want to place the form.

2. Choose Insert | Form | Form. FrontPage inserts the new form (with its dashed outline) into the page. The two default buttons (Submit and Reset) are also placed on the form (see Figure 10-5).

The beginnings of a custom form shows only the form boundaries and two buttons.

3. To make room for your fields above the buttons, place the text cursor to the left of the buttons and press ENTER to give yourself some blank lines.

4. Enter text and graphics using the standard editing tools discussed earlier in this book. Adding these elements to a form is just like building any other page.

5. To give the form a name, right-click anywhere in the form and choose Form Properties from the shortcut menu. Type the name for the form into the Form Name field near the bottom of the Form Properties dialog box.

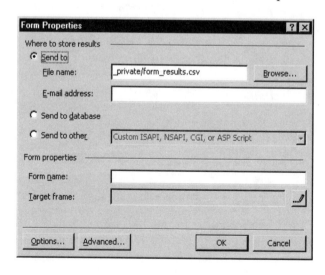

Save the Results

If you are not using the Form Page Wizard, you have a lot of options as to where the results go when someone submits the form. You can send the results to various types of text or HTML files, you can send the results in an e-mail, and you can choose which fields you want to see in the result set.

 *You can also apply these customizations to the form created by Form Page Wizard after the wizard finishes.*

To specify how the results get saved for a particular form, right-click in the form and choose Form Properties in the shortcut menu to open the Form Properties dialog box. In this dialog box you can set the name of the file where the results will go and the e-mail address to which the results will be sent. However, there are many more configuration options you can make to ensure that the results are handled just the way you want. To perform the rest of the configurations, click the Options button in the Form Properties dialog box. This opens the Saving Results dialog box (see Figure 10-6).

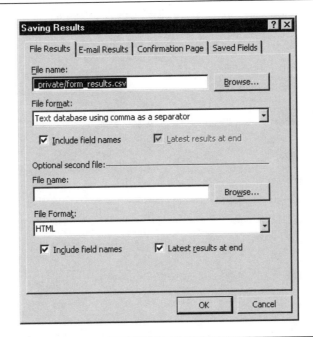

FIGURE 10-6   Use the many tabs in this dialog box to configure exactly how FrontPage should handle the form results.

Send Results to a File

The File Results tab (visible in Figure 10-6) lets you specify how to handle the results in a file. For a file, you can specify the following:

- **File name**   If you specified a filename for the results file in the Form Properties dialog box, the filename will be visible in the File Name field. You can change the filename if you wish, or click the Browse button and pick an existing file.

- **File format**   Use the File Format drop-down list to select the format of the result file. Table 10-1 details the available formats.

Format	Format Description
HTML	Plain HTML text in a Web page.
HTML definition list	HTML text formatted in a definition list. The "defined term" is the field name; nested below it (in the definition area) is the data entered by the user.
HTML bulleted list	HTML text formatted in a bulleted list. The content of each field (including the field name if you included it) is one bullet.
Formatted text within HTML	Standard formatted text, but inserted into a web page.
Formatted text	Standard formatted text in a text file. You can open and read such a file with Notepad or a word processor.
Text database using comma as a separator	All the data in one record is placed on a line (which may wrap) in the text file. The individual data elements are separated by commas.
Text database using tab as a separator	All the data in one record is placed on a line (which may wrap) in the text file. The individual data elements are separated by tabs.
Text database using space as a separator	All the data in one record is placed on a line (which may wrap) in the text file. The individual data elements are separated by spaces.

TABLE 10-1   The Available Formats for Form Results

- **Include field names**   Check the Include Field Names checkbox to include the field names in the results file. If you leave out the field names, the results file will be smaller, but you may have a difficult time telling which data is which!

- **Latest results at end**   Check the Latest Results At End checkbox to place the most recently submitted form results at the bottom of the file, rather than at the top (which is the default). This option is only available if you choose one of the HTML formats. The text formats *always* place the latest results at the end, and you can't change that (this checkbox is checked and grayed out).

- **Optional second file**   You can specify all the previous quantities for a second file. Using this option, you can (for example) send the results to both a text file and an HTML file.

Send Results to an E-Mail

Click the E-mail Results tab to specify the properties of a results e-mail.

Each time a reader submits the form, the results are gathered up into an e-mail by the FrontPage server and sent to an e-mail server for transmission.

For an e-mail, you can specify the following:

- **E-mail address**   Enter the e-mail address in the E-mail Address To Receive Results field. If you had previously entered an e-mail address in the Form Properties dialog box, it appears in this field.

- **E-mail format**   All the same format options detailed in Table 10-1 are available for composing an e-mail.

- **Include field names**   Check the Include Field Names checkbox to include the field names in the results file.

- **Specify the subject line**   Enter the subject for the e-mail in the Subject Line field. This is to help you figure out that this e-mail contains form results. If you want the subject line to contain the results from one of the form fields, check the Form Field Name checkbox and enter the name of the field into the Subject Line field.

- **Specify the reply-to line**   If you want to specify the contents of the Reply-To line in the e-mail, type the contents into the Reply-To Line field. If you want the Reply-To line to contain the results from one of the form fields, check the Form Field Name checkbox, and enter the name of the field into the Reply-To Line field. Normally, you *do* want to collect the reader's e-mail address, and populate it automatically into the Reply-To line to save you the trouble of addressing a reply.

Display a Custom Confirmation Page

It is considered good manners to show the reader some sort of confirmation that their data has been received. By default, FrontPage provides a simple confirmation page that sums up all the data submitted. However, you can specify a different confirmation page if you wish. This confirmation form can be a standard Web page that just acknowledges receipt of the data. As you will see later in this chapter, you can also build a specially formatted confirmation form using one of the general templates designed for this purpose.

To specify the URL of the confirmation Web page (whether a regular Web page or special confirmation form), use the Confirmation Page tab.

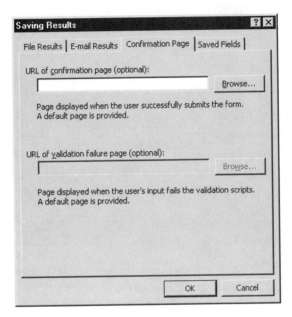

Enter the Web page into the URL Of Confirmation Page field.

As you will also see later in this chapter, you can specify validation criteria for data someone enters into a form. For example, you can make a field required—the reader is not allowed to leave it blank. If you wish to provide a Web page to tell a reader that the data they submitted is invalid, enter the URL for this Web page into the URL Of Validation Failure Page field. This field is grayed out until at least one field in the form has validation criteria.

Specify the Saved Fields

You don't have to include all the fields on the form in the result set (although I can't think of a reason to ask the reader to provide the information unless you are going to save it!). To specify which fields to save in the result set, use the Saved Fields tab.

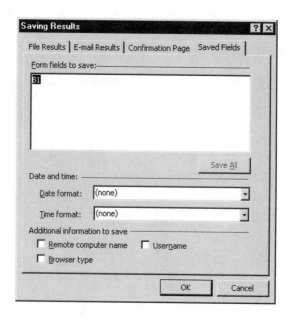

The Form Fields To Save text box initially lists all the fields on the form. You can select any of the fields and press BACKSPACE or DELETE to remove the field from the list. If you change your mind, you can bring back all the fields on the form by clicking the Save All button.

> **NOTE** *In our example, we haven't added any fields to the form yet, so the list of form fields to save is empty with the exception of the Submit button (B1).*

In addition to the fields in which the reader enters data, you can also save some information about the reader and his or her computer. If you want to include the remote computer name, username, or browser type, check the appropriate checkbox. This information is gathered automatically (without the reader knowing it) when the reader submits the form results.

You can also set the display format of any date or time fields in the form results. To do so, choose the date format you want to use from the Date Format drop-down list and choose the time format you want to use from the Time Format drop-down list.

Specify Uploaded File Properties

If you add a file upload field to your form (see "Add a File Upload Field," later in this chapter), you'll see an extra tab in the Saving Results dialog box: the File Upload tab.

A file upload field enables the reader to upload a file to the Web site. Use the Destination field in the File Upload tab to specify the destination for the uploaded file. This is the folder within the Web site where the uploaded files will be stored.

You can also specify a category for the uploaded files by checking one of the checkboxes in the Available Categories list, or by using the Categories button to define a new category and then picking that category.

> NOTE
>
> *Although you can specify a category for the uploaded files and pick a value from both the Assigned To drop-down list and the Review Status drop-down list, these values are not assigned to the uploaded files. Further, the Assigned To drop-down list and Review Status drop-down list are empty the next time you open the dialog box.*

Before you can upload files to the destination folder you selected, you'll need to configure that folder in a special way. To do so, right-click on the folder in the Folder List and choose Properties from the shortcut menu. This opens the Properties dialog box.

Clear the Allow Scripts To Be Run checkbox. This makes two additional checkboxes available in the bottom section of the dialog box:

- Check the Allow Anonymous Upload To This Directory checkbox.

- If you wish to allow files in the directory to be overwritten by files of the same name, check the Allow Uploaded Files To Overwrite Existing Filenames checkbox.

Send Results to a Discussion Form Handler

The Discussion Form Handler is designed to handle input from a discussion Web site—a Web site where people hold ongoing conversations, reading what others have said about a topic and replying. You can build a discussion Web site using a FrontPage wizard. You may wish to direct the output from your custom form to a discussion Web site. If you do, you must make some modifications to the form properties.

First, open the Form Properties dialog box, choose the Send To Other option, and select the Discussion Form Handler from the drop-down list. Click the Options button to open the Options For Discussion Form Handler dialog box with the Discussion tab displayed.

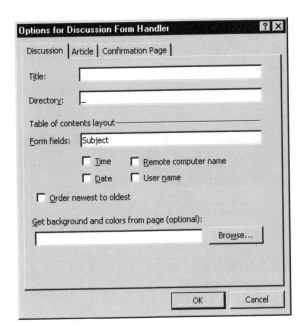

You can configure the following options:

- **Title**   Set the name of the discussion group by entering it in the Title field. This title appears in all the articles in the discussion Web site.

- **Directory**   Use the Directory field to specify the directory in which FrontPage should store all the articles in the discussion Web site. This directory must be hidden—which is why there is a leading underscore in the directory name.

- **Table of contents**   Use the Table Of Contents Layout section to customize how the table of contents will look. The table of contents is regenerated automatically each time someone submits an article. Use the Form Fields field to specify which fields appear for each article in the table of contents. Although Subject is the default, you can add other fields; just separate each field from the previous field with a space. Checking the Time and Date checkboxes displays the time and date that the article was submitted. Checking the Remote Computer Name and User Name provides this information about the author of the article. You can check the Order Newest To Oldest checkbox to display the articles in that order. Finally, you can specify a page from which to get the background and colors for the table of contents page. Enter the name of the page to use into the Get Background And Colors From Page field.

The Article tab lets you customize how each article (posting) will look in the discussion Web site.

You can include a Web page to provide the header and a Web page to provide the footer for each article. To do so, specify the URL of the Web page in the URL Of Header To Include and the URL Of Footer To Include fields. You can include the time and date on which the article was submitted, and the format for the time and date by choosing them from the Date Format and Time Format drop-down lists. You can also include the Remote Computer Name and User Name of the author of the article by checking the appropriate checkboxes.

Specify Hidden Fields

Sometimes it is helpful to include information that the reader did *not* enter in the form result set. This information could help you evaluate the results. An example of this sort of information is the version of the form the reader was using. To add your own information to the form so that it appears in the result set, you use *hidden fields*. For each hidden field, you specify two values: the field name and the value that goes with it. In our form-version example (and the following illustration), the field name might be "Version" and the value that goes with it could be "1.0". This is called a *name/value pair*.

To create and populate hidden fields, click the Advanced button in the Form Properties dialog box to open the Advanced Form Properties dialog box.

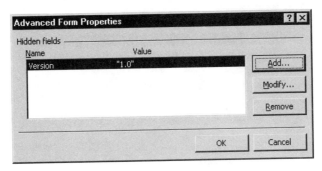

To create a hidden field and its value, click the Add button. In the resulting Name/Value Pair dialog box, enter the field name in the Name field and the associated value in the Value field. Then click OK to add the hidden field. At any time, you can select an existing pair and click Modify to change either the name or the value. You can also click Remove to remove the name/value pair from the list.

 *If you use the default confirmation form, the hidden fields will show on the confirmation form. If you don't want them to, build your own confirmation form!*

Add Fields to a Form

To insert a field into a form, choose Insert | Form, and then pick the type of field you want to add from the submenu that appears. There are 11 types of fields, including a one-line text box, a checkbox, radio buttons, and a drop-down list.

You can select a field and change the alignment of the field on the form using the alignment tools in the Formatting toolbar. For example, you can center the field on the page by clicking the Center button in the Formatting toolbar.

Once you have added a field to a form, you can change its properties by right-clicking the field and choosing the Properties entry from the shortcut menu. This entry may be called Form Field Properties, Group Box Properties, or Advanced Button Properties, depending on the type of field. We'll discuss the specifics of the field properties for each type of field in the next few sections.

From the Properties dialog box you can also specify the field formatting for Font, Paragraph, Border, Numbering (for a numbered list or bullets), and Position (discussed in Chapter 13). To do so, click the Style button to open the Modify Style dialog box, and click on the Format button to display a list of formatting options:

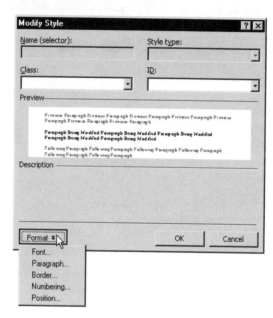

Make your choice from this list and then specify the formatting from the resulting dialog box. Realize, however, that once again FrontPage uses Cascading Style Sheets to format the field, so the formatting may not show up properly (or at all) in some browsers.

For most fields, you can also specify validation criteria. To do so, click the Validate button in the field's Properties dialog box. We'll discuss the validation options for each type of field in the next few sections.

Add a One-Line Text Box

The one-line text box provides you with a field that is one line high and up to 999 characters long. It is useful (mostly) for short strings, such as a name, address, phone number, or e-mail address. When you choose a one-line text, the field appears in the form. You can change the length of the field (but not the height) by clicking the field and dragging the sizing handles.

To change the properties of the one-line text box, choose Form Field Properties from the shortcut menu and use the resulting Text Box Properties dialog box.

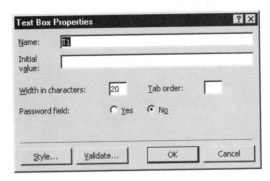

From the Text Box Properties dialog box, you can configure the field as follows:

■ **Change the name**   The default name for the field is not very informative, so enter the name you want in the Name field.

■ **Specify the initial value**   If you want the field to start off containing a default value, enter that value in the Initial Value field.

■ **Specify the field width**   Enter the length of the field (as it appears on the form) in the Width In Characters field. This is *not* the maximum amount of information the field can hold, which is actually set in the Validation dialog box.

■ **Set the tab order**   The Tab Order field sets the order in which the cursor moves through the fields on the form when you press the TAB key. This field only has an effect in Internet Explorer 4 or later. To remove the field from the tab order (so the cursor will *not* go into this field when you press the TAB key), enter **–1** in the Tab Order field.

■ **Password field**   Choose the Yes option if you want the text box to be a Password field. All this means is that anything the reader types in is masked with asterisks.

You can apply validation criteria to a one-line text box. Validating data enables you to reject data that doesn't meet your criteria. To establish validation criteria, click the Validate button to display the Text Box Validation dialog box.

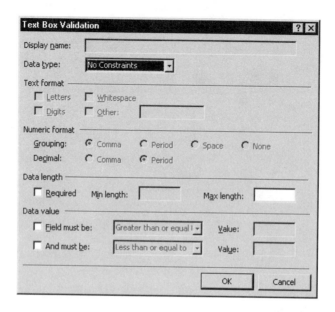

The first step in setting up the validation criteria is to pick the type of data you expect from the Data Type drop-down list. Different options make different portions of the dialog box available. The options are

■ **No constraints** This is the default. For this selection, you can establish the following criteria:

   ■ **The display name** This is the name the reader sees in an error dialog box if the field name (as configured in the Form Field Properties dialog box) is different from the label text alongside the field as it appears on the form. The Display Name field is available only after you establish a constraint of some kind in the Validation dialog box.

   ■ **Whether the field is mandatory** If a value must be filled in, check the Required checkbox in the Data Length section.

   ■ **The minimum and maximum length of the data** If you check the Required checkbox, you can specify the minimum (enter a value in the Min Length field) length of the data entered in the field. You can also enter the maximum (enter a value in the Max Length field) length of the data entered in the field regardless of whether the field is required or not.

   ■ **Valid value range** If you want to establish a valid range of values, check the Field Must Be checkbox, and choose a comparison (such as Greater than or equal to, Less than, and so on) from the drop-down list.

Use the Value field to specify the value to compare the field contents to. You can also establish a second criterion by checking the And Must Be checkbox. Then pick the second comparison from the adjacent drop-down list and type the value to compare to into the Value field. By using both comparison options, you can establish both ends of a range of valid values.

- **Text**   Choose Text if you want to treat the field contents strictly as a string of characters. In addition to the validation options noted previously, the options in the Text Format section enable you to establish whether to allow Letters, Digits, Whitespace, or Other special characters by checking one of these four checkboxes. You can allow one or more of these items—checking none of the checkboxes allows any characters at all. If you want to allow certain special characters, type them into the field adjacent to the Other checkbox, separated by commas.

- **Integer**   Choose Integer to allow only numbers without a decimal fraction. This choice grays out all the options in the Text Format section and makes the Grouping options available. Grouping indicates how numbers larger than 999 are displayed. For example, if you choose the Comma option, the number 1234 will be displayed as 1,234.

- **Number**   Choose Number to allow decimal numbers. This choice enables the same validation options as Integer, and adds the ability to specify whether you want the integer portion of the number separated from the fractional portion by a decimal point or a comma. Choose the appropriate Decimal option.

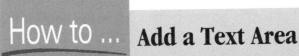

How to ...   Add a Text Area

The Text Area field provides you with a field into which the reader can type multiple lines. It is most useful for such things as comments, complaints, and other blocks of text that won't fit easily on a single line. When you choose a text area, the field appears in the form. You can change the height and width of the field by clicking the field and dragging the sizing handles.

To change the properties of the text area, use the Text Area Properties dialog box. The properties are identical to a one-line text box, except that you can specify the number of lines.

The validation for a text area is identical to a one-line text box—it even uses the same dialog box (Text Box Validation).

> **TIP** *Unless you resort to changing the Style (not recommended), any text label you place to the left of a text area is aligned with the bottom of the text area, which is not particularly attractive. To work around this limitation, place the label above the text area.*

Add a Checkbox

Use a checkbox for a list of fields in which it would be reasonable to check one or more of the available options. For example, you might ask readers what types of computers they own (PC, Mac, WinCE, Palm Pilot, etc.). You would provide a checkbox for each option, and the reader could check all that apply. To change the properties of a checkbox, choose Form Field Properties from the shortcut menu and use the resulting Check Box Properties dialog box.

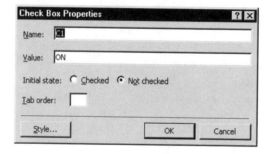

Name the checkbox field in the Name field, and set the value returned when the checkbox is checked in the Value field. The checkbox returns either the value in the Value field (checkbox is checked) or null (checkbox is cleared). You can also specify whether the checkbox should be initially checked or not by picking either the Checked option or the Not Checked option. Since a checkbox can only return two values, no validation is needed.

> **TIP** *If you intend to add up the number of times a checkbox was checked on a form (for example, using a spreadsheet), set the checked value to 1.*

Add Option Buttons

Option buttons provide you with a way to capture data when the reader must provide one—and only one—value from a relatively short list of possible values. One of the buttons in the list is always selected, and picking a different button in the list deselects the initially chosen button. Option buttons are useful for determining such data as gender (one value from a short list), whether someone owns a car (yes or no), or their current marital status.

To change the properties of an option button, right-click the option button and choose Form Field Properties from the shortcut menu to open the Option Button Properties dialog box.

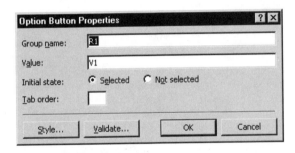

Set the group name for the option button in the Group Name field. All option buttons that work together must have the same group name. As with checkboxes, enter the value returned by the option button when it is selected in the Value field. You can choose whether the initial state of the radio button is Selected or Not Selected by selecting one of these options. However, only one option button in a group can be initially selected. Choosing another radio button to be initially selected deselects the first choice.

To validate an option button, use the Option Button Validation dialog box. For option buttons, you can only choose whether the data is required (check the Data Required checkbox). Making the data required for one option button in a group makes the data required for all the buttons in the group. In addition, making the data required enables the Display Name field. This field is where you can specify the text used to identify the option button in the error message that appears if you violate the data required requirement.

Add a Drop-Down Box

A drop-down box gives the reader another way to enter a choice—either a single choice from the list or multiple selections. You can use a drop-down box for the same sorts of things for which you use a checkbox (multiple selections) or radio buttons (a single selection).

When you insert a drop-down box on the form, it does not contain any data, and it is shown at a minimum size of about one character high and one character wide. Also, although sizing handles appear when you select the drop-down menu, you can only adjust the height (not the width) of the field by dragging it.

To set the properties of a drop-down box, choose Form Field Properties from the shortcut menu and use the resulting Drop-Down Box Properties dialog box.

Provide a name for the drop-down box in the Name field. The next thing you need to do is add values to the list. To do so, click the Add button to display the Add Choice dialog box.

Use the following steps to configure a choice:

1. In the Choice field, type the entry that will appear in the drop-down menu.

2. If you want the form to return the value you specified in the Choice field, leave the Specify Value checkbox cleared. However, if you want the form to return a different value when the choice is selected, check the Specify Value checkbox and enter the value in the Specify Value field. You might want to do this if the text of the choice on the form is long and descriptive but you only need a shortened version to perform data analysis.

3. Choose whether this entry will be initially Selected or Not Selected by picking one of these options. Only one of the items in the list can be initially selected—if you choose another one to be initially selected, your first choice will be unselected.

Once you have specified your list of choices, you can work with the choices, as follows:

■ To modify one of the items in the list, select it and click the Modify button. This opens the Edit Choice dialog box, which is identical to the Add Choice dialog box.

■ To delete one of the choices, select the choice and click the Remove button. The choice is removed from the list.

■ To rearrange the items in the list, click an item and then click Move Up or Move Down.

You can set the height of the drop-down menu by typing a value in the Height field. You can also enable multiple selections by choosing Yes or No in the Allow Multiple Selections section. If allowed, the reader can make multiple selections using standard techniques for making multiple selections in Windows. The simplest way is to click the first item, then hold down the CTRL key and click other items you want. CTRL-clicking a selected item a second time deselects it.

NOTE   *When you only allow single selections and a height of one line, the drop-down menu looks like a classic drop-down list, with a down arrow on the right side. Clicking this arrow drops the list down so you can see its contents. However, if you allow multiple selections or a height greater than one line, the "drop-down menu" becomes a scrolling text list.*

10

To validate the contents of a drop-down menu, you use the Drop-Down Box Validation dialog box.

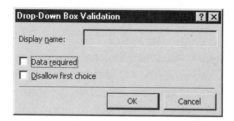

You can set the validation for a drop-down menu as follows:

■ Check the Data Required checkbox to ensure that at least one item in the list is selected. If you check the Data Required checkbox, you can enter the Display Name (used to warn readers when they don't supply a value in a required field).

■ If you specified that multiple selections are allowed, you can specify the limits on the number of items the reader can pick by typing values into the Minimum Items and/or Maximum Items fields. These two fields are missing from the validation dialog box if you don't allow multiple selections.

■ If you don't want the reader to be able to pick the first item in the list, check the Disallow First Choice checkbox. This enables you to make the first item an instruction, such as "Pick one item from the list." Clearly, you don't want to consider this item a valid choice!

Add a Push Button

A push-button field gives you a button on the form. There are three possible kinds of buttons: Normal, Submit, and Reset. The Submit and Reset buttons were mentioned earlier. The Submit type of button sends the form results to the designated destination, and each form must have at least one Submit type of button. The Reset type of button clears the form. A Normal type of button doesn't have any special functionality—it is just a button. You can, however, attach a hyperlink to a Normal type button, essentially providing a hyperlink on your form that looks like a button.

NOTE *Although sizing handles appear when you click a push button, you cannot adjust the size of a push button by clicking and dragging a sizing handle. The size is set automatically by the label you place in the button.*

You adjust the properties of a push button by right-clicking the button and choosing Form Field Properties from the shortcut menu to open the Push Button Properties dialog box.

Other than the name and tab order, the only properties you can set for a push button are the label that appears on the button (type this into the Value/label field) and the type of button (pick one of the Button Type options).

Push buttons cannot be validated.

> **TIP**
> *Just like any other graphic, you can attach a hyperlink to a push button by choosing Hyperlink from the button's shortcut menu, selecting the button and clicking the Hyperlink tool in the Standard toolbar, or choosing Insert | Hyperlink.*

Add an Advanced Button

Like a push button, an advanced button gives you a button on the form, and you can set the button type to Submit, Reset, or Normal. However, unlike a push button, you can set the width and height of an advanced button, and format the button without using Cascading Style Sheets.

When you first create an advanced button, the button text reads "Type Here". You can type in the button text and even press ENTER to split the name over multiple lines (the button automatically increases its height to contain the button text). To edit the button text, simply select it like any other text and edit it. You can also set the font, color, size, and effects by selecting the text and using the standard text formatting tools. Finally, you can select the button itself and set the text area background using the Highlight tool in the Formatting toolbar.

You can apply formatting to an advanced button from the options in the Format menu. However, if you select the advanced button and choose Format | Borders and Shading, the formatting is applied *not* to the button, but to the entire line of the form on which the button resides.

CAUTION *FrontPage uses a special hyperlink tag to display an advanced button: <button>. Since this is not a generally recognized tag, browsers earlier than Internet Explorer 5.0 and all versions of Netscape will not recognize the advanced button, and will fail to display it properly. For example, Netscape Navigator 4.7 will display only the button text. So, unless you can guarantee that all visitors to your site will have Internet Explorer 5.0 or later, don't use advanced buttons in your forms.*

You can adjust the properties of an advanced button by choosing Advanced Button Properties from the shortcut menu to open the Advanced Button Properties dialog box.

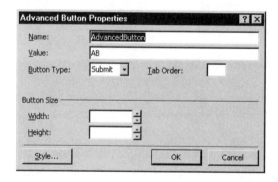

Like a push button, you can set the name, button type, and tab order for an advanced button. You can also specify a value in the Value field, although this value is not returned when the button is pushed (in fact, the Value field doesn't appear to do anything useful). Finally, you can specify the button size in pixels by specifying the width (in the Width spinner) and the height (in the Height spinner).

> **TIP**   *It is much easier to specify the button size by clicking on the edge of the advanced button so that the sizing handles are visible, and then clicking and dragging a handle.*

Add a File Upload Field

A file upload field enables someone to specify a file to upload to the Web site. The file is deposited in the Web site folder you specified, as described earlier in this chapter ("Specify Uploaded File Properties"). When you add a file upload field to a form (see Figure 10-7), it consists of two parts: a text box to specify the file to upload, and a Browse button that opens a Choose File dialog box where the reader can specify the file to upload.

To set the properties of a file upload field, choose Form Field Properties from the shortcut menu to open the File Upload Properties dialog box.

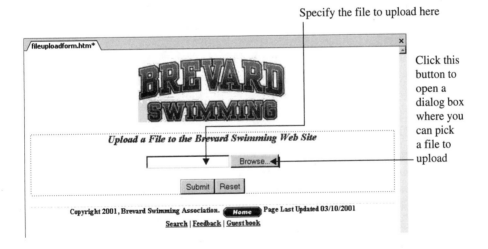

Specify the file to upload here

Click this button to open a dialog box where you can pick a file to upload

FIGURE 10-7   Use a file upload field to upload a file to the Web site, where others can retrieve it.

File Upload Properties

Name: F1

Initial value:

Width in characters: 20   Tab order:

Style...   OK   Cancel

You can set the field name, initial value (the name of the file to upload), width (in characters), and tab order.

Add a Picture Field

A form picture field is actually nothing more than a graphic that has the same functionality as the Submit button. That is, clicking the picture field submits the form results. You can't configure anything about a picture field except the name.

To add a picture field, choose Insert | Form | Picture. Pick the graphic from the Picture dialog box, as discussed in Chapter 3. FrontPage inserts the graphic into the form. You can adjust the size and graphic properties of the picture using all the standard techniques. Choosing either Form Field Properties or Picture Properties from the field's shortcut menu opens the Picture Properties dialog box. This dialog box looks exactly the same as a standard Picture dialog box, except that it has one additional tab called Form Field, where you can name the field.

Add a Form Label

Although you can type text alongside a form field to give the reader an idea of what the field is used for, this text is not considered the field's "label" as defined by HTML standards. Defining a field's label doesn't provide much of an advantage except that the default field description used when flagging validation errors is the field's label (if it exists). By defining a field's label, you don't have to add a Display Name in the Form Field Validation dialog box.

To define a form's label, insert the field as usual and add some descriptive text alongside the field—just the way you would expect. Then select both the text and the form field, and choose Insert | Form | Label. The text appears with a dotted line around it (see Figure 10-8) to indicate that HTML now identifies the text as the field's label.

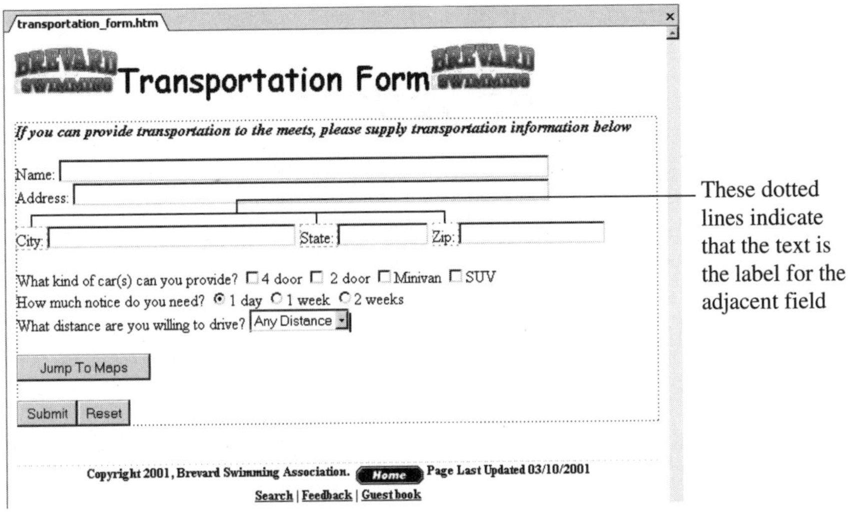

FIGURE 10-8   A label for a field is displayed with a dotted line around it.

Add a Group Box

A group box is simply a graphical element you can use for visually grouping related form fields.

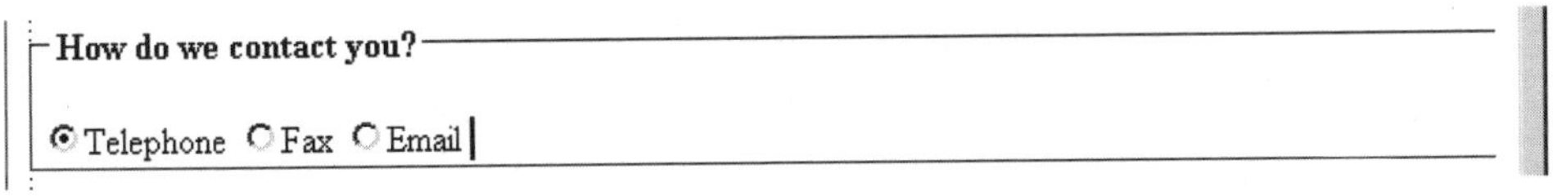

Once you have added the group box to the form, you can change the label in the upper-left corner by selecting the text and editing it. You can format the text using all the text formatting tools. You can also resize the group box by selecting it and dragging the sizing handles.

To change the properties of the group box, choose Group Box Properties from the shortcut menu to open the Group Box Properties dialog box.

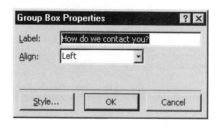

There are two fields you can set values for:

- **Label**   Changing the label changes the label text of the group box. As mentioned earlier, you can also select the group box label text and edit it directly.

- **Align**   Set the value in the Align drop-down list to Left, Center, or Right. This sets the alignment of the label text—*not* the alignment of any fields you add inside the group box. These fields are unaffected by the Align setting.

Of course, a group box is of little use unless you add fields to it. You can add fields inside a group box just like adding fields anywhere else on the form. Simply position the cursor inside the group box and choose a form field from the Insert | Form submenu.

 *If you want to apply the same text formatting to group box label text and to any text contained in the group box, click the group box to get the sizing handles to appear. Then apply the text formatting.*

Add a Search Form

One of the handiest of FrontPage's extended features is the ability to add a search form. With a search form, the reader can enter words or phrases, and the form returns a list of all the Web pages that contain those words or phrases. Since this list is actually a set of hyperlinks, the reader can just click one of the items in the list to jump right to that page (see Figure 10-9).

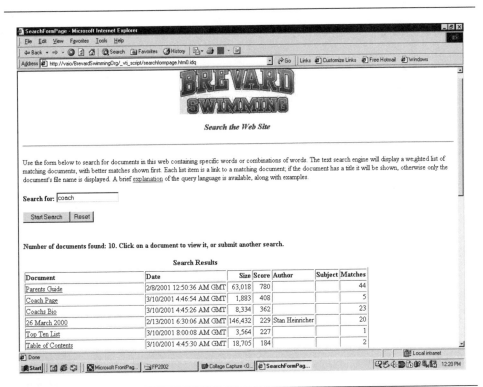

FIGURE 10-9   The results of a search are a set of clickable hyperlinks, making it very easy to go to a page of interest.

There are two ways to create a search form: create an entire search form page, or insert the search form component into an existing Web page.

Add a Search Form Page

To create a search form page, choose File | New Page or Web to open the New Page or Web Task Pane. Click Page Templates to open the Page Templates dialog box. Pick the Search Page icon and click OK. FrontPage creates a new search page (see Figure 10-10) that includes not only the operational elements for searching, but also a concise explanation of how to use the search facility.

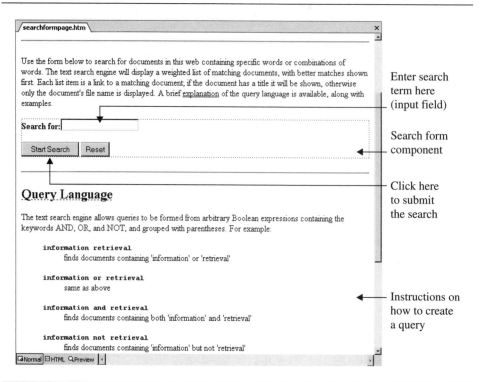

FIGURE 10-10 A search page includes the tools to perform a search, as well as instructions on how to do it.

Once you have your search page built, you can give it a title and save it just like any other page. You can also customize the properties of the search form component. To do so, right-click in the component and choose Search Form Properties from the shortcut menu to open the Search Form Properties dialog box.

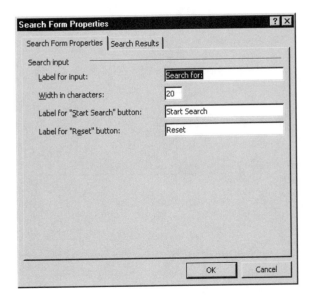

You can customize the search form using the following fields:

■ **Label for input**   To change the label for the field into which you type your search criteria, enter the label into this field.

■ **Width in characters**   To set the width of the Input field, type the number of characters into this field.

■ **Label for "Start Search" button**   To change the label for the button you click to start the search, type the label into this field.

■ **Label for "Reset" button**   To change the label for the button you click to clear the form, type the label into this field.

You can configure how you want the search results returned by clicking the Search Results tab.

10

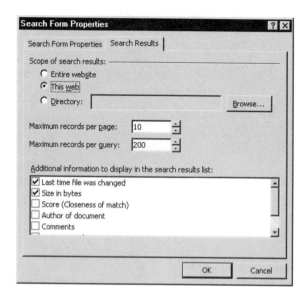

You can customize the search results as follows:

■ **Scope of search results** Choose one of the options in this section to limit the scope of the search. The options are

■ **Entire website** This option allows the search to proceed through (you guessed it!) the entire Web site.

■ **This web** This option limits the search to the current Web site. The results are the same as for the previous option unless you are viewing the contents of a subweb (a Web site contained within another Web site). If you *are* viewing the contents of a subweb, the search is limited to the subweb and ignores pages in other subwebs and in the parent Web site.

■ **Directory** Choose this option to limit the search to a particular directory within the current Web site. Select the directory by typing it into the field or clicking the Browse button and picking the directory from the resulting dialog box. This option is handy when your Web site contains multiple discussion groups (as mentioned earlier in this chapter), each in its own folder.

■ **Maximum records per page** To limit the number of records returned on each page of the search, set the limit in the Maximum Records Per Page spinner. If FrontPage finds more "hits" on your search term, it presents a button that enables you to view the next batch of pages that contain your search term.

- **Maximum records per query**   To limit the number of records returned by the entire query, set the limit in the Maximum Records Per Query spinner.

- **Additional information**   FrontPage can provide information about each of the documents in the list of documents that meet your search criteria. Check the checkbox for each item of information you want included. The items are

  - **Last time file was changed**   The date and time that the file was last modified.

  - **Size in bytes**   The size of the file.

  - **Score (Closeness of match)**   A score that indicates how closely the found file matches your search criteria.

  - **Author of document**   The "author" of the document. This field is only populated for Microsoft Office documents (such as Word documents) contained in the Web site. This field displays the contents of the Author field in the Summary tab of the document Properties dialog box.

  - **Comments**   Any comments attached to the found page. As with Author, this field is only populated for Microsoft Office documents contained in the Web site. It displays the contents of the Comments field in the Summary tab of the document Properties dialog box.

  - **Document subject**   Displays the contents of the Subject field in the Summary tab of a Microsoft Office document Properties dialog box.

  - **Matches**   Displays the number of matches within a given document.

Add a Web Search Component

To add the Web Search component to an existing page, choose Insert | Web Component. Choose Web Search from the Component Type list on the left side of the Insert Web Component dialog box and Current Web from the list on the right side. Click Finish to open the Search Form Properties dialog box (as discussed in the previous section). Customize the properties of the component and click OK to add the Web Search component to the page. Only the component itself is added to the page—the explanations on how to create a query are *not* included when you add the Web Search component.

Build a Form Using the Forms Templates

FrontPage provides templates for many general-purpose forms. These forms include a confirmation form, a feedback form, and a guest book. With several of these forms, you still need to do some setup work, but using one of the templates minimizes the amount of work you need to do.

Add a Confirmation Form

As mentioned earlier, you can use the Form Properties dialog box to specify a custom Web page that confirms the receipt of data submitted by someone on a form. This page is called a *confirmation form*. FrontPage provides a template for building a confirmation form that makes it relatively painless to build this page. Figure 10-11 shows a sample of what a confirmation form might look like.

The confirmation form in Figure 10-11 was automatically generated from the FrontPage confirmation form shown in Figure 10-12.

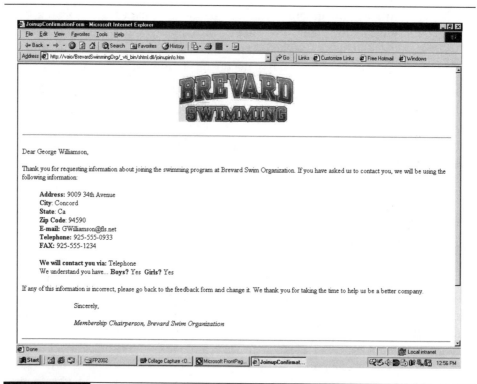

FIGURE 10-11   A good confirmation form should reflect the data submitted on the form.

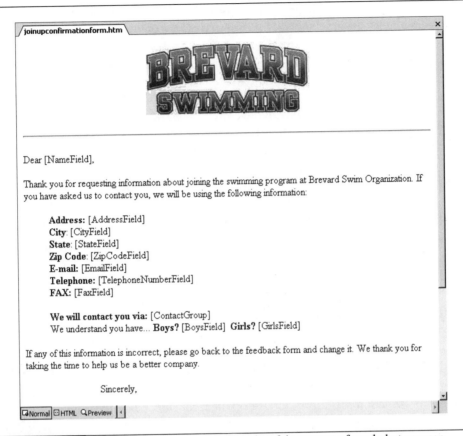

Dear [NameField],

Thank you for requesting information about joining the swimming program at Brevard Swim Organization. If you have asked us to contact you, we will be using the following information:

Address: [AddressField]
City: [CityField]
State: [StateField]
Zip Code: [ZipCodeField]
E-mail: [EmailField]
Telephone: [TelephoneNumberField]
FAX: [FaxField]

We will contact you via: [ContactGroup]
We understand you have... **Boys?** [BoysField] **Girls?** [GirlsField]

If any of this information is incorrect, please go back to the feedback form and change it. We thank you for taking the time to help us be a better company.

Sincerely,

FIGURE 10-12   Building a confirmation form is a fair amount of work, but you can customize exactly how you confirm the information you received.

To add a confirmation form, choose File | New Page or Web to display the New Page or Web Task Pane. Click on Page Templates, choose Confirmation Form from the Page Templates dialog box, and click OK.

NOTE *Realize that you don't have to build a confirmation form in order to achieve this functionality—FrontPage will provide a default confirmation form if you don't specify one. However, it is pretty ugly.*

The key to creating a good confirmation form is to specify the names of the fields on the submitted form whose contents you want to appear on the confirmation form. These fields appear within square brackets. When the reader sees the confirmation form in a browser, the confirmation fields in the square brackets are replaced with the actual value the reader placed in that field. The confirmation form generated by the template assumes that your form will have fields such as [username], [message type], [subject], and so on. If your original form does not include fields with these names, you must remove these references from the template-generated confirmation form. To change a field reference, you can either delete the field and add a field with the correct reference or change the existing field reference (both discussed shortly).

Normally, you won't want to be able to navigate to a confirmation page using hyperlinks, so don't add a confirmation page to the Navigation view. Or, if you do add it, deselect the Included In Navigation Bars option in the shortcut menu.

Modify the Confirmation Field Reference

To change an existing confirmation field reference, choose Confirmation Field Properties from the field's shortcut menu and change the name of the referenced field in the resulting dialog box.

Add a New Confirmation Field

To add a new field reference, you'll need to make a list of the field names on your submitted form. Switch to the confirmation form and choose Insert | Web Component to display the Insert Web Component dialog box. Choose Advanced Controls from the Component Type list on the left side of the dialog box, and select Confirmation Field from the list on the right side. Click Finish to display the Confirmation Field Properties dialog box, which has only a single field in it. Specify the name of the field from the submitted form to add to the confirmation form and click OK.

Add a Feedback Form

Feedback—about your Web site, your organization, or just about anything else—can be valuable in finding out what works and what doesn't. FrontPage provides a template for a feedback form, which is just a normal form (see Figure 10-13 for a sample).

To add a feedback form, choose File | New Page or Web to display the New Page or Web Task Pane. Click on Page Templates, choose Feedback Form from the Page Templates dialog box, and click OK.

Customize this form in any of the standard ways, including adding or removing fields, changing the text and graphics, applying validations to the fields (there aren't any by default), changing the values in the list, changing the type of file results, and attaching a confirmation form.

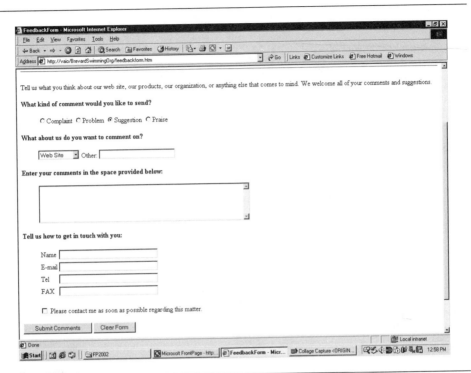

FIGURE 10-13 Use a feedback form to gather a reader's opinions.

> **TIP** *Remember to change the author and organization information at the bottom of the page. And change the copyright date (it reads 1999)!*

Build a Guest Book

The guest book is a form that enables people to make comments on a form, then displays a compilation of those comments on the same page as the form (see Figure 10-14).

The guest book "form" is actually a crafty combination of two FrontPage elements. The first element is a form into which you add your comments. These form results are saved into a HTML file in your Web. The second element is a FrontPage component called an *include page* (see Chapter 12 for more information). Basically, the included Web page—in this case, the form results HTML file—is embedded near the bottom of the guest book form. Thus, if you enter comments and press the Submit Comments button, these comments are written to the results HTML page. If you then refresh your browser, the results page updates and shows your comments—along with all the other comments that have been submitted. Pretty slick, eh?

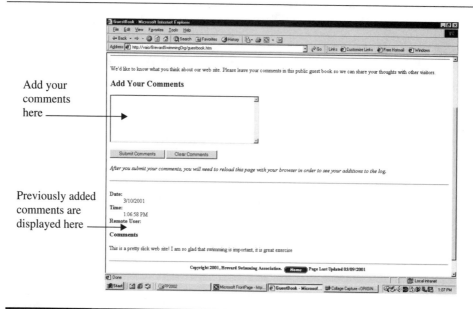

Add your
comments
here

Previously added
comments are
displayed here

FIGURE 10-14   Compile public comments in a guest book.

To add a feedback form, choose File | New Page or Web to display the New Page or Web Task Pane. Click on Page Templates, choose Guest Book from the Page Templates dialog box, and click OK. Once you have created the form, you can customize it just like any other form. You can even change the name of the file to which the results are sent—FrontPage will adjust the guest book page HTML to use the renamed results file. One thing you should *not* do is delete the filename for the results form or route only to an e-mail address. However, FrontPage will warn you if you make any changes like this that would invalidate the guest book form.

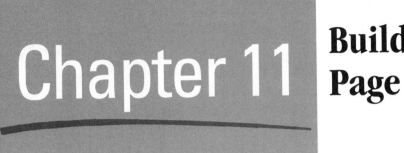

Chapter 11

Build a Frames Page

How to...

- Design frames pages
- Create and edit a frames page
- Use target frames
- Use FrontPage's frames templates
- Set up "no frames" support

Up to now, your Web site design has only allowed you to display a single page at any one time. This constraint puts a significant burden on the Web designer—you must provide navigation hyperlinks to other pages on every single page you build. Otherwise, a reader can get to a page and have no way to backtrack or move to another page except by using the built-in browser controls (the Back and Forward buttons). FrontPage eases this burden with shared borders and link bars, but the flexibility of these tools is somewhat limited. For example, you can't set the size of a shared border, and you must set up the Web hierarchy using Navigation view in order to specify which navigational hyperlinks appear in the Navigation bars.

NOTE *The major drawback to frames is that it is difficult for a reader to bookmark one of the pages on your site. With frames, the only URL you can see is the URL of the frames page (which contains the other pages—one in each frame). Thus, if you add any framed page to your Favorites or Bookmark list, and try to navigate back to that page, you return to the frames page, with its default contents visible.*

What Are Frames?

With frames, you can place multiple Web pages on the screen at the same time (see Figure 11-1) within a structure that you specify. This has the potential to make life much easier for someone visiting your site. For example, you can use one of the visible pages to display a list of hyperlinks to important sections of your site. When the reader clicks on a hyperlink, that page opens in another of the visible frame windows. The great advantage to frames is that you can keep your reader oriented as to where he or she is on your site. The links to other parts of the site (and to the home page) are always available. You can also use frames pages to display a constant header (with a company logo or name), footer, or both.

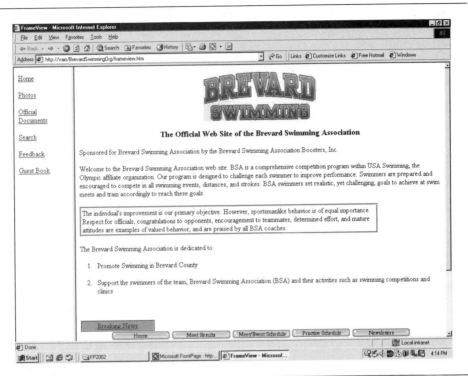

FIGURE 11-1 With multiple pages available, the reader can click a link in one window and have that page appear in another window on the screen.

Here are the essential parts of a frame setup:

■ **Frames page**   The frames page is the page that contains the other embedded pages. Each embedded page is contained within one frame of the frames page. The frames page is not visible to the reader, but it contains the frameset HTML tags that define the overall structure (size and number) of frames. In order to use frames, you will need to create a frames page.

TIP   *If you want your whole site to be framed, you should make your home page a frames page.*

■ **Frameset**   *Frameset* is what FrontPage calls the collection of frames that appear together in the frames pages. The code within the frameset tags (on the frames page) defines the layout of the frames page. The frameset is created automatically as you build the frames page.

11

- **One or more embedded pages** You need one initial page for each frame in the frames page. If you are using a simple content and main page layout (as shown in Figure 11-1), you need two embedded pages. If you use a more complex layout with additional frames, you need more embedded pages. Realize that the embedded pages themselves are just regular Web pages. There is nothing special about the pages, and these pages can be displayed in a nonframe environment as well. The magic of frames is all contained in the definition of the frames page.

Frame Design Considerations

Designing frame-based pages can be a tricky business, and it is easy to create frames that are hard to use. The first thing you need to understand when designing a frame-based environment is the difference between static elements and dynamic elements. A static element is a page that does not change as the reader navigates the site. The static page remains visible no matter what the reader does—it can be scrolled, but it is always present in its frame. The contents frame (at the left side of the window) in Figure 11-1 is static. A dynamic element, on the other hand, changes according to the reader's input. For example, when the reader clicks on a hyperlink in the contents frame, the page displayed in the main window (to the right of the contents frame in Figure 11-1) changes. Thus, the main window is dynamic.

As you design your frames environment, keep the following in mind:

- Minimize your static elements, and make them as small as possible. In general, static elements provide navigation and a reminder of what site the reader is viewing, and the main information is provided in the dynamic windows—so make the dynamic windows as large as possible.

- Don't use too many frames. The practical limit is about three, although you can get away with four if you keep three of them small. Adding too many frames to a page is confusing, and will force the reader to do too much scrolling in individual frames to see the information.

- Don't use frames just because you can. They do crowd up the screen, so they should only be used if they provide value to your Web site.

Create a Frames Page

Before you create a frames page, you should decide whether the embedded pages you are going to associate with the frames page will be new pages (which you can create as you create the frames page) or existing pages. It is somewhat simpler to associate existing pages with a frames page because there are fewer steps involved in building and saving the frames page. If you want to embed existing pages, make sure you have built the pages before starting on the steps below.

Choose and Populate a Template

To create a new frames page, use the following steps:

1. Choose File | New Page or Web to open the New Page or Web task pane. Choose Page Templates from the task pane to open the Page Templates dialog box, and click the Frames Pages tab, shown here.

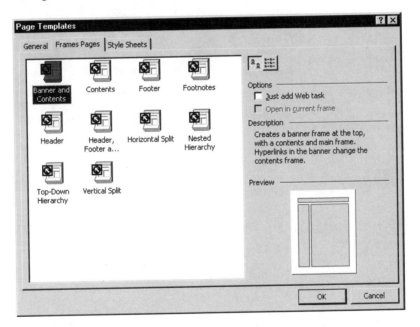

2. Click one of the templates and view the structure of the frames page that would result in the Preview section. When you have the layout you want, click OK to create the frames page (see Figure 11-2). The layout in this example places a navigational table of contents frame on the left side of the window, and the main window (which displays the page you choose from the hyperlinks in the left frame) on the right.

3. To embed an existing page in the right frame (or any other frame), click the Set Initial Page button. This opens the Insert Hyperlink dialog box.

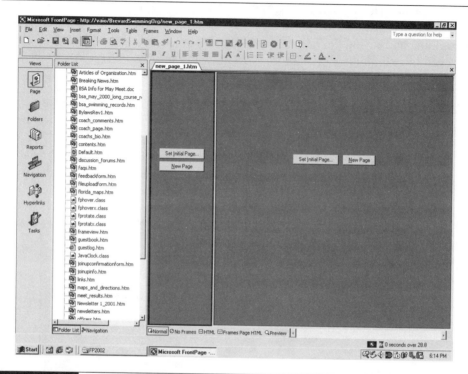

FIGURE 11-2 The new frames page shows you the structure, but not the contents, of the page.

Use the Insert Hyperlink dialog box to specify the address of the initial page to show in the frame.

4. Once the page's URL has been entered into the Address field, click OK to place the page in the frame.

> **TIP** *You can click and drag an existing page from the Folder List into the frame.*

You can now specify another existing page for the other frame. Alternatively, you can create a new page for the other frame. To create a new page, click the New Page button. This instantly creates a new, blank page in the frame. At this point, you can compose the page using any of FrontPage's tools. Remember to specify the page title from the Page Properties dialog box (choose Page Properties from the shortcut menu for the page).

One of the advantages to building the page within the frame structure is that you can see how the information on the page will be displayed. If you build the page normally (that is, not within the frame), you might find that the page doesn't work very well within the frame structure. One of the most common problems is that some of the information on the page is not visible because the frame is too small to show all the information you placed on the page.

Save the Frameset

Once you have your frames page set up the way you want, you need to save your work.

> **TIP**
>
> *Opening the Page Properties dialog box to change the page title of the frames page can be difficult. This is because right-clicking in the frames page does not bring up the page shortcut menu for the frames page—instead, it either displays the shortcut menu for a page in the individual frames (if you have assigned a page to the frame) or the Frame Properties shortcut menu (if you have not assigned a page). To easily access the shortcut menu for the frames page, click on a border between frames to highlight the outside of the frame page. Then choose File | Properties to open the Page Properties dialog box.*

The first time you save your work, FrontPage will prompt you to save the entire frameset—all the new pages you defined as well as the definition of the frames page. To save your work, use the following steps:

1. Choose File | Save. FrontPage opens the Save As dialog box. At the right side of the dialog box is a schematic of your frames page (see Figure 11-3).

2. For each new page, FrontPage highlights the section of the frames page in which the new page is embedded. Enter the filename for that page in the File Name field and click Save.

3. FrontPage saves the file and prompts you for the next new page (returns to step 2).

4. After all the new pages have been saved, FrontPage prompts you for the filename of the frames page itself. You can tell that the frames page is being saved because of the heavy border around the whole page (see Figure 11-4).

11

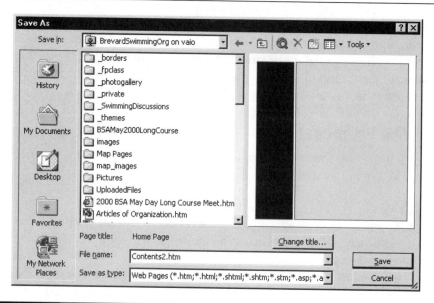

FIGURE 11-3 The Save As dialog box shows the structure of your frames page when you are saving a frameset.

> **TIP**
>
> *When viewing the list of pages on your Web site, it can be confusing to remember where each page fits into a frameset. Thus, it is helpful to name the pages with some indication of where the page is normally displayed. For example, you can name the contents page that goes in the left frame as "leftmenu.htm" or the page that goes in the top frame as "banner.htm".*

5. If you have not already assigned a title to the frames page, click the Change Title button and specify a new page title in the Set Page Title dialog box. Click OK to return to the Save As dialog box.

6. Enter the filename for the frames page and click Save.

> **NOTE**
>
> *If you make a change to a page in the frameset and want to save it right away, you can choose Frames | Save Page. This saves just the selected page. Using File | Save saves all the pages in the frameset, as well as any changes to the frames page itself (such as the frames' dimensions).*

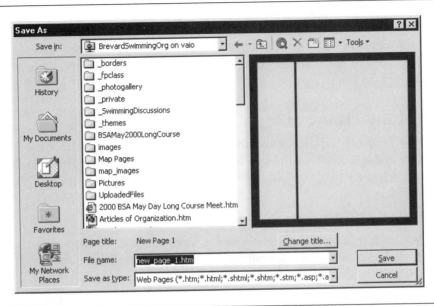

FIGURE 11-4   The heavy border around the frame shape indicates you are now saving the frames page definition.

Edit Pages in the Frameset

You can edit the pages visible within a frameset just as you would any other page. However, it can be quite awkward to work on a page if it is embedded within a small frame. To work around this, you can open the page normally from the Folder List and work on it in Page view. However, you must then save the page and open the frames page to see what the page will look like within the frame. There is a better way. Use the following steps to edit a page embedded in a frame:

1. Open the frames page so that you can see the page you want to work on.

2. Right-click on the page and choose Open Page in New Window from the shortcut menu. The page opens in normal Page view.

3. Edit the page as you normally would and save the results (choose File | Save).

4. Switch to the frames page by clicking on the page tab. If you like what you see, you are done. If not, click on the page tab for the embedded page and make more changes.

Edit the Frameset

Once you've created a frames page and the associated frameset, you aren't stuck with your design. You can change the size of each frame, as well as add or remove frames from the frameset.

Adjust the Frame Size

To adjust the size of a frame, move the mouse pointer over the border between two frames. Click and drag the border to increase or reduce the size of the frame. Adjacent frames automatically adjust their size to compensate for the size change.

Delete a Frame

You can delete a frame if you decide you no longer need it. The page associated with the frame, if any, is *not* deleted. To delete a frame, make sure the frame you want to delete is selected. Then choose Frames | Delete Frames.

Rename the Frames Page

You may decide to change the filename of the frames page. A good reason to do so would be to use the frames page as the home page for your Web site. In that case,

Split a Frame

You can split a frame into two frames. To do so, make sure the frame you want to split is selected. Then choose Frames | Split Frame. In the Split Frame dialog box, choose the option you want. Choose Split Into Columns to split the frame into vertical columns. Choose Split Into Rows to split the frame into horizontal rows. Choose OK to complete the split.

If you split the frame into columns, the leftmost column will contain the page originally associated with the frame you split. The rightmost column will display the standard buttons for associating a page with a frame: Set Initial Page and New Page. Use these buttons to associate a page with the new frame.

If you split the frame into rows, the uppermost row will contain the page originally associated with the frame you split. The lowest row will display the standard buttons for associating a page with a frame.

you'll want to change the filename of the frames page to Default.htm or Index.htm. You change the filename of a frames page just like any other page. One way is to locate the frames page file in the Folder List, and choose Rename from the page's shortcut menu. Then type in the new name.

Create an Inline Frame

If you want to display the contents of one page in another, you can use an inline frame (you can also use an include page, described in Chapter 13). To create an inline frame, choose Insert | Inline Frame. An inline frame works much like a regular frame—you can specify the size of the frame, and you can either specify an existing initial page or create a new page "on the fly" using the standard frame buttons.

11

NOTE *You can quickly create a new page in an inline frame by choosing New Inline Frame Page from the inline frame shortcut menu.*

You can also specify the alignment of the frame, choosing from all the same choices (and with the same results) as you would with a graphic. Inline frames are quite versatile in that you can resize them either by clicking and dragging the sizing handles or by using the Properties dialog box.

Another advantage of inline frames is that they are easy to create—just place the text cursor where you want the frame and choose Insert | Inline Frame. To configure an inline frame, choose Inline Frame Properties from the shortcut menu to display the Inline Frame Properties dialog box.

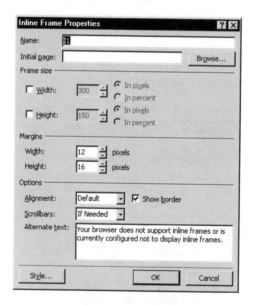

Besides the name (the significance of which is discussed in the next section), you can set the following properties:

- **Initial page** This is the page that will appear when the frame is first displayed. To choose this page from the dialog box, type in the address of the Web page or click the Browse button and select the page from the Edit Hyperlink dialog box that appears. You can also choose the initial page by clicking the Set Initial Page button in the frame.

- **Frame size** Set the width or height by checking the Width checkbox or Height checkbox and setting the size in the appropriate spinner. Choose whether to specify the size in pixels or in percent by picking either the In Pixels options or the In Percent option.

- ■ **Margins**   Set the width and height of the margins in pixels using the Width and Height spinners in the Margins section of the dialog box. These margins are the distances between the frame border and the page contained in the frame.

- ■ **Alignment**   Set the alignment of the inline frame on the page using the Alignment drop-down list. As mentioned earlier, the alignment options work exactly the same way as the graphics alignment options. For example, aligning the frame to the left places it against the left border of the page.

- ■ **Show border**   If you want the border of the inline frame to be visible, check the Show Border checkbox. If you clear the checkbox, the borders of the frame are invisible in Preview and in a browser (the borders are always visible in Normal Page mode).

- ■ **Scrollbars**   Choose whether to show scroll bars from the Scrollbars drop-down list. The three options are If Needed (shows if the embedded page is larger than the frame), Never (scroll bars are never shown) and Always (scroll bars are always shown).

- ■ **Alternate text**   Not all browsers can display inline frames—this feature takes advantage of HTML 4.0. If the reader's browser can't display inline frames, the browser will display the text in the Alternate Text field instead.

11

Modify the Frame Properties

To modify the frame properties, right-click in the frame and choose Frame Properties from the shortcut menu. This opens the Frame Properties dialog box.

Frame Properties	? ☒

Name: main

Initial page: Default.htm   Browse...

Frame size

Width: 1   Relative

Row height: 1   Relative

Margins

Width: 12

Height: 16

Options

☑ Resizable in browser   Frames Page...

Show scrollbars: If Needed

Style...   OK   Cancel

From the Frame Properties dialog box, you can configure the selected frame in the following ways:

- **Name**   Enter the frame's name in this field. This is *not* the name of the page; rather, it is the name of the frame, and it is used (as you'll see shortly) when specifying in which frame a hyperlinked page will open.

- **Initial page**   Enter the filename of the page that will open in this frame initially—that is, when you first activate this frames page, the page that will be displayed in this frame. You can click the Browse button to pick a page from the Edit Hyperlink dialog box.

- **Frame size**   Set the width and height using the appropriate spinners. The drop-down list alongside each quantity enables you to specify the width and height in Pixels, Percent (of the window), or Relative. Choose Pixels or Percent when you want a specific dimension (such as the width of the left column). Choose Relative when you want the frame to fill the rest of the window (examples of using Relative include the height of the left column, or both the width and height of the main window).

- **Margins**   Set the width and height of the frame margins in pixels. This invisible border is the distance between the frame border and the edge of the page that is embedded in the frame.

- **Resizable in browser**   Check this checkbox to allow the reader to resize the frame in his or her browser by clicking and dragging on a frame border. Of course, this does not change anything about the page as it is stored on the server, and the next time this person views the page, it is displayed in its default dimensions. If this checkbox is *not* checked, the reader cannot resize the frame while viewing the page.

- **Show scrollbars**   Choose the option you want from the drop-down list. The default value of If Needed displays scroll bars in the frame if the content is either too wide or too long to be displayed all at once.

- **Frames Page**   Click this button to display the Frames tab of the Page Properties (see Figure 11-5). In this tab, you can set the width of the borders using the Frame Spacing spinner. You can also show or hide the frame borders by checking or clearing the Show Borders checkbox.

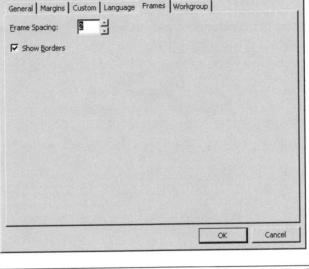

FIGURE 11-5   Use the Frames tab to set the border width and visibility for a frame.

Understand Target Frames

One of the trickier aspects of setting up a frames page is specifying in which frame a hyperlinked page will open. For example, take a look at Figure 11-6. When you click a hyperlink in the banner frame across the top of the screen, the hyperlinked page should open in the contents frame that runs down the left side. When you click a hyperlink in the contents frame, the hyperlinked page should open in the main window. And when you click a hyperlink in the main window, the hyperlinked page should open in the main window, replacing the current contents. But how do you make all that happen?

Set the Page Default Target Frame

The name of the frame in which a hyperlinked page will appear is set by an attribute called a *target frame*. You can set the target frame in one of two places.

Hyperlinks in this window should open in the main frame

Hyperlinks in this window should open in the contents frame

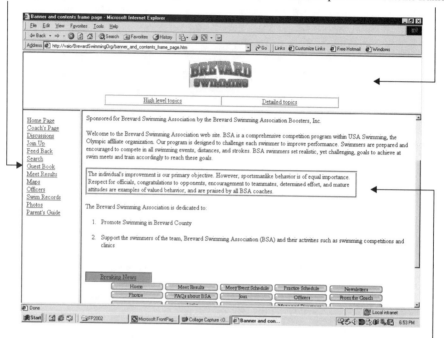

Hyperlinks in this window should open in the main frame (replacing the current page)

FIGURE 11-6 You must control where a hyperlinked page opens in order to make frames work the way you want.

First of all, you can set the default target frame for all hyperlinks on a page. To do so, open the Page Properties dialog box (see Figure 11-7). In the General tab is a field called Default Target Frame. This field specifies the name of the frame in which hyperlinks on that page will appear *if they are not overridden by the hyperlink itself* (more on this in a moment).

The contents of the Default Target Frame field are not directly editable. To set the value in this field, click the Change Target Frame button (the one with the pencil on it). This opens the Target Frame dialog box.

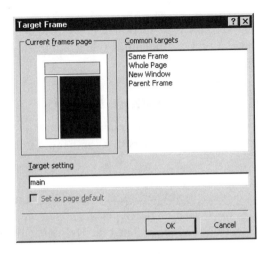

Although you can enter the name of the frame into the Target Setting field, it is much easier to simply click the frame in the graphic that you want to be the default target frame for the page. There are several additional options available to you in

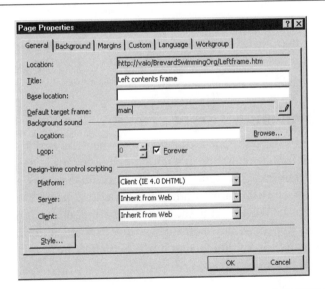

FIGURE 11-7   The Default Target Frame field specifies the name of the default frame for all hyperlinks on the page.

11

this dialog box, discussed in the next section. Click OK to choose the frame and close the Target Frame dialog box, then click OK again to close the Page Properties dialog box.

Direct Hyperlinks to Common Targets

In the Common Targets list in the Target Frame dialog box there are predefined targets that are understood by all browsers that can handle frames. Here is what they mean:

- **Same Frame**   Opens the hyperlinked page in the same frame window the current page uses. That is, the hyperlinked page replaces the current page in the same frame window. The other frames in the frameset are not affected.

- **Whole Page**   Closes the current frames window, and opens the hyperlinked page in the full browser window.

- **New Window**   Leaves the current frames window as it is and opens the hyperlinked page in a new instance of the browser.

- **Parent Frame**   This option only works for nested frames—that is, a frameset that exists in a page of another frameset. This option closes the current nested frameset and opens the hyperlinked page in the next higher frameset.

Define a Hyperlink Target Frame

You can also set the target frame for a hyperlink when you define the hyperlink itself. Any target frame you define in a hyperlink will override the default set for the page. Any hyperlink—text, graphics, buttons, or image maps—can have a target frame. To specify the target frame for a hyperlink, begin by defining the hyperlink in the usual way to get to the Insert Hyperlink dialog box. Alternatively, select an existing hyperlink and choose Hyperlink Properties from the shortcut menu to open the Edit Hyperlink dialog box. Then click the Target Frame button to open the Target Frame dialog box.

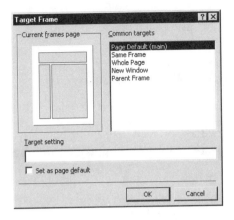

The Target Frame dialog box looks much like the one we saw previously, and you select a target frame the same way: Click the frame in the graphic that you want as the target frame. However, there are two important differences in this version of the Target Frame dialog box. First of all, there is another choice in the Common Targets list: Page Default. You can pick the page's default target frame as the hyperlink's target frame by clicking the Page Default selection. The other difference is the Set As Page Default checkbox (which was grayed out before). Once you pick a target frame for this hyperlink, you can make that target frame the default for the whole page by checking this checkbox. Any hyperlinks that use the page default will now use the target frame you define here.

Create Template-Based Pages for a Frameset

We've already mentioned that you can add pages to a frameset using either the Set Initial Page button or the New Page button. And, once you do, you can specify the target frame for the page using the Target Frame dialog box. However, if you choose the New Page button, FrontPage provides a blank Web page for the frame. What if you want to create a new page for a frameset based on one of the many useful templates provided with FrontPage?

You can create pages based on a template and add the page to a frameset, provided that the frame (in the frames page) to which you want to add the new page does not currently have a page associated with it (that is, the frame still shows the Set Initial Page button). To create and add a new page to a frameset, use the following steps:

1. Open the frameset to which you want to add the newly created page.

2. Pick the frame in the frameset where the page will appear.

3. Choose File | New Page or Web to open the New Page or Web task pane. Click Page Templates in the task pane to open the Page Templates dialog box.

4. In the Page Templates dialog box, click the Frames tab, pick a template, and be sure to check the Open In Current Frame checkbox. This checkbox is grayed out (unavailable) if the frameset has a page already associated with every frame.

5. Click OK to open the new page in the selected frame.

6. Right-click the page and choose Page Properties from the shortcut menu.

7. In the resulting Page Properties dialog box, click the Change Target Frame button (the one with the pencil on it). Use the Target Frame dialog box to set the default target frame for the page, and click OK to close the Target Frame dialog box.

8. Give the new page a title and any other configuration options you want in the Page Properties dialog box. Then click OK to close the Page Properties dialog box.

9. Make any changes you want to the page itself and then save your work. All hyperlinks on the new page will be directed to the specified target frame.

Save a Custom Frameset as a Template

You can spend quite a bit of time building a frameset to get it just the way you want. If you think you might want to use the frameset again, you can save it as a template so it will appear on the Frames tab of the New dialog box. To save a frameset as a template, use the following steps:

1. Open the frameset in Page view.

2. Choose File | Save As to open the Save As dialog box. The overall frame is highlighted on the right side of the dialog box.

3. In the Save As Type list, choose FrontPage Template (*.tem). Supply the name of the template in the File Name field.

4. Click the Save button. FrontPage opens the Save As Template dialog box.

5. Enter the title of the template, the name, and a description. If you want the template saved only as part of the current Web site (so it will only be available in the current Web site), check the Save Template In Current Web checkbox.

6. Click OK to finish saving the template.

7. If any of the pages in the frameset use graphics, FrontPage provides the Save Embedded Files dialog box. This is because graphics associated with a template are saved in a different place than the graphics associated with a regular page in a Web site.

8. Click OK to save the embedded files to the destination suggested by FrontPage and create the template.

The template will be available in the Frames tab of the New dialog box (which appears when you create a new Web page). As you can see from Figure 11-8, you can now choose your new template by its title, see a preview of it, and read the description.

Use FrontPage's Frame Templates

FrontPage supplies a number of useful frame-based templates for you to use. They are

- **Banner and Contents** This template creates a three-frame frameset. There is a banner that stretches across the top of the page, a contents frame that

11

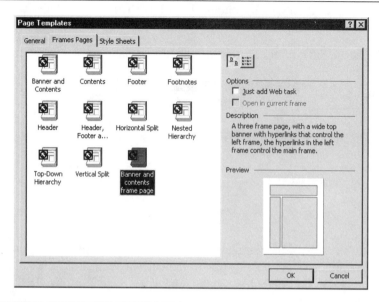

FIGURE 11-8   Pick your new template from the list of templates when you go to create
a new Web page.

stretches down the left side, and a main frame that fills most of the frameset.
Hyperlinks in the banner frame change the page in the contents frame, and
hyperlinks in the contents frame change the page in the main frame.

- **Contents**   This template creates a two-frame frameset. There is a
  contents frame that stretches down the left side and a main frame that fills
  the rest of the frameset. Hyperlinks in the contents frame change the page
  in the main frame.

- **Footer**   This template creates a two-frame frameset. There is a footer
  frame that stretches across the bottom of the screen, and a main frame that
  fills the rest of the frameset. Hyperlinks in the footer frame change the
  page in the main frame.

- **Footnotes**   This template creates a two-frame frameset. There is a
  footnotes frame that stretches across the bottom of the screen, and a main
  frame that fills the rest of the frameset. This template works the opposite to
  the Footer template—hyperlinks in the main frame change the page in the
  footnotes frame. This template is most often used to display a document in
  the main window that has footnote references. Each footnote reference in

the main window is a hyperlink that points to its footnote. Place all the footnotes on a single page, bookmark each footnote, and link the footnote references in the main page to the appropriate bookmark in the footnote page.

■ **Header** This template creates a two-frame frameset. There is a header frame that stretches across the top of the screen, and a main frame that fills the rest of the frameset. Hyperlinks in the header frame change the page in the main frame.

■ **Header, Footer and Contents** This template creates a four-frame frameset. There is a header frame that stretches across the top of the screen, a footer frame that stretches across the bottom of the screen, a contents frame that stretches down the left side of the screen, and a main frame that fills the rest of the frameset (see Figure 11-9). Hyperlinks in the header and footer frames change the page in the contents frame, and hyperlinks in the contents frame change the page in the main frame.

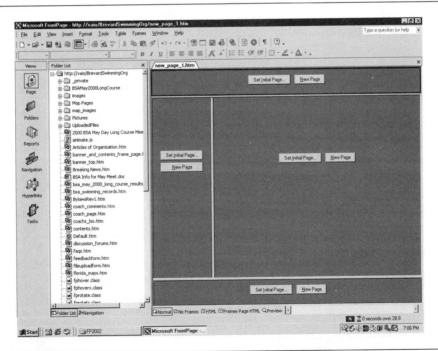

FIGURE 11-9 The complex Header, Footer and Contents frameset gives you four frames to work with.

■ **Horizontal Split** This template creates a two-frame frameset. The two frames split the screen horizontally, and each of the frames are independent: Hyperlinks in each frame replace the page in that frame.

■ **Nested Hierarchy** This template creates a hierarchical three-frame frameset (see Figure 11-10). The hyperlinks in the left frame change the page in the upper-right frame, and hyperlinks in the upper-right frame change the page in the lower-right frame.

■ **Top-Down Hierarchy** This template creates a hierarchical three-frame frameset, with each window stretching across the screen. The hyperlinks in the topmost frame change the page in the middle frame, and hyperlinks in the middle frame change the page in the bottom frame.

■ **Vertical Split** This template creates a two-frame frameset. The two frames split the screen vertically, and each of the frames are independent: Hyperlinks in each frame replace the page in that frame.

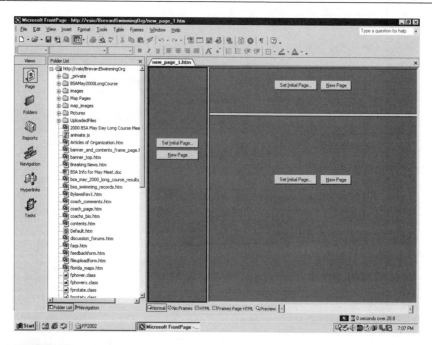

FIGURE 11-10 The Nested Hierarchy template establishes a hierarchy of linked pages from left to right, and then down.

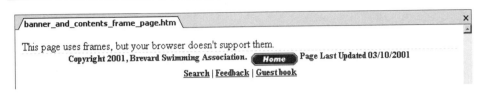

banner_and_contents_frame_page.htm   ×

This page uses frames, but your browser doesn't support them.
　　Copyright 2001, Brevard Swimming Association. (**Home**) Page Last Updated 03/10/2001
　　　　　　　　　　Search | Feedback | Guestbook

FIGURE 11-11   Use the No Frames version of a frames page to support
　　　　　　　　non-frame-enabled browsers.

Set Up "No Frames" Support

Although it is getting rarer, there are still people who surf the Internet with
browsers that don't support frames. You can provide a version of the frames page
for non-frame-enabled browsers. To do so, open the frames page in Page view. At
the bottom of the screen, you'll see a tab marked No Frames. Click it to view the
No Frames page (see Figure 11-11).

This "page" is not a new page (you won't see it in the Folder List, for example).
Instead, it is an alternate view of the frames page. By default, this page simply
contains the text "This page uses frames, but your browser doesn't support them."
However, you can customize this page just like any other page, including adding text
and graphics, shared borders, Navigation bars, and so on. Don't forget to save your
work when you are done.

NOTE *If you added shared borders to all pages in your Web site, the No Frames
page will already contain the shared borders (as the shared bottom border
visible in Figure 11-11 illustrates).*

11

Part III

Advanced Web Tools

Chapter 12

Add Content with Web Components

How to...

- Understand Web components
- Add various Web components to the page

In this chapter, we are going to cover some of the features that set FrontPage apart from other Web site creation tools. Web components enable you to add sophisticated features to your pages without programming.

It is important to keep in mind that because of the sophistication of these features, they must be used with caution. For example, Web components require a server-based Web site to function—they won't run on a disk-based Web. Furthermore, the server must have the FrontPage 2002 extensions installed.

 *A few of the items in the Insert | Web Component menu have been covered previously. These include the Confirmation Field, Search Form, Photo Gallery, and Link Bars.*

What Are Web Components?

Web components are where the real power of FrontPage starts to show. Web components (Microsoft called them webbots in earlier versions of FrontPage, and the HTML generated still reflects this heritage) automate certain processes that would otherwise have required you to write code in HTML or in a scripting language. When you add a Web component to a Web page, you are embedding some programming code in the Web page. This code executes when certain events occur. For example, the hover button code executes when the reader moves the mouse pointer on top of the button.

Place Web Components

In general, you add a Web component to a Web page by choosing Insert | Web Component, and choosing the component you want to add from the Insert Web Component dialog box. Most components require that you set some parameters that determine how the component operates—such as choosing the counter style for the hit counter. You may have to do some preparatory work, such as setting up the graphics to cycle for the Banner Ad Manager. This might seem like a lot of work, but compared to what it would take to implement this Web component using manual coding, FrontPage's Web components make your Web site construction work much easier.

Place a Banner Ad Manager

This Web component displays a list of images for a particular length of time, using a specified transition from one image to the next. Although originally designed for advertising, you can use the Banner Ad Manager to animate the heading of a page or even present an ongoing slide show. The Banner Ad Manager is usually displayed at the top of a page (hence the name), but you can actually place it anywhere on the page. It is a Java applet, and so will work in Netscape Navigator 3 and later, as well as in Internet Explorer 3 and later.

Before beginning, you'll need to either create or identify the various graphics you are going to use as the banners. In addition, you will need to make a note of the pixel height of the tallest image and the pixel width of the widest image so you'll know the largest dimension of the banner. For best results, the images should all be close to the same size.

To create a Banner Ad Manager, use the following steps:

1. Choose Insert | Web Component and select Dynamic Effects from the Component Type list. Choose Banner Ad Manager from the list on the right side of the dialog box and click Finish to open the Banner Ad Manager Properties dialog box.

12

2. Type the width of the widest image into the Width field, and the height of the tallest image in the Height field.

3. Select the transition between the images from the Transition Effect drop-down list. Various effects include dissolve, blinds, and box in or box out.

> **TIP** *The best way to choose a transition effect is to create one, save the page, and preview the page in your browser.*

4. Specify how long (in seconds) you want each image displayed using the Show Each Picture For (Seconds) field.

5. If you want the reader to be able to click the banner ad and jump to a hyperlinked page, specify the destination in the Link To field. You can either type in the URL of the destination page or click the Browse button to use the Select Banner Ad Hyperlink dialog box to choose the destination. This dialog box looks just like the Insert Hyperlink dialog box you should be familiar with.

6. Click the Add button to open the Add Picture For Banner Ad dialog box—which is just a standard FrontPage image file location dialog box. From here you can pick images in your current Web site, on your hard drive, or even on the Internet. Pick the image you want and click OK to return to the Banner Ad Manager dialog box. The image you picked is listed in the Pictures To Display list.

7. Continue adding images to the Pictures To Display list (up to a maximum of 10). If you want to rearrange the images in the list, choose a file and click Move Up or Move Down. If you change your mind about including a graphic, choose the file and click the Remove button.

8. Choose OK when you are finished specifying the images. In normal Page view, the first image in the list will appear. In preview Page view, the images will cycle just as you specified.

> **NOTE** *If you choose images outside your Web site, the Save Embedded Files dialog box will appear when you save the page so you can save the images into your Web site. You must do this—the Banner Ad Manager will not work if it tries to reference an image that is not in the current Web site. In other words, do not use the Set Action button to force the graphic reference to remain outside the Web site.*

If you click the banner ad in normal Page view, you'll see sizing handles. You can click and drag these sizing handles to adjust the size of the banner.

Adding a Hit Counter

A hit counter counts the number of times a page has been viewed—the number of "hits" on the page. This can give you some idea how popular a page is. Hit counters (see Figure 12-1) are popular on the Web. Typical hit counters use some explanatory text, such as "This page has been viewed" and the date the hit counter started counting.

The hit counter works properly in version 3 browsers (both Netscape and Internet Explorer) and later.

To create a hit counter, use the following steps:

1. Choose Insert | Web Component and select Hit Counter from the Component Type list. The right side of the dialog box displays the various styles for hit counters.

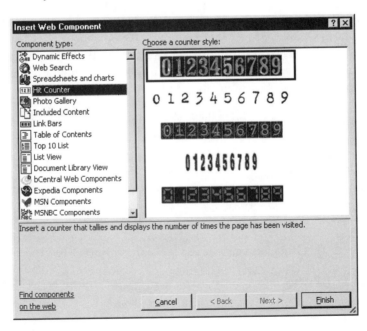

2. Select a style and click Finish to display the Hit Counter Properties dialog box.

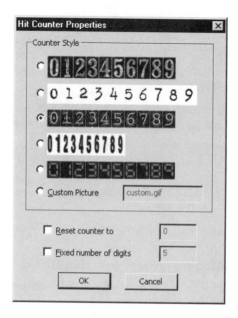

3. Select the style of the hit counter numbers by choosing one of the options in the Hit Counter Properties dialog box. If you choose the Custom Picture option, you must specify an image that includes all the numbers (0–9). The numbers *must* be evenly spaced. That is, all the rectangles that contain the numbers must be *exactly* the same size.

4. If you want to start the hit counter at a number other than 1, check the Reset Counter To checkbox and enter the starting number in the adjacent field.

This Page has been viewed **23** times since 3/10/01

Copyright 2001, Brevard Swimming Association. **Home** Page Last Updated 03/10/2001
Search | Feedback | Guestbook

FIGURE 12-1   A hit counter tells how many times a page has been viewed.

> TIP *You can also use the Reset Counter To checkbox to reset the counter to zero. You might want to do this when you first publish your page to the Internet, erasing the "hits" that resulted from testing the page.*

5. If you always want the same number of digits (for example, you want to see 00007 instead of 7), check the Fixed Number Of Digits checkbox and fill in the number of digits in the adjacent field.

6. Click OK to save the hit counter parameters.

The position of the hit counter on the page is indicated by the text [Hit Counter]. To view the hit counter, click on the Preview tab or preview the page in a browser.

Place a Hover Button

Have you ever seen a button on a Web site that seemed to know when the mouse pointer passed over it? Because such buttons seem to come to life when the mouse pointer hovers over it, these buttons are known as *hover buttons*. The hover buttons create Java applets, and therefore run just fine in version 3 (or later) of either Netscape Navigator or Internet Explorer. To add a hover button, place the cursor where you want to insert the button and choose Insert | Web Component. Select Dynamic Effects from the Component Type list and choose Hover Button from the list on the right side of the dialog box. Click Finish to open the Hover Button Properties dialog box.

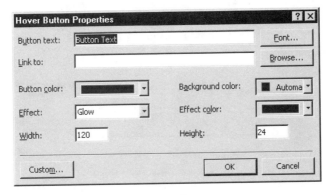

Configure the hover button as follows:

■ **Button text**   In this field, enter the text to be displayed on the button.

- **Font**   Click this button if you want to change the font properties. The resulting dialog box lets you change the font, style, size, and color of the button text. However, the list of fonts is limited to a few standard ones: Arial, MS Sans Serif, Courier New, and Times New Roman.

- **Link to**   Specify a hyperlink destination for the button in this field. If a reader clicks the button, the hyperlinked destination page will appear. You can click the Browse button to open the Select Hover Button Hyperlink dialog box—which is just a standard dialog box for creating hyperlinks.

- **Button color**   Set the color of the button using this drop-down list. This displays the standard color.

 You can also set a background color, but it doesn't seem to have any effect, because the button doesn't have a background.

- **Effect**   Use this drop-down list to pick the color effect when the mouse pointer hovers over the button. Choices include color fill, color average, glow, reverse glow, light glow, and beveling.

- **Effect color**   If you want the button to change color when the mouse pointer hovers over it, pick the color from this drop-down list. The drop-down list is identical to the Button Color drop-down list.

- **Width and Height**   Set the button width and height in the Width and Height fields, respectively.

If you want to customize the hover button further, click the Custom button to open the Custom dialog box.

In the Custom dialog box, you can configure the hover button with the following options:

- **Play sound**   You can play a sound either On Click or On Hover. To specify the sound, type in the filename of the sound in these fields, or click the Browse button to pick the sound file. However, because the hover button is a Java applet, only AU or SND sound files can be used. More common formats (such as WAV or MID) won't work.

- **Custom**   You can specify that the button use a custom image (specify an image in the Button field) and that the image change when the reader hovers the mouse pointer over the button (specify an image in the On Hover field). The advantage to using your own graphics is that you can use any combination of color and fonts. Clicking the Browse button opens a standard dialog box for locating and selecting a graphic image file.

To preview the button, save your page and switch to preview Page view. Move your mouse pointer over the button to see (and hear) the effect.

Place a Marquee

Marquees (the term is taken from Broadway and movie theatres) are boxes that have text scrolling through them. Marquees function only in Internet Explorer. They appear in Netscape Navigator, but do not scroll.

To insert a marquee, choose Insert | Web Component and select Dynamic Effects from the Component Type list. Choose Marquee from the list on the right side of the dialog box and click Finish to open the Marquee Properties dialog box.

12

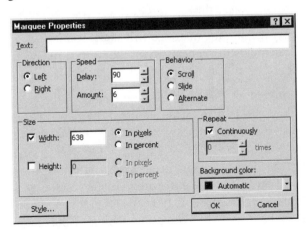

Configure the marquee as follows:

- **Text**   Place the text of the marquee in this field.

- **Direction**   Set the scroll direction by choosing the Left or Right option.

- **Speed**   Use the Delay spinner to set the delay. A large value causes the text to move in increments; a small value causes the text to move more smoothly.

- **Amount**   Set the distance the text moves with each cycle. A large value causes the text to move quickly (with a somewhat jerky movement), a small value causes the text to travel slowly, covering a shorter distance each time it moves.

- **Behavior**   Set the scroll behavior of the text using the options. Scroll causes the text to scroll in from one side and scroll off the other side. Slide causes the text to scroll onto the screen and stop. Alternate causes the text to scroll onto the screen, stop, disappear, and then scroll onto the screen again.

- **Width**   You can set the width of the marquee by checking the Width checkbox, setting the width in the adjacent field, and choosing whether the width is to be measured In Pixels or In Percent. If you don't set the width, the marquee width will be the entire width of the window.

- **Height**   You can set the height of the marquee by checking the Height checkbox, specifying the height in the adjacent field, and choosing whether the height is to be measured In Pixels or In Percent. If you don't set the height, the marquee height will be sufficient to hold the text with a small border. If you increase the text size, the marquee height will grow as well.

- **Repeat**   By default, the marquee will scroll continuously. If you want to set a specific number of repeats, clear the Continuously checkbox and set the number of repetitions in the adjacent spinner.

- **Background color**   Set the background color of the marquee by clicking the drop-down list to display the standard color tool. The Automatic choice ensures that the marquee background is the same as the page.

You can adjust the font and paragraph properties of the marquee using the standard formatting tools. To do so, select the marquee (sizing handles appear) and apply the formatting you want. For example, you can align the marquee on the page by using the alignment buttons in the Formatting toolbar. Note that the formatting applies to all the text in the marquee—you can't select just a portion of the marquee text. You can use the Font and Size drop-down lists in the Formatting toolbar, as well as the effects buttons (bold, italics, underline) and the Text color tool to set the properties of the marquee text. You can even choose Format | Font and specify all the font properties from the Font dialog box. In addition, you can click and drag a sizing handle to adjust the size of the marquee on the page.

> **TIP** *Want to use a graphic in the marquee? It's easy. Just choose Format | Borders And Shading, click the Shading tab, and specify a picture in the Background Picture field in the Patterns section. The chosen picture appears as a background to the marquee and the text scrolls over the picture. Make sure the background color is set to Automatic or you won't be able to see the picture. If the picture is too busy, you can center the marquee and decrease its width so that it appears in a section of the middle of the page. Change the background color of the marquee (in the Marquee Properties dialog box) to the same color as the page. That way, the marquee text scrolls across a solid color, but the background picture shows through at the edges of the marquee.*

Place an Include Page

One of the banes of the Web site designer is information that must be present in many places throughout a Web site. Examples might include your contact information or a set of graphics (such as a collection of logos). You can place such information on every page that needs it, but when the information changes, you must hunt down all its occurrences and change them. Of course, you've seen some tools—such as shared borders—that help this situation because they are the same on every page. But FrontPage offers another solution: Include Pages. The Include Page Web component inserts the contents of one page into other pages (sometimes referred to as "parent" pages). By using the Include Page component, you only have to build the information content once, and then repeat it as many times as you need by using the Include Page component on other pages. The advantage to this approach is if the information changes (your logo or your e-mail address, for example), you only need to change the data in the included page. Each page that uses the Include Page component will change automatically when the included page changes.

To use the Include Page Web component, choose Insert | Web Component and select Included Content from the Component Type list. Choose Page from the list on the right side of the dialog box and click Finish to open the Include Page Properties dialog box.

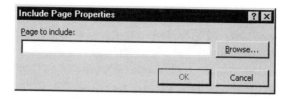

All you need to do is specify the URL of the page to include. You can either type in the URL or use the Browse button to open the Current Web dialog box and choose the file from a list.

Place a Scheduled Picture

The Scheduled Picture component places a picture on a Web page during a specified time period. If the time period has not yet arrived or has expired, an alternate picture is displayed (if one was specified) or nothing is displayed (if no alternate picture was specified). This component is especially useful when displaying graphics that are date-based. For example, a graphic related to Christmas or Valentine's Day would be a prime candidate for a scheduled picture.

To add a Scheduled Picture component to a page, Choose Insert | Web Component and select Included Content from the Component Type list. Choose Picture Based On Schedule from the list on the right side of the dialog box and click Finish to open the Scheduled Picture Properties dialog box.

In the dialog box, configure the Scheduled Picture using the following steps:

1. Use the During The Scheduled Time field to specify the image to display. You can either type in the URL of the image or click the Browse button to open the Picture dialog box and pick the image.

2. If you want an image to be displayed outside of the scheduled time, specify the image in the Before And After The Scheduled Time field. Once again, you can either type in the URL of the image or click the Browse button to pick the image. If you leave this field empty, no image is displayed outside of the specified time range when the reader views the page in a browser.

3. Use the fields in the Starting section to specify the beginning of the specified time.

4. Use the fields in the Ending section to specify the end of the specified time.

5. Click OK to finish defining the scheduled picture.

Save the page. As usual, if you picked an image that is not stored in the current Web site, you'll see the Save Embedded File dialog box to give you an opportunity to save the image within the Web site.

Although the image looks normal, the Scheduled Picture component does not behave like a regular image. You can select the image, but the Picture toolbar does not appear, so you don't have an opportunity to change the image. The shortcut menu for the image includes the item Scheduled Picture Properties, but it does not include Picture Properties, so you can't adjust the picture type, borders, or the other image properties. You can, however, adjust the alignment of the Scheduled Picture component using the alignment buttons in the Formatting toolbar. You can also assign a hyperlink to the Scheduled Picture component by choosing Hyperlink in the shortcut menu (or any of the other ways of inserting a hyperlink). However, you cannot assign hotspots to a Scheduled Picture component, so you cannot create an image map.

TIP   *If you want to schedule a graphic that contains an image map, use the Scheduled Include Page component (see the next section for details). Add the graphic to the page you are going to include (and schedule) and modify the graphic to add hotspots and hyperlinks.*

12

Place a Scheduled Include Page

A somewhat more versatile option than the Scheduled Picture component is the Scheduled Include Page. Like an Include Page, this component enables you to specify a page to be included in one or more parent pages. The difference is that you can schedule the included page—showing one page within the scheduled time, and a different page (or no page) outside the scheduled time.

To add a Scheduled Include Page component, Choose Insert | Web Component and select Included Content from the Component Type list. Choose Page Based On Schedule from the list on the right side of the dialog box and click Finish to open the Scheduled Include Page Properties dialog box. This displays the very same dialog box (except for the title) shown in the previous illustration. The only difference is that you fill in an HTML file (Web page) instead of an image.

Once you've inserted the Scheduled Include Page, you can't edit it in place or change its properties (the Page Properties entry in the shortcut menu refers to the main page, not the included page). However, you can simply open the included page itself and edit it just like any other page. The easiest way to accomplish this is to choose the Open Page In New Window option from the shortcut menu. Simply edit the included page in the normal Page view, save it, and switch back to the parent page to view the changes.

Place a Table of Contents

If you've got a complex site, you might wish to use the Table Of Contents component. This dynamic component creates a table of contents (see Figure 12-2) of the specified portion of your Web site. The Table Of Contents component traces the hyperlinks from a specified Web page. Thus, you can include all the pages that are linked from the home page or a subsection of your Web. When readers view the table of contents, they can jump to any page by clicking the entry (hyperlink) for that page.

NOTE *Since the Table Of Contents component uses the page titles as the text for the hyperlinks, make sure each page has a descriptive title.*

You can add a table of contents to your Web site either by using the Web component or by creating a table of contents page with one of the page templates provided by FrontPage.

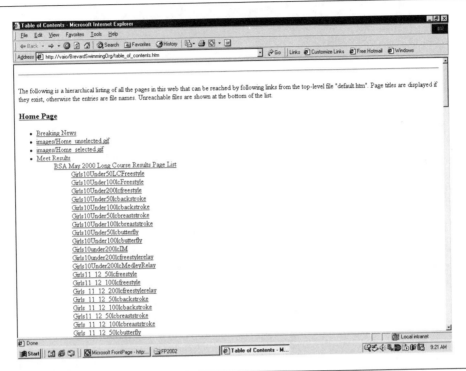

FIGURE 12-2   A table of contents makes it easy to jump to any page on your site.

12

 The Table of Contents component for an entire Web site shows all files that can be reached via a hyperlink. Thus, if you create a hover button (with its associated hyperlinks) and use custom images for the button (as described earlier in this chapter), these images will show up in the table of contents listing. There is no way to suppress this, so if you are planning to use a table of contents, you may wish to avoid using custom images hover buttons.

Add a Table of Contents Web Component for the Web Site

To add a Table Of Contents Web component to a page, Choose Insert | Web Component and select Table of Contents from the Component Type list. Choose For This Web Site from the list on the right side of the dialog box and click Finish to open the Table of Contents Properties dialog box.

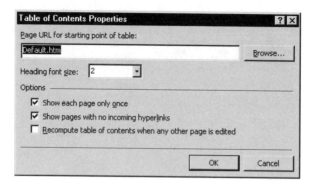

Configure the Table Of Contents Web component as follows:

- **Page URL for starting point of table**   Specify the page from which the table of contents starts in this field. The Web component follows all the hyperlinks from this page in constructing the entries in the table of contents. If you want all the linked pages in your site displayed in the table of contents, start from your home page. The starting page also determines which pages are displayed to the far left in the table of contents. Destination pages pointed to by hyperlinks on the starting page are indented one level in the table of contents.

- **Heading font size**   Choose the heading size from the drop-down list. The heading is taken from the page title of the starting page. For example, if the starting page is the home page, the text of the heading will reflect the page title of your home page. The heading is a hyperlink to the starting page.

> **TIP**   *Many Web designers place their table of contents right on their home page, and make the home page the starting point. In this case, you probably don't want the heading hyperlink, which points to the starting page—a circular reference that does you no good. To suppress the heading, simply choose None from the Heading Font Size drop-down list.*

- **Show each page only once**   Check this checkbox to keep a page that is the destination of many hyperlinks from appearing over and over in the table of contents. If you clear this checkbox, the page will be shown once for each hyperlink that points to it.

- **Show pages with no incoming hyperlinks**   Check this checkbox to show all pages on the site, including "orphan" pages that are not the destination of any hyperlink.

■ **Recompute table of contents when any other page is edited**   Check
this checkbox to automatically update the entries in the table of contents
whenever you edit a page. This can take a while for a large site, so you'll
probably want to leave this checkbox cleared. To manually update the table
of contents at the end of an editing session, open the page that contains the
Table Of Contents Web component and resave it.

Once you've created your table of contents, you can't actually view it in
FrontPage. In both normal and preview Page views, you'll see three dummy
entries, which you cannot edit. To view the table of contents, you must view
it using a browser and accessing the page through a server (as in Figure 12-2,
above). For a disk-based Web site, you must publish the Web site to the hosting
service and view the page in a browser. For a server-based Web site, you can view
the page using the Preview In Browser function.

Add a Table of Contents Based on Page Category

If you've gone to the trouble of setting up categories for your pages (as described
in Chapter 5), you can create a table of contents for pages in one or more of the
categories. To do so, choose Insert | Web Component and select Table Of Contents
from the Component Type list. Select Based On Page Category from the list on the
right side of the dialog box and click Finish to open the Categories Properties
dialog box.

12

Check the categories you want to include in the table of contents, and use the Sort Files By field to choose whether to sort the files by Document Title or Date Last Modified. You can choose to include the date on which the file was last modified and the file comments in the table of contents by checking the appropriate checkboxes.

As with the standard Table Of Contents Web component discussed in the last section, you must preview the table of contents based on a category in a browser on a server-based Web site.

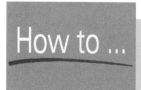

How to ... Create a Table of Contents Web Page

You may wish to simply create a separate page containing your table of contents, and link to the page from your home page using a link that might say "Site Table of Contents." You can certainly create an empty page and embed a Table Of Contents component in it, as discussed in the last section. However, you can also create a table of contents page using a FrontPage template. To do so, use the following steps:

1. Select File | New Page or Web to open the New Page or Web task pane.

2. Choose Page Templates from the task pane, and select the Table Of Contents template from the General tab.

3. Click OK to create the page (see Figure 12-3).

The created table of contents page contains the Table Of Contents component, as well as comments explaining the page setup, author and copyright placeholders, and explanatory text. The default starting page is the home page. If you want to change this (or any of the other properties of the Table Of Contents component), right-click in the component and choose Table Of Contents Properties from the shortcut menu. This opens the Table Of Contents Properties dialog box, discussed previously.

Place a Substitution

The Substitution component adds a field to your Web page that lets you show additional information to your visitors. When the page is displayed in the browser, the current contents of the specified field are displayed on the page. You can add two kinds of fields to the page using the Substitution component. The first type of field is

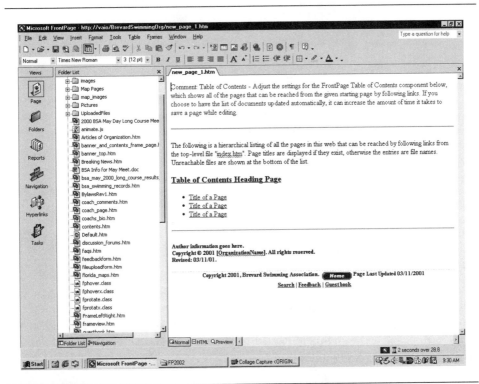

FIGURE 12-3   The table of contents page created by FrontPage instantly creates the page with no input necessary from you.

12

a page configuration variable. These variables include page author, description, the person who last modified the page, and the page URL. To set the contents of the field that the substitution uses for the description, use the following steps:

1. In the Folder view or Folder List, right-click the page for which you want to add a description. Choose Properties from the shortcut menu to open the Properties dialog box for the page.

2. Click the Summary tab.

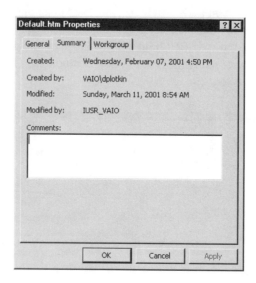

3. Enter the description for the page in the Comments field. This field is used for the description substitution.

The other type of field you can use in a Substitution component is used for Web settings parameters. These are field/value pairs you can set yourself and which are then associated with the Web site. A good reason to use a Web settings parameter would be to inform visitors to your site when the site last had a major upgrade, or perhaps what version of the site they are now viewing. To create a Web settings parameter, choose Tools | Web Settings, and click the Parameters tab. Then click Add to define the parameter. For more details on how to set up Web settings parameters, see Chapter 14.

To add a Substitution component to a page, choose Insert | Web Component and select Included Content from the Component Type list on the left side of the Insert Web Component dialog box. Choose Substitution from the list on the right side. Click Finish to open the Substitution Properties dialog box.

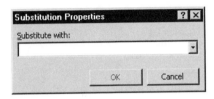

Pick the substitution you want to place on the page from the Substitute With drop-down list. The list includes any parameters you defined. Click OK and the component appears on the page.

Add Automatic Web Content

You've seen those nifty portal pages, such as My Yahoo, Excite, and MSN. Within limits, you can customize these pages to display news, weather, your horoscope, and even local TV listings. FrontPage enables you to place many of these same components on the pages of your FrontPage Web site. You can even add a component to search the Internet for information, courtesy of MSN.

NOTE *You must be connected to the Internet in order to insert and test these components. And, since some of the components use graphics that are loaded from the remote Web site (such as MSN), the graphics will not be displayed if you view the page while you are not connected to the Internet.*

12

To add automatic Web content components, choose Insert | Web Component and select either MSN Components or MSNBC Components from the Component Type list on the left side of the Insert Web Component dialog box. Choose the Web component you want to add from the list on the right side. For example, if you pick MSN Components from the Component Type list and select Search The Web With MSN, a small search form appears on the page.

NOTE   *The MSNBC components are quite useful as they provide a range of news headlines in various categories (Business, Living and Travel, News, Sports, Technology, and Weather). When a visitor to your site selects a particular headline, they can then read the entire story on the MSNBC Web site.*

Create Top Ten Lists on Your Web Site

When people visit your Web site, it can be helpful to know something about their visit—what pages on your site were most popular, what were the most often-used search strings, or perhaps what were the most popular sites from which they came. FrontPage provides the ability to track such information in its "top ten lists"—so named because these lists display the ten most popular items in the selected category. Each item in the list consists of the item name and the number of times that item occurred. For example, if you are listing the top ten visited pages, each item in the list displays the URL of the page and the number of times it was accessed. For visited pages, referring domains, and referring URLs, the listed item is a hyperlink to that page, domain, or referring URL.

NOTE   *In general, the information provided by top ten lists is not of much interest to visitors to your site. Instead, they are of much more interest to you as the Webmaster. Thus, you will probably wish to create a page that contains these lists and not provide hyperlinks that access the page. Instead, when you log onto your site, you can just type in the URL for the page containing the Top Ten lists so you can view it. Visitors to your site won't even know the page is there.*

To add a top ten list to your Web site, choose Insert | Web Component and select Top 10 List from the Component Type list on the left side of the Insert Web

Component dialog box. Then pick the type of list you want from the selections on the right side of the dialog box.

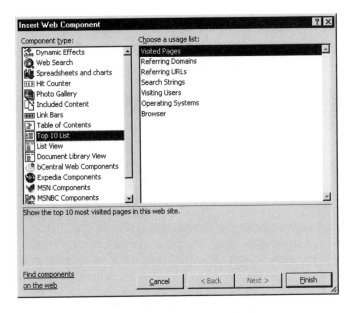

The types of top ten lists are

- **Visited Pages**   The most popular pages on your Web site. FrontPage determines this by the number of page views for each page.

- **Referring Domains**   The most popular domains visited by people just prior to coming to your site.

- **Referring URLs**   The most popular Web pages (identified by the address, or URL) visited by people just prior to coming to your site.

- **Search Strings**   The most popular search criteria that led people to find your site.

- **Visiting Users**   The log-in ID of the ten people who visited your site most often.

- **Operating Systems**   The most popular operating system among the people who visited your site.

- **Browser**   The most popular browsers used by people who visited your site.

Once you have selected a Top 10 List in the Insert Web Component dialog box, click Finish to display the Top 10 List Properties dialog box.

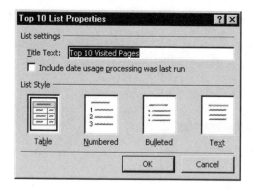

Enter the title for the list in the Title Text field, and choose the list style (Table, Numbered, Bulleted, or Text). Then click to insert the list into the page.

You can't actually see the list until you either publish the page to your Web site or preview the list in a browser for a server-based Web site. Of course, your Web site has to have a few visitors so that the data for the list can be compiled. If no one has visited your site, you will see a message notifying you that there is no usage data for the list.

In order for top ten components to work, the server logs must be turned on, the server must be configured to retrieve usage analysis data, and set to update frequently enough to make the results meaningful. By default, server logs are set to update only weekly, so the information in your top ten components can be quite out-of-date. If you are hosting your site on a remote server, you'll have to ask the server administrator to turn on the server logs, enable usage analysis, and change the update frequency. But if you are hosting your own IIS server in Windows 2000, and you have Administrator rights to the server, you can use the following steps to reconfigure the server:

1. Select Start | Settings | Control Panel to open the Control Panel.

2. Click on Administrative Tools, and then click on Microsoft SharePoint Administrator. This opens Internet Explorer to display the Microsoft SharePoint Server Administration page.

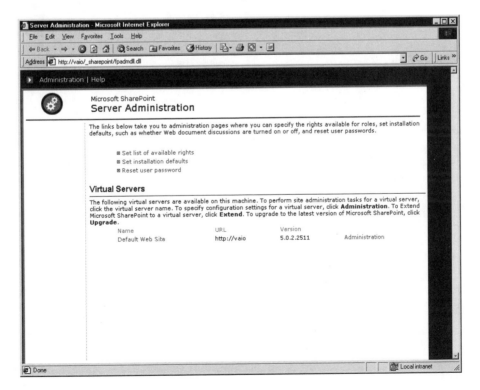

12

3. Click on *Administration* for the *Default Web Site* line to open the Virtual Server Administration page, and click Go To Site Administration for http:// servername. This opens the Site Administration page for your Web server.

4. In the Configure Usage Analysis Settings, click Change Usage Analysis Settings to open the Change Usage Analysis Settings page.

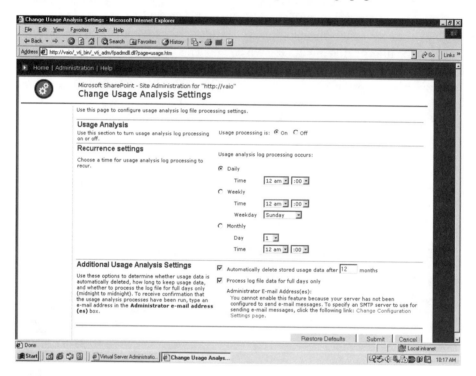

5. From this page, you can turn usage analysis on and off (using the options in the Usage Analysis section) as well as set how often the usage analysis log processing is to occur: Daily, Weekly, or Monthly. You can also set the time (for all three options), day of the week (for weekly processing), or date (for monthly processing).

6. Click Submit to make your changes.

NOTE *The settings you make here also affect the usage analysis reports discussed in Chapter 16.*

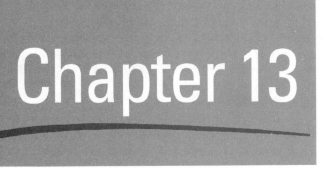

Chapter 13

Use Positioning, and Dynamic HTML

How to...

■ Apply Dynamic HTML effects

■ Position elements on the page

With Dynamic HTML (DHTML) you can use special commands to produce motion and special effects just by picking a few parameters. And you can precisely locate items on a page using the positioning features of FrontPage, bypassing the inherent limits of HTML.

Dynamic HTML is not supported except by the most modern of browsers, and even the latest revision of Internet Explorer and Netscape Navigator implement DHTML differently. The same is true of the positioning features, which depend on Cascading Style Sheets (CSS). CSS is not supported by older browsers and not implemented uniformly in even the latest browsers.

Work with Dynamic HTML Effects

One of the more recent developments has been the ability of web browsers to recognize and execute Dynamic HTML. With DHTML, you can create all sorts of animations and special effects—even write games that run in a browser. Of course, you need to know how to write code to pull most of this off. However, as with so many other things, FrontPage makes some of the more common animations and effects available without writing any program code.

Understand Events

The effects produced by DHTML must be triggered by an *event*. That is, an event must occur that triggers the script to run and produce the desired effect. In effect, the DHTML-aware browser waits for one of these events to occur in connection with the text or graphic to which the DHTML effect is attached. The events recognized by FrontPage are

■ **Click**   The reader clicked the text or graphic.

■ **Double Click**   The reader double-clicked the text or graphic.

■ **Mouse Over**   The reader moved the mouse over the text or graphic.

■ **Page Load**   The reader's browser loaded the page (usually due to a hyperlink).

Build a DHTML Effect

FrontPage provides the DHTML toolbar to add DHTML effects to a page (see Figure 13-1). If the toolbar is not visible, choose View | Toolbars | DHTML Effects.

There are three basic steps in defining a DHTML effect. Depending on the effect chosen, a fourth step may also be necessary. The steps are

1. Add the text or graphic to which the DHTML effect will be attached to the page. Adding the text or graphic works just like adding any other text or image—there is nothing special about the text or graphic—yet.

2. Select the text or graphic and pick the event to which you want to attach the effect. A list of events is available from the leftmost drop-down list (On) in the DHTML toolbar.

3. Choose the effect you want to use. The list of available effects depends on the chosen effect and whether you are attaching the effect to text or to a graphic. Table 13-1 shows the valid combinations of text/graphics, events, and effects. You choose the effect you want from the Apply drop-down list (second from left) in the DHTML toolbar.

4. If you chose an effect that requires additional information, you must specify this information. For example, if you specify that the text will fly off the screen, you must pick the direction. You choose the additional parameters from the rightmost drop-down list in the DHTML toolbar.

The DHTML effects available are as follows:

■ **Fly out (available for text and graphics)**   The text or graphic flies off the page when the event occurs. You must set where the item leaves the page. Options include choices such as To Top Right, To Bottom Left, To Top, and so on.

FIGURE 13-1   Use the DHTML toolbar to specify the events, effects, and parameters for a DHTML effect.

13

Attached to Text or Graphic	Available Event	DHTML Effect
Text	Click	Fly out, formatting
	Double Click	Fly out, Formatting
	Mouse Over	Formatting
	Page Load	Drop in by word, Elastic, Fly in, Hop, Spiral, Wave, Wipe, Zoom
Graphic	Click	Fly out, Swap picture
	Double Click	Fly out
	Mouse Over	Swap picture
	Page Load	Drop in by word, Elastic, Fly in, Hop, Spiral, Wave, Wipe, Zoom

TABLE 13-1   The Valid Combinations of Text/Graphics, Events, and Effects

- **Formatting (text only)**   The text changes format when the event occurs. There are two sets of parameters you can set: Choose Border and Choose Font. If you select Choose Border, FrontPage opens the Borders And Shading dialog box, where you can set border, border color, background and foreground color, border style, and any other options in this dialog box. If you select Choose Font, FrontPage opens the Font dialog box, where you can set font, size, color, and effects.

- **Swap picture (graphic only)**   The currently visible picture changes to display another picture. Select Choose Picture in the DHTML toolbar to open the Picture dialog box and select the alternate picture.

- **Drop in by word, Elastic, Fly in, Hop, Spiral, Wave, Wipe, Zoom** The set of effects available on page load are completely different than for the other events. These essentially consist of animation effects that automatically play when the page loads. Some of these options allow for additional parameters to be selected in the rightmost drop-down list. For example, Zoom has choices for Zoom In and Zoom Out, while Wipe has options that include Left To Right, Right To Left, and From Middle.

Edit the DHTML Effects

Once you've created DHTML effects, you can see where the effects are on the page by clicking the button at the far right end of the DHTML toolbar. This button is labeled Highlight Dynamic HTML Effects. When this button is depressed, FrontPage displays a blue bar on the page where the effects are in place (see

Figure 13-2). To edit the selected effect, click anywhere in the blue area. The DHTML toolbar will display the selected effect, and you can change it by making other selections from the toolbar.

NOTE   *Some effects—such as Fly In—apply to an entire line, and the blue bar stretches across the entire page. Other effects—such as Swap Picture—apply only to the selected item. Another oddity is that if you apply a Fly In effect to a picture, you can't click the picture to edit the effect after you apply it. Instead, you must click alongside the picture in the blue bar.*

To remove an effect, click in the blue bar for the effect you want to remove, and click the Remove Effect button in the DHTML toolbar.

NOTE   *Visitors to your site may never click an item that has an effect attached unless you give them a clue to do so. Unless you make it obvious that there is an effect, it may never be seen.*

13

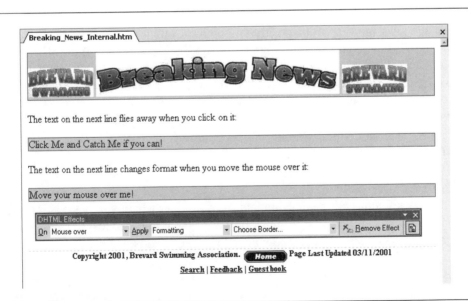

FIGURE 13-2   The blue bars indicate where DHTML effects have been applied to the page.

Specify Position on the Page

As you've been building your own Web pages, you may have noticed that getting text and graphics positioned exactly where you want them on the page can be quite a challenge. Extra spaces, tabs, and lines get ignored, making it difficult to get things where you want them. The problem is that the positioning tools in HTML are fairly coarse, and as a result Web authors have evolved tricks over the years to try and compensate. Examples include using tables and single-pixel graphic files that are used as spacers on the page. With the advent of Cascading Style Sheets (CSS), positioning items on a Web page has gotten much easier. However, it is important to remember that positioning code generated by FrontPage only works consistently with Internet Explorer 4 and later. Netscape Navigator 4 and later understands positioning code, but they are not fully compatible with FrontPage's implementation.

Differences in Positioning on the Page

There are three kinds of positioning possible when you use CSS. Each behaves quite differently. The three kinds of positioning are None (or static), Absolute, and Relative.

Static HTML Positioning

This is the most limiting of the positioning options, but it will work with any browser. With static HTML positioning, you are limited in your options of where to place text or graphics. For example, you can place a graphic flush against the left or right margins, or you can center it. But you can't place it (for example) 1.5 inches from the left margin, unless you use a trick such as placing the graphic in a table cell (see Figure 13-3) and make sure that the empty cell against the left margin is 1.5 inches wide—which can be a trick in itself. You also can't just plunk down a block of text in the middle of a page.

Absolute Positioning

Absolute positioning gives you complete freedom over where you place a graphic or block of text. Once you set the positioning for the graphic or text to be absolute, you can specify exactly where on the page the item should appear. The item's positioning coordinates are specified by the top-left corner of the item and are measured from a fixed (absolute) point—the upper-left corner of the page. The position of the item is completely ignored by graphics or text that use static positioning—static graphics or text will flow over the absolute positioned item as if it wasn't there. This behavior is termed as not being "in the text stream," because text does not flow around the graphic or block of text.

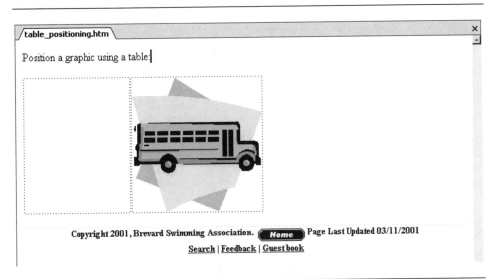

Position a graphic using a table:

Copyright 2001, Brevard Swimming Association. **Home** Page Last Updated 03/11/2001

Search | Feedback | Guestbook

FIGURE 13-3   You can position a graphic using a table with invisible borders to force a space between the graphic and the left margin.

To use absolute positioning, use the following steps:

1. Select the graphic or text block. Choose Format | Position to open the Position dialog box.

Position

Wrapping style

None   Left   Right

Positioning style

None   Absolute   Relative

Location and size

Left: Width:

Top: Height:

Z-Order:

OK   Cancel

13

To apply absolute positioning to a paragraph (text block), simply click in the paragraph to place the text cursor within the paragraph. The positioning style applies to the entire paragraph—you can't apply it to just selected text.

2. Choose Absolute from the Positioning Style section of the dialog box. You can use the Left and Top spinners to set the exact coordinates of the image or text block. The Width and Height spinners will already contain the dimensions of the image, although you adjust these if you wish.

3. Click OK. The image appears on the page in the position you specified.

You don't really need to specify the pixel coordinates in the dialog box. Instead, you can drag an absolute-positioned item to any position on the page. To do so, click the item to select it, and move the mouse pointer over the item until it becomes a four-headed arrow. Then click and drag the item to its destination.

It can be difficult to get the mouse pointer to turn into a four-headed arrow when attempting to drag a text block. However, it will do so if you move the mouse pointer between two of the sizing handles on the perimeter of the text block.

An alternative way to establish absolute positioning is to use the Positioning toolbar (see Figure 13-4). To open the Positioning toolbar, choose View | Toolbars | Positioning.

To set an element's positioning to absolute, select the element and click the button at the left end of the toolbar (this has already been done in Figure 13-4). You can then enter the desired position in the Left and Top fields.

Take a close look at Figure 13-4. See how the text disappears behind the picture, rather than wrapping around it? That is because the graphic has been positioned absolutely, so the text stream ignores it!

Relative Positioning

Relative positioning shares some of the traits of both absolute and static positioning. First of all, like static positioning, a relative-positioned item remains in the text stream, which means you can't place a relative-positioned item on top of another item. And if you move a relative-positioned item (by dragging or typing in the coordinates), other items on the page (except for absolute-positioned items)

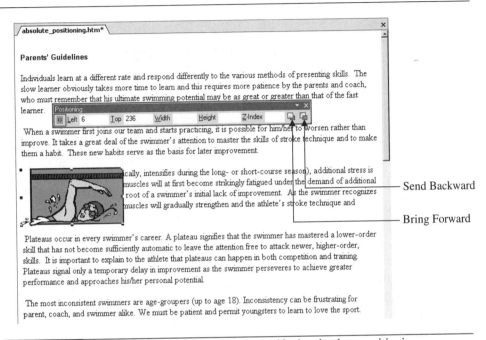

Send Backward

Bring Forward

Use the Positioning toolbar to specify the absolute-positioning parameters for an element on the page.

move out of the way, just as they would with a static-positioned item. You also can't drag a relative-positioned item freely, the way you can an absolute-positioned item. But you can open the Position dialog box and enter a Left and Top quantity to locate the item anywhere you want.

Another difference between relative positioning and absolute positioning is how the coordinates are measured. With absolute positioning, the zero point (point from which the coordinates are measured) is always the upper-left corner of the page. However, with relative positioning, the coordinates are measured *relative* to the item's position if it were statically positioned. Thus, if you place an item on the page, and switch its positioning to relative, you'll see the starting Left and Top values are 0,0. If you enter 10 in each field, the item will move 10 pixels right and down from *where it would have been if it were statically positioned*. This behavior leads to an odd occurrence. If you have text flowing around a graphic, and you use relative positioning to move the graphic, the text does *not* fill in the hole where the graphic was located.

NOTE *You cannot see the results of using relative positioning in the normal Page view. You must switch to preview Page view.*

13

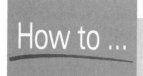 **Position Multiple Elements**

The freedom that absolute or relative positioning gives you in designing a Web page is great, but what if you want to keep several elements together as you position them? To do so, make sure you select all the elements you want to move as a single item before specifying either absolute or relative positioning. All the selected items will move together, and maintain their spatial relationship on the page as you move them. To select multiple items, click on the first item, hold down the CTRL key, and click on the additional items.

Layer Items

With absolute positioning, you can stack multiple images on a page. As a result, you need a way to specify the stacking order. This order is called z-ordering or z-indexing (because the z axis in algebra is the one that represents depth—while the x axis is width and the y axis is height). For example, say you wanted to stack three images: a table, a saucer, and a coffee cup. The table would be the lowest layer, the saucer would be the next layer, and the coffee cup would be the highest layer. To achieve this result, remember that the layers are specified relative to each other, with the highest number being the top layer. In our example, therefore, the table might be layer 0, the saucer would be layer 1, and the coffee cup would be layer 2. You could also skip layers to allow for adding more items in between the existing items later (for example, the table, saucer, and cup could be layers 1, 4, and 7). You can use negative layers, too. The table could be –5, the saucer could be –3, and the cup could be –1. It really doesn't matter, as long as you get the order right.

To set the z-order, you can use either the Position dialog box or the Positioning toolbar. In the Position dialog box, set the z-order in the Z-Order spinner. In the Positioning toolbar, set this quantity in the Z-Index field at the right end of the toolbar. You can also adjust the z-index of an object by selecting the object and clicking the Bring Forward button in the Positioning toolbar (second from the right) or the Send Backward button (far right).

Chapter 14

Set Page Options and Web Settings

How to...

- Specify browser compatibility
- Choose Web technology
- Color code and format HTML source
- Add user-defined parameters to a Web site
- Set the language options
- Set the navigation options

There are a lot of items you can configure about your Web site using the Page Options dialog box and the Web Settings dialog box. Both of these are available from the Tools menu. Although the defaults work most of the time, you should at least be aware of the options available to configure how your Web site will work.

Set Up the Page Options

To set up the page options, choose Tools | Page Options to display the Page Options dialog box.

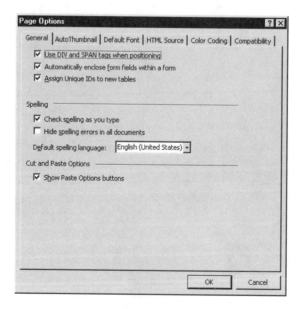

Set the Options in the General Tab

Set the options in the General tab as follows:

- **Use DIV and SPAN tags when positioning**   If you want to allow FrontPage to use DIV and SPAN HTML positioning tags, check this checkbox. The DIV tag is used to align elements within a portion of the document (called a division). You can enclose several HTML statements between DIV tags, and apply only a single ALIGN attribute to align everything between the DIV tags. The SPAN tag is used to align a portion of text within another tag. For example, you can surround HTML text with SPAN tags, and only the HTML text within the SPAN tags will have the specified alignment—the balance of the text will be unaffected.

- **Automatically enclose form fields within a form**   If you want FrontPage to create a new form the first time you add a form field to a page, check this checkbox. This is usually best, since if you forget to enclose a form field with a form, the field won't work.

The Assign Unique IDs To New Tables option will be covered in Chapter 19. The spell-checker options and cut-and-paste options in this dialog box were covered in Chapter 2.

Set Up Compatibility and Web Page Technologies

There are a lot of combinations of hardware and software on the Internet. Different browsers and different versions of browsers have different capabilities, and even the server software can affect which capabilities of a Web site will be available. You may not be familiar with the subtle (and sometimes not-so-subtle) differences between the various browsers and server software, but FrontPage is. You can use the Compatibility tab (see Figure 14-1) to tell FrontPage what browsers and server software you are designing for, and FrontPage will disable the unsupported features. For example, if you choose Netscape Navigator 4 and later as the browser you are designing for, then features such as ActiveX controls (which are only understood by Internet Explorer) will be turned off. FrontPage won't allow you to embed ActiveX controls to your Web site (see Chapter 15 for more information on ActiveX).

14

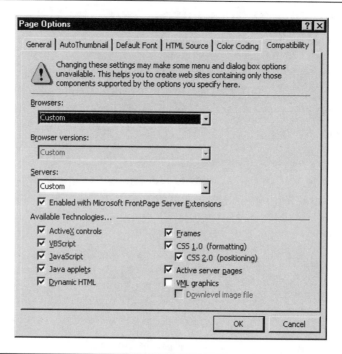

FIGURE 14-1   The Compatibility tab lets you choose which browser and server
software you are designing for.

Configure the Compatibility tab as follows:

- **Browsers**   Select the browser(s) you want to design for from the
  drop-down list. Choices include such well-known browsers as Netscape
  Navigator, Microsoft Internet Explorer, and Microsoft Web TV. Although
  you can select only one choice from the list, one of the options enables
  you to select Netscape Navigator *and* Internet Explorer. In this case, the
  features that are supported by both will be available, and any features
  unsupported by either one will be turned off.

- **Browser versions**   Select the version of the browser(s) you want to
  design for from the drop-down list. You can choose to design for 3.0
  browsers and later, 4.0 browsers and later, or 5.0 browsers and later.
  However, the list of choices does *not* include the ability to design for
  (for example) 4.0 browsers (and later) of one browser and 5.0 browsers
  (and later) of the other. Once you select the browser(s) and version, the
  checkboxes in the Technologies section reflect the capabilities of these

choices. For example, if you select Netscape Navigator Only from the Browsers list and 4.0 browsers and later from the Browser Versions list, both the ActiveX and VBScript checkbox are cleared.

■ **Servers**   Select the server software running on the host server from the drop-down list. You'll probably have to ask your Web presence provider (WPP) to provide this information. Once again, any Technologies checkboxes that are unsupported by the server are cleared in the Technologies section.

■ **Enabled with Microsoft FrontPage server extensions**   If the host server has the FrontPage extensions installed, make sure this checkbox is checked. Although this doesn't affect anything in the Technologies section, you will be warned when you try to publish the Web site to the server.

CAUTION   *Clearing the Enabled With Microsoft FrontPage Server Extensions checkbox will* not *cause FrontPage to warn you when you use a FrontPage component that requires these extensions. Instead, you will only get a warning when you publish the Web site. At that time, you'll have to go back and remove any of the listed problem components from the Web site—or at least not publish the pages containing the component.*

■ **Available Technologies**   Check the checkboxes for all technologies you want to enable, and clear the checkboxes for technologies you don't want to allow on your Web site. Again, you won't be warned if you use one of these disallowed technologies until you publish your Web site. Also, if you make selections from the Browser, Browser Versions, or Servers drop-down lists that affect the checkboxes in the Technologies section, and then manually modify the state of these checkboxes, it may cause one or more of the drop-down lists to reset to the Custom setting. This indicates you have made a technology selection that is not consistent with the previous Browser, Browser Version, or Server selections.

14

Format HTML Source Code

Although you can largely ignore the HTML code written by FrontPage, if you choose to view this code (click the HTML tab in Page view), the code can be somewhat overwhelming. To help with this situation, FrontPage enables you to customize the way in which the HTML source code is presented. You can customize the HTML code in two main ways: by color coding, and by specifying exactly how the HTML code is laid out on the page.

Color Code the HTML Source

With color coding, you can assign different colors to different types of HTML code. For example, you can use one color for tags (HTML commands) and another color for scripts. This makes it much easier to understand the HTML code and find what you're looking for. To specify the color coding for HTML code, use the Color Coding tab in the Page Options dialog box.

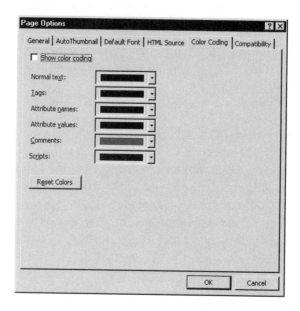

Configure the colors as follows:

- **Show color coding** To activate color coding, check this checkbox. When this checkbox is cleared, all text in the HTML Page view is shown in black.

- **Normal text** The displayed text contents of a page is the normal text. To set the color of the normal text, choose from the Normal Text color tool. Clicking the arrow in the color tool displays the standard color tool, from which you can pick a standard color, or click More Colors to pick any color your computer can display. Note that this color applies only to the normal text in the HTML Page view—it does not affect the color of the contents in the normal Page view.

- **Tags** HTML uses special commands, called tags. If you view the HTML code, you'll see the tags in braces, such as <strong>. To set the color for the tags, choose from the Tags color tool.

- **Attribute names/Attribute values** Much of HTML code is made up of attribute name/value pairs. For example, to align text to the center of the page, you might see a tag that looks like <hr align="center">. The "hr" part of the command (as well as the enclosing braces) is considered the tag and has its color set by the Tags color tool, as discussed in the previous bullet. The "align" portion is considered the attribute name, and has its color set by the Attribute Names color tool. The "center" portion is considered the attribute value, and has its color set by the Attribute Values color tool.

- **Comments** Comments are blocks of text that are ignored by a standard HTML browser. Originally, comments were used by HTML programmers to annotate their code, but FrontPage has expanded this use considerably. Essentially, any special FrontPage feature that is not part of standard HTML (such as any of the components) is implemented in the HTML code as a comment. Browsers that are FrontPage-aware will read these comments and execute the component, while non-FrontPage-aware browsers will ignore the special code because it is considered a comment. To set the color of comments, choose the color from the Comments color tool.

NOTE *This usage of "comments" is not the same as FrontPage comments discussed earlier. A FrontPage comment is actually a special component of FrontPage. Setting the color of comments in the Color Coding tab of the Page Options dialog box does not change the color of a FrontPage comment in the normal Page view.*

14

- **Scripts** If you add JavaScripts or Visual Basic scripts to your Web page (either by writing them yourself or using a feature of FrontPage that adds them automatically), you can set the color of the script text by choosing it from the Scripts color tool.

TIP *It is pretty easy to come up with an ugly and difficult-to-read color scheme. If you need to reset the colors to their default values, just click the Reset Colors button.*

Customize the HTML Formatting

FrontPage provides many more options for customizing how a page's HTML is displayed. These options are available from the HTML Source tab of the Page Options dialog box.

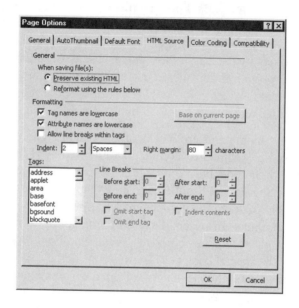

Pick one of the two formatting options in the General section of the dialog box. These options are

■ **Preserve existing HTML** Selecting this option tells FrontPage to ignore the formatting instructions in the rest of this dialog box and *not* reformat the HTML.

■ **Reformat using the rules below** Selecting this option tells FrontPage to reformat the HTML using the instructions you specify. When you save the page, FrontPage applies the formatting changes to all the HTML on the page. These settings are also applied to any subsequent pages you create.

 *You won't see the changes in the HTML Page view until you switch to normal Page view and then back to HTML Page view.*

The Formatting section in the center of the dialog box enables you to set the formatting options that are the same for all tags on the page. The options are

- **Tag names are lowercase**   Check this checkbox to specify that tag names are lowercase. Since this is the default for HTML generated by FrontPage, you won't see any changes in the HTML code unless you have added your own HTML (and the tag names are uppercase).

- **Attribute names are lowercase**   Check this checkbox to specify that attribute (described previously) names are lowercase. Again, since this is the default, you won't see any changes in the HTML code unless you have added your own HTML (and attribute names are uppercase).

- **Allow line breaks within tags**   Some tags can be quite long, as they may include a whole host of attributes and values. Normally, FrontPage will keep a tag (and its attributes) on a single line in the HTML code, regardless of the margins you set. To read an entire tag, you'll have to scroll left and right. If you want to allow the tag to wrap to a second line so that you don't have to scroll left and right to read it, check this checkbox. It is usually best to leave this checkbox cleared, as it is easier to follow what is going on if an entire tag is on a single line.

- **Indent**   To indent each line containing a tag, set the amount of the indent from the Indent spinner. Choose whether to indent using spaces or tabs from the adjacent drop-down list.

- **Right margin**   Use the Right Margin spinner to set the right margin of the HTML Page view. Text automatically wraps at the right margin.

The Tags section of the dialog box (near the bottom) is where you can specify formatting rules that vary by tag. For example, you can format the *caption* tag one way and the *body* tag completely differently. To set the formatting for a particular tag, choose the tag from the Tags list, and use the following options:

- **Set line breaks**   Line breaks enable you to use blank lines in the HTML code to provide a visual break between tags (remember that most tags come in pairs—a begin tag and an end tag). You can add blank lines before the start tag command (Before Start), between the start tag and the HTML affected by the tag (After Start), between the HTML and the end tag (Before End) and between the end tag and the next set of HTML (After End).

- **Omit start tag, Omit end tag**   Some tags don't require either the start tag or the end tag. Where available, you can check one of these checkboxes to

14

omit the unneeded tag. For most tags these options are grayed out and unavailable, and you'll have to accept the default. In general, it really isn't necessary to change the values provided by FrontPage—using the defaults guarantees your code will work.

- ■ **Indent contents**   If you want to indent the HTML between the start tag and end tag, check the Indent Contents checkbox. This simply makes the contents a little easier to see, especially if you choose *not* to use extra line breaks (described above).

 *If you change your mind and want to reformat the HTML on the page back to the FrontPage defaults, click the Reset button.*

Set the Default Font

When you don't specify a font to use for text on a FrontPage Web page, FrontPage needs to know what default font it should use. You set this quantity from the Default Font tab of the Page Options dialog box.

Page Options	? ✕

General | AutoThumbnail | Default Font | HTML Source | Color Coding | Compatibility |

Select the font FrontPage should use for each language when no font is specified for text

Language (character set):

Thai
Traditional Chinese (Big5)
Turkish
Unicode
Unicode (Big-Endian)
Unicode (UTF-8)
US/Western European
Vietnamese

Default proportional font: Times New Roman

Default fixed-width font: Courier New

OK   Cancel

Choose the character set you want to use from the Language list. Virtually all the readers of this book will want to use the US/Western European option. You need to specify a default proportional font and a default fixed-width font from the appropriate drop-down lists. A proportional font is a font in which each letter takes up a different amount of space. For example, the letter "i" takes up less room than the letter "W." A fixed-width font is a font in which each letter takes up the same amount of room. Unfortunately, both the Default Proportional Font drop-down list and the Default Fixed-Width Font drop-down list show *all* the fonts you have installed on your computer. For example, the Default Fixed-Width Font drop-down list displays options for Arial and Times New Roman, despite the fact that both of these are proportional fonts. Thus, it is up to you to know which type of font is which, and choose accordingly.

A good choice for a default proportional font is either Times New Roman or Arial, both of which are proportional fonts and are available on virtually all computers. A good choice for a default fixed-width font is Courier New.

Specify the Web Site Settings

You can set configuration options for the Web site as a whole. To do so, choose Tools | Web Settings to open the Web Settings dialog box.

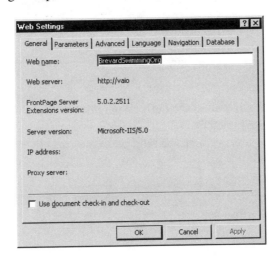

Change the Web Site Name

If you decide you don't like the name of your Web site, you can change it. Simply type the new name into the Web Name field of the General tab.

14

Add Parameters

As mentioned in Chapter 12, you can specify parameters and place them in a Web page using the Substitution component. To get these parameters to appear in the drop-down list from which you select the substitution items, you must add them to the Web site. Each parameter consists of a parameter name and the value assigned to that parameter. Examples of parameters you might want to use include the version of the site or the last time a major update was done.

To add parameters to a Web site, click the Parameters tab of the Web Setting dialog box, shown here (along with a few parameters I defined).

This tab displays a list of all the defined parameters, showing both the name and the value of the parameter.

To add a new parameter, click the Add button to open the Add Name And Value dialog box.

Type a name for the parameter into the Name field and the associated value into the Value field. Then click OK to add the parameter to the list of parameters. To change a name or value, select the parameter from the list and click Modify. To delete the parameter, select the parameter from the list and click Remove.

Set the Scripting Language

FrontPage has the capability of creating scripts to support its special features and components in either JavaScript or Visual Basic. To specify the default scripting language to use, switch to the Advanced tab of the Web Settings dialog box. Choose the scripting language from the Client drop-down list.

> **TIP**   *Only Internet Explorer can execute Visual Basic scripts, so unless you want to lock out all the users of Netscape Navigator (not a good idea), choose JavaScript as the default. Both browsers can execute JavaScript scripts.*

How to ...   Show Documents in Hidden Directories

When viewing files in the Folder List, there are some folders and files you don't normally see. These include the folders that FrontPage uses for its own bookkeeping, such as the folders for themes, borders, and the folder (usually called "_private") that holds form results. These folders all have names that are prefaced by an underscore ("_"). It can be useful to view these folders on occasion. To do so, click the Advanced tab of the Web Settings dialog box, and check the Show Hidden Files And Folders checkbox.

14

Delete Temporary Files

If you create or open a Web site on a server, FrontPage creates temporary files on your local hard drive that cache the information on the server. This makes it possible to open and work with files much more quickly because the files don't have to load from the server every time you access them. However, if many people are working on the Web site at once, the temporary files can get out of synch with the Web site on the server. Your first clue about this may be that your Web management reports suddenly stop showing certain pages, or hyperlinks no longer work even though you didn't change either the hyperlink or the target of the hyperlink. If this happens, you need to synchronize your local temporary files with the latest information on the server. To do so, click the Delete Files button in the Temporary Files section of the Advanced tab. The next time you open the Web site on the server, it will take longer because FrontPage has to reload all the information. However, the information should now be accurate.

Set the Navigation Options

If you have used Navigation bars (see Chapter 9), you already know that you can't directly customize the text of the buttons that appear in the Navigation bar. To change the text for buttons that refer to other pages in your Web site, you must change the icon title for the page in Navigation view. But what about the text for the navigation buttons that enable you to move back and forward in the stream of pages you are viewing, as well as navigate up to the parent page and to the home page? To change the button text for these buttons, switch to the Navigation tab in the Web Settings dialog box.

Enter the button text for the Home Page, Parent Page, Previous Page, and Next Page in the fields on this tab.

If you wish to return to FrontPage's default values, click the Default button.

Set the Server Message Language

FrontPage uses the server message language to determine which language to use to display messages from the FrontPage server extensions. These include edit error messages, as well as error messages displayed to the site visitor when an operation fails. Examples of these types of messages include the failure of a search to work or a form validation error. The server message language is also used when the FrontPage extensions generate Web pages, such as the default form submission confirmation pages. To specify the server message language, click the Language tab of the Web Settings dialog box and choose the language from the Server Message Language drop-down list.

Set the Default Page Encoding

When FrontPage stores the information on a Web page, it uses a feature called "encoding." The contents of the page are encoded using an encoding scheme, and it is important to choose the right one for the language. For example, if a Web page is written in Chinese, it won't be saved properly if the encoding scheme is US/Western European (the default). To set the encoding scheme to use, click the Language tab of the Web Settings dialog box and choose the encoding scheme from the Default Page Encoding drop-down list.

FrontPage (and all the Office applications) are sensitive to the type of keyboard attached to the computer, and will automatically choose an encoding scheme consistent with the keyboard unless you check the Ignore The Keyboard When Deciding The Encoding Of New Page checkbox.

14

Chapter 15

Use Java Applets and ActiveX Controls

How to...

- ■ Find Java applets
- ■ Add Java applets to your site
- ■ Configure Java applets
- ■ Find ActiveX controls
- ■ Add ActiveX controls to your site

There is a lot you can do to add functionality to your Web site with HTML and Dynamic HTML. In addition, you can add variety and some measure of interactivity to your Web pages using Java applets and ActiveX controls. Java applets are created using the Java programming language, while ActiveX controls are created using a variety of different programming languages—but the programming must conform to Microsoft's standards for creating these special controls. However, you don't have to be a programmer to use Java applets or ActiveX controls on your Web pages. You can find a ready supply of prebuilt applets and controls on the Internet, and you can use them in your Web site without any knowledge of how they were programmed. Both Java applets and ActiveX controls use sets of parameters (defined by the programmer), and as long as the documentation tells you what the parameters are and the valid values you can use for each, you can customize Java applets and ActiveX controls within the bounds set by the programmer.

Automate Your Web Site with Java Applets

A Java *applet* is a small application (which is why it is called an "applet") created in the Java programming language. An applet can be downloaded with a Web page and executed by any browser that includes a Java virtual machine—basically, version 3 or greater of either Internet Explorer or Netscape Navigator. Although Java applets don't strictly need to be run from within a browser, that is their major use. Java is platform-independent—that is, as long as the browser is Java-aware, the applet (and thus the functionality of your Web site) will run on a PC, Mac, Sun, or other computer. And, since the Java code executes locally on the reader's computer, it can be quite fast.

Find Java Applets

Programming a Java applet is not especially difficult, but unless you are a programmer and equipped with the right tools, it may well be a task you don't feel up to. Don't despair—the Internet contains a huge number of Java applets you can download and use. Some are free, some are shareware (which require you to pay a nominal fee if you continue to use an applet you downloaded and tried out), and some must be purchased outright. Table 15-1 is a list of just some of the places you can obtain Java applets.

URL	Description
www.gamelan.com	No Java applets, but lots of information about programming in Java, including tutorials. Also, Java development kits for sale.
www.jars.com	A compendium of Java, JavaScript, ActiveX, and others. Categorized and rated, with links to the sites that contain the actual applets/scripts/controls.
softwaredev.earthweb.com /directories/ pages/dir.java.html	A large collection of categorized Java applets. Most applets are well documented, and you can search for applets that do what you need. Many of the listings include the applet tag code, so you can just copy and paste it into your Web pages.
www.javaboutique.internet.com	An amazing collection of Java applets, categorized and rated. You can download applets and generally view documentation on how to set the parameters. Also includes a search engine, tutorials, and reviews of Java software.
Java.sun.com/applets	An excellent applet resource, including a long list of sites where you can find applets, as well as some of the more popular applets themselves. As you might expect from Sun, this is a well-done site.

TABLE 15-1   A Few of the Many Java Resource Web Sites

15

Some very interesting *Java applet construction sets* are appearing on the market as well. These are toolkits in which you can specify what you want your applet to do, and the tool will write the Java code for you. For example, there are several of these toolkits that construct banners. You can specify how large you want the banner to be, the background color, the text content, how fast and in what direction you want the text to scroll, and so on. Once you've got the banner looking the way you want it, you can generate your own Java applet. For some really good quality toolkits of this type, check out www.coffeecup.com. This site includes downloadable demo versions of all their software.

Add a Java Applet to a Page

Once you have obtained the Java applets you want, you are ready to add them to your Web page. To do so, use the following steps:

1. Copy the applet file and any support files into the same folder as the page to which you will be adding the applet. You'll recognize the applet file because it has an extension of .CLASS (or less frequently, .CLA). Many Java applets use graphics and small text files when they are running, so be sure to copy them all.

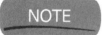 *When you download a Java applet, the download file (usually a zip file) will probably include the applet file, the support files, and any documentation on how to configure the applet.*

2. Choose Insert | Web Component and select Advanced Controls from the Insert Web Component dialog box. Choose Java Applet from the list on the right side of the dialog box. Click Finish to open the Java Applet Properties dialog box (see Figure 15-1).

3. Use the Java applet documentation to fill out the Java Applet Properties dialog box (step-by-step instructions for filling out this dialog box are included in the next section). At a minimum, you must enter the name of the .CLASS file into the Applet Source field.

4. Click OK to add the Java applet to your page (see Figure 15-2). FrontPage places a placeholder on the page to show how large the applet will appear.

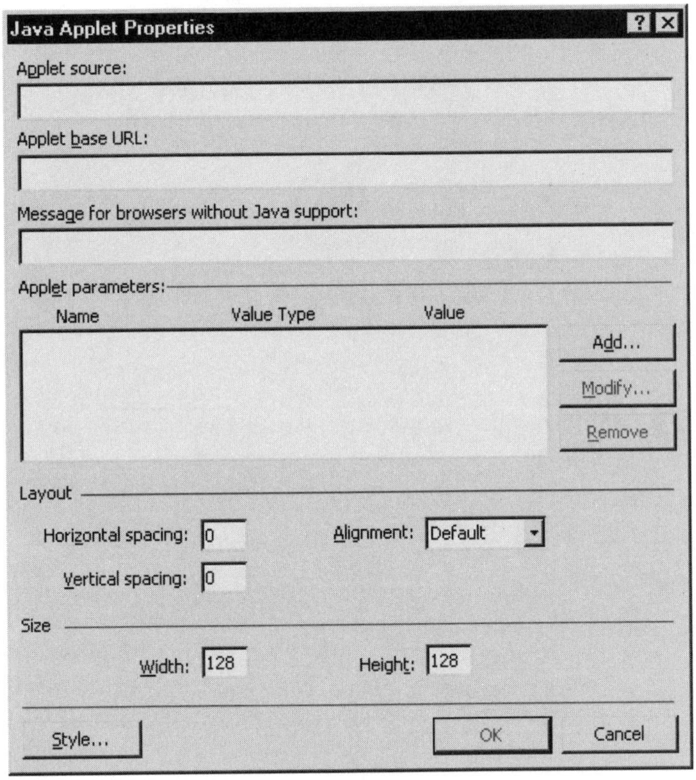

FIGURE 15-1   Specify the applet and set up its parameters using the Java Applet Properties dialog box.

5. To see the Java applet in action, click on the Preview tab in Page view. After a few moments, the Java applet will start up and run. Figure 15-3 shows a clock (one of the most popular types of simple Java applets) running on the page.

If you want to see how the Java applet appears in HTML, switch to the HTML Page view and look over the HTML code between the <applet> tags. Figure 15-4 shows how an applet with many parameters might look in HTML.

15

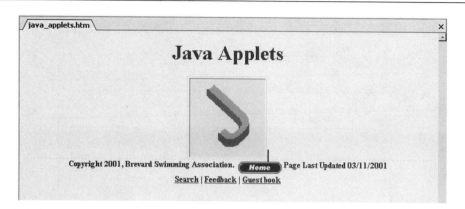

FIGURE 15-2 The placeholder shows where the Java applet output will appear on the Web page.

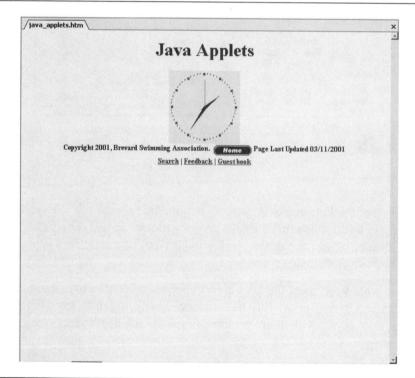

FIGURE 15-3 Switch to the preview Page view to see the Java applet in action.

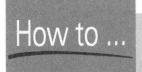 **Duplicate a Java Applet on Many Different Pages**

Want to duplicate a Java applet on many different pages, complete with all the parameters settings? Here's how:

1. Add and configure the applet on one page.

2. Switch to the HTML Page view for that page and copy all the text between the <applet> tags.

3. Paste that text into the HTML Page view of any other pages—voila!

Just remember that all these pages must be in the same folder for this to work.

```
java_applets.htm                                                          ✕
<html>

<head>
<meta http-equiv="Content-Language" content="en-us">
<meta name="GENERATOR" content="Microsoft FrontPage 5.0">
<meta name="ProgId" content="FrontPage.Editor.Document">
<meta http-equiv="Content-Type" content="text/html; charset=windows-1252">
<title>Java Applets</title>
<meta name="Microsoft Border" content="b, default">
</head>

<body>

<h1 align="center"><font color="#0000FF">Java Applets</font></h1>
<p align="center">
<applet width="250" height="250" code="JavaClock.class">
  <param name="sHandColor" value="green">
  <param name="backcolor" value="red">
  <param name="fontcolor" value="green">
  <param name="fontsize" value="24">
  <param name="hHandColor" value="blue">
  <param name="mHandColor" value="blue">
  <param name="typeface" value="Heritage">
</applet></p>

</body>

</html>

Normal  HTML  Preview
```

15

FIGURE 15-4   Use the HTML Page view to see how the applet looks in HTML.

Configure the Java Applet

You can control quite a bit about the applet with the Java Applet Properties dialog box (refer back to Figure 15-1). Configure the applet as follows:

- **Applet source** Enter the name of the Java applet file in this field. This is the .CLASS or .CLA file. Note that the name is case-sensitive. If you type the name in incorrectly, you'll still see the placeholder for the applet when you click OK, but nothing will appear on the page (except a gray rectangle) when you preview the page.

- **Applet base URL** As long as the applet files are in the same directory as the page, you can leave this field blank. If the applet is *not* stored in the same folder (not recommended), you'll have to enter the URL of the page into this field.

- **Message for browsers without Java support** Although it is rare for browsers to not support Java applets, you should enter the message that someone will see if their browser does not support Java. This is especially true these days, when people may turn off the Java support in their browsers to protect themselves against malicious applets.

- **Horizontal spacing** Set the amount of spacing to the left and right of the applet.

- **Vertical spacing** Set the amount of spacing above and below the applet.

- **Alignment** This drop-down list lets you specify how the applet is displayed on the page. The Left, Right, and Center options specify the horizontal alignment. The rest of the options specify how text alongside the applet will be aligned. The values work identically to the alignment options for graphics, as detailed in Chapter 3.

- **Width/Height** The documentation for the Java applet should provide you with the recommended width and height, and you can enter the quantities in these fields. You can also size the applet on the page by clicking on the applet placeholder to display the sizing handles. Drag the sizing handles to adjust the size.

The center section of the Java Applet Properties dialog box is used to specify parameters that affect how the applet looks and works. For example, the clock applet uses parameters to specify the typeface, size, and color of the font used to display the digital time, the color of the hands in the analog version, the background color, and many other quantities.

There is no standard set of parameters for Java applets—the programmer specifies the parameters. The documentation for the applet should tell you what parameters are available and what their valid values are.

To add a parameter to the Java Applet Properties dialog box, click the Add button to open the Set Attribute Value dialog box (see Figure 15-5). Enter the parameter name in the Name field, check the Specify Value checkbox, and enter the value in the Data, Ref, or Object fields (following the configuration instructions).

TIP *If the documentation simply specifies a value for an attribute, enter the value in the Data field.*

NOTE *Not all Java applets use parameters. Some just are what they are.*

To change the name or value assigned to a parameter, click the Modify button to reopen the Set Value Attribute dialog box. If you decide you don't need the parameter, select it and click Remove.

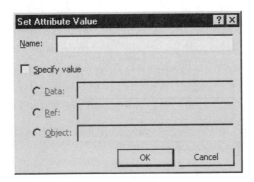

15

FIGURE 15-5   Choose the values of parameters to configure the Java applet.

CAUTION *Much has been written about the malicious use of Java applets. Although most applets are safe, there are a few twisted individuals who create Java applets that can potentially do damage to your machine. Obviously, you don't want to use such applets yourself, and you certainly don't want to post these applets on your Web site. It is best to try out unknown Java applets on a test machine (if you have one), and only download Java applets from trusted Web sites (such as those listed in Table 15-1).*

Automate Your Web with ActiveX Controls

An alternative to Java applets is ActiveX controls. Invented by Microsoft, ActiveX controls are similar to Java applets in that they typically (although not always) implement small, self-contained pieces of functionality. And like Java applets, they can be embedded in Web pages and configured. They are often used to provide controls: sliders, media players, calendars, spreadsheets, progress bars, and so on. ActiveX controls can significantly extend the functionality of the browser, enabling you (if you are a proficient programmer) to customize Internet Explorer both in appearance and function. Unfortunately, however, ActiveX controls only work in Internet Explorer—Netscape Navigator users won't be able to take advantage of ActiveX controls.

ActiveX controls come in three flavors:

- Embedded ActiveX controls appear as rectangular windows in a Web page. You may not be able to tell the difference between the control and a graphic—at least until you begin exploring the interactivity of the control, something you can't do with a plain graphic!

- A full-screen ActiveX control takes over the entire browser window and displays its own contents. With this type of control, the browser window can display information that is not supported by the browser.

- Hidden ActiveX controls are not visible, but add functionality to the browser that wouldn't otherwise be available.

URL	Description
softwaredev.earthweb.com /directories/ pages/dir.activex.html	A large collection of categorized ActiveX controls. Most controls are well documented, and you can search for controls that do what you need. You can also purchase controls.
download.cnet.com	One of the really big shareware boards, with many ActiveX controls available. Put in "ActiveX" as a search term.
www.longbright.freeserve.co.uk/	The self-proclaimed "unofficial guide to ActiveX."
www.jars.com	A compendium of Java, JavaScript, ActiveX, and others. Categorized and rated, with links to the sites that contain the actual applets/scripts/controls.

TABLE 15-2   Just a Few of the Sites You Can Use to Obtain ActiveX Controls

Find ActiveX Controls

Building your own ActiveX controls requires a fair degree of programming skill. However, as with Java applets, a large number of ActiveX controls are available on the Internet. Table 15-2 lists just a few of the sites where you can find information on programming ActiveX and obtain prebuilt ActiveX controls.

Add ActiveX Controls to the Page

To add an ActiveX control to your Web page, use the following steps:

1. Choose Insert | Web Component and select Advanced Controls from the Insert Web Component dialog box. Choose ActiveX Control from the list on the right side of the dialog box. Click Next to display a list of available ActiveX controls.

15

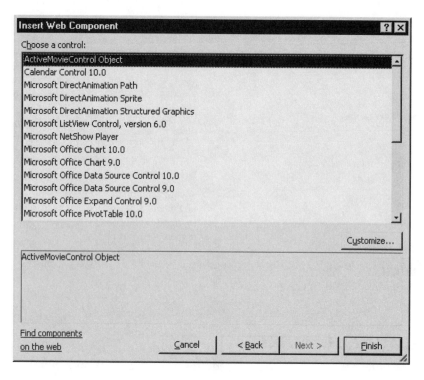

2. Click the ActiveX control you want to insert into the page and click Finish.

3. The ActiveX control appears on the page (see Figure 15-6). You can switch to preview Page view if you want, although many of the controls look the same in normal and preview Page views.

NOTE *Although there are quite a few ActiveX controls in the Insert Web Component dialog box, you actually have access to many more. To see a list of all the controls installed on your computer, click the Customize button in the Insert Web Component dialog box. A long list of controls appears in the Customize ActiveX Control List dialog box. Each has a checkbox next to it. Check the checkbox for the controls you want to see in the Insert Web Component dialog box, and clear the checkbox for the controls you don't want to see.*

The calendar ActiveX control is one of the most popular—and a handy addition to many Web pages.

If you'd like to see how the ActiveX control is implemented in HTML, switch to the HTML Page view (see Figure 15-7). The code for the ActiveX control is between the <object> tags.

Configure the ActiveX Control

To configure an ActiveX control, double-click on the control or choose ActiveX Control Properties from the shortcut menu. This opens the ActiveX Control Properties dialog box (see Figure 15-8). It is very important to understand that the dialog box for each control is different—we'll cover the common aspects of the dialog box.

To set the values for the specialized tabs, such as the General tab, you'll have to have some documentation about the ActiveX control. Some of the controls are pretty self-explanatory, but others are something of a mystery. The good news is that many ActiveX controls have built-in help. For example, if you click the Help button on the calendar's ActiveX Control Properties dialog box, you'll get a list of

15

```
activex_controls.htm                                                    ×
<meta name="ProgId" content="FrontPage.Editor.Document">
<meta http-equiv="Content-Type" content="text/html; charset=windows-1252">
<title>ActiveX Controls</title>
<meta name="Microsoft Border" content="b, default">
</head>

<body>

<h1 align="center"><font color="#0000FF">ActiveX Controls</font></h1>
<p align="center">
<object classid="clsid:8E27C92B-1264-101C-8A2F-040224009C02" id="Calendar1">
  <param name="_Version" value="524288">
  <param name="_ExtentX" value="7620">
  <param name="_ExtentY" value="5080">
  <param name="_StockProps" value="1">
  <param name="BackColor" value="-2147483633">
  <param name="Year" value="2001">
  <param name="Month" value="3">
  <param name="Day" value="11">
  <param name="DayLength" value="1">
  <param name="MonthLength" value="1">
  <param name="DayFontColor" value="0">
  <param name="FirstDay" value="7">
  <param name="GridCellEffect" value="1">
  <param name="GridFontColor" value="10485760">
  <param name="GridLinesColor" value="-2147483632">
  <param name="ShowDateSelectors" value="-1">
  <param name="ShowDays" value="-1">
  <param name="ShowHorizontalGrid" value="-1">
  <param name="ShowTitle" value="-1">
  <param name="ShowVerticalGrid" value="-1">
  <param name="TitleFontColor" value="10485760">
  <param name="ValueIsNull" value="0">
</object>
</p>

</body>

[Normal] [HTML] [Preview]
```

FIGURE 15-7   The code between the <object> tags belongs to the ActiveX control.

the various parameters and what they mean, as well as guidance on how to set the options in the ActiveX Control Properties dialog box.

All ActiveX controls have at least the Object Tag tab and the Parameters tab, and these tabs are the same for all controls. The Object Tag tab is displayed in Figure 15-9.

Configure the Object Tag tab as follows:

- **Name**   Type a name for the control into this field. This name makes it easier to find the control in the HTML code later (you can just search for the name).

- **Alignment**   This drop-down list lets you specify how the applet is displayed on the page. The Left, Right, and Center options in this list

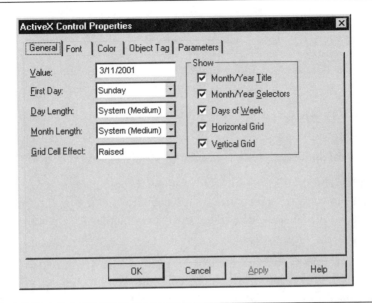

FIGURE 15-8 The General tab of the calendar's ActiveX Control Properties dialog box is very specific to a calendar—you won't see these settings in the spreadsheet ActiveX control.

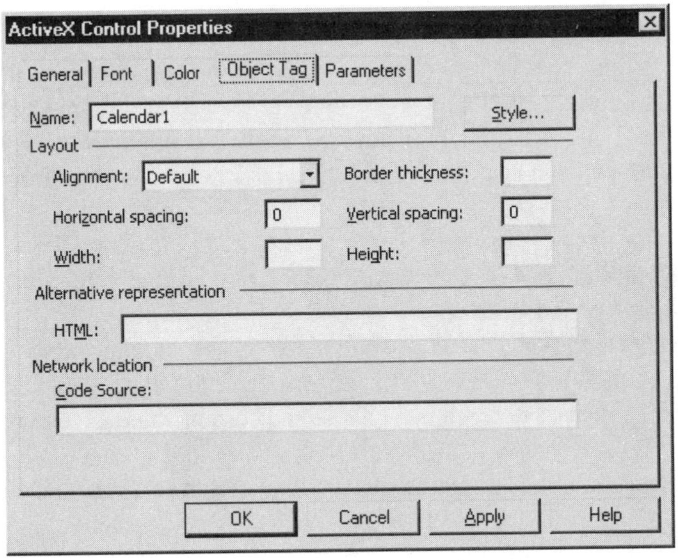

FIGURE 15-9 Set the general properties of the ActiveX control in the Object Tag tab.

specify the horizontal alignment. The rest of the options specify how text alongside the control will be aligned. The values work identically to the alignment options for graphics, as detailed in Chapter 3.

- **Border thickness** The thickness of the border (in pixels) around the control. Leave this blank if you don't want a border displayed.

- **Horizontal spacing** Set the amount of spacing to the left and right of the applet.

- **Vertical spacing** Set the amount of spacing above and below the applet.

- **Width/Height** Enter the width and height into the appropriate fields. You can also size the control on the page by clicking on the control to display the sizing handles. Drag the sizing handles to adjust the size.

- **HTML** Enter the HTML code to display on the page if the browser doesn't support ActiveX controls or if the reader has turned off ActiveX support in his or her browser. For example, you could enter **<H1> Your Browser Does Not Support ActiveX </H1>**.

- **Code Source** If the code for the ActiveX control does not reside within your Web site, you must provide the location where the code *is* located in this field.

The Parameters tab (see Figure 15-10) gives you an opportunity to modify how the ActiveX control behaves, somewhat similar to the parameters in Java applets.

To add a parameter, click the Add button to open the Edit Object Parameter dialog box (see Figure 15-11). You can type a new parameter into the Name field, but unlike Java, you can also pick an existing parameter from the drop-down Name list.

Enter a value in one of the fields in the Value area of the dialog box (Data, Page, or Object) by selecting one of the options and entering a value in the adjacent field. Click OK when you're done.

You can also modify the value of a parameter by selecting the parameter from the list and clicking the Modify button, which opens the Edit Object Parameter dialog box. This time, however, the parameter name and current value are prepopulated in the fields.

Finally, you can remove a parameter by choosing it from the list and clicking Remove.

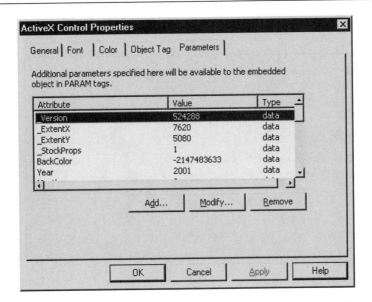

FIGURE 15-10   Choose a parameter to modify and change how the control works.

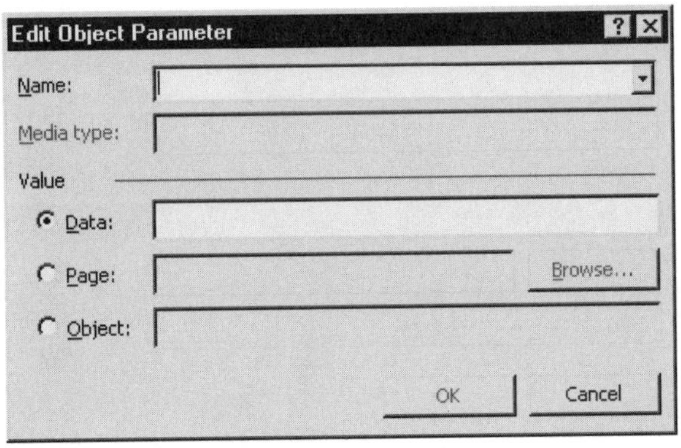

FIGURE 15-11   Choose or enter a parameter in the Name field to work with that
parameter.

15

Chapter 16

Manage Your Web Site with Tasks and Reports

How to...

- Use the task list
- Add a task manually
- Add a task to build pages
- Manage the tasks
- Run reports
- View and understand report results
- Filter the report results
- Quickly fix problem areas
- Change the publishing status of your pages

When you first begin building a Web site, you will probably focus on the mechanics of building the pages: typing in and formatting the text, adding the graphics, laying out the tables, specifying the hyperlinks, and making good use of forms and frames. But how do you manage the task of building and maintaining your Web site? It seems like there are so many things to be done, and you may be constantly thinking of new ways to improve your site. Tasks can help with getting organized, reminding you of the things you need to take care of.

Another issue you may worry about is keeping track of everything on your site. Did you get all the hyperlinks right? Are any of the pages too slow to load? Reports can help you find problems with your site, and you can use reports to navigate right to the problem areas in your web site.

Keep Track of the Work with Tasks

When you are building a large Web site with many pages, wouldn't it be helpful to be able to make a list of the pages you think you need—perhaps a few fixes that come to mind—and even jot down some long-term development plans (such as adding a search page)? FrontPage's Task view can help you get organized and stay organized as you build your Web site.

What Are Tasks?

Think of the Task view as your "to do" list. You can list new tasks, mark tasks as in-progress or completed, and prioritize the tasks. The Task view (see Figure 16-1) provides a consolidated view of tasks you have identified. Each of the tasks in the list is something you or someone on your team needs to take care of to finish the Web site.

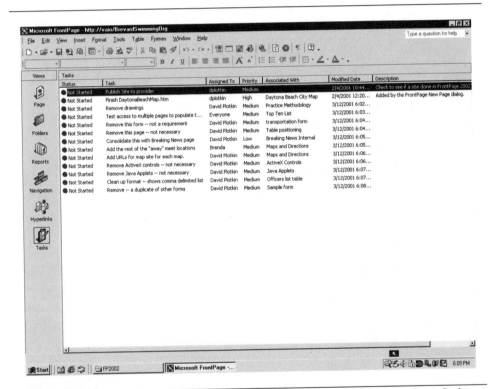

FIGURE 16-1   The Task view shows you everything you still need to get done. Isn't that jolly?

Add New Tasks

Before you can work with the tasks, you need to add them to the task list. There are quite a few ways to add tasks, and the techniques for adding tasks vary depending on which view you are using and whether you have a page selected in that view when you create the task.

Add a Task Manually in Task View

To add a new task in Task view, right-click in a blank area of the Task view, and choose Add Task from the shortcut menu, or choose Edit | Tasks | Add Task. Either way, the New Task dialog box appears (see Figure 16-2).

You can also create a new task in Report view using Edit | Tasks | Add Task. Then configure the task as described below.

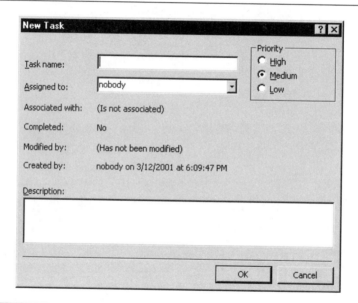

FIGURE 16-2 Specify the parameters of a new task in the New Task dialog box.

An important thing to notice in the New Task dialog box is that the Associated With field displays the value (Is Not Associated). This indicates that the manually created task is not associated with any page. As you'll see later, when a task is associated with a page, FrontPage provides a certain amount of automation to help you manage the task as you edit the page. However, this is not possible with tasks created in the Task view or Report view. These nonassociated tasks are appropriate for general Web tasks, such as publishing the Web site, changing the theme, adjusting the Navigation bars, and so on. Configure the new task as follows:

- **Task name**   Enter a descriptive name for the task. This is the text that appears in the Task column of the Task view, so you should think carefully about the name you choose.

- **Assigned to**   Enter the name (or some other identifier, such as e-mail address) for the person responsible for completing this task. You can type the identifier into the field, or click the down arrow and select from a drop-down list of previously assigned people. The contents of this field appear in the Assigned To column of the Task view.

- **Priority**   Set the task priority by selecting High, Medium, or Low. This quantity appears in the Priority column of the Task view.

- **Description**   Enter a description for the task. This text appears in the Description column of the Task view.

NOTE   *You cannot change the Associated, Completed, Modified By, or Created By fields. These are automatically filled in by FrontPage.*

Click OK to create the task. The new task appears in the Task view, with a status of Not Started.

Add a Task in Page View

To create a new task in Page view, display the page to which you want to associate the task, then choose Edit | Tasks | Add Task to open the New Task dialog box. It looks just like the New Task dialog box displayed in Figure 16-2, except that now the task is associated with the open page. After filling out the New Task dialog box, click OK to create the task. To see the new task, switch to the Task view.

16

 *If you create a task without first displaying a page or selecting a file in the Folder List, the task will not be associated with any page.*

Add a Task from the Folder List

If you can see the Folder List, you can quickly create a task associated with any page in the list. To do so, select the page and choose Edit | Tasks | Add Task to open the New Task dialog box. Fill in the New Task dialog box as described previously, and click OK to create a task associated with the selected page.

In Folder view, you can select a page from the list of files (see Figure 16-3) and add a task associated with that page by choosing Edit | Tasks | Add Task to open the New Task dialog box. Configure the task and click OK to create it.

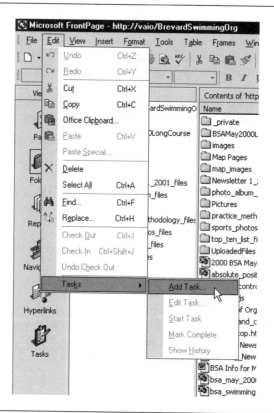

FIGURE 16-3　Select a page in the list of files, and add a task associated with that page.

Add a Task in Other Views

You can add a new task from the Navigation view or Hyperlink view. Either of these views displays icons for pages in the main window of the screen. To add a task associated with a page, click the page, then select Edit | Tasks | Add Task to open the New Task dialog box. Configure the task and click OK to create.

NOTE *If you choose Edit | Tasks | Add Task without first selecting a page, the created task will not be associated with any page.*

Create a Task When You Create a Page

FrontPage makes it easy to create a task when you create a page. By using this feature, you can come back and build the page later. This makes an excellent planning tool—just specify a page you need, create a task to build the page later, and repeat the process until you have all the pages queued up to build. Using this technique, you don't have to stop your planning process to actually build the pages.

To create a task as you create a page, use the following steps:

1. Choose File | New Page or Web to display the New Page or Web task pane. Click Page Templates to display the Page Template dialog box.

2. Pick the template you want to use from the Page Templates dialog box.

3. Check the Just Add Web Task checkbox (see Figure 16-4).

4. Choose OK. FrontPage opens the Save As dialog box.

5. Type the filename for the page into the File Name field.

6. Click the Change Title button to change the page title. Type the title into the Set Page Title dialog box and click OK.

7. Click Save to create the page and a task to remind you to finish the page later. The task is titled "Finish *FileName*" where *FileName* is the name you gave the page. You can rename the task in the Task view if you wish, as detailed in the next section.

CAUTION *If you cancel the new page from the Save As dialog (by clicking the Cancel button), the new task is still created, but it is associated with an unknown page. You'll need to delete the task as detailed in the next section.*

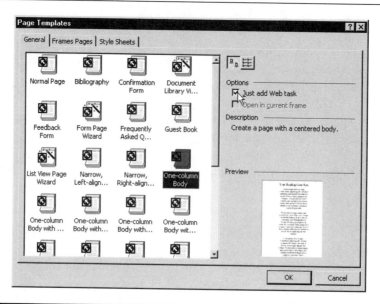

Check the Just Add Web Task checkbox to avoid having to build the page right now.

Delete a Task

If you need to remove a task from the Task view, select the task and either press the DELETE key or select Edit | Delete. Confirm that you want the task deleted by clicking Yes in the Confirm Delete dialog box and the task disappears.

Manually Adjust Task Properties

From the Task view, you can manage your tasks manually, changing the status of the task as well as its properties. Once you select the task, here is what you can do from the Task view:

- Double-click the task in Task view (or choose Edit Task from the shortcut menu) to open the Task Details dialog box (see Figure 16-5). This dialog box works identically to the New Task dialog box, except that if the task is associated with a page, the dialog box has one additional button, Start Task. Clicking the button opens the page associated with the task in Page view.

- Change the task title by clicking the text in the Task column. This makes the text editable so you can type in a new title.

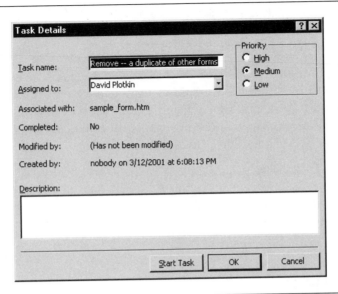

FIGURE 16-5   Change the properties of an existing task—and start the task—from the
Task Details dialog box.

- Change the person the task is assigned to. Click the entry in the Assigned
  To column and either type in a new name or choose an existing name from
  the drop-down list.

- Change the priority of the task. Click the entry in the Priority column and
  select the priority from the drop-down list.

- Change the description by clicking the text in the Description column. This
  makes the text editable so you can type in a new description.

NOTE   *You cannot change the contents of either the Associated With column or
the Modified Date column. FrontPage sets these automatically.*

16

Each task has a shortcut menu, accessed by right-clicking the task, from which
you make selections to manage the task. The shortcut menu contains the following
elements:

- **Edit Task**   This opens the Task Details dialog box.

- **Start Task**   This option is available only if the task is associated with a page. Selecting this option opens the page in Page view. You can also choose Edit | Tasks | Start Task.

- **Mark Complete**   This changes the status of the task from either Not Started or In Progress to Completed. Once a task has been completed, it will appear in the task list only until you refresh the list of tasks (choose View | Refresh). Upon refreshing the list, all completed tasks disappear. You can also choose Edit | Tasks | Mark Complete.

- **Delete Task**   This deletes the task from the Task view.

If you want to see all the tasks for this Web site, including completed tasks, choose Edit | Tasks | Show History. This toggle displays the completed tasks in the list. Select this option again to turn it off.

Perform Tasks

If a task is associated with a Web page, you can "start the task" by clicking the Start Task button in the Task Details dialog box. Alternatively, you can start it by right-clicking to bring up the shortcut menu and selecting Start Task, or by selecting Start Task from the Edit | Tasks menu. Starting the task opens the associated page in the Page view. Once the page is open, you can customize the page any way you want using any of FrontPage's tools. When you save the page, FrontPage will query you (see Figure 16-6) about whether you want the task marked as completed. If you do, click Yes. When you return to the Task view, you will find that the task status has changed to Completed. If you click No, the task status will change to In Progress. You can reopen the page from the Task view and make additional changes, and upon saving the page FrontPage will once again query you about whether to mark the task as completed.

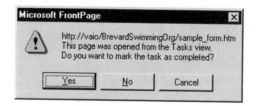

FIGURE 16-6   If you want, FrontPage will mark the task as completed when you save a page.

 *FrontPage will only query you to mark the task as completed if you open the page from the Task view by starting the task. If you open the page any other way, FrontPage won't prompt you about the task.*

Check Your Site with Web Site Reports

FrontPage provides a set of 13 reports that will help you manage your Web site and find (and fix) problems. By using these reports religiously, you can avoid Web no-nos such as broken hyperlinks, pages that take too long to load, and pages containing outdated information.

Access the Reports

To begin working with reports, click the Reports icon in the Views bar. If this is the first time you've used the Reports tool, the Site Summary report appears (see Figure 16-7). You can also view this report by choosing it from the Report toolbar or selecting View | Reports | Site Summary.

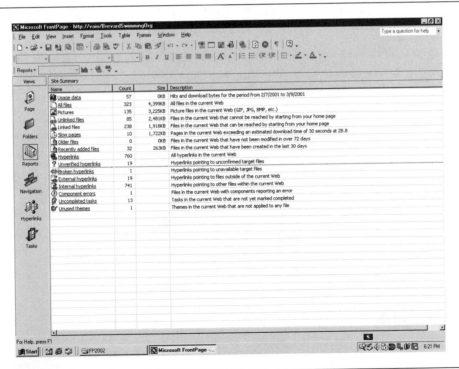

FIGURE 16-7   The Site Summary report shows you the results of the various FrontPage reports at a glance.

16

You can run any of the FrontPage reports (including a few that *don't* appear in the Site Summary report) from the drop-down list in the Reporting toolbar (see Figure 16-8) or from the submenu that appears when you choose View | Reports.

To make the Reports toolbar visible, choose View | Toolbars | Reporting.

Set the Report Parameters

If you take a quick look at the Site Summary report, you'll see some reports that list pages that load slowly, or that have been added recently, or perhaps are considered old. You can configure the reports to specify the parameters used by these reports. To do so, choose Tools | Options to open the Options dialog box. Then click the Reports View tab (see Figure 16-9).

Set the parameters for the reports as follows:

- **"Recent" files are less than** Choose what you consider recent files. Files that were added to the site more recently than the number days you specified are considered recent and are included in the Recently Added Files list.

- **"Older" files are older than** Choose what you consider old files. Files that were added to the site more than the specified number of days ago are included in the Older Files list.

FIGURE 16-8   Select the report you want to run from the Reporting toolbar.

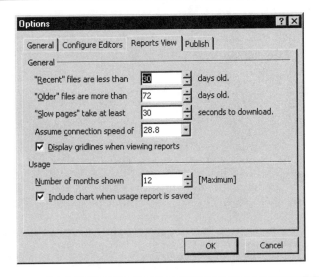

FIGURE 16-9   Use the Reports View tab in the Options dialog box to set report parameters.

■ **"Slow pages" take at least**   Choose what you consider to be the length of time it takes a slow page to download.

■ **Assume connection speed of**   Choose the speed of the Internet connection you want to use when calculating slow pages. Common speeds between 14.4 and T3 are available in the drop-down list. The default value of 28.8 is usually a good one to use.

■ **Display gridlines when viewing reports**   If you want to see the grid in the Reports view, check this checkbox.

■ **Usage data**   FrontPage has a whole collection of usage reports, including page hits (monthly, weekly, daily), visiting users, referring domains, and many others. To set the number of months of data included in the usage reports, use the Number Of Months Shown spinner. If you want a chart created that graphically displays the data (available for some of the usage reports), check the Include Chart When Usage Report Is Saved checkbox.

16

Work with Files in the Report View

Many of the reports available list files that meet certain criteria, such as files that load slowly or recently added files. You can work directly with the files in the reports by right-clicking on a file and choosing an option from the shortcut menu. The options available are

■ **Open**   Opens the file in the default editor. For example, opening a HTM file normally displays it in the FrontPage editor.

■ **Open With**   Opens the file using the editor that you specify. When you choose Open With, a list of compatible editors is displayed in the Open With Editor dialog box. Pick the one you want and click OK.

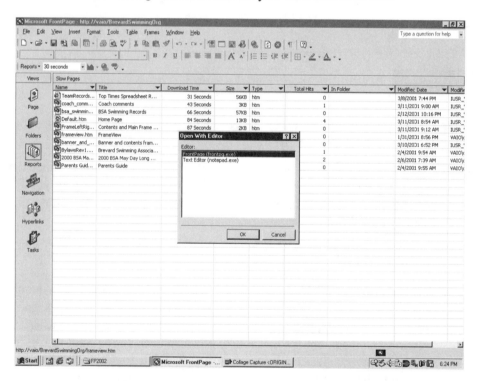

■ **Preview in Browser**   Displays the file in a browser. If you have multiple browsers on your computer, you will be given the chance to pick which browser you want to use.

- ■ **Cut/Copy**   Cuts or copies the text line (including all the column contents) to the clipboard.

- ■ **Copy Report**   Copies the contents of the entire report to the clipboard.

- ■ **Paste**   This option is available only if you used Cut or Copy—it is not available if you used Copy Report. Further, pasting over another line in a report does not change that line. In other words, this option doesn't actually do anything.

- ■ **Rename**   Makes the filename (in the Name column) editable. Type in the new name and press RETURN to change the filename. FrontPage automatically changes any pages where the file is referenced or used.

- ■ **Delete**   Removes the file from your Web site. Any references to the file will become invalid.

- ■ **Publish Selected Files**   Enables you to publish the single file to your Web site. Making this selection opens the Publish Destination dialog box, where you can specify where you want to publish the file. For more information on publishing files, see Chapter 17.

- ■ **Don't Publish**   This is a toggle that changes the status of the file to Don't Publish (checked) or Publish (unchecked). Files that have a status of Don't Publish will not be published (surprise!) when you publish your Web site.

- ■ **Properties**   Opens the Properties dialog box for the file.

TIP   *If you want to save the contents of a report, use Copy Report from the shortcut menu to place the report on the clipboard. Then, open Excel and paste the report into Excel. Each of the cells in the original report (intersection of columns and rows) is pasted into a cell in Excel, and you even get the column headings (in bold, no less!).*

Sort the Report Results

16

You can sort the results in any of the reports by any of the columns. To sort the results on a column, click on the column heading. The first time you click on a column heading, FrontPage sorts the results in ascending (lowest to highest) order. Clicking on the column heading again sorts the results in descending (highest to lowest) order.

Rearrange the Report Columns

If you don't care for the order of the columns in the report, you can click on a column header and drag it to a new position. As you drag the column header, a dark gray rectangle indicates where the column will be positioned when you release the mouse button.

Filter the Report Results

The reports that FrontPage provides all follow a common format—rows of information with columns (and headings) that tell you what the information means. You can see a sample in Figure 16-7, above. However, many of the reports can be overwhelming, providing too much information to easily work with. For example, even a moderate-size Web site can contain hundreds of files, so finding a particular file—or a specific set of files—in the All Files report can be difficult. Further, as mentioned earlier, a single report displays both broken hyperlinks and good hyperlinks. What do you do if you only want to see the broken ones?

Fortunately, FrontPage provides a way to filter the reports so you can choose what you want to see. At the top of each column is the column heading, and alongside each heading is small down arrow (see Figure 16-10). Clicking on the down arrow exposes a list of potential filters.

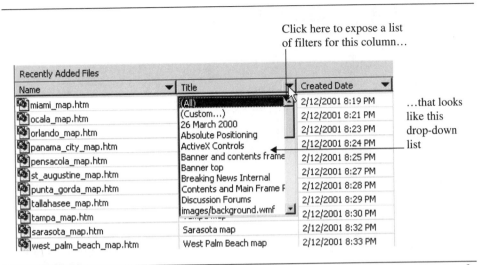

Click here to expose a list
of filters for this column…

…that looks
like this
drop-down
list

FIGURE 16-10   Filters available for each column help you narrow down the amount of information you see.

The entries in the filter drop-down list include the following items:

- **(All)**   Click this entry to remove any filters you have set and view all the records in the report.

- **A list of all unique values**   Most of the list consists of all unique values for the items in the report. For example, the filter for Type in any of the file reports lists all the types of files (CLASS, GIF, HTM, JPG, etc.). The Status column in the Broken Hyperlinks report displays the values *Broken* and *OK*. If you choose a value from the list, only items that meet the selected criteria (files of the specified type, or only broken hyperlink, for example) will be displayed in the report.

- **(Custom…)**   Choosing this entry enables you to create your own custom filter, as described below.

The real power of filters is the Custom AutoFilter, accessed by choosing (Custom…) from any of the filter drop-down lists. When you do, the Custom AutoFilter dialog box appears.

16

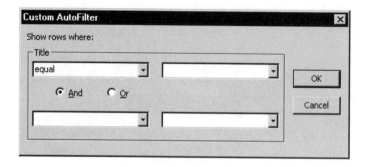

To specify the filter criteria, use the following steps:

1. Choose the comparison function from the top-left drop-down list. The list includes Equal, Not Equal, Is Greater Than, Is Less Than, Begins With, Does Not Begin With, Ends With, Does Not End With, Contains, and Does Not Contain.

2. Specify the value to which the value in the column will be compared in the top-right drop-down list. You can either choose from the list of unique existing values, or type in a value for comparison. You cannot, however, use wildcards such as "*" to match any string the way you can with many other filtering tools.

If any of the records in the report have a blank in the filtered column, the values (Blanks) and (NonBlanks) appear at the end of the list, making it easy to pick these values if you wish.

3. If you wish to add a second criterion (comparison function and value) for the column, enter it in the bottom two drop-down lists. Choosing the And option means that only records that meet *both* criteria will be displayed. Choosing the Or option means that records that meet *either* criterion will be displayed.

4. Click OK to engage the filter and view the results.

NOTE *You can specify a filter on multiple columns if you wish. For example, you can choose to view only broken hyperlinks (set in the Status column) for page titles greater than "B". Only files that meet both criteria will be visible. For example, if the page Breaking News has broken hyperlinks, it will display because it meets both criteria. However, even if the page After the Meet has broken hyperlinks, you won't see it in the report because the page title is not greater than "B".*

Understand the Site Summary Report

The Site Summary report gives you a quick idea of any problems with your site. For example, if the Site Summary report lists a few broken hyperlinks, you'll want to check those on the more detailed report. To run any of the available detailed reports whose summaries appear in the Site Summary report, click the name of the report you want to run (the name is shown in blue underline) in the Site Summary report. The entries in the Site Summary report that do *not* have their own detail reports are

- **Pictures** A summary of the files in the Web site that are image files. These files are listed among the files in the All Files report.

- **Linked files** This line lists a summary of all the files in the Web site that can be reached via hyperlinks. This is the counterpart of the Unlinked Files report, which does have a detailed report.

- **Hyperlinks, Unverified hyperlinks, External hyperlinks, Internal hyperlinks, Broken hyperlinks** All of these entries in the Site Summary report take you to the Broken Hyperlinks report. From the Broken Hyperlinks report, you can inspect and fix any broken or unverified hyperlinks. You can also filter the report to show you just the type of hyperlinks you want to see.

- **Uncompleted tasks** Clicking this summary switches you to the Task view.

- **Unused themes** If you changed your mind about using a theme while you were building your site, your Web site will still contain the now-unused files for that theme. These files can take up a fair amount of space. To get rid of

16

the unused theme files, click the Unused Theme entry in the Site Summary report. FrontPage will confirm that you want to eliminate the unused files (and recalculate the hyperlinks in the process). Confirm that you want to do this by clicking Yes, and the files will be removed.

The Site Summary report contains the following columns:

- **Name**   The name of the report being summarized.

- **Count**   The number of records that meet the report criteria. For the Broken Hyperlinks report, for example, the Count column contains the number of broken hyperlinks.

- **Size**   For reports that return multiple files, this is the total size (in KB) of all the included files. Of course, many reports don't have files associated with them. These include the various hyperlink reports, unfinished tasks, and component errors.

- **Description**   A description of what the summary report measures.

After you have made changes, such as repairing broken hyperlinks or removing unused theme files, you can refresh the Site Summary report by pressing F5 *or selecting View | Refresh.*

Details of the Files Reports

The Files reports include the All Files, Recently Added Files, Recently Changed Files, and Older Files.

All Files Report

The All Files report (see Figure 16-11) provides a listing of the major files in your Web site. You can get an idea of how much space your Web site will take up by adding up the file sizes. Just remember to display all the hidden files if you want a complete picture of all the files that make up your Web site. Showing the hidden files displays an accurate size for your Web site, but it also can be overwhelming, since it includes theme files, files needed to make up shared borders, and a whole host of other hidden or support files. To show the hidden files, choose Tools | Web Settings, and click the Advanced tab. Then check the Show Hidden Files And Folders checkbox.

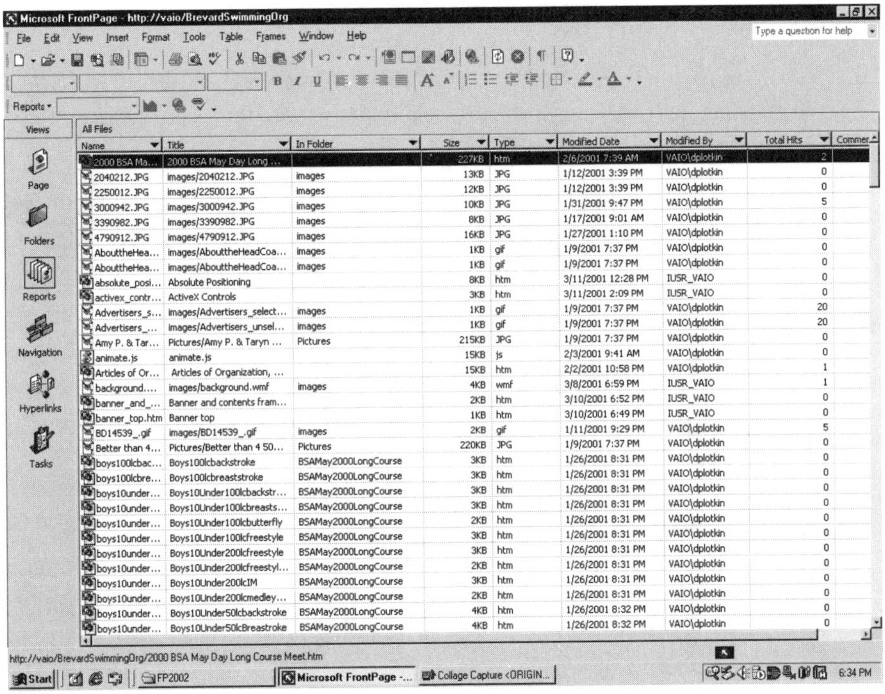

FIGURE 16-11   The All Files report lists all the files in your Web site.

You can change the contents of the Name, Title, and Comments columns. To do so, click in the column for the file you want to modify to make the column editable. Type in the new contents for that column.

The All Files Report includes the following columns:

■ **Title**   The title of the file. If the file is not a page (for example, a graphic, a Java applet, and so on), this is just the filename.

■ **In Folder**   The folder in which the file resides. The folder is relative to the root folder for the Web site.

■ **Size**   The file size (in KB).

■ **Type**   The type of file. For example, page files are type HTM, while most graphics are either GIF or JPG.

16

- **Modified Date**   The date and time the file was last modified. If the file has never been modified, this column contains the creation time and date.

- **Modified By**   The identifier for the person who last modified this file. If the file has never been modified, this is the identifier of the person who created the file.

- **Total Hits**   The number of times this file has been viewed by visitors to your site. The contents of this column are only valid if you are collecting usage data (see "Details of the Usage Reports," later in this chapter).

- **Comments**   General comments about the file.

You can open the files listed in the All Files report. To do so, double-click a file. The file opens in the editor associated with that file type. For example, HTM files normally open in the FrontPage editor.

Recently Added Files

The Recently Added Files report shows you a list of files that have been added to the site, well, recently (the default is files that have been added in the last 30 days). This is especially useful if more than one person is working on the site. Using this report, you can keep track of what is new on the site. To modify a page, double-click it in the report to open the page in Page view.

You can adjust what FrontPage considers a "recently added file" either from the Reports View tab in the Options dialog box (covered previously) or from the Reporting toolbar. When viewing the Recently Added Files report, a second drop-down list appears in the Reporting toolbar. Click this drop-down list and select how recently the file must have been added for it to show up in the report.

The columns in the Recently Added Files report are identical to the All Files report except that the Modified Date is replaced by the Created Date, and the Comments column is missing. As with the All Files report, you can select a file in the report and click the name or title to modify it.

Recently Changed Files

The Recently Changed Files report shows you a list of (can you guess) recently changed files. Using this report, you can keep track of what pages have been modified.

You can adjust what FrontPage considers a "recently changed file" either from the Reports View tab in the Options dialog box (covered previously) or from the Reporting toolbar. When viewing the Recently Changed Files report, a second drop-down list appears in the Reporting toolbar. Click this drop-down list and select how recently the file must have been changed for it to show up in the report.

The columns in the Recently Changed Files report are identical to the Recently Added Files. As with the All Files report, you can select a file in the report and click the name or title to modify it.

Older Files

The Older Files report shows you a list of files that are older than a certain date. The default value is files that are older than 72 days. Use this list to keep an eye on files that might be getting outdated.

You can adjust what FrontPage considers an "older file" either from the Reports View tab in the Options dialog box (covered previously) or from the Reporting toolbar. When viewing the Older Files report, a second drop-down list appears in the Reporting toolbar. Click this drop-down list and select the age of the file you want displayed as an older file.

The columns in the Older Files report are identical to the Recently Changed report, except that this report displays both the Created Date and the Modified Date. As with the All Files report, you can select a file in the report and click the name or title to modify it.

Details of the Problems Reports

Problems reports include Unlinked Files, Slow Pages, Broken Hyperlinks, and Component Errors.

Unlinked Files

The Unlinked Files report lists any page file in your Web site that cannot be reached by starting from your home page. This is either because the link is missing (you forgot to create it) or the link that was supposed to point to the page is broken. Another reason is that you decided you didn't need the page any longer, deleted the links, but neglected to delete the page. The Unlinked Files report also lists any graphic elements that are not used in the Web site. You may wish to get rid of these elements to save space. You can remove a file directly from the Unlinked Files report. To do so, select the file and choose Delete from the shortcut menu.

The columns in the Unlinked Files report are identical to the All Files report except that the Comments column is missing. You can open the files listed in the Unlinked Files report by double-clicking the file. However, this doesn't really help you find where the link to the page (if there should be one) should have originated. Instead, it probably makes more sense to add a task to the task list to investigate and add the link. Note that you *don't* need this task associated with the unlinked file, as it is not necessary to open the unlinked file to fix the problem.

16

Slow Pages

The Slow Pages report lets you know which pages will take a long time to load into a reader's browser. This report injects a dose of reality into your Web design, because many Web creators forget that most people will be viewing their pages over a dial-up modem connection. If the page takes too long to load, the reader might well give up and go elsewhere. To modify the page, double-click it in the report to open the page in Page view.

TIP *You can see the estimated load time for a page as you are working on the page. The load time is near the right end of the status bar along with the assumed connection speed. Oddly, this connection speed has nothing to do with the connection speed assumed for slow pages. To change the assumed connection speed used for calculating download time, right-click the connection speed and choose the connection speed from the shortcut menu (see Figure 16-12).*

The normal cause of a slow page download is one or more large graphics. You can reduce the size of graphics (and improve the page download speed) by shrinking the size of the graphic, reducing the number of colors, or using a thumbnail so the reader can decide by viewing the thumbnail whether to view the full graphic. To adjust the size or number of colors in a graphic, you will need to use a graphic tool. For more information on using the Auto Thumbnail feature, see Chapter 8.

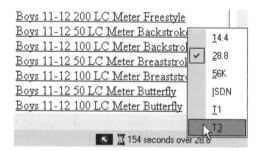

FIGURE 16-12 Select the assumed connection for calculating page download time from the shortcut menu.

It is considered good Web etiquette to note that a page has a long download time on hyperlinks that point to that page. That way, at least the reader will be warned that they have to be patient!

You can adjust what FrontPage considers a slow page either from the Reports View tab in the Options dialog box (covered previously) or from the Reporting toolbar. When viewing the Slow Pages report, a second drop-down list appears in the Reporting toolbar. Click this drop-down list (see Figure 16-13) and select the amount of time a page must take to download before FrontPage considers it a slow page.

The columns in the Slow Pages report are identical to the All Files report, except that the Slow Pages report is missing the Comments column and has an additional column (Download Time) that states the download time in seconds. As with the All Files report, you can select a file in the report and click the name or title to modify it.

Broken Hyperlinks

The Broken Hyperlinks report displays not only broken hyperlinks—hyperlinks with known invalid destinations—but unverified hyperlinks as well (see Figure 16-14). To reach the Broken Hyperlinks report, you can click any of the following in the Site Summary report: Hyperlinks, Broken Hyperlinks, Unverified Hyperlinks, External Hyperlinks, and Internal Hyperlinks.

16

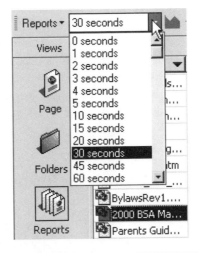

FIGURE 16-13   Select the time it takes before a page is considered slow from the Reporting toolbar.

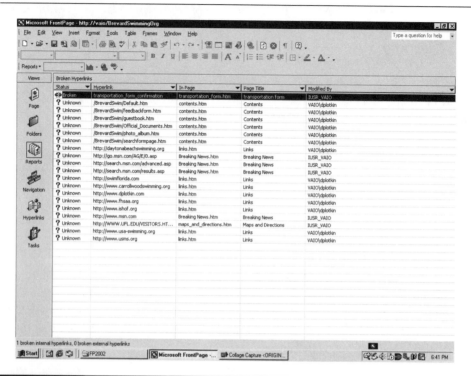

FIGURE 16-14 Check out broken hyperlinks as well as unverified hyperlinks with the Broken Hyperlinks report.

Broken hyperlinks (shown with a status of Broken in the report) are a major pain to someone browsing your Web site. There is very little more frustrating than searching for a particular piece of information, only to be stymied by a broken hyperlink. In addition, broken hyperlinks make the Webmaster (that would be you!) look silly. Thus, the Broken Hyperlink report is one of the most important you'll use in managing your Web site.

NOTE *You can repair broken hyperlinks right from the Broken Hyperlinks report. For details, see "Repair Broken Hyperlinks" later in this chapter.*

As mentioned earlier, the Broken Hyperlinks report also shows you unverified hyperlinks—hyperlinks that may or may not be broken. These are shown with a status of Unknown in the Broken Hyperlinks report. Details on how to repair or verify unverified hyperlinks are discussed in "Verify Hyperlinks," later in this chapter.

The columns in the Broken Hyperlinks report are

- **Status**   The status of the hyperlink. It is either Broken, Unknown, or OK.

If none of your hyperlinks are of a certain status, that status won't be available from the Status filter. For example, if none of your hyperlinks are Unknown, the value Unknown won't be in the Status list.

- **Hyperlink**   The destination of the hyperlink.
- **In Page**   The filename of the page in which the hyperlink is located.
- **Page Title**   The page title of the page in which the hyperlink is located.
- **Modified By**   The person who last modified the page in which the hyperlink is located.

None of the columns in the report are directly modifiable.

Component Errors

As discussed earlier, components add quite a bit of functionality and interactivity to your Web site. However, because components may need other support files, something can go wrong with a component. The Component Errors report lists any components that are not functioning properly. To edit the page on which the component is located, double-click the entry to open the page in Page view. The details of the error are displayed in the Errors column. If you want to read the full text in the Errors column, you can right-click the entry and choose Properties from the shortcut menu. This opens the Properties dialog box, showing the Errors tab, where you can easily read the entire error message.

As with the All Files report, you can select a file in the report and click the name or title to modify it.

Repair Broken Hyperlinks

You can repair broken hyperlinks right from the Broken Hyperlinks report. To do so, use the following steps:

1. Either double-click a broken hyperlink entry or choose Edit Hyperlink from the shortcut menu to open the Edit Hyperlink dialog box (see Figure 16-15).

16

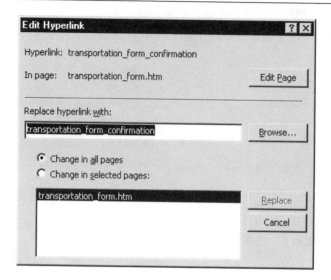

FIGURE 16-15 Use the Edit Hyperlink dialog box to repair a broken hyperlink.

2. Enter the correct hyperlink in the Replace Hyperlink With field (this may take some research!). You can click the Browse button to open the Select Hyperlink dialog box and choose the hyperlink from your Web site or the Internet.

3. Select the option to decide how you want to apply the correction: Change In All Pages or Change In Selected Pages.

4. If you select Change In Selected Pages, select the pages to which you want to apply the change.

5. Click the Replace button to make the hyperlink replacement.

You can also click the Edit Page button to open the page containing the broken hyperlink in Page view. You can then manually edit the hyperlink properties to fix the broken hyperlink.

The Broken Hyperlinks report also enables you to jump directly to the page containing the broken hyperlink, where you can edit the hyperlink to correct the destination. Simply right-click the broken hyperlink entry in the report, and choose Edit Page from the shortcut menu.

You can add a task to go back and fix the broken hyperlink later. Choose Edit | Tasks | Add Task to open the New Task dialog box, which you saw earlier in this chapter. Unfortunately, FrontPage does not associate a task created in this way with the page containing the broken hyperlink.

Details of the Workflow Reports

FrontPage includes several other reports that will help you manage the Web development process. These reports include the Review Status, Assigned To, Categories, and Publish Status reports.

Review Status

The Review Status report (see Figure 16-16) gives you an overview of all the files in your Web site and their review status.

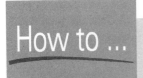

How to ... Verify Hyperlinks

The Broken Hyperlinks report also displays unverified hyperlinks—hyperlinks that may or may not be broken. Typically, these are links outside your Web site that FrontPage has not verified actually exist. The shortcut menu for unverified hyperlinks (which have a status of Unknown in the report) include many of the same choices as broken hyperlinks: Edit Hyperlink, Edit Page, and Add Task. These options work the same as for broken hyperlinks. However, unverified hyperlinks have an additional option: Verify Hyperlink. If you select this option (and are connected to the Internet), FrontPage will notify you that it is verifying the link. If it fails to find the destination you specified, the link status becomes Broken. However, if it does find the link you specified, the link status becomes OK.

16

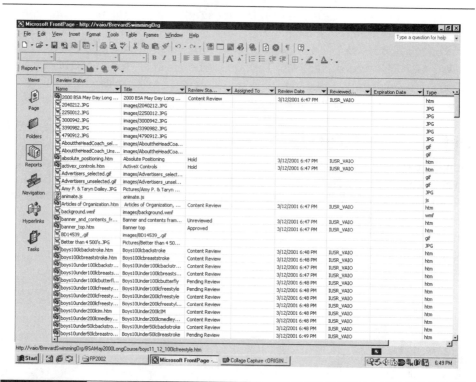

FIGURE 16-16 Use the Review Status report to manage the status of the pages in your Web site.

Typically, you don't care about the review status of anything except Web pages. To quickly filter the report results so that you see only Web pages, click on the small down arrow in the Type column and choose htm from the list.

The columns in this report are

■ **Name** The filename of the file. You can click the contents of this column to make it editable, and change the name if you wish.

■ **Title** The page title of the file. You can click the contents of this column to make it editable, and change the title if you wish.

■ **Review Status**   The current review status. To change the review status, click the contents of this column and choose a value from the drop-down list. Alternatively, you can type in another review status. Any status you type into the list becomes available in the list of statuses for other files. You can also change the value in this field from the Workgroup tab of the Page Properties dialog box (choose Properties from the shortcut menu).

■ **Assigned To**   The person who is responsible for this page. To change the assignee, click the contents of this column and choose a value from the drop-down list. Alternatively, you can type in another assignee. Any name (or other identifier) you type into the list becomes available in the list of assignees for other files. You can also change the value in this field from the Workgroup tab of the Page Properties dialog box (choose Properties from the shortcut menu).

■ **Review Date**   The date on which the review status was last changed. Try it—go to the Review Status column and choose or add a new value. The review date changes to today's date. This column is not directly editable.

■ **Reviewed By**   The identifier for the person who last changed the review status. This column is not directly editable.

■ **Type**   The file type (for example, HTM, JPG, GIF, and so on).

■ **In Folder**   The folder in which the file is located.

■ **Expiration Date**   The date on which the file expires. To change the expiration date, click on the drop-down list and choose None (removes any expiration date), Expired (sets the value in the column to Expired), or Custom. If you choose Custom, FrontPage opens the Date and Time dialog box (as shown in Figure 16-17) where you can enter the date and time on which the file expires. Once you select a date and time, FrontPage evaluates the date/time and enters either Expired (the date and time specified has passed) or the date and time you entered (the date and time is still in the future).

16

TIP   *To choose the expiration date from a calendar, click the down arrow in the Date and Time dialog box and use the Calendar tool to pick a date.*

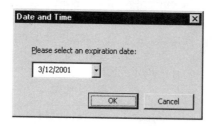

FIGURE 16-17   Pick the date and time on which the file expires from the Date and Time dialog box.

To edit a page in Page view, double-click the file's entry in the report.

Assigned To

The Assigned To report displays who is responsible for developing a particular Web page. The columns in the Assigned To report are

- **Name**   The filename of the file. You can click the contents of this column to make it editable, and change the name if you wish.

- **Title**   The page title of the file. You can click the contents of this column to make it editable, and change the title if you wish.

- **Assigned To**   The person who is responsible for this page. To change the assignee, click the contents of this column and choose a value from the drop-down list. Alternatively, you can type in another assignee. Any name (or other identifier) you type into the list becomes available in the list of assignees for other files. You can also change the value in this field from the Workgroup tab of the Page Properties dialog box (choose Properties from the shortcut menu).

- **Assign Date**   The date on which a person was assigned responsibility for the page. This is the last date a value was entered or changed in the Assigned To column. This column is not directly editable.

- **Assigned By**   The identifier for the person who last changed the assignment. This column is not directly editable.

- **Comments**   The page comments. You can click the contents of this column to make it editable and change the comments if you wish. You can also change the value in this field from the Summary tab of the Page Properties dialog box (choose Properties from the shortcut menu).

- ■ **Type**   The file type (for example, HTM, JPG, GIF, and so on).
- ■ **In Folder**   The folder in which the file is located.

To edit a page in Page view, double-click the file's entry in the report.

Categories

The Categories report lists all the categories that have been assigned to a page in the Categories column. You can't directly edit the contents of the Categories column. Instead, choose Properties from the shortcut menu and choose the Workgroup tab in the Properties dialog box. As discussed earlier in this book, check off the categories you want to assign to the page. These categories then appear in the Categories column of the Categories report.

> NOTE   *You can filter the list on a single category by choosing the category from the drop-down list in the Reports toolbar. If you do filter this way, FrontPage ignores any filter you apply in the Category column.*

To edit a page in Page view, double-click the file's entry in the report. As with the All Files report, you can select a file in the report and click the name or title to modify it.

Change the Publish Status

The Publish Status report (see Figure 16-18) displays every file in your Web site and whether the file is slated to be published the next time you publish your site. This report is how you control which pages get published. If the file's status is Publish, the page will be sent to the host server the next time you publish your Web site. If the file's status is Don't Publish, the page will not be sent to the host server when you publish your Web site. To edit any page listed in the report in Page view, double-click the file.

The columns in the report are

- ■ **Name**   The filename of the file. You can click the contents of this column to make it editable and change the name if you wish.

16

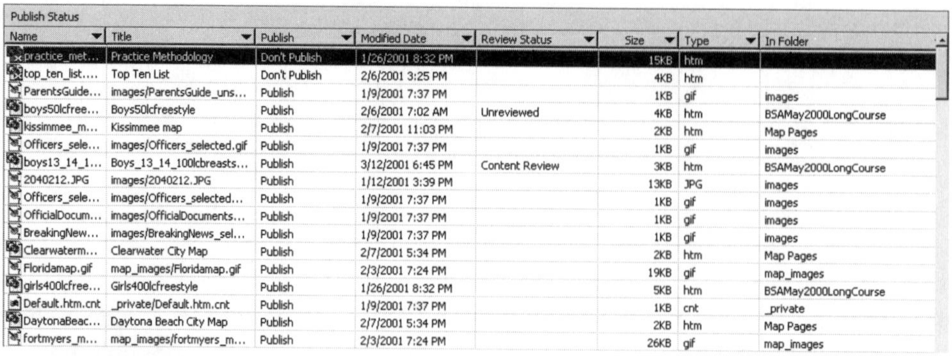

Publish Status

Name	Title	Publish	Modified Date	Review Status	Size	Type	In Folder
practice_met...	Practice Methodology	Don't Publish	1/26/2001 8:32 PM		15KB	htm	
top_ten_list....	Top Ten List	Don't Publish	2/6/2001 3:25 PM		4KB	htm	
ParentsGuide...	images/ParentsGuide_uns...	Publish	1/9/2001 7:37 PM		1KB	gif	images
boys50lcfree...	Boys50lcfreestyle	Publish	2/6/2001 7:02 AM	Unreviewed	4KB	htm	BSAMay2000LongCourse
kissimmee_m...	Kissimmee map	Publish	2/7/2001 11:03 PM		2KB	htm	Map Pages
Officers_sele...	images/Officers_selected.gif	Publish	1/9/2001 7:37 PM		1KB	gif	images
boys13_14_1...	Boys_13_14_100lcbreasts...	Publish	3/12/2001 6:45 PM	Content Review	3KB	htm	BSAMay2000LongCourse
2040212.JPG	images/2040212.JPG	Publish	1/12/2001 3:39 PM		13KB	JPG	images
Officers_sele...	images/Officers_selected...	Publish	1/9/2001 7:37 PM		1KB	gif	images
OfficialDocum...	images/OfficialDocuments...	Publish	1/9/2001 7:37 PM		1KB	gif	images
BreakingNew...	images/BreakingNews_sel...	Publish	1/9/2001 7:37 PM		1KB	gif	images
Clearwaterm...	Clearwater City Map	Publish	2/7/2001 5:34 PM		2KB	htm	Map Pages
Floridamap.gif	map_images/Floridamap.gif	Publish	2/3/2001 7:24 PM		19KB	gif	map_images
girls400lcfree...	Girls400lcfreestyle	Publish	1/26/2001 8:32 PM		5KB	htm	BSAMay2000LongCourse
Default.htm.cnt	_private/Default.htm.cnt	Publish	1/9/2001 7:37 PM		1KB	cnt	_private
DaytonaBeac...	Daytona Beach City Map	Publish	2/7/2001 5:34 PM		2KB	htm	Map Pages
fortmyers_m...	map_images/fortmyers_m...	Publish	2/3/2001 7:24 PM		26KB	gif	map_images

FIGURE 16-18 The Publish Status report is where you control whether to publish a page or not.

- **Title** The page title of the file. You can click the contents of this column to make it editable, and change the title if you wish.
- **Publish** The publishing status. To change the status, click the column and select a value (Publish or Don't Publish) from the drop-down list.
- **Modified Date** The date on which the file was last changed.
- **Review Status** The current review status. To change the review status, click the contents of this column and choose a value from the drop-down list. Alternatively, you can type in another review status. Any status you type into the list becomes available in the list of statuses for other files. You can also change the value in this field from the Workgroup tab of the Page Properties dialog box (choose Properties from the shortcut menu).
- **Size** The size of the file (in KB).
- **Type** The file type (for example, HTM, JPG, GIF, and so on).
- **In Folder** The folder in which the file is located.

Details of the Usage Reports

The Usage reports help you analyze what pages on your site are most (and least) popular, as well as summarizing information about the people who visited your site. There are three major categories of reports included in the Usage reports: Time-Based Summaries, Page Hits, and General Information Counts.

NOTE   *The usage information has to be collected by the server that hosts your Web site. The server must be configured by your Web presence provider (WPP) to provide usage information. You can also test some usage information using a local server-based Web site. However, information such as top referrer, top referring domain, etc., can only be collected on a remote server. Also, if usage information is not being collected, all the usage reports will be blank.*

Time-Based Summary Reports

The time-based summary reports include the Usage Summary, Monthly Summary, Weekly Summary, and Daily Summary reports.

The Usage Summary (see Figure 16-19) lists summary data items, such as the total visits to the site, top referring Web site, most popular Web browser, and other general information. Clicking on one of the hyperlinked items (such as Total Visits) takes you to a Monthly Summary report.

The Monthly Usage Summary report summarizes information by month for the following columns:

- **Month**   The month for which the summary information is provided. You can set the number of lines in the report (one for each month) by using the Reports View tab of the Options dialog box (choose Tools | Options). Select the number of months from the Number Of Months Shown spinner.

- **Visits**   The number of unique visits to your Web site during that month.

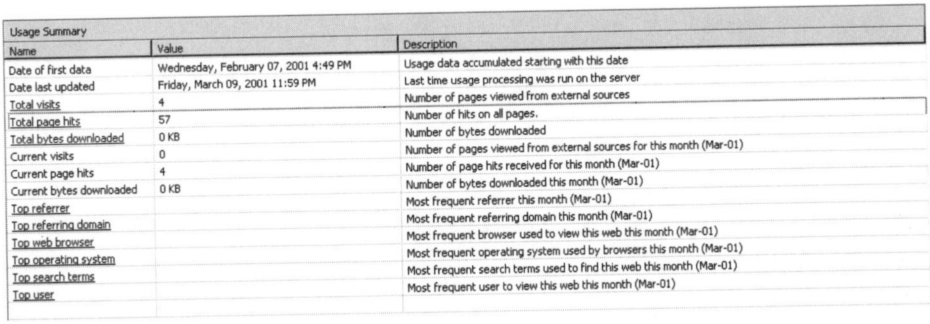

Usage Summary

Name	Value	Description
Date of first data	Wednesday, February 07, 2001 4:49 PM	Usage data accumulated starting with this date
Date last updated	Friday, March 09, 2001 11:59 PM	Last time usage processing was run on the server
Total visits	4	Number of pages viewed from external sources
Total page hits	57	Number of hits on all pages.
Total bytes downloaded	0 KB	Number of bytes downloaded
Current visits	0	Number of pages viewed from external sources for this month (Mar-01)
Current page hits	4	Number of page hits received for this month (Mar-01)
Current bytes downloaded	0 KB	Number of bytes downloaded this month (Mar-01)
Top referrer		Most frequent referrer this month (Mar-01)
Top referring domain		Most frequent referring domain this month (Mar-01)
Top web browser		Most frequent browser used to view this web this month (Mar-01)
Top operating system		Most frequent operating system used by browsers this month (Mar-01)
Top search terms		Most frequent search terms used to find this web this month (Mar-01)
Top user		Most frequent user to view this web this month (Mar-01)

16

FIGURE 16-19   The Usage Summary report gives you a quick summary of your Web site statistics.

■ **Hits**   The number of unique page hits for that month.

■ **Total Hits**   The total number of page hits for the month.

■ **Download Size**   The total amount of information downloaded from you site. This amount is only populated if you make files available for download on your site.

The Weekly Summary report summarizes information by week. It is similar to the Monthly Summary report, except that each line in the report represents one week, with the date range for that week being shown in the Week column. The Weekly Summary report does not show the download size; instead, it has a new column entitled Percentage Of Hits, which calculates and displays the percentage of the total hits on the site that occurred during that week.

Week	Visits	Hits	Total Hits	Percentage Of Hits
3/4/2001-3/9/2001	0	4	183	7%
2/25/2001-3/3/2001	0	1	180	1%
2/18/2001-2/24/2001	0	0	0	0%
2/11/2001-2/17/2001	0	2	72	3%
2/4/2001-2/10/2001	4	50	438	87%

The Daily Summary report summarizes information by day. It is identical to the Weekly Summary report, except that each line in the report represents one day, with the date being shown in the Day column.

Page Hits Reports

There are three Page Hits reports: Monthly Page Hits, Weekly Page Hits, and Daily Page Hits. Each of the reports displays columns for Name (filename), Title (page title), In Folder (the folder containing the file), and Total Hits (hits on that page for the time period).

The Monthly Page Hits report (see Figure 16-20) lists one column for each month from the current month back. The default is to go back one year, but you can change the number of months from the Reports View tab of the Options dialog box (choose Tools | Options). The Weekly Page Hits report lists one column for each week for the past month. The Daily Page Hits report lists one column for each day for the past week.

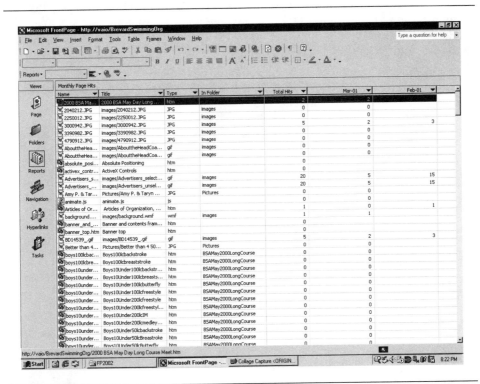

| FIGURE 16-20 | Check out the number of hits on a page during each month using the Monthly Page Hits report. |

General Information Count Reports

The General Information Count reports provide counts for Visiting Users, Operating Systems, Browsers, Referring Domains, Referring URLs, and Search Strings. Each of these counts is provided in a different report, but except for the first column (which details what is being counted), all the reports display the same information:

- **Count**   The number of times a particular value of Visiting User, Operating System, etc. occurs for the given time period.

- **Percentage**   The overall percentage of the total that this value represents.

Graphing the Usage Reports

The long lists of numbers presented in the Usage reports can be overwhelming. It is often easier to understand trends by viewing your data in a graphical format. To produce a graph of the report you are currently viewing, click on the arrow alongside the small Graph icon in the Reporting toolbar to display a list of available graphs.

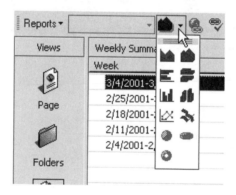

Select the type of graph you want from the list and FrontPage displays the graph for you.

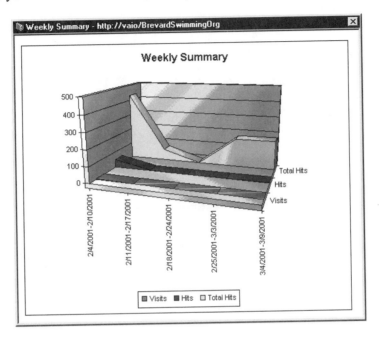

Chapter 17

Publish Your Web Site

How to...

■ Test and review your site for errors

■ Find a WPP that supports the FrontPage server extensions

■ Publish your FrontPage Web site to a host server

The time has finally come—your carefully crafted Web site is done. However, you still have a few things left to do. First, you need to make sure the Web site is error-free—errors in your Web site make you look foolish. You also need to find a WPP (Web presence provider) to host your Web site, and you'll have to publish your Web site to the host's server.

Test and Review Your Site

No matter how carefully you crafted your Web site while you were building it, there are bound to be some errors in it. Perhaps it is a misspelled word, a broken hyperlink, a page that takes forever to load, a page you thought you had linked in but hadn't, and so on. The more complex your site, the higher the likelihood that there are at least a few small items that need correcting. Don't despair! You have already learned how to use the tools you need to ensure that your Web site is correct and error-free.

Spell Check and Read the Site Contents

The first step in error-checking your site is to use the spell checker, as covered in Chapter 2. This may seem obvious, but the wealth of spelling mistakes on existing Web sites makes it painfully clear that many site designers don't bother with this fundamental step. Yet very few things make you look sillier and call the credibility of your Web site into question more than obvious spelling errors.

Unfortunately, it is not enough to simply run the spell checker and accept the suggested corrections. Often, the silliest mistake is substituting one word for another. This can happen due to a typo (for example, substituting *haste* for *waste*) or misspelling (substituting *to* for *too*), but either way, the spell checker won't catch this sort of mistake. Until smarter spell checkers come along, it will be up to you to catch these types of errors by carefully proofreading the text on each Web page. Even better is to have someone else proofread your pages—it is very difficult to proof your own work.

Find Errors with Reports

FrontPage provides you with a number of reports (covered in Chapter 16) you can use to find problems with your Web site—and easily fix those problems. These reports include Broken Hyperlinks, Component Errors, and Unlinked Files.

Broken and Unverified Hyperlinks

Have you ever gone to a Web site, clicked a hyperlink, and gotten a message (typically with the heading "404 Not Found") that informs you the hyperlink points to a nonexistent page? I don't know about you, but I usually have some choice things to say about the Webmaster for that site! FrontPage includes reports that let you know if there are problems with your hyperlinks. If either the Broken Hyperlinks or the Unverified Hyperlinks (or both) line in the Site Summary report displays a number other than zero, you know you have problems. As mentioned in Chapter 16, the unverified hyperlinks are not necessarily broken, but FrontPage has not ensured that they are indeed valid, so you should verify each hyperlink (you'll need to be connected to the Internet to do so), and repair any hyperlinks that point to nonexistent destinations. The easiest way to verify a hyperlink is to right-click the unverified link and choose Verify Hyperlink from the shortcut menu.

You also need to repair any broken hyperlinks from the Broken Hyperlinks report. The easiest way to accomplish this is to right-click the broken hyperlink, and choose either Edit Hyperlink or Edit Page from the shortcut menu. Edit the hyperlink's destination either from the dialog box (Edit Hyperlink) or from the page (Edit Page) to point to a valid destination or to remove the hyperlink.

Component Errors

Components are advanced items you can add to a Web page (see Chapter 12 for more information). Component errors are items that will not work properly once the Web site is published to the host server. For example, if you are publishing a FrontPage 2002 Web site to a server that does not have FrontPage extensions installed, certain components won't work. This type of component error is often beyond your control unless you are willing to switch hosts. About all you can do is remove the components from your Web site.

There are component errors you *can* fix, however. For example, you can add a substitution to a Web page by choosing Insert | Web Component, choosing Included Content from the list of Component types, and selecting Substitution from the right side of the dialog box. One of the items you can add as a substitution is a

17

Web parameter (choose Tools | Web Settings and click on the Parameters tab to specify a parameter). If you reference a parameter in a substitution that doesn't exist, you'll get a component error. You either need to remove the substitution or define the parameter.

Unlinked Files

Technically, unlinked files may not be a problem—other than visitors to your site can't see these files, so why publish them in the first place? But you should inspect the list of files, because if a Web page shows up in this list that you expected readers to be able to access, you'll need to add a link to the page. Also, if you publish unlinked pages, any search form on your site might find these pages during a search.

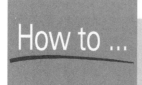 **Find a WPP that Supports FrontPage Server Extensions**

If you don't have a Web presence provider (WPP) that supports FrontPage server extensions, you're going to need to find one. The first way is to peruse the major computer magazines—many of these have advertisements for WPPs. These advertisements will usually state whether FrontPage server extensions are supported. The advertisements will also usually state other important parameters, such as how much disk space, bandwidth, and number of e-mail accounts are included with the account.

Another way to find a WPP is to choose File | Publish Web to display the Publish Web dialog box. Make sure you are connected to the Internet and click the hyperlink labeled Click Here To Learn More. This opens your Web browser and directs it to Microsoft's Web site at http://www.microsoftwpp.com/wppsearch/. Here, you can search for a WPP by company, location, and services offered.

Publish Your Web Site to a WPP Host Server

Once you get an account on a host server, you need to publish your site.
"Publishing" consists of transmitting the Web site files over the Internet to the host
server. FrontPage makes this relatively simple, especially if the host server has the
FrontPage server extensions installed. To publish your site, you need to know
three things:

- The URL (destination on the Internet) for publishing

- Your username on the host server

- Your password

Once you sign up for Web hosting services, the Web presence provider should
supply all three of these items to you. The URL is usually in the format of http://
www.servername.net/username/ or something similar. Just make sure you write down
all three of these important items or you won't be able to publish your Web site!

Publishing to a Server with FrontPage Server Extensions

To publish your Web site to a host server that supports the FrontPage server
extensions, use the following steps:

1. Select File | Publish Web. If you've never published the Web site before,
   FrontPage opens the Publish Destination dialog box.

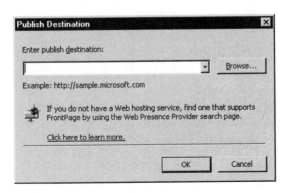

NOTE *Once you've published your Web site, FrontPage remembers the destination. Thus, FrontPage won't display the Publish Destination dialog box, and prompts you for your username and password instead (see step 3). If you need to change the publishing destination for your site, see the Tip below (step 5).*

2. Type the URL to which you are going to publish your Web site. For example, it might look like http://www.*servername*.net/*username*/.

CAUTION *When publishing to a server that has the FrontPage server extensions enabled for your account, always use http:// as the beginning of the location to which to publish your Web site. This prefix uses FrontPage's special publishing mechanism. Publishing using a prefix of ftp:// (or using another FTP tool) can corrupt the server extensions on your account, requiring the host to reinstall them for you.*

3. Enter your username and password in the dialog box.

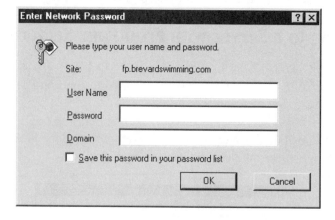

4. Click OK to open the Publish Web dialog box.

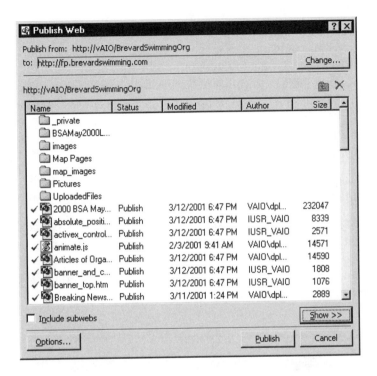

TIP *You can change the publishing destination from the Publish Web dialog box. Simply click on the Change button to open the Publish Destination dialog box.*

5. To publish any subwebs of the selected Web site, check the Include Subwebs checkbox.

6. If you wish to configure the publishing options, click the Options button to open the Options dialog box, displaying the Publish tab (see Figure 17-1). Your options are

■ **Publish changed pages only**   Choose this option if you want to publish just the pages that have changed on the Web site. Otherwise, choose All Pages, Overwriting Pages Already On Destination.

17

■ **Determine changes between source and target**   If you choose to publish only the files that have changed, you need to specify how FrontPage is going to figure out *which* files have changed. If you want FrontPage to compare the files between the source (your PC) and the destination (your hosted Web site), choose Determine Changes By Comparing Source And Destination Webs. If you would rather use the file timestamps, choose Use Source File Timestamps To Determine Changes Since Last Publish.

■ **Log the publishing changes**   If you want to keep track of exactly what was published, check the Log Changes During Publish checkbox.

7. If you just want to publish your Web site, you can click on the Publish button and wait while your Web site is published (if you are not connected to the Internet, click Connect when FrontPage prompts you). However, you have much more control over exactly what happens during the publishing operation, as detailed below.

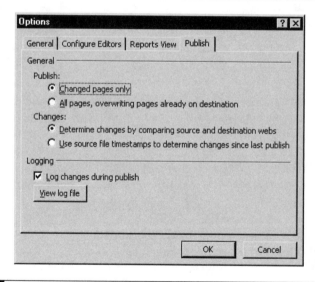

FIGURE 17-1   Use the Publish Tab of the Options dialog box to configure your Web publishing options.

8. FrontPage begins publishing your pages to the Web site. You can watch the progress as it proceeds.

9. Once the publishing finishes successfully, FrontPage prompts you to click the supplied hyperlink to view your published site.

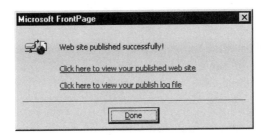

Control Web Publishing with the Expanded Publish Web Dialog Box

The Publish Web dialog box provides a considerable degree of control over how you can publish your Web site. First of all, you can compare the Web site on your PC with the hosted Web site on the server. To do so, click the Show >> button to expand the Publish Web dialog box.

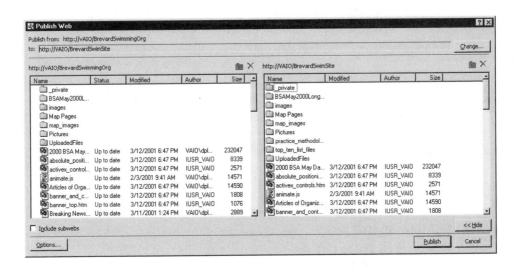

17

The area on the left side of the expanded dialog box displays the FrontPage Web site on your local machine. The area on the right side displays the Web site on the remote server. Using this expanded view, you can compare the two sites, comparing files, modification date, author, and file size. The Status column in the left window gives you an idea of what you'll need to do to bring the two Web sites into "synch." The Status column can contain four values:

- **Publish**   This value indicates that the file on your local machine is different—and more recent—than the file on the remote server. This file will be published.

- **Don't Publish**   If you have set any files to a status of Don't Publish, this value will appear in the Status column for that file.

- **Up to date**   This value indicates that the file on your local machine and the file on the remote server are identical, and thus the file does not need to be published again.

- **Conflict**   This value indicates that the file on your local machine is not only different from the file on the remote server, but the remote file is more up-to-date. Thus, publishing the local file will overwrite a more recent file and may not be a good idea. This condition occurs for files that are updated on the remote server, such as the guest book or form results files. In this case, it is best to use drag and drop (see below) to copy the file from the remote server to your local machine.

The shortcut menu available for the files in the left window (your local machine) gives you considerable power. In addition to the standard items such as Cut, Copy, Paste, Rename, and Delete, you can use the following commands:

- **Change the Publish Status**   You can change the publish status of any file on the left side of the dialog box by choosing the Don't Publish toggle from the shortcut menu. When this menu item is selected (checked), the file won't be published.

- **Publish Selected Files**   Choose one or more files on the left side of the Publish Web dialog box and select this menu item to publish just the files you have selected.

■ **Delete a File**   You can delete a file from either the left side of the dialog box (the FrontPage Web site on your local PC) or the right side (the Web site on the remote host). This is *not* recommended, as you can foul up a Web site pretty good by deleting random files! But if you know you no longer need a file on the remote host, go ahead and delete it. Good examples are the default files (such as "under construction" graphics) provided by WPPs when you sign up for a site.

You can also delete a file by selecting it and clicking on the small X near the upper-right corner of either the left or right windows in the Publish Web dialog box.

Publish Your Web Using Drag and Drop

You can publish files or folders from your local PC to the remote host by dragging and dropping a file from the left side window of the Publish Web dialog box to the right-side window. You can also retrieve files or folders from the remote host by dragging them from the right-side window to the left-side window of the Web Publish dialog box. This can be extremely handy for retrieving uploaded files and updating your local copy of the Web site for changes made to the remote Web site by someone else. It is *especially* useful to retrieve files that are automatically updated on the Web site—such as the hit counter (Default.htm.cnt in the _private folder), feedback and form result documents, the guest book, and even the contents of database updated by a form (see Chapter 18).

If you want to work with files that are inside a folder (such as images), double-click on the folder in the Publish Web dialog box to display the contents of the folder.

Publish to an FTP Server

If (and only if) the server to which you are publishing does not have the FrontPage server extensions installed, you can use File Transfer Protocol (FTP) to publish your Web site. Of course, none of the advanced features of FrontPage will work (more about this a little later in the chapter), but a basic Web site can be published without the extensions. Since most of the free hosting services on the Internet do *not* have FrontPage extensions, you may be stuck with such a service if you can't afford to pay for Web hosting.

17

Many Internet service providers (ISPs) provide their members with free space that can be used to host a small Web site. This feature is often not publicized (I wonder why?). For example, as of this writing, America Online, MSN, Yahoo, Excite, and CompuServe provide such space.

Send Your Web Site to an FTP Server

Publishing to an FTP server is not very different from publishing to a FrontPage server. To do so, use the following steps:

1. Select File | Publish Web to open the Publish Web dialog box.

2. When prompted, enter your username and password and click OK.

3. Type the URL to which you are going to publish your Web site. This time, it will begin with ftp://—for example, ftp://server.host.net/username/subdirectory.

4. Click the Publish button. If you are not connected to the Internet, just click Connect when FrontPage prompts you.

5. FrontPage begins publishing your Web site. Once the publishing process has completed, you can click the supplied link to view the site.

If your site uses any features or components of FrontPage that won't work without the FrontPage Server extensions, you will be warned when you try to publish your Web site. You really should remove these components before publishing. Otherwise, you'll get strange results. For example, if you try to use a search form, the only result you'll get is a page that tells you that FrontPage extensions are not installed. Guess how I know that?

Establish an FTP Location

If you regularly publish to several FTP locations, you may wish to save those locations so you can select them from a list, rather than typing in a rather long and convoluted address. To do so, use the following steps:

1. Choose File | Publish Web to open the Publish Web dialog box (or the Publish Destination dialog box if you've never published the site before—and skip to step 3).

2. Click the Change button to open the Publish Destination dialog box.

3. Click the Browse button to open the New Publish Location dialog box.

4. From the Look In drop-down list, pick Add/Modify FTP Locations.

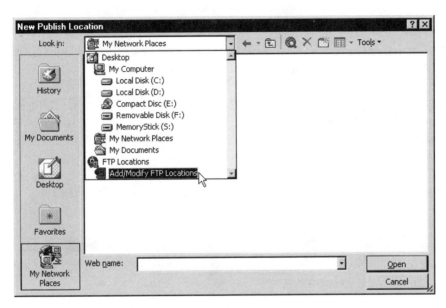

5. FrontPage opens the Add/Modify FTP Locations dialog box.

6. Type the full URL of the location to which you want to publish your pages into the Name Of FTP Site field.

7. Choose the User option, and type your username in the adjacent drop-down list. Enter the password that goes with this username.

8. Click Add to add the combination of the URL, username, and password to the list of FTP sites at the bottom of the dialog box.

To change a previously defined FTP location, select the location from the list of sites in the FTP Sites list. Make any changes to the FTP site, username, and password. Then click Modify. To delete a previously defined FTP location, select the location from the list of sites and click Remove.

Once you've specified a set of FTP locations, you can click the Browse button in the Publish Destination dialog box, choose FTP Locations from the Look In drop-down list, and pick an FTP site from the list.

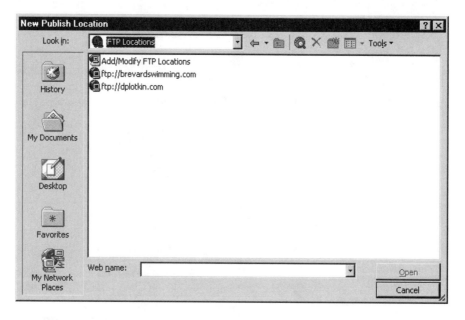

Limitations for Publishing to an FTP Server

As alluded to above, a number of the features and components of FrontPage 2002 won't work if you publish to an FTP server using FrontPage 2002 because they require the FrontPage extensions. If you attempt to publish Web pages that include any of these features or components, you'll be warned when you try to publish.

The features and components that won't work without the FrontPage extensions include the following:

- Form handler (including discussion group forms, registration forms, and search forms)
- Shared borders
- Include pages
- Scheduled pages and graphics
- Hit counter
- Top ten lists
- Subwebs
- Cascading Style Sheets
- Customized themes
- Dynamic HTML
- Usage analysis reports

Part IV

Database Integration and Advanced Formatting

Chapter 18

Route Form Results to a Database

How to...

- Store form results in a database table
- Specify the columns into which field data is placed
- Create a new database for your form results
- Connect to an existing database on a Web server or network computer
- Verify that the database connection is working

Earlier in this book, we discussed how to build forms and how to place the results from the form into a text or HTML file. There is a lot you can do with these results, but there are also some significant limits.

Why Use a Database?

Once you start to get a significant number of results (say, several hundred or a thousand), keeping form results in a text or HTML file gets unwieldy. It is very hard to analyze the results looking for trends and statistics. However, a database is *designed* to handle a large volume of data. In addition, most databases have tools available to enable you to run reports, archive old data, find or replace all records that contain specified information, and in general, "mine" your data for valuable information. Thus, if you anticipate that a form will generate a lot of data that could prove of value, you may well be better off routing the form results to a database.

Another very good reason to route form results to a database is if you need a database application to process those results. For example, if you take orders on your Web site, you are likely to want to create an order form and send the results to your orders database. Sending the information to a text or HTML file would be counterproductive in this instance.

Store Data in a Table

As you may be aware, a database consists of one or more *tables*. The results from a form are stored in a single table, which FrontPage will create for you if you wish. Each row in the table contains a single set of form results. That is, each time someone submits the form, a new row is created in the table to contain those results. Each field on the form corresponds to a column in the table. The table columns do not have to have the same name as the form fields, but it is less confusing if they do. For example, if you build a form with fields called Last_Name and First_Name, the data submitted will normally go into columns called Last_Name and First_Name in the table. Table 18-1 shows a sample of what a database table might look like after three form submissions. The top row displays the column names.

NOTE   *The first column in this table illustrates a common database requirement: the need for a column that uniquely identifies each row in the database. While this unique identifier can be a collection of multiple columns, it is more typical to use a unique and meaningless number. If you allow FrontPage to create your database table for you, the default behavior is to automatically create the unique identifier column and populate this column with a unique number when the form is submitted. You do not need a field on your form for this column. However, if you already assign a unique identifier to the person submitting the form results (such as a customer ID), you can have the person fill in that value on the form and use that column as the unique identifier. To override FrontPage's unique ID behavior, choose Tool | Page Options. In the General tab of the Page Options dialog box, clear the Assign Unique IDs To New Tables checkbox.*

Basics of Database Connections

In order to send form results to a database, you must establish a connection between FrontPage and the target database. At its simplest level, you can instruct FrontPage to create a connection to an Access database using point and click (and we'll show you how shortly). In fact, FrontPage can build an Access database and the connection to the database all in one step. However, database connections are completely separate from the database itself—you can connect to a database using more than one database connection, and you can reuse a database connection to connect to the database from multiple forms. If you aren't using an Access database

ID	Last_Name	First_Name	Occupation
1	Jones	Sam	Data Administrator
2	Smith	Mary	Police Officer
3	Greenlee	Sarah	Hotelier

TABLE 18-1   Sample Database Results from Three Form Submissions

18

running on your local machine, however, database connections can become considerably more complex. The type of database connection you create will depend not only on the database you are trying to connect to, but where that database is located. There are four possibilities for database connections:

- Access database running on your local machine (and published to the Web server along with your FrontPage Web)

- Any other database (such as FoxPro, Paradox, dBase, Approach, and so on) running on your local machine (and published to the Web server along with your FrontPage Web site)

- A database running on a Web host server

- A database running on a network server

Each of these possibilities requires that you perform a different set of tasks to set up the connection to the database. And, in most cases, you will need special information provided by a network administrator, database administrator (DBA), or Web host administrator to set up the connection.

Something else you will need is a special piece of software known as a *driver*. The driver software translates the commands from FrontPage into commands that can be understood by the database. Drivers come in two flavors: native drivers and open database connectivity (ODBC) drivers. Native drivers are usually very fast and efficient, because they are designed to work specifically with a particular database and are optimized for that database. ODBC drivers are usually slower, but may be more widely available. Virtually every database on the market today has ODBC drivers available. Both native and ODBC drivers must be installed on your machine before you can set up a connection to a database using the driver.

You may already have ODBC database drivers installed on your computer. Internet Explorer, Windows 98, Windows NT 4 and Windows 2000 all install some ODBC drivers during the installation process. To check for the drivers, click the Start button and choose Settings | Control Panel to open the Control Panel. If the Control Panel includes an icon labeled either ODBC Data Sources or ODBC, you have at least some ODBC drivers installed. In Windows 2000, you have to open the Administrative Tools and look for Data Sources (ODBC). To view the list of drivers, double-click the ODBC icon to open the associated dialog box. Click the Drivers tab (see Figure 18-1).

Only 32-bit ODBC drivers are supported by Windows 95/98; Windows NT supports both 16-bit and 32-bit drivers. Thus, if you're unable to get your form

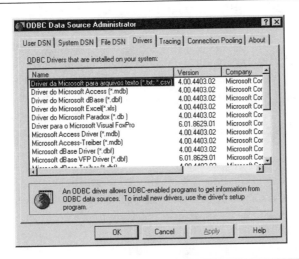

results to successfully route to a database, you may need to update your ODBC
drivers. To do so, you can log on to Microsoft's Universal Data Access Web site
at http://www.microsoft.com/data/odbc.

Connections on the Web Server

The Web server to which you publish forms that use database-based results must
be configured properly. At a minimum, the server must have the FrontPage server
extensions installed, as well as the Microsoft Data Access Components. If you are
testing a server-based Web site on your local machine, installing the Office Web
Server on IIS running in Windows 2000 provides all the functionality you need.

If you are using an Access database to store your results, and that database
resides within your Web site, it should work as long as these requirements are met.

If you want to use any other type of database or if the database does *not* reside
within your Web site, you must set up a connection known as a *system DSN* in
order to connect to the database. The parameters for setting up this connection
must be supplied to you by the hosting service. Most hosting services charge extra
for each DSN you require (you need one for each different type of database you
send form results to).

Many sites offer ODBC database support. However, in order to set up the
ODBC connection and have it point to your database, you must either configure

18

the Web host server's ODBC connection using the server's ODBC Data Source Administrator or have the Web hosting service set up this connection for you. This latter option is the most likely one, since most Web hosting services will not let you change the ODBC Data Source Administrator settings on the host server.

Some hosting services may also offer native database support (Microsoft SQL Server is a common option and is also included with Office Web Server), but the native support varies widely by site. In addition, the Web site must support active server pages (ASP) because a form that sends its results to a database must be an active server page.

> NOTE *ASP is a technology for dynamically generating Web pages from the contents of a database—or populating a database from the contents of a Web page. Support for ASP is built into Microsoft Personal Web Server and IIS, so you can test routing form results to a database using server-based Web sites on your own PC if you are using PWS 4.0 or IIS 5.0.*

Save Form Results to a New Access Database

The quickest and easiest way to save form results to a database is to use an Access database that resides within your Web site. You don't need to do anything special to set this up, and FrontPage will even create the database you need. Of course, to view and manipulate the contents of the database you do need a copy of Access, but given that Access is inexpensive and easy to use (at least, in comparison with the other databases available), using Access isn't a bad choice.

> NOTE *When Access databases get very large (in excess of 10,000 records) performance gets to be a problem, and you'll need to consider stepping up to a more "industrial-strength" database.*

To route the results of a form to a new Access database, use the following steps:

1. Create the form from which you want to route the results to a database. You can use any techniques you want, including the Form Page Wizard or one of the form templates, or you can build the form from scratch. Save the page (File | Save) and give the page a name that ends with the extension .asp.

NOTE *The ending .asp (which stands for active server page) is necessary for the form to correctly route the results of the form to the database. If you don't use the .asp ending at this point, FrontPage will warn you that the form won't work when you later save the form after inserting the database information.*

2. Right-click in the form and choose Form Properties from the shortcut menu. This opens the Form Properties dialog box. Choose the Send To Database option (see Figure 18-2). Don't click OK yet.

3. Click the Options button to open the Options For Saving Results To Database dialog box (see Figure 18-3).

4. Click the Create Database button. FrontPage creates an Access database with the same name as the form whose results are being saved to the database, and places the Access database file into the fpdb directory.

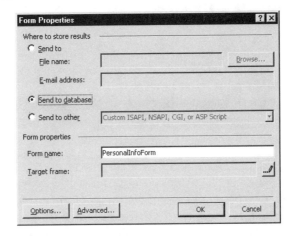

FIGURE 18-2   The first step in routing form results to a database is to choose this option in the Form Properties dialog box.

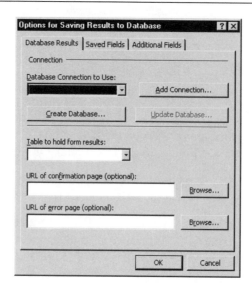

FIGURE 18-3   Use the Options For Saving Results To Database dialog box to set up the database into which the form results will be placed.

Once this operation is complete, FrontPage confirms the creation of the database, as shown here.

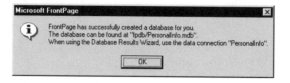

NOTE

If the form page contains more than a single form element, FrontPage will create multiple Access databases. Each Access database is named for the form, but contains a sequential number at the end of the database name. For example, if you have an HTML page entitled Interest_Form that contains three form elements, the Access databases will be named Interest_Form1.mdb, Interest_Form2.mdb, and Interest_Form3.mdb. Each Access database contains a single table called Results.

5. If you wish, you can specify a confirmation page and error page, just as with any other form. Use the URL Of Confirmation Page field and the URL Of Error Page field to do so.

6. The new Access database contains only a single table, called Results. In addition, FrontPage creates a database connection (displayed in the Database Connection To Use drop-down list) and connects FrontPage to the new database through that connection (see Figure 18-4).

7. Click the Saved Fields tab (see Figure 18-5) to see how the form fields are associated with the database columns.

SHORTCUT *To quickly associate all the fields on the form with their database columns, make sure you are on the Database Results tab and click the Update Database button. This is especially handy if you rename some of the fields on the form.*

8. Click OK to return to the Form Properties dialog box. Click OK again to finish creating the database and associating the form results with it.

9. Choose File | Save to save the form. If you did not use the .asp extension earlier when naming the form, FrontPage saves the form but warns you that it won't work unless you rename it to use the .asp extension. Click OK to get past this warning.

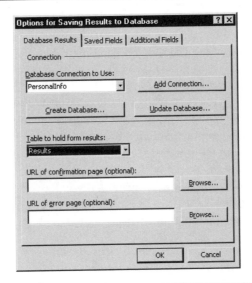

FIGURE 18-4 This version of the Options For Saving Results To Database dialog box shows the new database connection and the table entitled Results.

18

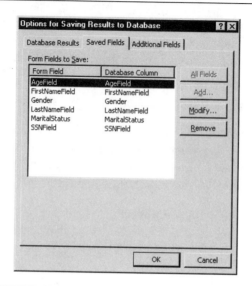

The Saved Fields tab shows you the database columns associated with the fields on the form.

10. If FrontPage warned you about the form name (previous step), rename the form by right-clicking it in the Folder List and choosing Rename from the shortcut menu. Change the extension to .asp and press ENTER. FrontPage will warn you that the file may become unusable, but click Yes to complete the rename.

To test the form, you must be using a server-based Web site and open it in a browser—just previewing the page generates an error when you try to submit the form. However, if you open the page in a browser (and are using a server-based Web site), you can fill in the information and submit the results to the database by clicking the Submit button. To actually view the submitted data, double-click the Access database to open it in Access—provided you have Access installed on your computer. Once the database is open, double-click the Results table in Access's main dialog box to open the table in Browse mode (see Figure 18-6).

CAUTION *If you have Access, you can change the structure of the table, including changing the table name, column names, and even data types. However, if you do, FrontPage won't be able to route the form results to the database correctly. You'll need to manually associate form fields with the renamed table and columns (as discussed shortly). So, unless you really know what you are doing, resist the temptation to change the Results table structure in Access.*

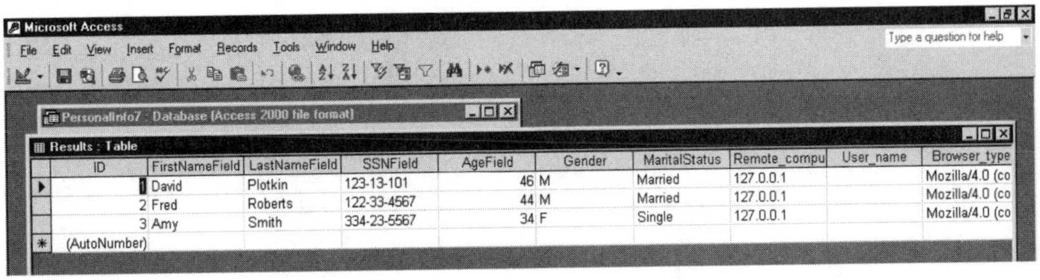

FIGURE 18-6   Use Microsoft Access to view the contents of the Results table.

Send Results to a Different Table

You aren't stuck just using the one automatically generated table in a database to store your form results. For example, you might wish to create an Access database that contains multiple tables, one for each set of form results. This could be handy if you use many forms and just want to download one Access database file from the web site that contains all the form results. Or, you might have an existing Access database that you imported into your web site (as detailed later in this chapter). Assuming that you know enough about Access to create tables, you can direct the results of a form to any table in the database.

> **NOTE**   *This technique for selecting a table will actually work for any database to which you establish a connection (as discussed later in this chapter). However, remote databases (such as an Oracle database running on a network or a web server) are usually protected, and you need special permissions to create tables or modify the structure of existing tables. These permissions are much more restrictive than the permissions you need to simply dump data into those tables. Thus, it is normal for network or web server databases that you will have to request that a database administrator (DBA) add a new table or modify the structure of an existing table.*

To select an existing table in a database to store the form results, use the following steps:

1. Open the web page (.asp) that contains the form. Right-click the form portion of the web page, and choose Form Properties from the shortcut menu. Click the Options button to open the Options For Saving Results To Database dialog box.

18

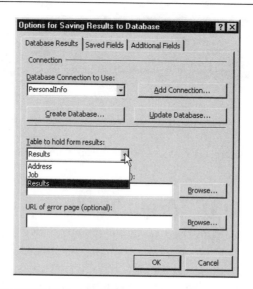

FIGURE 18-7   Select the table to which you want to route the form results from the drop-down list.

2. Click the Table To Hold Form Results drop-down list (see Figure 18-7). The drop-down list contains a list of all the tables in the database.

3. Assuming that the alternate table contains columns with the same name as the form fields, simply click OK in the Options For Saving Results To Database dialog box and the Form Properties dialog box to route the results to a different table.

NOTE   *If the database columns are named differently than the form fields, you'll have to manually associate the fields with the columns, as detailed in the next section.*

Change the Field-To-Column Mapping

You have complete control over how the fields on a form are mapped to database columns. You can break the link between a field and a column (handy if you need to delete a form field), or manually establish a link between a field and a column (handy if you need to add another field to the form). You can also modify the mapping, sending the results from a form field to a different database column than the one to which it is currently mapped.

NOTE   *Although you will normally be working with the Saved Fields tab in the Options For Saving Results To Database dialog box, everything in this section that applies to the Saved Fields tab also works for the Additional Fields tab. The Additional Fields tab contains the field mappings for the Browser Type, Remote Computer Name, Timestamp, and Username.*

Delete a Form Field

If you decide you no longer need a form field, you can delete the field from the form. However, this action does *not* remove the mapping from the (now-nonexistent) field to the database column. To remove the mapping, open the Form Properties dialog box and click the Options button to open the Options For Saving Results To Database dialog box. Click the Saved Fields tab, and select the deleted form field and its associated database column (see Figure 18-8). Click the Remove button to remove it from the list.

NOTE   *Deleting the mapping between a form field and a database column does not remove the column from the database table. The column remains, but it will always be empty.*

Add a Form Field

If you decide to add a field to a form, it will not be associated with a database column initially. You can correct this situation in one of two ways: add the column to a table manually and associate the column with the field, or let FrontPage add the column for you. Obviously, letting FrontPage add the column for you is easier, but this only works for databases under your control, such as an Access database within your own Web site. As mentioned, remote databases (such as an Oracle database on a network or the Web server) are well protected, and you need special permissions to modify their structure. Thus, you may have to request that the column be added to the table in the remote database.

18

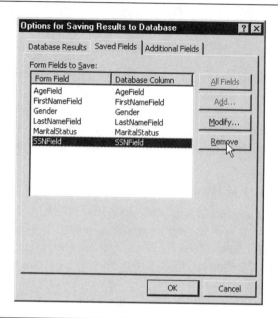

FIGURE 18-8   Use the Remove button to delete a mapping between a form field and a
database column.

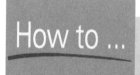 **Add a Column to a Local Access Database**

Adding a column for the new form field to a local Access database couldn't be
simpler. Use the following steps:

1. Add the field to the form, making sure to give it a descriptive name. To
    change the name of the form field, right-click it and choose Form Field
    Properties from the shortcut menu. Then fill in the name in the Properties
    dialog box and click OK.

2. Save the form. You must do this or step 4 won't work properly.

3. Right-click the form portion of the Web page and choose Form Properties from the shortcut menu. Click the Options button to open the Options For Saving Results To Database dialog box.

4. Click the Update Database button. FrontPage automatically adds the new column to the database. Click OK twice to complete the operation.

The next time someone submits the form, this new column will contain the contents of the new field. Older records, of course, will have no data in the new field.

Associate a New Field with a Column in a Remote Database

If the database structure is not under your local control, you will need to either make the changes to the database yourself using tools specially designed for that purpose or request that the change be made for you by a database administrator. Once the new column has been added to the table in the database, proceed to create the new field and associate it with the column as follows:

1. Add the field to the form, making sure to give it a descriptive name. To change the name of the form field, right-click it and choose Form Field Properties from the shortcut menu. Then fill in the name in the Properties dialog box and click OK. Save the form.

2. Right-click the form portion of the Web page and choose Form Properties from the shortcut menu. Click the Options button to open the Options For Saving Results To Database dialog box.

18

3. Click the Saved Fields tab, and select the new form field. This field won't have a Database Column associated with it.

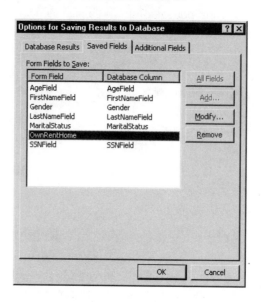

4. Click Modify to open the Modify Field dialog box.

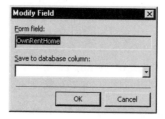

5. Click the Save To Database Column drop-down list to display a list of all the database columns not currently associated with a form field.

6. Select the column you want to associate with the new field and click OK to complete the operation and return to the Saved Fields tab.

NOTE   *You can also use this technique to associate a form field with a column in a local Access database if you want.*

Add and Delete Form Field Mappings

If you simply want to break the connection between a form field and a database column, you can click the Remove button in the Saved Fields tab of the Options For Saving Results To Database dialog box. The field remains on the form, but its results no longer go to any database column. You might want to do this prior to remapping a different field to this same column. As mentioned earlier, you can only modify the field mapping to point to a column that is *not* currently associated with a form field. Thus, you might need to break an existing connection first.

NOTE   *If you remove the field and its database column and click OK, the next time you open the Options For Saving Results To Database dialog box, the form field will be redisplayed in the Form Field list—but it won't be associated with any database column.*

Once you have removed a field from the Saved Fields tab, both the Add button and All Fields button become available. Clicking the All Fields button redisplays any removed form fields, but they are no longer associated with a database column. This makes it easy to choose the unassociated form field, and then click Modify to associate the form field with another database column.

If you choose the Add button, the Add Field dialog box appears (see Figure 18-9). The top portion of the dialog box displays all form fields that are unassociated with a

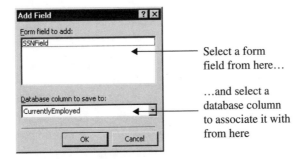

FIGURE 18-9   Use the Add Field dialog box to associate a currently unmapped form field to a currently unmapped database column.

database column. The Database Column To Save To drop-down list contains a list of all the database columns that are currently unassociated with a form field.

To associate a form field with a database column, select the field from the Form Field To Add list, and choose the database column to associate it with from the Database Column To Save To drop-down list. Then click OK.

Connect to a Database

If you are not going to use the automatic database connection created by FrontPage, you will need to define your own database connection. To open the dialog box you'll need, you do one of two things. Your first option is to choose Tools | Web Settings and click the Database tab. Alternatively, you can right-click a form and choose Form Properties from the shortcut menu. Once the Form Properties dialog box opens, click the Options button, then click the Add Connection button. Either way, the Database tab of the Web Settings dialog box is displayed (see Figure 18-10).

Click the Add button to open the New Database Connection dialog box (see Figure 18-11).

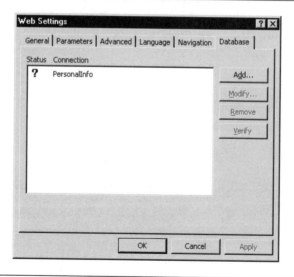

FIGURE 18-10   Use the Database Tab of the Web Settings dialog box to define a new database connection.

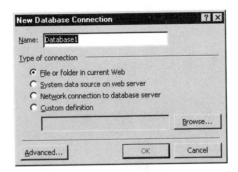

FIGURE 18-11   Specify the name and type of the new database connection in the New
Database Connection dialog box.

The first step in defining a new database connection is to type the identifying
name into the Name field. Next, you'll need to pick the type of database connection
to create by selecting one of the options in the Type Of Connection section. The
four types of connection are

- **File or folder in current web**   Use this option to identify a file or a
  folder that actually contains the database. For example, an Access database
  is contained in a file with an .mdb extension.

- **System data source on web server**   This option enables you to select
  a system data source connected to a database on the Web server. The
  system data source will probably have to be set up for you by a database
  administrator with the authority to do so. It is unlikely you'll have the
  permissions to create the system data source yourself.

- **Network connection to database server**   This option lets you specify
  a particular database on a server and connect to that database. A database
  administrator is likely to have to set up the necessary permissions in order
  for you to connect to the database, as well as supplied the variety of values
  you will need in order to connect to the network database.

- **Custom definition**   This option simply allows you to select a file to use
  to specify how to connect to a database. The file must have been created
  by someone who is knowledgeable about the specifics of connecting to the
  database, and who can supply you with the values you'll need to configure
  the connection (such as the connection string).

18

Once you select the type of connection you want, follow the instructions for the type of connection you selected, as detailed in the next few sections.

Create a Connection to a File or Folder in the Current Web

To create a connection to a file or folder in the current Web, click the Browse button to open the Database Files In Current Web dialog box (see Figure 18-12).

Select the type of database file or folder you want from the Files Of Type drop-down list. This list contains a list of all the drivers for the local database you have installed. Select the file or folder from the large central area of the dialog box, or type it into the URL field and click OK to close the dialog box.

If you need to specify any additional parameters in order to connect to the database (you don't normally need to for local databases), click the Advanced button to open the Advanced Connection Properties dialog box (see Figure 18-13).

Fill in any necessary information in the following fields:

■ **Username** If you need to supply a username to access the database, supply the value in this field. This should be a username with permission to write data to the database, as capturing the results from a form requires writing those results into the database.

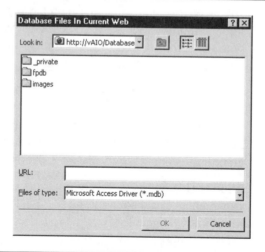

FIGURE 18-12 Select a file type and a file to specify the database file or folder.

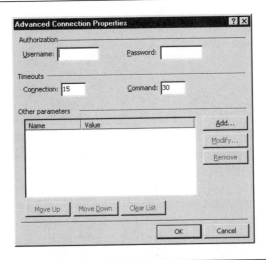

FIGURE 18-13   Specify the additional parameters for connecting to the database using the Advanced Connection Properties dialog box.

■ **Password**   If the username requires a password, enter it in this field.

■ **Connection**   In the Timeouts section, fill in the number of seconds you want FrontPage to wait before timing out when attempting to establish a connection with the database. Filling in a low value may cause the connection to fail even if a connection was available (but slow). Filling in a high value may cause you to wait (and wait) for a connection that is simply not available. The default of 15 seconds is a reasonable compromise, although you may have to tune this number for your database—especially if that database is located on a network server.

■ **Command**   In the Timeouts section, fill in the number of seconds you want FrontPage to wait before timing out when attempting to execute a command (such as writing a record) to the database.

■ **Other parameters**   If the database connection requires any special name/value parameter pairs, click the Add button to open the Add Parameter dialog box (see Figure 18-14). Fill in the Name and Value, and click OK to add the parameters.

If you have multiple parameters, you can rearrange them in the Advanced Connection Properties dialog box by clicking the Move Up or Move Down button.

18

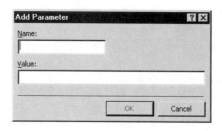

 FIGURE 18-14   Add parameters to connect to the database using the Add Parameter dialog box.

You can empty the list of parameters by clicking the Clear List button. You can also select a parameter and change either the name or the value by clicking the Modify button, or delete the parameter by clicking the Remove button.

> NOTE   *The Advanced Connection Properties dialog box is identical for two of the other options: System Data Source On Web Server, and Network Connection To Database Server. The Advanced Connection Properties dialog box is different for the Custom Configuration option and will be covered in that section.*

Create a Connection Using a System Data Source on a Web Server

To create a connection using a system data source on a Web server, select the System Data Source option and click the Browse button to open the System Data Sources On Web Server dialog box (see Figure 18-15).

Select the system data source you want from the list and click OK. The name of the system data source appears near the bottom of the New Database Connection dialog box. If you need to enter any of the information in the Advanced Connection Properties dialog box, click the Advanced button and proceed as explained previously.

Create a Connection Using a Network Connection to a Database Server

To create a connection using a network connection to a database server, select the Network Connection option and click the Browse button to open the Network Database Connection dialog box (see Figure 18-16).

FIGURE 18-15 Specify the system data source to use to connect to the database on the Web server.

Fill in the following fields in this dialog box:

■ **Type of database driver** Use this drop-down list to select the database driver to use. The list will include any native database drivers or ODBC drivers you have installed.

■ **Server name** Fill in the server name. This will have to be supplied to you by the database's database administrator.

■ **Database name** Fill in the name of the database on the selected server. This too will have to be supplied to you by the database administrator.

FIGURE 18-16 Specify the details of connecting to a network database using the Network Database Connection dialog box.

18

Click OK to return to the New Database connection dialog box. The database name and server name (in the format databasename@servername) appear near the bottom of the dialog box. If you need to enter any of the information in the Advanced Connection Properties dialog box, click the Advanced button and proceed as explained previously.

Create a Connection Using a Custom Definition

If the database to which you want to connect cannot use a native or ODBC driver, a database administrator can create a file data source name (file DSN) that contains the necessary parameters for connecting to the database on the Web server. You can then import the file DSN into your Web site and connect to create a new custom database connection. You can also connect to a universal data link (UDL) file. Basically, both the file DSN and UDL are just files (albeit fairly complex ones) that you can use to create a database connection. You also have the opportunity (as discussed shortly) to define a custom connection string using the Advanced Connection Properties dialog box.

There are two kinds of authentication that occur with a custom definition file: the browse-time authentication and the author-time authentication (these distinctions are not necessary with the other database connection options). The author-time authentication (username and password) is used by FrontPage to open a connection to the database. The browse-time authentication (also username and password) is used to open a connection when filling in a form in a browser. Here are the rules for setting up author-time authentication:

- When you use a custom database connection file (either a file DSN or UDL), the author-time authentication information must be in the file.

- When you use a custom definition string, the author-time authentication must be present in the connection string. The connection string syntax varies by database, but it is usually of the form UID=*username*, PWD=*password*, where *username* is the author-time username, and *password* is the author-time password.

To connect to a database using a custom connection, select the Custom Definition option and click the Browse button to open the Connection Files In Current Web dialog box (see Figure 18-17).

FIGURE 18-17   Use the Connection Files In Current Web dialog box to specify a file DSN or UDL file that contains the parameters.

Choose either a data source name or a universal data link from the Files Of Type drop-down list. Then select the file itself from the dialog box or type the filename into the URL field. Click OK to close the Connection Files In Current Web dialog box.

To edit a connection string, click the Advanced button to open the Advanced Connection Properties dialog box (see Figure 18-18).

In addition to the Username, Password, Connection (in the Timeouts section), and Command fields (discussed earlier), you can fill in values in the Connection String field.

There are several additional requirements that need to be met in order for the custom connection to work. They are

■ You must not use a file DSN to connect to a database file in the current Web site, because the file DSN will contain file paths that are incorrect for the Web server. Use the File Or Folder In Current Web connection instead.

■ It is best to include timeouts and any other name/value parameters in the file DSN.

■ The database driver referred to by the file DSN or connection string must be present on the Web server for the connection to work properly.

18

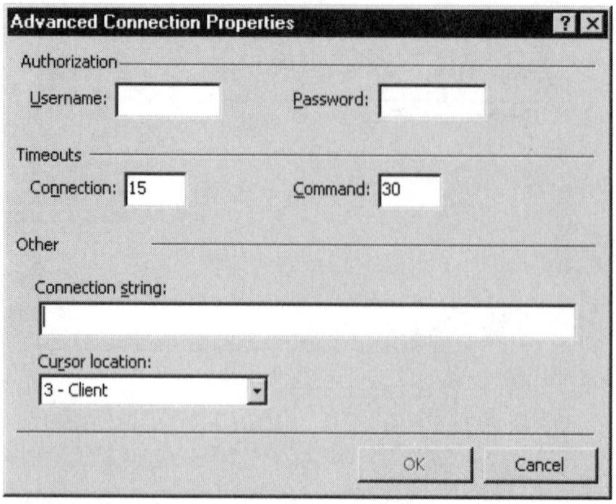

FIGURE 18-18   Fill in the connection string in the Advanced Connection Properties dialog box.

Modify or Remove a Database Connection

Once you have built one or more database connections, you can modify the connection by selecting it in the Database tab of the Web Settings dialog box and clicking the Modify button. This reopens the Database Connection Properties dialog box so you can modify any of the parameters or change any of the information in the Advanced Connection Properties dialog box.

If you no longer need a connection, you can select that connection and click Remove to discard it.

Verify a Database Connection

If you have built a database connection but not tested it, a question mark will appear in the Status column next to the connection name in the Database tab of the Web Settings dialog box (choose Tools | Web Settings).

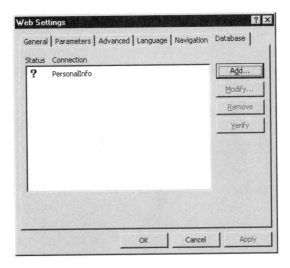

To make sure the database connection is working properly, select the connection and click the Verify button. If FrontPage is able to successfully verify the database connection, the question mark in the Status column will change to a checkmark. If FrontPage cannot successfully verify the connection, you can modify the connection to get it working by clicking the Modify button.

Import an Access Database into Your Web Site

If you are knowledgeable about databases, you may have already constructed and populated the Access database you want to use with your Web site. If so, you'll need to import the database into your Web site before using it to capture data from forms (as explained in this chapter) or to display data in a form (as explained in the next chapter). FrontPage makes it easy to import an Access database, and even offers to build the database connection automatically.

To import an Access database, use the following steps:

1. Choose File | Import to open the Import dialog box.

18

2. Click Add File to open the Add File To Import List dialog box, and pick the database you want to import.

3. Click Open to return to the Import dialog box with the database added to the list of files to import.

4. Click OK. FrontPage displays the Add Database Connection dialog box.

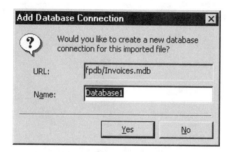

5. Fill in the name of the database connection in the Name field and click Yes. FrontPage imports the database and creates the database connection for accessing the database.

Chapter 19

Present Database Contents Using the Database Results Wizard

How to...

- Do the preparatory work to use a database
- Specify the data to display
- Set up filtering and sort order
- Provide an interactive search form
- Format the returned records
- View the results in a browser

If the information you want to display in your Web pages is fairly static, creating the Web pages by typing in text and adding graphics works fine. However, there are times when building such static pages is not appropriate. This is especially true if the information changes fairly frequently or if there is a lot of information people might want to search through. Examples of such data might include

- Available products your company sells. Not only might the actual products themselves change, but their current availability can vary from one moment to the next.
- A membership list for your organization.
- Computer applications by category. This list is especially volatile if you include shareware, as shareware programs arrive and disappear more frequently than commercial software.
- Results from sports competitions, where people might wish to search by race, competitor name, or team.

> **TIP** *Any time your information consists of a long list, it is a prime candidate for the techniques discussed in this chapter.*

Typically, you might consider keeping this kind of information in a database application, making it easy to add new information and modify existing information. If you do use a database, you can display the contents of the database in a dynamic Web page, and even include an embedded search form to help readers find specific information. For example, if you categorize the products you sell, you could allow readers to type in a category of product they are interested in, and just display that category in a table on the Web page.

Another excellent candidate for inclusion in a database (and subsequent display on a dynamic Web page) is information that people who visit your site can update themselves, such as membership information and preferences. First, you create a search form in which a reader inputs their username and password so you can find their record. By capturing the data the reader enters directly into the database (using the techniques discussed in Chapter 18), the information is not only updated, but the reader can see the new information (taken from the database) on the screen immediately.

FrontPage's Database Results Wizard makes it fairly straightforward to build a Web page that takes its source data from a database. Although the Database Results Wizard is more complex than other wizards, it still reduces to manageable proportions the complexity of what was previously an extraordinarily difficult task.

Perform Initial Setup

There are a few things you'll need before beginning work on a Web page to display the contents of a database. First of all, you'll need the database itself. You have all the same options for source databases that were discussed in Chapter 18: a local file in your Web site, a database running on the Web server, or a database running on a network server. Unlike routing form results to a database, however, you do *not* have the opportunity to create a new database while setting up the Web page. You must have the database designed and built prior to building the Web page.

You will also need a connection to the database. Setting up the connection works exactly as described in Chapter 18, and you *do* have the opportunity to define a new connection while building the Web page. Just be sure you have all the necessary setup work done ahead of time, including installing any necessary ODBC or native database drivers and obtaining permissions from the database administrator (if necessary).

> NOTE   *For the gruesome details of setting up connections to network or Web host databases, see Chapter 18.*

Finally, you'll need the structure of the database, called the *schema*. This includes the names of tables, the names of the columns in those tables, and their data types (for example, numeric, character, date, and so on). You will also need to understand the purpose of each column so you can make an informed decision as to what information is stored there.

19

Configure the Database Results Wizard

To display the contents of a database on a Web page, you need to create the Web page and then run the Database Results Wizard. The Database Results Wizard places a *database region* on the page. This database region is a table or list that contains the specified columns from the database. When you publish the page to a Web server running FrontPage extensions, the contents of the table is populated with data from the database. If you built a server-based Web site using Microsoft Personal Web Server 4 or IIS 5.0, you can also preview the page in a browser to see the database results.

Create the Initial Web Page

The first step is to create the Web page. Choose File | New Page or Web to open the New Page Or Web task pane, choose Page Templates from the task pane, and select the normal Page template from the Page Templates dialog box. When the new page appears, right-click and select Page Properties from the shortcut menu, then fill in the title. Choose File | Save and enter the name you want in the File Name field. It is very important to use the .asp ending, as you are creating a dynamic Web page.

NOTE   *If you don't name the file using an .asp ending, FrontPage will complain when you save the page after running the Database Results Wizard. You'll need to rename the page at that point if you want the page to operate correctly.*

After you have created the Web page, run the Database Results Wizard by clicking the page and choosing Insert | Database | Results to open the first panel of the Database Results Wizard.

Specify the Data to Display

The first panel of the Database Results Wizard (see Figure 19-1) lets you select the database connection for the database that contains the data for the web page.

You have three options for the database connection. First, you can use the sample Northwind database that comes with Access (provided you installed it) by selecting the Use A Sample Database Connection option. You can choose an existing database connection by selecting the Use An Existing Database Connection option and selecting the connection from the drop-down list. Finally, you can define a new database connection (as discussed in Chapter 18) by choosing the Use A New Database Connection option and clicking the Create button.

When you are done selecting the database connection, click Next to continue.

The second panel of the Database Results Wizard (see Figure 19-2) lets you either select a record source or create a custom SQL query.

Choose a Record Source

To choose a record source, click the Record Source option and choose the source from the drop-down list. This list contains all the tables in the target database, as well as any views that exist. A *view* is a logical grouping of physical data with filters and sorting applied—Access queries are actually views. Thus, if the source is an Access database, the drop-down list contains any queries (displayed with the word VIEW after the query name).

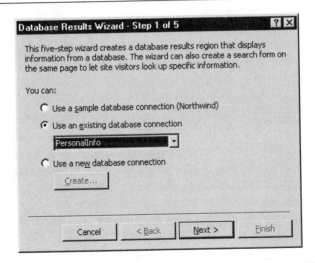

FIGURE 19-1   Select the database record source from the first panel of the Database Results Wizard.

19

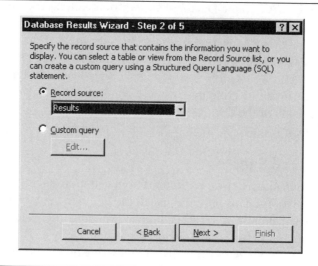

FIGURE 19-2   Select a table or view, or create a custom query using the second panel of the Database Results Wizard.

NOTE   *Although the Database Results Wizard enables you to select fields and establish selection criteria and sort order, if you are familiar with Access (and are using an Access database as your source) or your database's View facility, you may want to consider building the view using your database and then just using it as your record source in FrontPage. For example, an Access query (and most other database View facilities) enables you to join multiple tables (connected by foreign keys), include the columns you want, establish filtering and sorting criteria, group by the value in a column, and add calculated results. Not only is this considerably more power than is provided by the Database Results Wizard, but if you frequently change the sort or filtering criteria, you can just adjust the criteria in the database View facility and you won't have to modify the database results properties on the Web page.*

When you are done selecting a record source, click Next to move to the next step.

Create a Custom Query

You can create a custom query by choosing the Custom Query option in the second panel of the Database Results Wizard and clicking the Edit button to open the Custom Query dialog box.

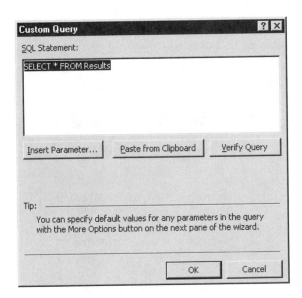

The Custom Query dialog box enables you to enter an SQL query that returns results from the database. You can (if you know what you are doing) create a complex query that returns exactly what you want from the database. To build the SQL query, simply type it into the Custom Query dialog box. To check the syntax of the query, click the Verify Query button. If all is well, FrontPage will confirm the correctness of the query. If there is an error, FrontPage will report that as well. The initial error message doesn't contain much information, but if you click the Details button, you'll get a lot more information.

NOTE *The error messages returned can be quite unnerving. For example, if you misspell the name of a table, FrontPage initially reports an error that it was unable to retrieve schema information from the query. However, if you scroll down far enough, you'll see a reasonably clear error message.*

If you want to write your query in another tool (such as a SQL editor), you can copy it from that tool (provided the other tool supports clipboard activities) and paste it into the Custom Query dialog box by clicking the Paste From Clipboard button.

As we will discuss in more detail later, you can set up a search form into which the reader can enter values for information they are looking for. For example, if you were querying a database of swimming races, you could create a search form field called RaceGender, and if the reader was looking only for girl's races, he or she could type **Girls** into this field. If you are creating a custom query, you will

19

want to add a WHERE clause to the SQL to select those records where a particular column matches the value in the search form field. To do this, create the WHERE clause in the Custom Query dialog box and click the Insert Parameter button. This opens the Insert Form Field Parameter dialog box.

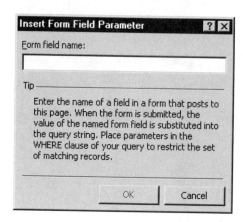

Type the name of the search form field into the Insert Form Field Parameter dialog box and click OK. This inserts the search form field name (surrounded by double colons) into the Custom Query dialog box, which might then look like this:

```
Select * from RaceResults where RaceGender = ::RaceGender::;
```

When the query is submitted to the database, the contents of the search form field (input by the reader on the search form) are used to replace the reference to the search form field (::RaceGender:: in this example). This gives you considerable power—including using "like" matching and enabling the reader to use wildcards (which are not supported by the Database Result Wizard's normal search form).

When you are done creating the custom query, click OK to return to the Database Results Wizard, and click Next to go to the next step.

Select the Columns to Display

You can choose the columns to include in the database results region from the third panel of the Database Results Wizard (see Figure 19-3).

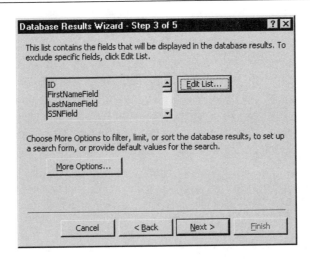

Select the columns to include by clicking the Edit List button.

Click the Edit List button to open the Displayed Fields dialog box.

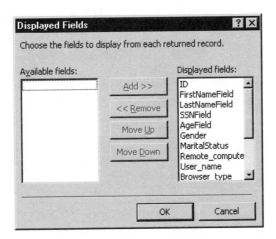

The Available Fields list shows all the fields in the record source that are *not* included in the database region of the Web page. The Displayed Fields list shows all the columns in the record source that are included. To remove a field from the Displayed Fields list, select the field and click the Remove button. To add a field from the Available Fields list, select the field and click the Add button.

The columns displayed in the database region on the Web page are arranged in the order in which they appear in the Displayed Fields list. To change the order of the fields, click a field and use the Move Up or Move Down button.

If you want to establish filtering criteria, set up a search form for returning results from the database, or specify sort order, click the More Options button to open the More Options dialog box (see Figure 19-4).

Establish Filtering Criteria

To establish filtering criteria, click the Criteria button to open the Criteria dialog box (see Figure 19-5).

The Criteria dialog box displays any criteria you have specified to filter the records returned from the database. For example, if you only wanted to see races where the race gender was "girls," you would specify that condition in the Criteria dialog box.

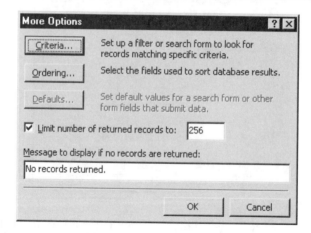

FIGURE 19-4 More options include sorting and filtering.

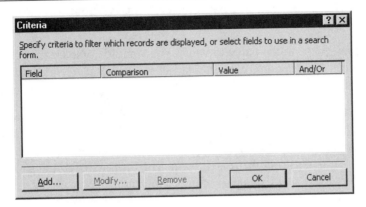

FIGURE 19-5   Add filtering criteria to filter the records returned from the database.

To add criteria, click the Add button to open the Add Criteria dialog box.

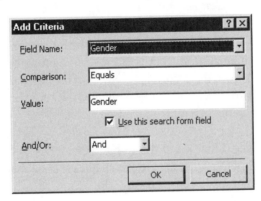

Specify the criteria using the following fields:

- **Field Name**   Use the drop-down list to specify the name of the field whose contents you will be inspecting for a value matching your specification. The list contains every column in the table or view—the field does *not* have to be one of those displayed in the database region of the page.

- **Comparison**   Choose the operation you want to use to compare the Field Name to the Value. Options include Equals, Not Equals, Less Than, Not

Less Than, Greater Than, Not Greater Than, Is Null, and Is Not Null. For the comparisons Is Null and Is Not Null, the Value field is not available.

■ **Value** Type in the value to which you want to compare the Field Name. You can also type in a character string (such as RaceGender) that names a search field.

■ **Use this search form field** If you check this checkbox, the value in the Value field will be used as the name for a field on a search form. Later in the Database Results Wizard, you will be offered the opportunity to have the wizard construct the search form. The form will automatically contain any field you specify as part of the filter criteria.

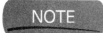
The search form field name must begin with a letter and cannot use spaces. This is because the search form field is used as part of a custom ASP script (which you never see). If you violate these constraints when naming the search form field, FrontPage will warn you, but it will allow you to name the field in a way that will cause an error later when the script executes.

■ **And/Or** Choose either And or Or to connect the current criteria to the next criteria (if any). If you connect two criteria together with an And, *both* must be true before the record is returned in the database results region. If you connect two criteria together with an Or, if either condition is true the record will be returned in the database region.

If you check the Use This Search Form Field checkbox to use the value in the Value field as a form field name, the criteria displays the Value quantity in square brackets, indicating that it is a search form field.

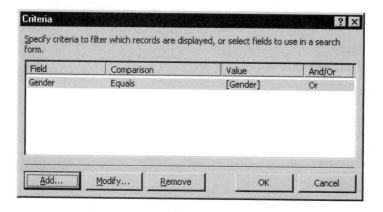

You can delete a criterion by selecting it and clicking the Remove button. To change the criterion, select it and click the Modify button. When you are done creating criterion, click OK to return to the More Options dialog box.

Specify the Record Sort Order

To specify the order in which returned records will be displayed, click the Ordering button to open the Ordering dialog box.

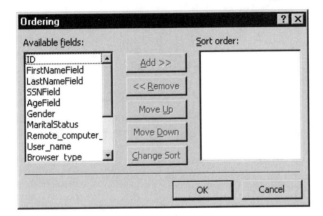

The Available Fields list displays all the available fields on which you can sort. To sort on a field, select it and click the Add button to move the field to the Sort Order list. To remove a field from the Sort Order list, click it and select Remove. If you choose more than one field to sort on, you can change the order of the fields in the Sort Order list using the Move Up and Move Down buttons. The order is important, because the records are sorted first on the topmost field. Any records that have the same value for the topmost field are then sorted by the second field and so on.

TIP   *Strictly speaking, the sort field does not have to be one that is displayed on the page, but readers will be confused about how order was established if you sort on a nondisplayed field.*

By default, any fields you add to the Sort Order list are sorted in ascending order—the lowest value first, then the next higher value, and so on. If you wish to change the type of sort (from ascending to descending or from descending to ascending), select the field and click the Change Sort button. The yellow rectangle alongside the sort field changes to indicate whether the sort order is ascending

19

(pointing up) or descending (pointing down). The Ordering dialog box might look like the following if you built a two-level sort (ascending on both columns):

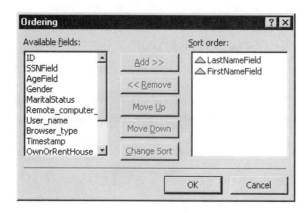

Establish Defaults for Search Form Fields

If you specified any search form fields when establishing criteria, the Default button in the More Options dialog box becomes available. Clicking the Default button opens the Defaults dialog box.

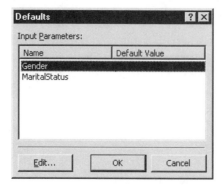

You can use the Defaults dialog box to establish default values for any of the fields on the search form. That is, if the reader does not enter any value in the field, the value submitted to the database during the query will be the default value. This is handy if you know that a search form field will normally be populated with a particular value.

To specify a default value, select the search form field from the Defaults dialog box and click the Edit button to open the Default Value dialog box.

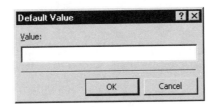

Fill in the value and click OK. Once you are done with the Defaults dialog box, click OK to return to the More Options dialog box.

Database columns have data types (for example, character, date, number, and so on). If you specify a default value that does not match the data type of the database column, the search will return no records—and, depending on the database, may also return an error. This behavior will also occur if the reader inputs a value to the search field that does not match the data type, so you may want to add instructions to the search form about what data type the search form field (and thus the database) is expecting.

Limit the Number of Returned Records

Databases can be really huge, and an injudicious search could return a lot of records. This could take quite a while over a dial-up line. Because of this, you can set the maximum number of records that a database search will return to the Web page. To do so, check the Limit Number Of Returned Records To checkbox, and enter the number in the adjacent field.

If you do decide to limit the number of records, be sure to add a note to the Web page telling the reader what the maximum number of records allowed has been limited to. Otherwise, readers may think they have retrieved all the records matching their criteria (and indeed, they may want to see them all), which could be misleading.

Specify the No Records Message

A highly selective query might return no records, so it is best to specify a message telling readers that no records matched their query. Type this message into the Message To Display If No Records Are Returned field.

 *The default message (No records matched your query) is uninformative because it doesn't tell the reader what to do next. You should change the message to give readers an idea of what to try next if they don't get any records. Perhaps a better message would be "No records were returned. Try removing one or more conditions from your query."*

Once you have finished specifying the items in the More Options dialog box, click OK to close it and return to the Database Results Wizard. Then click Next to move to the next panel.

Select the Results Format

The next step is to select how you want the database results presented. There are three options: as a table, as a list, or as a drop-down list.

Return Results as a Table

The most common method of presenting the results from a database query is as a table. Choosing Table – One Record Per Row from the drop-down list in the Database Results Wizard gives you the following version of the fourth panel:

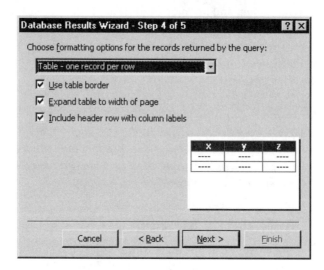

You have the following options:

- **Use table border**   Checking this checkbox displays the table boundary and cell outlines as a solid grid. Leaving this checkbox cleared makes the borders invisible in a browser or in Preview mode.

- ■ **Expand table to width of page**   Checking this checkbox expands the table to fill the page width. You may not want to do this if the data returned is very small, but normally you will want to check this option.

- ■ **Include header row with column labels**   Checking this checkbox adds a row at the top of the table. This extra row contains the column names. Since column names from databases can often be quite cryptic, you may want to edit the header row after the Database Results Wizard finishes.

Return Results as a List

If you select List – One Field Per Item from the drop-down list, you get the following version of the fourth panel of the Database Results Wizard:

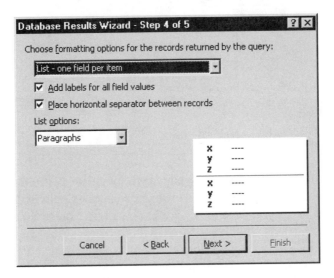

This option presents the data as a list, with one field on each line. The following options are available:

- ■ **Add labels for all field values**   Since a plain list of values is pretty confusing, you'll probably want to check this checkbox to ensure that each field has a label. The label is just the database column name (which can be cryptic), but it's better than nothing, and you can customize the label on the Web page once the Database Results Wizard finishes.

- ■ **Place horizontal separator between records**   Checking this checkbox places a horizontal break between the set of items that make up each record. This gives you a visual cue where one record ends and another begins.

19

- ■ **List options** Select the list formatting from this drop-down list. Options include standard paragraphs, bulleted list, numbered list, definition list, text fields, and even a table.

Return Results as a Drop-Down List

Choosing Drop-Down List – One Record Per Item gives you the following version of the fourth panel of the Database Results Wizard:

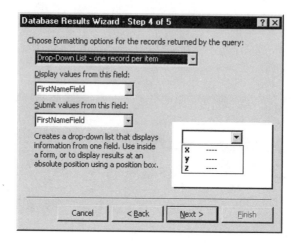

This option is especially useful if you want to populate a drop-down list in a form from the contents of a database. However, since each item in the list is one record in the database, you have to be careful about how you populate the database table. If the table includes multiple records with the same value, those values will show up multiple times in the drop-down list (unless, of course, you built your own SQL query and used "SELECT Distinct").

To specify how the drop-down list will behave, you must specify two quantities: the field to display values in from the drop-down list, and the field that contains the value you want to submit using the form. The reason is that frequently you will have two fields in your database: one that contains a code (such as "F") and one that contains a description (such as "Girls"). The person filling out the form will need to see the description in the drop-down list, but you may wish to submit (and store) the code instead. Thus, you would select the field containing the description to use for the Display Values From This Field drop-down list and the field containing the code to use for the Submit Values From This Field.

 *Of course, you can set both fields to the same value—in which case the reader will see the same field you are submitting and storing.*

Finish with the Database Results Wizard

The last panel of the Database Results Wizard (see Figure 19-6) lets you set grouping options and automatically create the search form right on the same page with the database results region.

Group Your Records

There are two options available for visually grouping your records in the database region of the Web page. Display All Records Together does just that—all the records are returned in the table, with no breaks between records. This works fine if you don't expect a lot of records to be returned. The other option—Split Records Into Groups—enables you to enter the number of records to display at once in the table or list (see Figure 19-7). To move to the next group of records or the previous

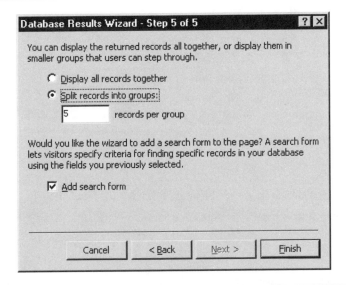

FIGURE 19-6   Set the number of records to group together and whether to create a search form automatically on the last panel.

19

group of records, use the navigation buttons at the bottom of the database region. This option is handy if you expect many records to be returned.

You can use the Split Records Into Groups setting to break records across printed pages.

Records returned from the database ⎯

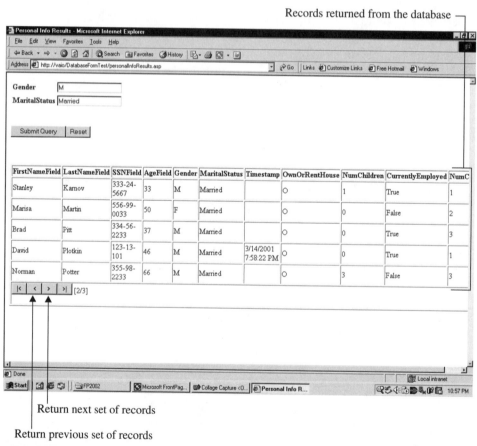

Return next set of records

Return previous set of records

FIGURE 19-7   Grouping records in the database region can make them easier to read and to print out.

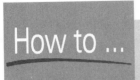

Create the Search Form Automatically

One of the most powerful options available in FrontPage 2000 is the ability to return selected records from the database using a search form. If you created filter criteria earlier (using the Criteria dialog box) that uses search form fields, the Add Search Form checkbox is enabled. Checking this checkbox instructs the Database Results Wizard to create the search form above the database results region on the Web page. The search form will automatically include all search fields you specified as part of the criteria.

Grouping records is not available if you chose the option to return the database records in a drop-down list.

Work with the Database Results Web Page

To finish creating the database results Web page, click the Finish button on the last panel of the Database Results Wizard. This inserts the database region and the search form (if you specified one) into the Web page, similar to Figure 19-8.

Modify the Layout

The default layout that results from running the Database Results Wizard isn't bad, but it can be improved to make it easier to use.

CAUTION

Do not change the column names enclosed in << >>! These refer to the data source column in the database, and if you change these column names, no data will be returned for that column. Also, depending on the database, you may get an error when you try to retrieve data. Note, though, that if you change the structure of the record source (say, by using your database tool to change the column name), you will need to reflect that change in the column names on the page. The easiest way to do that is to right-click the column name, choose Database Column Value Properties from the shortcut menu, and choose the new column name to display from the Column To Display drop-down list in the Database Column Value dialog box.

19

Search form section   Database column headings

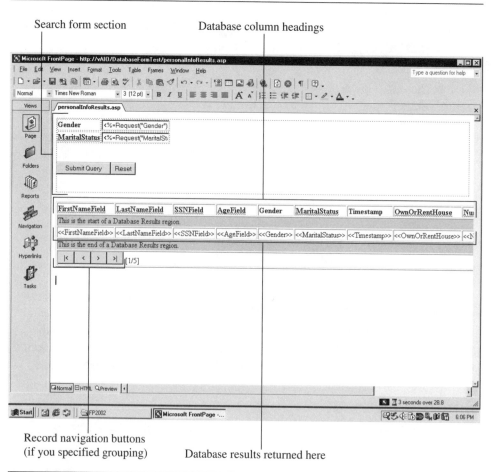

Record navigation buttons
(if you specified grouping)   Database results returned here

FIGURE 19-8   The "finished" database results Web page, ready for customization and use.

Here are some areas to focus on:

■ **Table headings** If you returned your results as a table, the column headings are the database column names. These can be cryptic and hard to read, so consider replacing them with more descriptive headings.

TIP

It is a proven fact that database results are used more frequently and to better effect when the reader understands what the data means. Add a hyperlink to each column heading that jumps to another page where the meaning of that column is explained in great detail. Experienced users can ignore the link, but new users can easily find out what the data means.

- **List field names** If you returned your results as a list, the list field names are the database column names. As with table headings, consider replacing them with more descriptive names.

- **Search form instructions** You'll notice that the search form contains no instructions on how to use it. You'll probably want to add instructions telling the reader how to enter the data they are searching for. In addition, if you added multiple fields, you'll want to explain how the fields are connected (with an And or an Or) and what that means for the returned database results.

- **Search form field names** Spaces are not allowed in the search form field names, and the default label for the field is the field name. You'll probably want to change the label to make it easier to read.

- **Search form field valid values** Often, only a certain set of valid values are allowed for a particular field. For example, the RaceGender field used in this example allows only two values: Girls and Boys. However, if readers do not know which values are valid, they may keep trying values that return no records, which is very frustrating. And if there are a lot of possible values (such as is the case with RaceName or RaceAge), the chances that the reader will type in an invalid value are much greater. It *is* possible to convert the search form field to a drop-down list (as discussed later in this chapter), but it is pretty complicated and even requires that you write a simple custom query (which I'll show you how to do). Instead, you may want to figure out a way to inform the reader which values are valid. One way is to add a note to the form. Another way (which works better if there are a lot of valid values) is to add a hyperlink alongside the search form field, perhaps labeled Valid Values. The reader can click the hyperlink to navigate to another page where the valid values are detailed, along with their meanings.

View the Results

To view the database Web page in action, you'll have to publish the page and open it in a browser. Either publish the page to your Web hosting service and open it on the Internet or, if you created the Web as a server-based Web site in Personal Web Server 4 or IIS, simply display the page and choose File | Preview In Browser. It may take a moment or two for the page to open, since the database results must be retrieved and formatted. Eventually, however, you should see the database results on your Web page (see Figure 19-9).

19

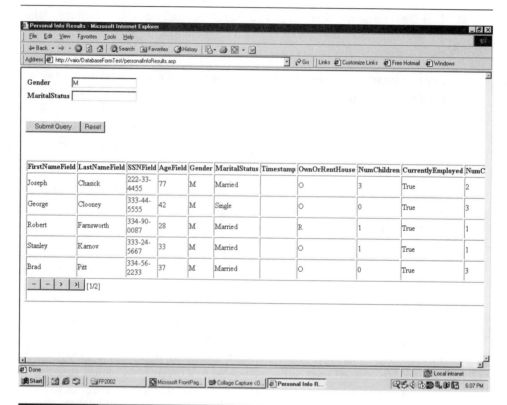

FIGURE 19-9   The database results are returned in a browser running on a Web server.

NOTE   *If you take a look at the HTML version of the Web page, you'll notice that unless you created a custom query, the automatically generated SQL query that retrieves data from the database actually retrieves everything (Select * from...), then filters out the columns you don't want. This method of retrieving records can seriously affect performance, especially if you have one or more nondisplayed fields that contain large amounts of data (such as a long description field). If you are noticing poor performance, this may be the reason. Unfortunately, the only way to fix this is to create a custom query that obtains just the needed data from the database.*

Advanced Techniques for Finding Database Records

As mentioned earlier, when FrontPage creates a search form, the fields in the form are simply text fields into which you must type the value you want to search for. If the values are fairly complicated, such as the names of the races in a swim meet, the probability is relatively high that the reader will type in a value that doesn't exist in the database. For example, one of the races is *100 Yard Breaststroke*. But if you accidentally typed it in as *100 Yard Breastroke* (a common misspelling), no records will be returned by a search—probably leaving the reader wondering what happened.

Ideally, what you'd like to do is pick a value from a list of valid values, presented in a drop-down list. To do that, though, you'll have to do more work. First, build a standard form that includes a Database Results component and a search form, as described earlier in this chapter. Make sure that you include (in the Criteria under the More Options button) criteria based on all the fields you are going to want to search on. In the example below, we have built a standard Database Results component with a search form that includes gender (RaceGender), age range (RaceAge), and the name of the race itself (RaceName)—and cleaned up the field names.

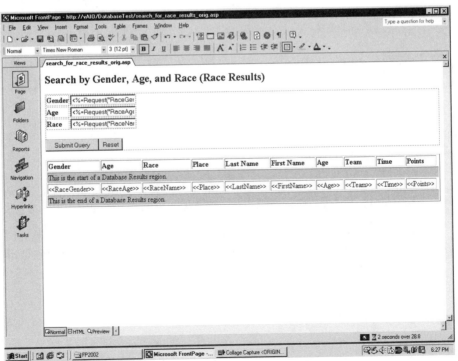

At this point, the form looks just like what we discussed previously.

The next step is to select and delete the search fields in the search form. This causes the table cell containing the search field to shrink, but don't worry about that.

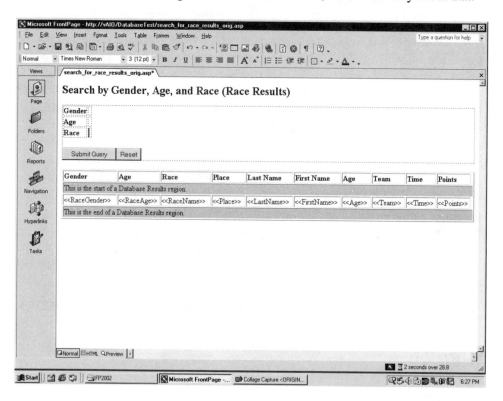

To replace each search field with a drop-down list, use the following steps for each search field (the example below will illustrate this for the RaceName field, labeled Race on the form):

1. Click in the table cell where you want to insert the drop-down list. Choose Insert | Database | Results to open the Database Results Wizard dialog box.

2. In step 1, choose the Use An Existing Database Connection option and select the same database connection you used to build the form originally. Then click Next to continue.

3. In step 2 of the Database Results Wizard, choose the Custom Query option and click the Edit button to open the Custom Query dialog box.

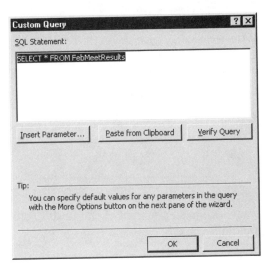

4. Type in the SQL query that returns a list of all the unique values in the database for the column you want to search on. The syntax is
   `SELECT Distinct(ColumnName) FROM DatabaseName`
   For example, if you wanted to search on the RaceName column in the FebMeetResults database, you would type in the following SQL query:

   `SELECT Distinct(RaceName) FROM FebMeetResults`

5. Make sure you typed everything correctly (and selected a valid column name and database name) by clicking the Verify Query button. If the query verifies OK, proceed to the next step by clicking OK in the Custom Query dialog box and then clicking Next in the Database Results Wizard. Otherwise correct the query.

6. Step 3 of the Database Results Wizard should display the single field you named in the custom query—click Next to continue.

7. In step 4 of the Database Results Wizard, click on the drop-down list at the top of the dialog box and select Drop-Down List – One Record Per Item. Both of the other two drop-down lists should display the name of the column you used in the custom query.

19

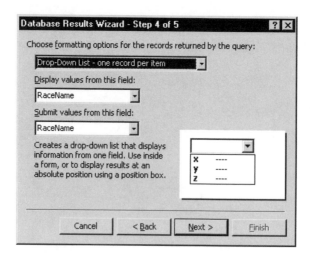

8. Click Next to advance to step 5, then click Finish to close the Database Results Wizard dialog box.

If you now look at the search form, you can see that the Database Results component you just built is embedded in the search form.

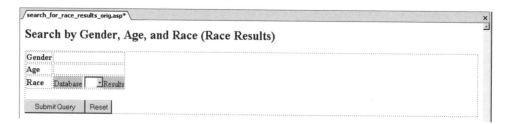

Repeat the above procedure for all drop-down lists you want in your search form. If your Web site is server-based, preview it in a browser to see the result. Click on the search form field drop-down list to see a list of the distinct values in that column in the database (the result of the custom query you built).

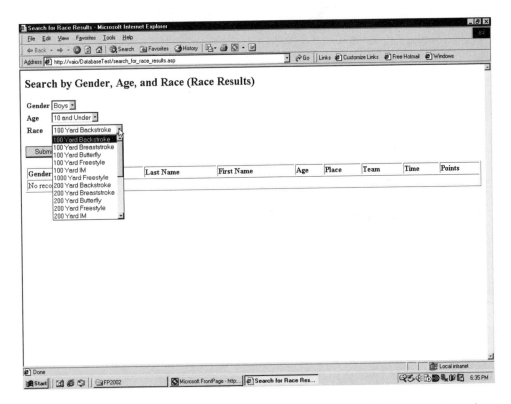

When you make a selection from the drop-down list, the field returns the value you just selected, making it available to the search form. When you click the Submit Query button in the search form, the search is carried out in the database, returning the records that match your query. And since you are absolutely, positively guaranteed that the value you picked exists in the database, you won't get any search results that contain no records.

NOTE   *Of course, if you use multiple search fields, and combine them with And clauses, you may still get empty search results. For example, you can pick RaceGender of Boys, RaceAge of 10 and Under, and RaceName of 1000 Yard Freestyle. These are all valid values in the database, but because boys age ten and under don't swim 1,000 yards freestyle, the combination of the three criteria won't return any records.*

Chapter 20

Build a Database Web Site Using the Database Interface Wizard Template

How To...

- Create a new Web site with the Database Wizard
- Create a new database or use an existing database with the Database Wizard
- Use the Results page
- Use the Submission page
- Work with the Database Editor forms
- Protect your database with a login

Although FrontPage makes it easier than it has ever been before to send form results to a database (see Chapter 18) and display the contents of a database in a form (see Chapter 19), it is still quite a bit of work to set all this up—after all, it took us two entire chapters to understand how to add this functionality to a Web site. With FrontPage 2002, Microsoft has added the Database Interface Wizard template. This is a Web site template that automates much of the process of creating a database-driven Web site. This powerful tool asks you a set of questions and then constructs forms for collecting new records, and viewing existing records. In addition, you can instruct the Database Interface Wizard template to create the forms (collectively called the "Database Editor") that enable you to update existing records, delete records, and view a single record from a list. You can even have the Database Interface Wizard template create a login screen to control who has access to your data.

Create a New Site with the Database Interface Wizard

To create a new site with the Database Interface Wizard, use the following steps:

1. Choose File | New Page or Web to open the New Page or Web task pane. Click Web Site Templates in the task pane to open the Web Site Templates dialog box.

2. Fill in the location of the Web site in the Specify The Location Of The New Web field. Make sure to specify a server-based Web site if you want to be able to preview and test the database in a browser on your local machine.

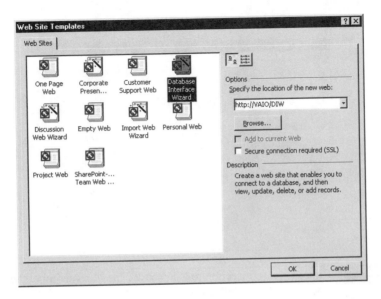

3. Choose the Database Interface Wizard from the list of available templates and click OK.

> **TIP**   *You can use the Database Interface Wizard template to implement a database within an existing Web site. To do so, first create a Web site as usual, and use the techniques discussed in Chapter 18 to create a connection to a database. In the Web Site Templates dialog box, check the Add To Current Web checkbox. This procedure enables the option to choose an existing database connection in the next step of the Database Interface Wizard.*

4. From the next panel of the Database Interface Wizard (see Figure 20-1), choose how you want to connect to the database. Your options are

■ **Create a new Access database within your Web site**   Walks you through the process of building a new, one-table Access database.

■ **Use an existing database connection**   Enables you to connect to an existing database connection. However, unless you took advantage of the tip above, there won't be any database connections available to choose from.

■ **Use a sample database connection (Northwind)**   This option imports the sample Northwind Access database into your Web site and creates a database connection for it called "Sample".

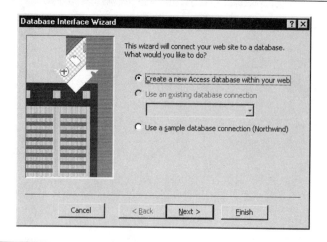

FIGURE 20-1 Choose your connection to a database from this version of the Database
Interface Wizard dialog box.

Exactly what happens next depends on the option you selected above. We'll
cover each of the options in the next few sections.

Create a New Access Database Within Your Web Site

If you select the option to create a new Access database within your Web site and
click Next, the next panel of the Database Interface Wizard requests the name of
the database connection.

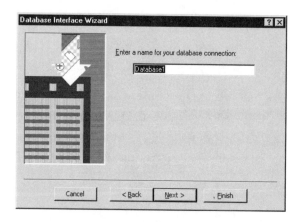

Enter the name and click Next to proceed. The next panel of the wizard enables
you to define the columns in the Results table of the database.

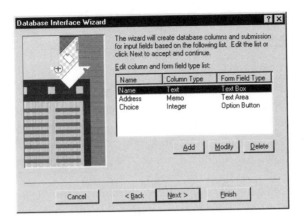

NOTE   *The table is always called "Results"—you do not get an opportunity to rename it.*

There are few default columns provided. Each column has a Name, Column Type, and Form Field Type (defined below).

To add a new column to the database table, click the Add button. This opens a new version of the Database Interface Wizard in which you can define the following items:

- ■ **Column Name**   The name of the column in the table.

- ■ **Column Type**   The Column Type defines what kind of data the database will expect in the column (text, integer, float, double, date, etc.). Select the column type from drop-down list.

- ■ **Form Field Input Type**   The Form Field Type defines what kind of form field will be available for data input (text box, drop-down box, option button, or text area). Pick the form field input type from the drop-down list.

- ■ **Number of options**   This field is only available if you picked a form field input type of option button because FrontPage needs to know how many option buttons to place on the form.

You can also modify any of the columns by selecting the column and clicking the Modify button. Or, if you don't need a column, you can select it and click Delete to remove it altogether.

Once you have finished defining the database table columns, click Next to proceed. FrontPage takes a moment to create the database and connect to it. When prompted, click Next to proceed.

From here, the rest of the Database Interface Wizard proceeds as described in the "Specify the Forms To Build" section later in this chapter.

Use an Existing Database Connection

If you've chosen to add the results of the Database Interface Wizard to an existing Web site, and that Web site already has at least one existing database connection, you can choose the database connection to use from the Use An Existing Database Connection drop-down list (visible in Figure 20-1). Click Next to continue.

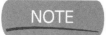 *If you chose Use A Sample Database Connection (Northwind), the steps you follow are identical to those outlined in this section. FrontPage simply adds the Northwind database to the current Web site before moving on to the steps below.*

The next panel of the Database Interface Wizard enables you to pick which table or view in the database you want to use as your data source.

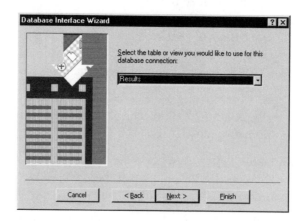

Select the table or view from the drop-down list in the dialog box and click Next to continue. The next panel displays a list of columns, their column type, and the form field type, as described in the previous section.

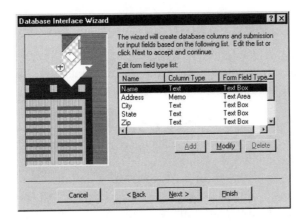

However, because you are using an existing database, you cannot add or delete columns, and selecting a column and clicking Modify enables you to change only the Form Field Input Type—everything else is grayed out and unavailable.

Once you have made any adjustments to the Form Field Input Type (and returned to the main Database Interface Wizard dialog box), click Next to continue. From here on, follow the procedure discussed in the "Specify the Forms To Build" section later in this chapter.

20

Specify the Forms to Build

The next panel of the Database Interface Wizard (see Figure 20-2) enables you to pick which forms you want the wizard to build automatically. You can check one, two, or all three of the checkboxes. Here is what they mean:

- **Results Page** Provides a form with a Database Results region (as detailed in Chapter 19). The form presents the contents of the database and includes a hyperlink to the Submission form (if you create a Submission form). The default layout of this form is relatively ugly and groups records in sets of five. However, you can use the techniques detailed in Chapter 19 to customize the database results region on the form.

- **Submission Form** Provides a form that routes the submitted contents into the database, as described in Chapter 18. You can customize this form (and will probably want to, at least to make the field labels more friendly). This form includes a hyperlink to the Results page, if you created a Results page.

- **Database Editor** Provides a set of forms you can use to update existing records, add new records, view individual records, and even delete records from the database. If you wish, you can even protect the Database Editor screens with a login ID and password.

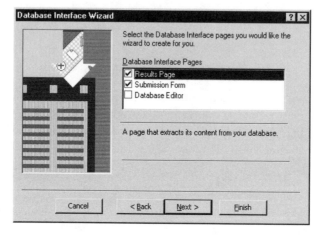

FIGURE 20-2 Select the forms you want the wizard to build from this dialog box.

If you chose to include the Database Editor, the next panel in the Database Interface Wizard offers you the option of setting up a username and password to protect your Database Editor.

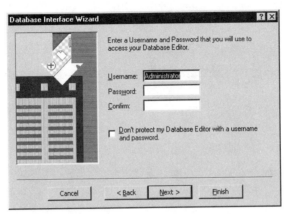

If you *don't* want to have to log in and provide a username and password each time you (or anyone else) use the Database Editor screens, check the Don't Protect My Database Editor With A Username And Password checkbox. Otherwise, enter a username in the Username field, and type the password twice: once in the Password field and once in the Confirm field. Then click Next to continue.

If you set up username and password protection as described in the previous paragraph, FrontPage displays a login screen each time someone tries to access one of the Database Editor screens. The user will need to know both the username and password in order to gain access to the screens. This protection does not apply to the Submission form—so don't provide a Submission form if you don't want anyone entering new records without having to supply a username and password.

In the final panel, the Database Interface Wizard informs you where the forms you requested will be placed. Click Finish to create the forms.

Understand the Database Interface Wizard Results

Once you turn the wizard loose, FrontPage gets busy and creates the forms you requested. This section assumes you instructed FrontPage to create them all, and discusses each one in turn. A certain amount of customization is also a good idea, and this section describes how to do that as well.

The Results Page

The Results page (see Figure 20-3) displays the contents of the database in a table. The data is displayed in a Database Results component, as described in Chapter 19.

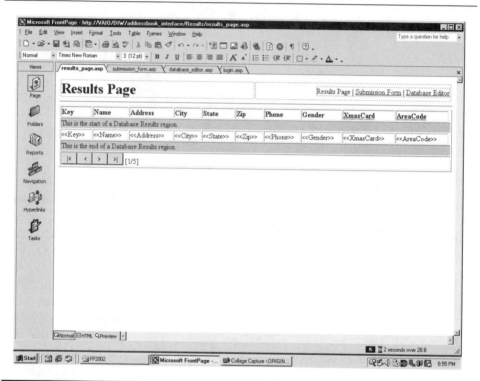

FIGURE 20-3 FrontPage uses a Database Results component to display the contents of a database table.

You can customize the Results page to make it easier to view. Some of the things you'll probably want to change are

- **Column Headings**   The default column headings are just the column names in the database table. These tend to be cryptic and difficult to read. Select each column heading and replace it with more informative text.

- **Adjust the number of listed records**   By default, the database region lists the records in groups of five. For any reasonably sized database, this doesn't provide enough records. To adjust the number of records, right-click in the Database Results and pick Database Results Properties to open the Database Results Wizard, described in Chapter 19. Step through the wizard to step 5, where you can set the number of records in a group or suppress grouping altogether.

- **Add a search form**   The Results form (and its associated Database Results component) does not include a search form to locate records that meet a certain criteria. This can make it absurdly difficult to find what you are looking for. To fix this situation, right-click in the Database Results and pick Database Results Properties to open the Database Results Wizard. Step through the wizard until you reach step 3, and click the More Options button to open the More Options dialog box. Click the Criteria button and establish the criteria for finding records, as described in Chapter 19. Don't forget to check the Add Search Form checkbox in step 5 (it is actually checked by default).

- **Sort the results**   Unless you really want to see the contents of the database in whatever order they were entered, you'll need to establish a sort order. Once again, right-click in the Database Results and pick Database Results Properties to open the Database Results Wizard. Step through the wizard until you reach step 3, and click the More Options button to open the More Options dialog box. Click the Ordering button and establish the sort order you want, as described in Chapter 19.

The Submission Form

The Submission form enables you to do one thing: enter new records into the database. It is simply a form that sends its results to a database, as described in Chapter 18.

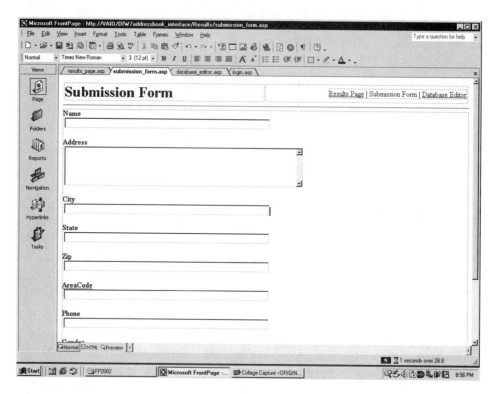

Once again, you are probably going to want to customize the form in the following ways:

- **Field names** The default field names are just the column names in the database table. These tend to be cryptic and difficult to read. Select each field name and replace it with more informative text.

- **Option buttons** If you are using option buttons, the labels for the buttons are something like "Option 1", "Option 2", and so on. The only exception to this is if you choose a Boolean data type for the column—then the labels are "True" and "False". Select each option button label and change it to make it more descriptive of what values are being placed in the database. The default value inserted into the database when an option button is selected is also "Option 1", "Option 2", etc., except for Boolean, in which case the values are 0 (false) and 1 (true). To set your own values, you'll need to right-click on each option button field, choose Form Field Properties from the shortcut menu, and change the value in the Value field.

■ **Drop-down boxes**   If you are using drop-down boxes, the Database Interface Wizard uses "Option 0", "Option 1", and so on as the values in the list (and also as the values to place in the database). The only exception to this is if you chose a Boolean data type for the column—then the values are "True" and "False". To specify your own values, right-click on the drop-down box and choose Form Field Properties to open the Drop-Down Box Properties dialog box. To change the entry, select it in the Drop-Down Box Properties dialog box, click Modify, and change the values in the Choice field and the Specify Value field.

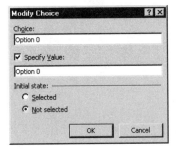

CAUTION   *If you are in the habit of using spaces when you name columns in your database, you'll have to stop using spaces, and remove any spaces in existing column names (and table names, too). This is because the Database Interface Wizard writes a set of custom scripts for updating the database, and these scripts won't work if the table name, column name, or form field name (group name for an option button) contain a space. The default that the Database Interface Wizard uses for group names or field names is the column name—which includes any spaces. FrontPage does not warn you of the errors—the first time you'll find out about them is when you try to use the forms in a browser.*

20

The Home Page

The Database Interface Wizard provides a simple Home page (Default.htm) with links to the Results page, Submission form, and the Database Editor.

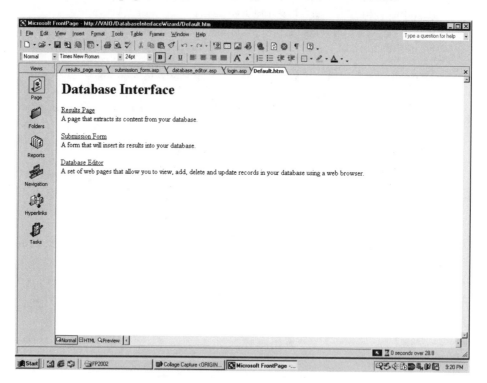

The Database Editor

If you decided to include the Database Editor forms, the Database Interface Wizard creates a whole series of forms for you, including the Log In form (provided you asked for one), the Database Editor form, the new record (Submission) form, and an edit form for changing existing records.

The Login Form

The Database Editor Login form (see Figure 20-4) provides a place for someone to enter a username and password.

Once they click the Login button, FrontPage checks them against the values you specified when you built the form. If they match, the user is allowed access to

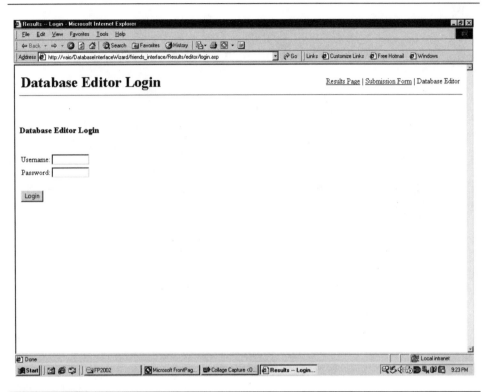

FIGURE 20-4   A user must type in the correct username and password in order to access the Database Editor forms.

the Database Editor. If not, the user is given another opportunity to enter the correct values.

When setting up your Web site, you don't need to provide a link to the login screen (login.asp). Instead, you can provide a link directly to the Database Editor form (database_editor.asp), and FrontPage will display the login screen automatically.

20

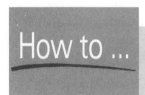 **Change the Username and Password**

If you want to change the username and password assigned to the Database Editor, it is pretty easy. Double-click on the file login.asa in the folder list to open the file.

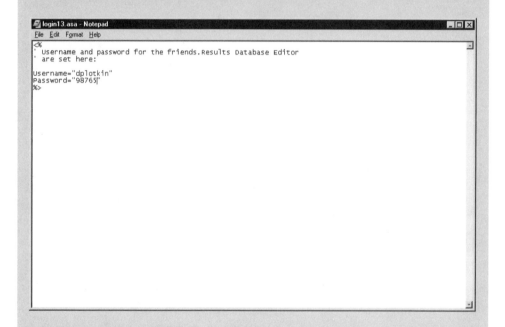

Change the entries for username and password in the login.asa file and save the results (File | Save).

The Database Editor Form

The Database Editor form (see Figure 20-5) is the heart of Database Editor. From this form, you can get to any of the other Database Editor forms (except the login form). Thus, the Database Editor form is the form that your application should provide a link to in order to edit the database contents.

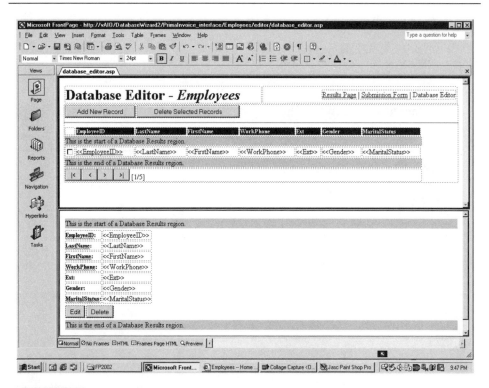

FIGURE 20-5   Link to the Database Editor form to allow readers to modify the database contents.

Previewing the Database Editor form in a browser (see Figure 20-6) clearly shows how the form functions.

The Database Editor form is actually a frameset consisting of a top frame and a bottom frame. The top frame displays the list.asp page, which itself contains a Database Results component. This component is used to display a list of database records. As described in Chapter 19, you can customize the component if you wish. The bottom frame displays the detail.asp page, which also contains a Database Results component. This component displays all the fields in a single record.

Here is what you can do with the Database Editor form:

■ **View a single record**   In the top frame, scroll through the listed records (using the provided buttons). When you find a record you want to view in the bottom frame, click on the hyperlink in the first column of the list (the primary key of the record). This displays the detail for the record in the bottom frame.

20

Click here to select this
record for deletion

Click here to view the detail of the
selected record in the bottom frame

Click here to open   Click here to delete any records
the Submission form   you have checked off

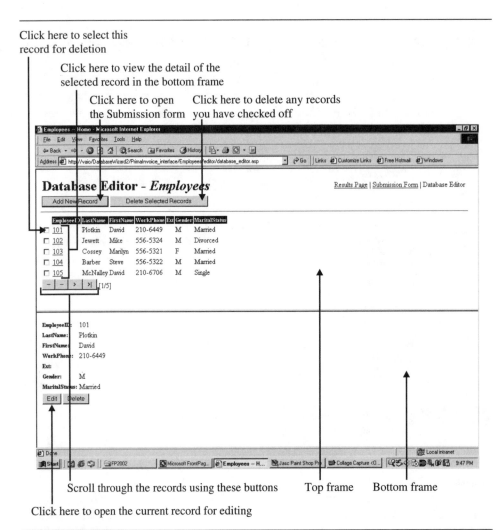

Scroll through the records using these buttons   Top frame   Bottom frame

Click here to open the current record for editing

FIGURE 20-6   Need to modify the contents of a database from a browser? No problem…

TIP   *View the properties of the hyperlink (right-click on the hyperlink and choose Hyperlink Properties from the shortcut menu). You'll discover that the hyperlink is accessing the database to recover the record where the primary key matches the value of the selected record in the list in the top frame. In order for this to work, you must structure your database records to use a single-column primary key.*

■ **Delete selected records**   To delete one or more records, check the checkbox alongside the records you want to delete. Then click the Delete Selected Records button. After confirming, the records are removed from the database. You can only select visible records. That is, if you check off a record, use the Forward button to scroll to the next set of records, then scroll back, you'll find that the original record is no longer checked.

■ **Update a record**   Clicking the Edit button displays the Edit form (discussed later in this chapter) with the data from the selected record displayed. You can change any of the data in a record and click OK to update the database record.

■ **Create a new record**   Click the Add A New Record button to display the Submission form, from which you can create a new record, and click OK to add the record to the database. Although this form looks exactly like the Submission form discussed earlier, it is *not* the same Web page, so if you have added a Submission form *and* the Database Editor form set, you'll have to customize both versions of the Submission form. Thus, if you are going to have the Database Interface Wizard create the Database Editor form set, you may wish to forgo creating the Submission form.

The Edit Form

You can update a database record using the Edit form (edit.asp).

When you click the Edit button in the Database Editor form, the edit form opens, displaying the selected record. All the fields are present *except* the primary key, thus you can't use this form to add a new record (you use the Submission form for that). What makes the Edit form unique is that it displays the contents of the record in the form, ready for you to edit. When you click OK, the updated contents are written back to the database.

As you should recall, you had the option to represent fields from the database as text boxes, text areas, drop-down boxes, or option buttons. As mentioned earlier, if you choose to use drop-down boxes or option buttons, you have a fair amount of customization to do in order to set up the correct values to be written to the database and add meaningful labels. There is another, even more significant disadvantage to using drop-down boxes and option buttons: When a record is retrieved from the database, any text box or text area fields display the contents of that column in the database. However, drop-down boxes and option buttons *do not*. A drop-down box or option button always shows the default value. You can change the value and click OK to save the result. *But if you don't reset the value in a drop-down box or an option button to the correct value for that record, the default value is what gets written back to the database.* This is a serious problem, and one that should make you think hard before using drop-down boxes or option buttons in an edit form (its not a problem in a new record, where you have to set all the values anyway).

For example, take a look at this screen.

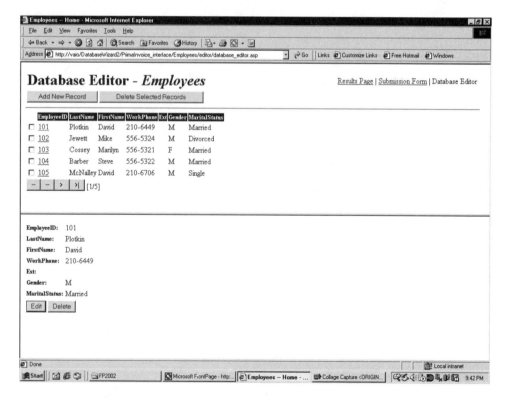

Note how the detail record in the bottom frame shows that this individual is married (and male). When you click the Edit button for this record, however, the resulting record comes up with a value of *Single* in the Marital Status drop-down box (and no gender).

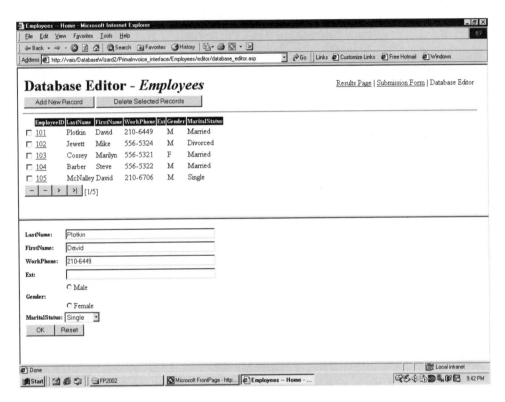

If you click OK at this point, the record will be written back to the database as Single (and no gender).

Index

INTERNATIONAL CONTACT INFORMATION

AUSTRALIA
McGraw-Hill Book Company Australia Pty. Ltd.
TEL +61-2-9417-9899
FAX +61-2-9417-5687
http://www.mcgraw-hill.com.au
books-it_sydney@mcgraw-hill.com

CANADA
McGraw-Hill Ryerson Ltd.
TEL +905-430-5000
FAX +905-430-5020
http://www.mcgrawhill.ca

GREECE, MIDDLE EAST,
NORTHERN AFRICA
McGraw-Hill Hellas
TEL +30-1-656-0990-3-4
FAX +30-1-654-5525

MEXICO (Also serving Latin America)
McGraw-Hill Interamericana Editores S.A. de C.V.
TEL +525-117-1583
FAX +525-117-1589
http://www.mcgraw-hill.com.mx
fernando_castellanos@mcgraw-hill.com

SINGAPORE (Serving Asia)
McGraw-Hill Book Company
TEL +65-863-1580
FAX +65-862-3354
http://www.mcgraw-hill.com.sg
mghasia@mcgraw-hill.com

SOUTH AFRICA
McGraw-Hill South Africa
TEL +27-11-622-7512
FAX +27-11-622-9045
robyn_swanepoel@mcgraw-hill.com

UNITED KINGDOM & EUROPE
(Excluding Southern Europe)
McGraw-Hill Education Europe
TEL +44-1-628-502500
FAX +44-1-628-770224
http://www.mcgraw-hill.co.uk
computing_neurope@mcgraw-hill.com

ALL OTHER INQUIRIES Contact:
Osborne/McGraw-Hill
TEL +1-510-549-6600
FAX +1-510-883-7600
http://www.osborne.com
omg_international@mcgraw-hill.com